Understanding Religious Conversion

UNDERSTANDING
Religious Conversion

The Case of Saint Augustine

DONG YOUNG KIM

☙PICKWICK *Publications* · Eugene, Oregon

UNDERSTANDING RELIGIOUS CONVERSION:
The Case of Saint Augustine

Copyright © 2012 Dong Young Kim. All rights reserved. Except for brief quotations in critical publications or reviews, no part of this book may be reproduced in any manner without prior written permission from the publisher. Write: Permissions, Wipf and Stock Publishers, 199 W. 8th Ave., Suite 3, Eugene, OR 97401.

Pickwick Publications
An Imprint of Wipf and Stock Publishers
199 W. 8th Ave., Suite 3
Eugene, OR 97401

www.wipfandstock.com

New Revised Standard Version Bible, copyright 1989, Division of Christian Education of the National Council of the Churches of Christ in the United States of America. Used by permission. All rights reserved.

ISBN 13: 978-1-61097-617-6

Cataloging-in-Publication data:

Kim, Dong Young.

Understanding religious conversion : the case of saint Augustine / Dong Young Kim, with a foreword by John Berthrong.

xvi + 404 p. ; 23 cm. Includes bibliographical references and index.

ISBN 13: 978-1-61097-617-6

1. Conversion—Christianity. 2. Augustine, Saint, Bishop of Hippo. 3. Psychology, Religious. 4. Religion and sociology. Religion and science. 5. I. Berthrong, John H., 1946– II. Title.

BL639 K67 2012

Manufactured in the U.S.A.

Contents

Foreword by John Berthrong vii
Preface ix
Acknowledgments xi
Abbreviations xiii

1 Facing the Challenge:
   An Interdisciplinary Approach to the Issue 1

2 Exploring Insights:
   Search for Studies of Religious Conversion 15

3 Illustrating the Case of St. Augustine:
   His Main Life History and Thought 95

4 Getting Insights:
   Critical Search for Interpretations of Augustine's Conversion 151

5 Playing Together:
   An Integrated Understanding of Augustine's Conversion 263

6 Sharing the Conversion Narrative in Our Midst:
   Reflections and Implications 357

Appendix:
The Implications of the Role of Augustine's Unnamed Woman in His Conversion 369

Bibliography 375
Index

Foreword

IT IS A PLEASURE to write the foreword for Dong Young Kim's *Understanding Religion Conversion: The Case of Saint Augustine*. I first have to confess that Augustine is not in my main research field. I am a scholar of world religions in general and Chinese Neo-Confucianism in particular (i.e., Song and post-Song Neo-Confucianism). But as every theologian and philosopher in the West I grew up reading Augustine and, of course, the account of his famous conversion. Moreover, conversion is certainly an important topic for comparative theology, as conversions of various sorts occur and are important in diverse religious communities and traditions. Along with St. Paul, St. Augustine certainly had the second most famous conversion in the Christian tradition, or at least one of the best-chronicled and fascinating narrative conversion stories ever told.

Kim has crafted an exhaustively researched and readable account of Augustine's process of conversion. Among the many memorable retellings of Augustine's story, he has focused on the process of the conversion by employing the interdisciplinary framework of Lewis Rambo. Armed with an integrated narrative method to interpret Augustine's conversion, Kim has effectively linked the best current studies of religious conversion in the literature with an intense and careful re-reading of Augustine's works (e.g., *Confessions*) and the best current critical historical, socio-cultural, psychological, and theological studies of Augustine. It allows the reader to discover, or rediscover, whole aspects of a familiar story from a unique new perspective.

Along with a relatively unique and comprehensive methodological approach to Augustine's conversion, Kim mastered a huge amount of primary and secondary material pertaining to the project. I joked with him (but with a serious point) that the bibliography of the book is

Foreword

worth the price of admission. It is truly an exhaustive example of fine scholarship.

The appeal of Kim's book is that is retells a familiar story from an interdisciplinary perspective and sustains it claims with an exemplary command of the primary and secondary scholarly background. It is written clearly and with a great passion for the topic. It will be of great interest to historians of religion, comparative theologians, social scientists, and members of the religious community fascinated by the never-ending impact of conversion.

John Berthrong
Professor of Comparative Philosophy and Theology
Boston University

Preface

THIS BOOK ILLUSTRATES THE merits of an interdisciplinary approach to religious conversion by employing Lewis Rambo's systemic stage model to illumine the *process* of St. Augustine's conversion. Previous studies of Augustine's conversion have commonly explored his narrative of transformation from the perspective of one specific discipline, such as theology, history, or psychology. In doing so, they have necessarily restricted attention to a limited set of questions and problems. By bringing these disciplines into a structured, critical conversation, this study demonstrates how formulating and responding to the interplay among personal, social, cultural, and religious dimensions of Augustine's conversion process may eventuate in the consideration of issues previously unarticulated and thus unaddressed.

Rambo formulates a model of religious change that consists of what he calls context, crisis, quest, encounter, interaction, commitment, and consequences. Change is explained by drawing upon the research and scholarship of psychologists, sociologists, anthropologists, and religionists, in conjunction with the contributions of theologians.

This study unfolds in the following chapters: 1. introduction; 2. search for scholarship about religious conversion, with emphasis on explication of Rambo's model; 3. case illustration of St. Augustine, drawn from a close reading of the *Confessions*; 4. critical search for scholarship about Augustine's conversion; 5. interdisciplinary interpretation of Augustine's conversion; and 6. reflections and implications for scholars of conversion and for pastoral caregivers.

This book demonstrates how Augustine's conversion experience was deeply influenced by 1) psychological distress and crisis; 2) the quest to know himself and the divine; 3) interactions with significant others; 4) participation in Christian communities; 5) philosophical

Preface

and cultural changes; and 6) the encounter with the divine. As such, this study reveals the value of interpreting Augustine's conversion as an evolving process constituted in multiple factors that can be differentiated from one another, yet clearly interact with one another. Based on the coherent portrayal of Augustine's narrative of transformation, this study provides a multi-dimensional pattern of the conversion process as described the *Confessions* (and his other works). It examines the implications of constructing an interdisciplinary approach to Augustine's conversion narrative for both the academy and the Christian community.

Acknowledgments

I would like to thank God for God's steadfast love and presence in the midst of my spiritual journey and learning. I would also like to thank St. Augustine for his unexpected invitation to share his spiritual pilgrimage and for his challenge to move into a better integrated life in the service of God and the service of others.

I am deeply grateful to Chris R. Schlauch and Claire E. Wolfteich for their compassionate guidance and encouragement—"faithfully companioning"—during my study at Boston University School of Theology in order to learn "something more" in the academy and to recognize the value of Christian life in solitude and community. I am also grateful to John Berthrong who has engaged in a critical and mutually-informing dialogue for successfully completing this work and for guiding my future study of conversion.

I would like to extend gratitude to Virgina Samuel, Arthur Pressley, James W. Jones, A. Johan Noordsij, Brita Gill-Austern, Kwok Pui Lan, Courtney T. Goto, and George S. Stavros who provided their support, direction, and challenges in order to realize the importance of earnest learning and to become a scholar.

My sincere thanks to Christian Amondson, Robin Parry, Ian Creeger, K. C. Hanson, and other members of Pickwick Publications who have provided their hospitality, guidance, friendship, and insights during the publication process of this work. Without their unique support, this book would have never been a reality.

Finally, I feel deep appreciation for my family members and my church members in South Korea and the United States who have supported me with prayer, encouragement, and hope. With love and joy, I dedicate this work to my parents, Chang Keun and Dal Soon Kim, my mother-in-law, Jung Sook Lee, my wife Young Mi, and my two children,

Acknowledgments

Joo Yeob and Jung In, who are God's loving gifts and who are *together* with me in my spiritual journey.

Abbreviations

ABBREVIATIONS OF AUGUSTINE'S WORKS

bapt.	*De baptismo*	On Baptism, against the Donatists
b. vita.	*De beata vita*	On the Happy Life
c. ep. Man.	*Contra epistulam Manichaei quam vocant fundamenti*	Against the Epistle of Manichaeus Called Fundamental
c. Faust.	*Contra Faustum Manicheum*	Reply to Faustus the Manichean
c. Jul. imp.	*Contra Julianum opus imperfectum*	Against Julian, an Unfinished Book
civ. Dei	*De civitate Dei*	City of God
c. litt. Pet.	*Contra litteras Petiliani*	To the Letters of Petilian, the Donatist
conf.	*Confessiones*	Confessions
corrept.	*De correptione et gratia*	On Rebuke and Grace
Cresc.	*Ad Cresconium grammaticum partis Donati*	To Cresconius, a Donatist Grammarian
div. qu.	*De diversis quaestionibus octoginta tribus*	Miscellany of Eighty-Three Questions

Abbreviations

doc. Chr.	*De doctrina Christiana*	Teaching Christianity
duab. an.	*De duabus animabus*	On the Two Souls, against the Manichaeans
ench.	*Enchiridion ad Laurentium de fide spe et caritate*	The Enchiridion (On Faith, Hope, and Love)
en. Ps.	*Enarrationes in Psalmos*	Expositions of the Psalms
ep. (epp.)	*Epistulae*	Letters
ep. Jo.	*In epistulam Joannis ad Parthos tractatus*	Homilies on the First Letter of John
ex. Gal.	*Expositio Epistulae ad Galatas*	Commentary on the Letter to the Galatians
f. et op.	*De fide et operibus*	On Faith and Works
gr. et pecc. or.	*De gratia Christi et de peccato originali*	On the Grace of Christ and Original Sin
Gn. litt.	*De Genesi ad litterat*	The Literal Meaning of Genesis
Jo. ev. tr.	*In Johannis evangelium tractatus*	Homilies on the Gospel of John
nat. et gr.	*De natura et gratia*	On Nature and Grace
ord.	*De ordine*	On Order
pecc. mer.	*De peccatorum meritis et remissione et de baptismo parvulorum*	On the Merits and Remission of Sins, and on the Baptism of Infants
praed. sanct.	*De praedestinatione sanctorum*	On the Predestination of the Saints
quant.	*De animae quantitate*	On the Greatness of the Soul
reg.	*Regula*	The Rule

retr.	*Retractationes*	The Retractions
s.	*Sermones*	Sermons
Simpl.	*Ad Simplicianum*	Miscellany of Questions in Response to Simplician
sol.	*Soliloquiorum libri duo*	The Soliloquies
Trin.	*De Trinitate*	On the Holy Trinity

OTHER ABBREVIATIONS

Ambrose, *sacr.*	*The Sacraments*
Hippolytus, *apost. const.*	*Apostolic Constitutions*
Leo I, *ep.*	*Letters*
Plotinus, *enn.*	*Enneads*
Possidius, *v. Aug.*	*The Life of Saint Augustine*
ACW	*Ancient Christian Writers: The Works of Fathers in Translation.* Edited by W. J. Burghardt and Thomas Comeford. 66 vols. New York: Newman, 1946–2012.
FC	*The Fathers of the Church.* Edited by Ludwig Schopp. 45 vols. New York: Cima, 1947–63.
NPNF	*A Select Library of the Nicene and Post-Nicene Fathers of the Christian Church.* Edited by Philip Schaff. 28 vols. Reprint. Grand Rapids: Eerdmans, 1956–2007.
WSA	*The Works of Saint Augustine: A Translation for the 21st Century.* Edited by John E. Rotelle. pt. I: 26 vols; pt. II: 4 vols; pt. III: 20 vols. New York: New City Press, 1990–2009.

1

Facing the Challenge
An Interdisciplinary Approach to the Issue

> A conversion experience is the process that happens around a conversion event. The conversion event is the pinnacle of the assortment of information, pressures, inquiries, circumstances, etc., that coalesce at a specific moment to inaugurate new awareness, or a new "level" of living. The conversion experience is the sum total of what happens in the life of a person before, during, and after the conversion event. A conversion experience is thus a process comprising the conversion event accompanied by antecedent and subsequent factors.
>
> —Robert A. Rennie[1]

STATEMENT OF THE PROBLEM

THE PURPOSE OF THIS book is to achieve an integrated understanding of the religious conversion process from an interdisciplinary perspective.[2] More specifically, this study investigates how personal, social, cultural,

---

1. Rennie, "Elements," 34–35.

2. The term *integrated* refers to the coordination of a series of ideas and approaches when reinterpreting the lived experience ("conversion") of Augustine. It is not just additive, juxtaposed, or multidisciplinary, but interrelated, coherent, or interdisciplinary.

and religious factors might have affected the process of Augustine's conversion by using the lens of Rambo's model of religious change. Augustine's narrative of conversion illustrates well the complex and multidimensional process of human transformation. Previous studies have tended to examine this dynamic process of Augustine's conversion from the perspective of one theoretical discipline. They have not critically integrated religious and social science perspectives for understanding Augustine's conversion. This study addresses this lacuna by exploring the interrelated impact of personal, social, cultural, and religious components on Augustine's lifelong process of transformation.

Religious conversion is a complicated and multi-layered process of religious change, which involves the total reorientation and transformation of one's life. Because of the complexity of the phenomenon of religious change, scholars have presented various understandings of conversion from different perspectives. For example, psychologists have primarily focused on the individual convert's crisis, need, and mental development.[3] Sociologists have articulated conversion as the result of forces mobilized and shaped by social institutions.[4] They have paid attention to social influence and change through affiliation with a religious group. Anthropologists have examined the cultural factors in a specific context.[5] They describe conversion as a process that must be intricately related to the worldview and structure of the culture. Theologians have primarily emphasized the dominant influence of God on the process of human transformation.[6] They assert that the consideration of one's encounter with God is essential for a more accurate understanding of the Christian conversion phenomenon. There is no single theoretical discipline that can encompass the various interpretations of the religious conversion process. Thus, there is a need for more

---

3. Conn, *Christian Conversion*; Fowler, *Becoming Adult*; Gillespie, *Dynamics*; James, *Religious Experience*; Ullman, *Transformed Self*; Zinnbauer and Pargament, "Spiritual Conversion."

4. Ammerman, *Bible Believers*, "Religious Identities"; Bainbridge, "Sociology"; Kilbourne and Richardson, "Communalization," "Paradigm Conflict"; Lofland and Stark, "World-Saver"; Snow and Machalek, "Sociology."

5. Austin-Broos, "Anthropology"; Hefner, "World Building"; Horton, "African Conversion," "Rationality"; Norris, "Converting"; Robertson, "Conversion"; Tippett, "Conversion," "Cultural Anthropology."

6. Gaiser, "Biblical Theology"; Gelpi, *Charism and Sacrament*, *Conversion Experience*; Marquardt, "Christian Conversion"; McKim, "Mainline Protestant"; Peace, *Conversion*; Smith, *Beginning Well*; Wells, *Turning*.

critical and integrative dialogue among theological and social scientific studies of conversion.

Since the late fourth century, St. Augustine has been a great role model for millions of religious people in facilitating a profound spiritual journey. This means that Augustine has remained influential in the psychological and spiritual lives of people across a range of cultures and times. The *Confessions* is both a personal prayer of honest self-disclosure before God and a public act in which Augustine's need to justify the reality of his conversion, both his turning away from Manichaeism and turning toward Christianity, led him to confess inwardly in his heart as well as outwardly before many witnesses in the Christian community (*conf.* 10.1.1). As a scholar in the fields of pastoral psychology and spirituality, and as a pastor in the Christian community, I face the challenge of providing a more integrated reinterpretation of Augustine's conversion for those scholars who have ignored the social scientific interpretation of Augustine's conversion (especially a psychoanalytic interpretation), for academics in the social sciences whose disciplines have not paid attention to the impact of the transforming power of the divine on the process of religious change, and for theologically oriented Christian pastoral caregivers of conversion who may be unaware of the influence of personal, social, and cultural factors on the process of human transformation.

Lewis Rambo's holistic model of conversion stresses the importance of integrating critically religious/theological and social science perspectives in order to understand better the complexity and richness of religious change. Rambo argues that the study of conversion must include the following components: the person, society, culture, and religion. As such, he carries out the perspectives of psychology, sociology, anthropology, and religious studies into critical dialogue and proposes a model of religious change which consists of context, crisis, quest, encounter, interaction, commitment, and consequences.[7] He assumes that "(a) conversion is a process over time, not a single event; (b) conversion is contextual and thereby influences and is influenced by a matrix of relationships, expectations, and situations; and (c) factors in the conversion process are multiple, interactive, and cumulative."[8] His model

---

7. Rambo, *Religious Conversion*, 7–18.
8. Ibid., 5.

helps us to examine the complicated and multi-dimensional elements of human religious change.

This book employs Rambo's model of conversion in order to formulate an interdisciplinary method for developing a more interrelated understanding of Augustine's conversion narrative in his *Confessions*. In other words, this study seeks to apply Rambo's interdisciplinary approach to the case of Augustine's conversion process. In doing so, it presents a more coherent picture of how the multiple factors involved in Augustine's conversion are knit together. It attempts to identify how and why St. Augustine converted to Christianity and to understand what specific experiences led him to conversion. Through the critical and integrative conversation of personal, social, cultural, and religious dimensions, this study shows that Augustine's conversion process was heavily affected by

1) the experience of psychological distress and crisis (e.g., *conf.* 7.7.11, 8.5.10, 8.12.28; *en. Ps.* 119.6),

2) the quest for knowing himself and the divine (e.g., *conf.* 7.10.16, 9.1.1; *sol.* 1.2.7, 2.1.1; *ord.* 2.18.47),

3) interactions with significant others, including Christians (e.g., Ambrose [*conf.* 5.13.23–5.14.25, 6.3.3–4, 9.6.14]; Simplicianus [8.2.3–5, 8.5.10]; Ponticianus [8.6.14–15, 8.7.16–17]; Alypius [8.8.19, 8.11.27, 8.12.30]; Monica [6.2.2, 9.7.15, 9.10.23–26]; his unmarried wife [6.15.25]),

4) participation in Christian communities (e.g., 5.13.23–5.14.25, 9.6.14),

5) the experience of cultural change related to the Neoplatonic heritage and the Christian monastic movement (e.g., 7.9.14–7.23, 8.6.14–15; Possidius, *v. Aug.* 3, 5), and

6) the encounter with the divine (e.g., 8.12.28–29, 9.1.1).

SIGNIFICANCE OF THE STUDY

Research Significance

This book is significant for promoting an integrated understanding of the diversity and complexity of the religious conversion process through the critical conversation of psychological, social, cultural, and theological perspectives, by using a case study of Augustine's conversion. Scholars have provided various interpretations of Augustine's conversion experience in different disciplines. For example, William James explores the process of interior transformation from the divided self to the integration of the self in relation to one's experience with the divine ("a More") from a perspective of psychology of religion. In this vein, he describes Augustine's conversion as a psychological process of unifying Augustine's divided self.[9] James contributes by advancing his psychological approach to conversion as a conflict resolution in the profound experience of interior transformation ("twice born").

Freudian psychoanalysts have focused on the oedipal conflict and a sense of guilt in the interpretation of Augustine's conversion experience.[10] From a Freudian view, Augustine's conversion experience is, in part, an effort to resolve his oedipal conflict. Freudian psychologists have explained Augustine's self-reproach, his oedipal guilt, and his obsessive personality within Augustine's relationships with his father (Patricius) and with his mother (Monica) in terms of triadic relationships between parents and child. However, Freudian psychoanalytic interpretations display certain hermeneutic limitations. First, because Freudian psychologists elucidate Augustine's personality and his conversion in terms of a model of a person derived from the study of psychopathology, they risk reducing all of Augustine's mental processes to psychopathological processes. Second, because Freudian psychologists examine Augustine's personality and his experiences with reference to a particular period in childhood (the "oedipal" period), they neglect the exploration of the influences of Augustine's experiences and events that occurred before or after that time. Third, Freudian psychologists customarily focus on Augustine's experiences

---

9. James, *Religious Experience*, 171–76.

10. Bakan, "Some Thoughts"; Dittes, "Continuities"; Dodds, "Augustine's *Confessions*"; Kligerman, "Psychological Study"; Pruyser, "Psychological Examination"; Rigby, "Paul Ricoeur."

as more or less "autonomous" or "isolated" from other persons in his life. As such, they mute appreciation of the ongoing interaction between Augustine and other persons.

In addressing this weakness, post-Freudian psychologists have emphasized pre-oedipal experiences/anxieties, a sense of shame, and narcissism to interpret Augustine's conversion experience.[11] From a post-Freudian view, Augustine's conversion is an earnest effort to be healed through a process of self-exposure and self-examination, to overcome pre-oedipal anxiety and a sense of shame, and to promote loving relationships with others and the divine. Post-Freudian interpretations explain Augustine's *Confessions* as a record of the process of self-becoming through developmental and progressive maturity rather than a record of a pathological personality. These interpretations provide insights into the interaction between Augustine's psychological development and his ongoing relationships with others/Other in the process of his conversion.

From a social perspective, scholars have focused on the communal and institutional dimension of Augustine's conversion process.[12] They have explained the influence of others' conversion stories on Augustine's conversion. In doing so, they have investigated how significant others had affected the transforming process of Augustine in light of interpersonal bonds within the Christian communities. From anthropological and philosophical perspectives, scholars have explained the impact of the Christian monastic movement, Neoplatonism, and the North African context on Augustine's thought and his conversion.[13] The anthropological interpretation helps us examine Augustine's cultural and intellectual changes, resulting in the reconstruction of his identity, worldview, and belief. These social and cultural interpretations elucidate the impact of institutional and cultural factors on the complex process of Augustine's transformation. However, on the whole, these interpretations neglect to investigate Augustine's inner division and

---

11. Capps, "Augustine as Narcissist," *Depleted Self*, "Parabolic Events," "Self-Reproach," "Scourge of Shame," "Vicious Cycle"; Dixon, *Augustine*; Gay, "Augustine"; Niño, "Restoration"; Paffenroth, "Book Nine"; Parsons, "St. Augustine."

12. Kreider, *Change*; Kreidler, "Conversion"; Matter, "Conversions(s)"; O'Brien, "Approach"; Van Fleteren, "Augustine's Theory"; Wills, *Augustine's Conversion*.

13. Cary, *Augustine's Invention*, "Book Seven," "Interiority"; Chadwick, *Augustine*; Dobell, *Augustine's Intellectual Conversion*; Harrison, *Augustine*; Lancel, *Saint Augustine*; Lawless, *Augustine*; O'Meara, *Young Augustine*; Zumkeller, *Augustine's Ideal*.

restlessness in his mind as well as to articulate both the interior journey toward union with the divine and the unique transformation of the individual in Augustine's own conversion in terms of knowing oneself and knowing the divine.

From a theological perspective, Augustine scholars have primarily explored the efficacy of the transforming power of God in Augustine's conversion in light of sin, God's grace, and conversion.[14] They describe Augustine's sin as his proud disobedience to God in a sense of guilt and self-exaltation. In this vein, Augustine's conversion experience involves the transformation from the bondage of concupiscence and sin to the state of humility and continence through God's grace. The contribution of the theological interpretation is the examination of the interaction of Augustine's experience of inherited concupiscence and original sin, his experience of the gratuity of God's grace, and his surrender to God. However, this interpretation tends to consider the personal, social, and cultural factors as subordinate to the theological factor (e.g., sin and God's grace) in the process of Augustine's transformation.

Although scholars have presented various ways to understand Augustine's conversion, most of the aforementioned studies have explored Augustine's conversion process from the perspective of a specific theoretical discipline. In other words, the contributions of their conversion studies have tended to stand in separation from one another, because the perspectives are formulated independently of one another.

Using the lens of Lewis Rambo's model of conversion, this book demonstrates that the understanding of Augustine's conversion is enriched by an interdisciplinary approach, which pays attention to the personal and socio-cultural contexts of his time and the religious dimension of his conversion. By critically extending the contributions of the literature, this study presents a more integrated picture of how personal, social, cultural, and religious/theological components interact with one another in the dynamic process of Augustine's conversion. In doing so, it sheds light on the reciprocity of Augustine's interior journey toward encounter with God and his sense of belonging with others within Christian communities in terms of knowing oneself, others, and the divine. Further, this study looks at how Augustine gradually

---

14. Burrell, "Reading the *Confessions*"; Holtzen, "Therapeutic Nature"; Quinn, *Companion*; Russell, "Augustine"; Stark, "Dynamics"; Starnes, *Augustine's Conversion*; TeSelle, "Augustine as Client," *Augustine the Theologian*; Vaught, *Encounters*.

reconstructed his identity, worldview, and belief through intensive interactions with significant others and through affiliations with religious groups, influenced by the Christian monastic movement and the Neoplatonic heritage of the late fourth century.

Practical and Pastoral Significance

In addition, this book is significant for providing a more holistic and multi-dimensional pattern of the conversion process as described in the *Confessions* for experiencing and reflecting on religious change in both the academic field and the Christian community. The *Confessions* is a pilgrim's book that affirms solidarity with fellow human persons going through the common struggle to answer the same crucial question Augustine put to himself.[15] This critical study of Augustine's conversion process gives us an insight into a need for appropriate pastoral care and ministry in the Christian community.

Scholars have presented various paradigms of Augustine's conversion process from the *Confessions*. For example, in "Restoration of the Self: A Therapeutic Paradigm from Augustine's *Confessions*," by using concepts of Heinz Kohut's self psychology, Andrés G. Niño proposes a therapeutic paradigm of the conversion process from Augustine's *Confessions* as follows: 1) recognition of self-fragmentation, 2) return to interiority, 3) recollection in dialogue with God, 4) movement beyond the boundaries of the self, and 5) creative responses in continuity. Niño's paradigm elucidates the therapeutic and loving relationships between the experience of the self and the experience of the divine in Augustine's conversion. Although this paradigm seeks to explain the process of Augustine's self-becoming in terms of the fragmentation and restoration of the self, it tends to neglect the interaction of the experience of the self with the experience of others in light of the impact of others' conversion experiences/stories on Augustine's own conversion. In "Saint Augustine's *Confessions* and the Use of Introspection in Counseling," Timothy A. Sisemore suggests the developmental stages of the conversion process as follows: 1) self-examination through introspection, 2) facing motives, 3) seeing God's grace, and 4) reorientation

---

15. Dixon, *Augustine*, 2; Gay, "Augustine," 193; Kotze, *Augustine's Confessions*, 3; McMahon, *Medieval Meditative Ascent*, 129; Niño, "Restoration," 16; O'Meara, *Young Augustine*, xxvii; TeSelle, "Augustine as Client," 93; Vaught, *Encounters*, ix–x.

to the beauty of God. Sisemore's paradigm explores the relationship between the integration of Augustine's self and his need for God's grace. Although this paradigm uses a psychological perspective, it is inadequate for explaining psychological development from early life experiences and the influence of parental and familial relationships on later life experiences. In *Early Christian Mystics*, Bernard McGinn and Patricia F. McGinn propose a model of Augustine's spiritual journey of the soul's ascent to God mapped out in Neoplatonic terms as follows: 1) an initial withdrawal from the sense world (*conf.* 7.17.23), 2) an interior movement into the depths of the soul (7.10.16), and 3) a movement above the soul to a vision of God (7.17.23). McGinns' model articulates Augustine's interior journey toward God in terms of Neoplatonic and Christian spirituality. However, it is inadequate for explaining the lifelong effects of conversion on Augustine's relationships with himself, others, and the divine for facilitating psychological development and spiritual maturity. Previous studies have not suggested an interdisciplinary and multi-layered pattern to articulate the complex and interrelated factors of Augustine's conversion process.

Through a critical conversation with previous studies within Rambo's interdisciplinary framework, this book contributes by suggesting a more comprehensive pattern of the conversion process from the *Confessions* in order to look at the influence of personal, social, cultural, and theological components on Augustine's conversion. In doing so, this study attempts to characterize more effectively and practically Augustine's conversion experience in light of "universalizing Augustine's story" of conversion. The holistic and multi-dimensional pattern includes the separate yet mutually-informing elements:

1) the expression of one's restless feelings in psychological crisis and spiritual darkness (e.g., *conf.* 8.5.10);

2) entrance into one's inwardness with the divine (e.g., 7.10.16);

3) the confession of one's powerlessness to the divine (e.g., 1.1.1);

4) the experience of loving care and support from other people in the Christian community (e.g., 8.2.3–5);

5) confrontation with philosophical and cultural changes resulting in the reconstruction of personal and religious identity, worldview, and belief (e.g., 8.6.14–15, 8.12.30);

6) the experience of the transformation of "the God representation"[16] (e.g., 1.12.19, 10.28.39); and

7) the re-creation of one's loving relationships with oneself, others, and the divine (e.g., 13.22.32).

This pattern of the conversion process can help both academics who have explored the complicated and multi-faceted phenomenon of religious conversion, and pastoral caregivers in the Christian community who have guided others to understand the impact of the personal, social, and cultural components on the process of human transformation as well as the influence of the transforming power of the divine on the process of religious change.

METHOD OF INVESTIGATION

This book uses an interdisciplinary method for exploring the complex and multi-dimensional process of religious conversion. This study uses Lewis Rambo's approach to religious conversion in order to formulate a methodological framework. In *Understanding Religious Conversion*, Rambo suggests an interdisciplinary approach to describe how conversion occurs through the mediation of personal, social, cultural, and religious components. Rambo highlights the idea that human beings are individuals embedded in immediate social contexts as well as in larger cultures and religious traditions, so that any attempt to explain conversion must be interdisciplinary: "Good scholarship should start with rich description of the phenomenon, and with respect for its integrity."[17] Rambo openly states his stance as a Christian and as a scholar of conversion, at which point he repudiates a tendency to understand religious conversion within "mere" psychological, sociological, or anthropological terms. For Rambo, the appreciation of the religious dimension of conversion and respect for personal accounts of encounters with the divine are essential for a more accurate perception of this complex phenomenon. Rambo argues that psychological, sociological, anthropo-

---

16. *The God representation* refers to an internal structure through which one's experience of and relationship with God is mediated. From an interdisciplinary approach, the God representation evolves throughout the human life span, influenced by the complex interaction of the person with personal, social, cultural, and religious forces (see Rizzuto, *Birth*; Spero, *Religious Objects* ; Spiro, "Collective Representations").

17. Rambo, *Religious Conversion*, 11.

logical, and theological disciplines are all equally pertinent to the study of religious conversion. Following Rambo, I realize that one particular discipline alone (e.g., psychology) is not sufficient to understand the nature and process of religious change. I demonstrate that 1) religious conversion is usually an evolving process in which many aspects of a person's life may be affected, and that 2) the study of religious conversion is enriched by an interdisciplinary approach, which examines coherently the personal and socio-cultural contexts of the convert and the religious dimension of conversion.

Rambo's model guides us to investigate a range of personal, social, cultural, and religious factors in the process of Augustine's conversion. In this study, the term *person* refers to an individual being, which includes the psyche (the mind and emotions), the body, and the soul. The term *society* means the system or condition of living together as a community in such a group, which includes "the interaction between individuals and their environmental matrix, and the relationships between individuals and the expectations of the group in which they are involved."[18] The term *culture* denotes "a manifestation of human creativity and a powerful force in the shaping and renewal of individuals, groups, and societies."[19] The term *religion* has to do with "the human concern, both individual and collective, with the spiritual, transcendent, or supernatural realm of existence."[20] The categories of the person, society, culture, and religion help us foster a critical conversation between social science and theology/religion that elucidates the diversity and complexity of religious conversion. In other words, these categories help us to use critically and collaboratively religious/theological and social science perspectives for an integrated reinterpretation of Augustine's transformational process.

DEFINITION OF RELIGIOUS CONVERSION

Conversion: The key biblical words for conversion are *naham* and *shûv* in Hebrew, and *metanoia* and *epistrophé* in Greek. The first word in each pair, *naham* and *metanoia*, emphasizes repentance and specifies

---

18. Rambo, *Religious Conversion*, 9; Dixon, *Augustine*, 14.
19. Rambo, *Religious Conversion*, 9; Dixon, *Augustine*, 15.
20. Rambo, *Religious Conversion*, 177.

a "turning *from*" (sin), while the second in each pair, *shûv* and *epistrophé*, indicates a "turning *toward*" (God).²¹ In classical Latin, and in Augustine's works as well, *conversio* and *convertere* refer to "the act of returning or becoming, the effect of a change, whether in a spiritual or in a material sense."²² From a perspective of psychology of religion, William James notes that, "To be converted, to be regenerated, to receive grace, to experience religion, to gain an assurance, are so many phrases which denote the process, gradual or sudden, by which a self . . . becomes unified and consciously right superior and happy."²³ From a sociological perspective, William S. Bainbridge conceptualizes conversion as "the joining of a new religious fellowship."²⁴ From an anthropological perspective, Diane Austin-Broos explains conversion as a process, which involves "an encultured being arriving at a particular place."²⁵ From a theological perspective, Donald K. McKim defines conversion as "one's turning or response to God's call in Jesus Christ in faith and repentance."²⁶ From a perspective that integrates psychology, sociology, anthropology, and religion, Lewis Rambo describes conversion as "a process of religious change that takes place in a dynamic force field of people, events, ideologies, institutions, expectations, and orientations."²⁷ From an interdisciplinary perspective, my definition of the term *religious conversion* has to do with the complex and multidimensional process of religious change that brings about the total reorientation and transformation of one's life, influenced by the interplay of personal, social, cultural, and religious components.

OUTLINE OF CHAPTERS

This book consists of six chapters: Following an introduction, chapter 2 explores critical insights by way of search for scholarship about religious conversion within the disciplines of psychology, sociology, anthropology, and theology. Then this chapter introduces Lewis Rambo's

21. Conn, "Conversion," 214–15.
22. Reta, "Conversion," 239.
23. James, *Religious Experience*, 189.
24. Bainbridge, "Sociology," 187.
25. Austin-Broos, "Anthropology," 2.
26. McKim, *Westminster Dictionary*, 62.
27. Rambo, *Religious Conversion*, 5.

Facing the Challenge

model of religious change, which brings together psychological, social, cultural, and theological aspects and integrates them into a process model. Chapter 3 describes the case of Augustine's conversion experience in order to illustrate the process of religious change. Then this chapter intends to provide a sufficient account of Augustine's main life history and some of his basic thought to create a better understanding of the process of his conversion.

Chapter 4 attempts to get insights through critical search for scholarship about Augustine's conversion from psychological, sociological, anthropological, and theological perspectives. More specifically, while succinctly rehearing each (discipline) of the contributions of religious conversion as discussed in chapter two, this chapter moves from a multidisciplinary presentation, seriatim, of the range of interpretations of Augustine's conversion to an interdisciplinary conversation between and among the interpretations of his conversion. As such, it presents specific interdisciplinary questions that intend to extend critically the contributions of the literature by bringing together various disciplines: How might we investigate the interrelated influence of personal, social, cultural, and religious factors on the *process* of Augustine's conversion? How had Augustine's psychological crises affected his earnest quests for knowing himself and the divine? How were Augustine's interior journey for union with God and his search for community with others knit together in the process of his conversion? How had significant other people in the Christian community provided love, support, and belonging to fulfill Augustine's psychological needs and to make up for his frustration with his deprivations in the social and cultural conditions of his time? How had Augustine reshaped his (personal and religious) identity, worldview, and belief through his interactions with others, and through his participation in Christian communities, and through his experiences of cultural change?[28]

Based on the critical and integrative questions of chapter 4, chapter 5 presents an integrated reinterpretation of Augustine's conversion through the mutually-informing conversation of the personal, social, cultural, and religious dimensions within Rambo's interdisciplinary

---

28. In addition, this chapter asks: How were Augustine's interpersonal relationships, his God representations, and his encounters with God bound together in his conversion process? How were Augustine's relationships with himself, others, and the divine related to his psychological development and spiritual maturity?

framework. In other words, it shows a coherent and integrated picture of how the complicated and multi-layered components of Augustine's conversion process interact with one another. In doing so, this chapter explains how and why Augustine converted to Christianity and what specific experiences led him to conversion. Following this reinterpretation, it intends to present additionally a holistic pattern of the conversion process from the *Confessions*. Chapter 6, as a conclusion, explores the implications of understanding Augustine's conversion for scholars of religious conversion and pastoral caregivers in the Christian community.

2

Exploring Insights
Search for Studies of Religious Conversion

> [Most of] the published material on conversion resembled a metropolitan train yard crowded with separate tracks that ran parallel to each other, where each individual train had its own assigned track and never crossed over to another.... Only a few scholars of conversion were aware that the subject was traversed by more than one track, and that there could even be more than one train on each track.
>
> —Lewis R. Rambo[1]

THIS CHAPTER EXPLORES CRITICAL insights by way of search for studies of religious conversion within the disciplines of psychology, sociology, anthropology, and theology. Then it introduces Lewis Rambo's theory of religious conversion, which brings together psychological, social, cultural, and theological perspectives and integrates them into a process model.

---

1. Rambo, *Religious Conversion*, xiv.

PSYCHOLOGICAL STUDIES OF CONVERSION

Psychological theorists and researchers have examined the underlying personal factors involved when individuals convert to various religious orientations. There is no common understanding and explanation of the phenomenon of religious change. In "A Psychology of Conversion: From All Angles," Sara Savage describes the diverse interpretations of conversion among the scholars of different schools:

> sudden conversion vs. gradual conversion;
> adolescent conversion vs. mid-life conversion;
> conversion preceded by crisis vs. no crisis;
> conversion as passive vs. conversion as active;
> negative mental health outcomes vs. positive mental health outcomes;
> conversion as socially constructed vs. spiritually inspired;
> the individual self as a goal vs. self-in-relationship as a goal.[2]

Mindful of the complexity and diversity of conversion studies undertaken by psychologists, this section of the literature review focuses on four main themes because they are valid for investigating the personal dimension of the human transformation process and because they are helpful to establish an integrated understanding of religious change. These main themes are 1) conversion and regressive psychopathology; 2) conversion, crisis, and the unification of the divided self; 3) conversion, intellectual arousal, and cognitive satisfaction; and 4) conversion, identity, and human development.

Conversion and Regressive Psychopathology

Freudian scholars have tended to regard religious conversion as a regressive, disintegrative, and pathological phenomenon. In *The Future of an Illusion*, Sigmund Freud, who has strongly affected the psychoanalytic study of conversion, describes the term *illusion* as the distortion of objective perception. According to Freud, *religion* refers to an illusion, which involves the distortion of the reality of the human condition: "[Religion] comprises a system of wishful illusions together with a disavowal of reality . . . in a state of blissful hallucinatory confusion."[3] Freud insists that religion is only fantasy; it is "an attempt to master

---

2. Savage, *Psychology*, 2.
3. Freud, *Future of an Illusion*, 55–56.

the sensory world in which we are situated by means of the wishful world which we have developed within us as a result of biological and psychological necessities."[4] In this vein, religion is an anxious search for substitutes for an unpleasant reality. For Freud, religion as an illusion involves human projection from the early experiences of infantile helplessness: "Biologically speaking, religiousness is to be traced to the small human child's long-drawn-out helplessness and need of help; and when at a later date he perceives how truly forlorn and weak he is when confronted with the great forces of life, he feels his condition as he did in childhood, and attempts to deny his own despondency by a regressive revival of the forces which protected his infancy."[5] In this sense, Freud characterizes religion as a universal obsessive neurosis of humankind: "One might venture to regard obsessional neurosis as a pathological counterpart of the formation of a religion, and to describe that neurosis as an individual religiosity and religion as a universal obsessional neurosis."[6] Freud contends that "of the three powers [art, philosophy, and religion] which may dispute the basic position of science, religion alone is to be taken seriously as an enemy."[7] For this reason, Freud's whole purpose in regard to religion is to unmask the completely irrational, fantastic, illusionary nature of religion, and to overcome religion as merely human projection and a universal obsessive neurosis of humankind.

Freud reverses the Genesis text of the Bible from "God created man in His own image" to say "Man created God in his."[8] Freud remains interested throughout his life in the process by which humankind creates God in his/her own image. Thus, in his clinical studies, Freud has explored the process of the formation of the "image" or idea of the divine ("the concept of God") in an individual psyche. For Freud, the image of a divine Being [God] originates from an imaginary enlargement of the father figure based on one's relation with the natural father: "the god of each of them is formed in the likeness of his father, that his personal relation to God depends on his relation to his father the flesh and oscillates and changes along with that relation, and that at bottom

---

4. Freud, *Introductory Lectures*, 207.
5. Freud, *Leonardo da Vinci*, 83–84.
6. Freud, "Obsessive Acts," 126–27.
7. Freud, *Introductory Lectures*, 198.
8. Freud, *Psychopathology*, 33.

God is nothing other than an exalted father."[9] As such, Freud's task is to explain the emergence of the God idea in the history of humanity and individuals.

Freud asserts that religious conversion emerges from the Oedipus complex, the relationship with the father. He writes,

> It roused in him [a young boy] a longing for his mother which sprang from his Oedipus complex, and this was immediately completed by a feeling of indignation against his father. . . . But the outcome of the struggle was displayed once again in the sphere of religion and it was of a kind pre-determined by the fate of the Oedipus complex: complete submission to the will of God the Father. The young man became a believer and accepted everything he had been taught since his childhood about God and Jesus Christ. He had had a religious experience and had undergone a conversion.[10]

For Freud, religious conversion is a matter of surrendering to the father's or Father's will. As a young boy acknowledges the superior power of his father and so puts to rest the Oedipus complex, the convert accepts the omnipotence of God and resolves this Oedipus situation, which has been displaced into the sphere of religion.[11] This means that for Freud, religious conversion is rooted in the oedipal complex of the person in childhood which is deeply related to the infantile compensation for the harshness of life, an illusory way of protecting oneself against one's own helplessness. In that sense, for Freud, religious ritual has to do with pathological expression of infantile wishes—an irrational and obsessive action—in order to deal with one's sense of helplessness, anxiety, and guilt.

Following Freud, Freudian psychoanalysts tend to describe religious conversion as a regressive pathology. For example, Leon Salzman regards conversion as a regressive defense against repressed hostility toward authority. He identifies repressed resentment for authority figures as the motivating force for conversion: "the conversion experience has represented a method of solving the conflict arising from the hatred toward the father. . . . [It] may be used for conflict with any authority

---

9. Freud, *Totem and Taboo*, 182; see 183–87.
10. Freud, "Religious Experience," 245–46.
11. Ibid. See Scroggs and Douglas, "Issues," 210.

figure, whether the father, the mother, or other significant persons."[12] In "Types of Religious Conversion," Salzman analyzes specific case studies of converts who had manifested regressive behaviors in order to confirm the psychological characteristics of the pathological conversion. He finds that sudden converts were characterized by "extreme dependency on strong, omnipotent figures." These converts tended to have unusually repressed hatred toward their fathers or toward authority. As a result, Salzman posits six pathological characteristics of the regressive conversion as follows:

> (1) The convert has an exaggerated, irrational intensity of belief in the new doctrine; in many converts, however, though they may remain in the new faith the ardor does not continue at the same high level; (2) The convert is more concerned with the form and doctrine than with the greater principle of his new belief; (3) his attitude toward his previous belief is one of contempt, hatred and denial, and he rejects the possibility that there might be any truth in it; (4) he is intolerant toward all deviates, with frequent acting-out by denouncing and endangering previous friends and associates; (5) he shows crusading zeal and a need to involve others by seeking new conversions; and (6) he engages in masochistic and sadistic activities, displaying a need for martyrdom and self-punishment.[13]

Like Salzman, in "The Personalities of Sudden Religious Converts," John P. Kildahl considers conversion as a regressive psychopathology. Kildahl administers a set of psychological tests to twenty first-year theological students who had experienced sudden religious conversions. He finds that sudden converts tended to be less intelligent and to score higher on the hysteria scale. He concludes that sudden converts tended to be more emotional, subject to mood swings, excitable, fearful, and showed relatively less independence and creativity.[14]

In response to the results of the psychoanalytic studies of conversion, Rambo notes that the psychoanalytic tradition has influenced the recognition of the importance of childhood, the unconscious, and the possibility of pathology in the conversion experience. Rambo insists that psychoanalytic scholars have viewed conversion as "a coping

---

12. Salzman, "Psychology," 187.
13. Salzman, "Types," 18–19.
14. Kildahl, "Personalities," 40–44.

device with the goal of guilt resolution, hostility management, and the identification of the person with the father figure," and that they have guided readers to interpret conversion as "a regressive, disintegrative, and pathological phenomenon."[15] Rambo comments that most psychoanalysts have depended on narrow and restrictive case studies in order to demonstrate the regressive pathology of religious conversion. This means that they have usually studied either small numbers of mentally ill patients or those persons affiliated with deviant religious organizations. These psychoanalysts have emphasized the person's "guilt, terror, grief, and emotional deprivations, sufferings, and desires." Thus, for them, conversion is inherently associated with emotional illness and pathological regression.[16]

Conversion, Crisis, and the Unification of the Divided Self

Psychologists of religion have explored the correlation between one's emotional crisis, the unification of the divided self, and religious change. In doing so, they have viewed religious conversion as a progressive and regenerative phenomenon (while assuming or preserving the presence or activity of the religious subject—the divine, the sacred, or God—in the process of human transformation). The empirical research of the early pioneers in the field of psychology of religion suggests that religious conversion often occurs during and after a period of stress, despair, even crisis. In *The Varieties of Religious Experience*, William James, who has deeply influenced the study of conversion within the psychology of religion, describes the term *religion* as a personal experience with the divine ("a More"). James writes, "Religion . . . shall mean for us *the feeling, acts, and experiences of individual men in their solitude, so far as they apprehend themselves to stand in relation to whatever they may consider the divine*."[17] For James, experience is the core of living itself; it is also multifaceted. In this vein, the varieties of religious experience are closely related to the varieties of human experience.

Unlike Freud, James asserts that personal religious experience is rooted and centered in the mystical states of consciousness. He notes

---

15. Rambo, "Bibliography," 155.
16. Ibid.; *Religious Conversion*, 142; "Theories," 266.
17. James, *Religious Experience*, 31. Italics in the original.

that "In mystic states we both become one with the Absolute and we become aware of our oneness."[18] This means that the primordial and solitary experience of the person lies in his or her inner union with the divine. James delineates four characteristics that identify an experience as mystical: 1) *Ineffability*—Like states of feeling, mystical experiences cannot be adequately expressed in words and thus can only be known by those who have them; 2) *Noetic quality*—Mystical states are experienced as states of knowledge, as sources of deeply significant illuminations; 3) *Transciency*—Mystical experiences are fleeting, lasting at most an hour or two. While tending to elude full recollection in normal states of mind, mystical experiences leave a lasting impression on the inner life and are immediately recognized when they recur; 4) *Passivity*—Although mystical states can be actively facilitated through meditation and other spiritual disciplines, the mystic may feel grasped by the Other beyond a sense of personal control.[19]

According to James, there are two basic styles in religious life; one is "the healthy-minded way" and the other is "the morbid-minded way." The healthy-minded person tends to ignore the reality of evil in the world because he or she has a view that life is basically good and joyous. However, the morbid-minded person ("the sick soul") vividly perceives the pervasiveness of evil in the world because he or she is preoccupied with suffering. For James, whereas the healthy-minded person tends to be usually "once born," the morbid-minded person tends to be "twice born" in order to be happy after experiencing inner transformation within mystical states.[20] James defines religious conversion as follows:

> To be converted, to be regenerated, to receive grace, to experience religion, to gain an assurance, are so many phrases which denote the process, gradual or sudden, by which a self hitherto divided, and consciously wrong inferior and unhappy, becomes unified and consciously right superior and happy, in consequence of its firmer hold upon religious realities.[21]

James employs Edwin D. Starbuck's concept of two types of conversion: the first is the *volitional type*—a voluntary way—in which the regenerative change is usually gradual, and consists in the building

18. Ibid., 419.
19. Ibid., 380–82. See Wulff, *Psychology of Religion*, 487–88.
20. James, *Religious Experience*, 162–68, 488.
21. Ibid., 189.

up of a new set of moral and spiritual habits; the second is the *self-surrender type*—an involuntary way—in which the personal will must be given up, at which point rapid change usually happens.[22] Although he acknowledges the gradual changes of growth in the volitional type of conversion, James concentrates on the self-surrender type of conversion—a way of mystical experience—in order to explain that the discordant personality of the sick of soul tends to be transformed by the intervention of the divine, and that his or her divided self tends to be integrated in the inner communion with the Other. In this vein, he describes conversion as "*a process of struggling away from sin rather than of striving towards righteousness.*"[23] James summarizes the characteristics of religious life which result from the religious conversion experience:

> 1. That the visible world is part of a more spiritual universe from which it draws its chief significance;
>
> 2. That union or harmonious relation with that higher universe is our true end;
>
> 3. That prayer or inner communion with the spirit thereof—be that spirit "God" or "law"—is a process wherein work is really done, and spiritual energy flows in and produces effects, psychological or material, within the phenomenal world;
>
> 4. A new zest which adds itself like a gift to life, and takes the form either of lyrical enchantment or of appeal to earnestness and heroism;
>
> 5. An assurance of safety and a temper of peace, and in relation to others, a preponderance of loving affection.[24]

Like James, Edwin D. Starbuck emphasizes the positive and regenerative effects of religious conversion. During his statistical study of conversion, he attempts to discover "the mental and spiritual processes at work during conversion, rather than to establish any doctrine."[25] In the examination of 192 records of respondents, Starbuck finds that anxiety, fear, a feeling of incompleteness, and a sense of sin were the prominent characteristics of the pre-conversion state. He also finds that

22. Ibid., 206–9.
23. Ibid., 209.
24. Ibid., 485–86.
25. Starbuck, *Psychology of Religion*, 21.

during the "normal" conversion, the personal will of the individual was surrendered, which was necessary before greater harmony could be achieved. Starbuck insists that the converts resolved their sense of sin, dejection, confusion, and depression through the conversion experience. As a result, he asserts that religious conversion becomes a means to alleviate the emotional distress of the individual and plays a role in enhancing the convert's religious awakening and growth. Starbuck concludes,

> It may in countless cases be a perfectly normal psychologic[al] crisis, marking the transition from the child's world to the wider world of youth, or from that of youth to that of maturity. . . . After conversion they almost invariably set out with new and high resolves; their attitude towards life had been transformed; in the presence of the new life old habits had apparently passed away, new interests and enthusiasm had been awakened; motives and purposes had been purified, higher ideals aroused; frequently the personality seemed entirely changed.[26]

Contemporary researchers have continued to examine the progressive and integrative aspects of religious conversion for the mental health of the person in terms of the resolution of emotional crisis.[27] In *The Transformed Self: The Psychology of Religious Conversion*, Chana Ullman describes religious conversion as "the occasion of a dramatic change in a person's life and on core elements of a person's self."[28] She focuses on the significance of emotional needs and attachments in the process of conversion to authoritarian religious traditions: "Conversion is best understood in the context of the individual life. It occurs on a background of emotional upheaval and promises relief by a new attachment."[29] Ullman studies forty religious converts from different religious groups (Judaism, Roman Catholicism, Bahai, and Hare Krishna), and a group of thirty religiously affiliated non-converts (Jewish and Catholic) who served as a matched control group. Ullman finds that the common pre-conversion state of a much larger percentage of

26. Ibid., ix, 355.
27. Carl W. Christensen insists that the psychoanalytic studies of conversion have contributed to the exploration of the psychopathological element of religious experience/belief. For Christensen, however, psychiatrists have tended to forget that "religion is a normal part of man's individual and cultural life" ("Religious Conversion," 17).
28. Ullman, *Transformed Self*, xv.
29. Ibid., xvii.

the converts (in comparison to the control group) was characterized by great emotional crisis—"feelings of despair, doubts of self-worth, fear of rejection, and estrangement from others." She also finds that most converts had experienced stressful and broken relationships with their fathers during childhood, at which point they would tend to move forward the quest for a perfect figure of Father (the divine or God). She demonstrates that conversion offered relief from the emotional struggles in which the converts found themselves, while seeking out connection and love within the context of religious faith and affiliation. For Ullman, the converts had experienced a positive sense of self through the process of merging with an idealized and powerful god figure in light of the correlation between the extension of the self and identification with the divine. As a result, Ullman concludes that emotional factors (e.g., emotional turmoil or distress) have played a prominent role in precipitating and establishing the psychodynamic conceptualizations of the conversion experience.

In the same way, Joel Allison views conversion as adaptive and positive: "we find tentative support for viewing conversion phenomena as a means of promoting personality integration."[30] After conducting an empirical study of young male converts, Allison finds that most converts had perceived the figures of their actual fathers as weak, ineffective, or absent. Consequently, he asserts that conversion functioned as a progressive, adaptive, and healthy process for young converts, in that these converts were able to move away from dependence upon and enmeshment with the mother and to replace the abnormal figures of their actual fathers with "a positive and powerful paternal figure," namely God.[31]

Like Ullman and Allison, Charles W. Stewart and Kenneth I. Pargament regard religious conversion as positive and integrative. They both consider conversion as a way of using religiosity to cope with the stress and crises of the person, while preserving the role of the divine or the sacred in the process of human transformation. In "The Religious Experience of Two Adolescent Girls," Stewart presents developmental studies of two normal adolescents who had religious experiences. He finds that the converts had experienced difficult relationships with others (e.g., parents, friends, church members, or God) before the

30. Allison, "Empirical Studies," 32.
31. Allison, "Religious Conversion," 23–38.

conversion, which is understood as a part of their total life history. He also finds that during the conversion experience, the youth had maintained inner integration in the face of their problems and had proceeded to reconciliation with the external world and with the divine. As a result, Stewart concludes,

> Religious conversion can be a means of creatively coping with, particularly, the interpersonal stress in one's environment and a healthy problem-solving activity. It is as such not a result of motives of deprivation but of motives of mystery, when the youth interiorizes his problem and "waits on" a new orientation of the self to the environment. The healing of alienation with his God and a reconciliation enabling him to cope with his external world with his God-given powers have been the age-long way of symbolizing the drama in religious terms.[32]

Likewise, Pargament understands conversion within a religious coping process of the person with respect to the role of the divine in the conversion process. He defines religion as "a process, a search for significance in ways related to the sacred."[33] For Pargament, coping refers to a process of actively searching for ways of solving various problems. Religious coping involves the relief or resolution of the emotional turmoil or enduring stress of the person within an encounter with the sacred. For Pargament, religious conversion is "an effort to re-create life, the individual experiences a dramatic change of the self, a change in which the self becomes identified with the sacred."[34] It involves the identification of the self with one of three types of sacred objects: "a spiritual force (spiritual conversion), a religious group (religious group conversion), or the whole of humanity (universal conversion)."[35]

In a more specific and extended view, Zinnbauer and Pargament define spiritual conversion—one type of religious conversion—"as a radical change in the self in response to a great deal of perceived stress through which the self became identified with a spiritual force."[36] Influenced by James, Zinnbauer and Pargament argue that the process of spiritual conversion includes six key elements: 1) the experience of

---

32. Stewart, "Religious Experience," 55.
33. Pargament, *Psychology of Religion*, 32.
34. Ibid., 248.
35. Ibid., 254.
36. Zinnbauer and Pargament, "Spiritual Conversion," 173.

life stress; 2) a divided sense of self; 3) motivation for radical change; 4) a unified sense of self; 5) the sacred becomes incorporated into the self; and 6) a life transformed.[37] According to Mahoney and Pargament, there are two key functions of spiritual conversion both psychologically (i.e., changes in the search for significance) and spiritually (i.e., changes in the sacred's role in one's life). In this vein, this spiritual conversion, which is related to "the interior world of religious conversion," involves a two-tiered reorientation in the relationship between the self and the sacred; it stimulates a change of the core destination of a person's life, and the person transforms his/her life pathway to reach this destination. This transformation may bring shifts in relationships, habits, patterns of thought, emotional reactions, and, more generally, a new sense of guidance in the journey of life.[38]

In order both to examine the nature and to test the definition of spiritual conversion, in "Spiritual Conversion: A Study of Religious Change among College Students," Zinnbauer and Pargament have studied a sample of 130 Christian college students, including religious converts and non-converts. They discover that in comparison with non-converts, most converts did experience more emotional stress and a greater sense of personal inadequacy/limitation before their conversions. They also discover that in conversion experiences, the religious converts underwent positive life transformation and significant improvements in their sense of self, self-esteem, self-confidence, and self-identity, and that in the post-conversion experiences, the converts had typically undertaken both greater improvement in their sense of adequacy/competence and higher connection between the self and the sacred. As a result, Zinnbauer and Pargament conclude and confirm that spiritual conversion plays an essential role in promoting a radical transformation in the self in response to emotional crises through which the self becomes identified with a spiritual force.

Conversion, Intellectual Arousal, and Cognitive Satisfaction

Some scholars have examined the role of human intellectual arousal and cognitive satisfaction in the conversion process. In "The Implications

---

37. Ibid., 167.
38. Mahoney and Pargament, "Sacred Changes," 483.

of Cognitive-Experiential Self-Theory for Research in Social Psychology and Personality," Seymour Epstein focuses on the intellectual and cognitive elements of conversion that are the fundamental motivations for the religious change of the person, while respecting the affective elements of that transformation. According to Epstein, individuals process information and acquire memory structures (schemas about self, others, and the world) to adapt to their surroundings by two systems—the rational and the experiential—and these two systems operate by different rules. For Epstein, information processing in the rational system is dispassionate, based upon analytical thinking and socially mediated knowledge, while information processing in the experiential system is driven by emotion.[39] Epstein explores how a person's quest for change is related to his or her motivational structures and proposes a model of motivation which includes four basic factors for human transformation: the need to experience pleasure and avoid pain, the need for a conceptual system, the need to enhance self-esteem, and the need to establish and maintain relationships.[40] For Epstein, the force of each of these motivations varies among different persons at different times and in different circumstances. Epstein points out that intellectual arousal and cognitive satisfaction are rooted in the human need for a conceptual system. Consequently, he asserts that these intellectual arousal and cognitive satisfaction are fundamental motivations for the religious change of the person; that is, they play a prominent role in facilitating the psychodynamic conceptualizations of the human experience of conversion.

Similar to Epstein, John Lofland and Norman Skonovd emphasize the role of intellectual variables in conversion experiences. For Lofland and Skonovd, the intellectual convert actively seeks out knowledge about religious or spiritual issues through books, television, articles, lectures, and other media that do not involve significant social contact. With intellectual conversion there is little or no social pressure; the searching and eventual conversion may happen over a moderate length of time, emotional arousal is tame, and the belief of the person precedes his or her participation in religious community. Lofland and Skonovd assert that conversion can be a result of personal intellectual exploration and the intellectual convert is a person who loves knowing

39. Epstein, "Integration," 709.
40. Epstein, "Implications," 283–310.

truth and searches for the meaning of life. For Lofland and Skonovd, although it is not common, the intellectual mode of conversion is probably on the increase because of the increasingly "privatized" nature of religion and of contemporary life in western society as well as the ever-increasing presence of "disembodied" media of religious communication (e.g., magazines, specialized newspapers, movies, video, "electronic church," etc.).[41]

Like Lofland and Skonovd, in "The Pleasure of Believing: Toward a Naturalistic Explanation of Religious Conversions," Fabrice Clement articulates the relationship between conversion and intellectual arousal from a cognitive point of view. Clement regards converts as "the truth seekers" who both engage in the rational quest for the ultimate and search for the meaning of life in a normal mental process. He employs Alison Gopnik's theory of the knowing process of the child to explore the intellectual or epistemic element of the conversion experience. According to Clement, Gopnik as a developmental psychologist finds that children tend to use extensively their energy to explain their environments: "explanation is to cognition as orgasm is to reproduction."[42] Gopnik views this highly positive and provocative force as an explanatory orgasm, which corresponds to the "aha" experience when the child understands a former unresolved problem and reaches intellectual satisfaction.

Based on the theory of Gopnik, Clement examines how this "aha-experience" of the person is related to the intellectual or epistemic dimension of the conversion process.[43] He proposes that conversion takes place in the "sophisticated mental apparatus" of the person. In order to seek out actively the meaning of life, the person engages in the rational quest for truth or the ultimate. In experiencing conversion, this person finds answers to his or her existential problems. Thus, he or she reaches cognitive satisfaction and gains a feeling of comprehensiveness, totality, and wholeness. For Clement, the intellectual or epistemic drive of the person—one of the human motives—leads him or her to the conversion process. Clement stresses the use of the cognitive energy of the person to understand his or her conversion experience.[44]

41. Lofland and Skonovd, "Conversion Motifs," 376–77.
42. Clement, "Pleasure of Believing," 74.
43. Clement, "Pleasure of Believing," 71, 74–75, 86.
44. Ibid., 76–86.

Conversion and Human Development

Psychologists have explored the connection between religious conversion and the process of human development in terms of the self/person-in-relationship.[45] In *The Dynamics of Religious Conversion*, V. Bailey Gillespie describes religious conversion as "a way of change" in the whole personality and orientation of the person, a change which involves his or her identity formation in the process of human development. For Gillespie, religious conversion plays an essential role "in the construction of personal identity, pointing a life in a particular direction, giving it an aim, giving it new meaning and purpose."[46] Gillespie writes that religious conversion includes the following constituent elements:

> 1) a unifying quality for self, which includes self-integration, wholeness, and possible reorganization and integration; 2) a positive behavior; 3) an intensity of commitment to an ideology, usually thought of as occurring within the Christian tradition as a confrontation with ultimates but may include change with any subjective religious quality; 4) . . . a decisive "change or returning to" brought on suddenly or gradually, seen as either instantaneous or incubational; 5) a sense of belonging or understanding of personal identity itself. The "triggers of change" may be influenced by personality, gender differences, environment, mystical experience, or practical (pedagogical) influences.[47]

Gillespie claims that religious conversion is a means by which one acquires a personal identity. Influenced by Erik H. Erikson, Gillespie regards identity formation as "the way to become" in which one experiences a sense of the self, integration, and continuity in the dynamic process of the life cycle.[48] For Gillespie, the person's new identity forged in the dynamics of change is closely related to one's profound relationships

---

45. As such, scholars have paid attention to the role of the age or developmental stage of the person in the conversion process. Some scholars have hypothesized that religious conversion is more likely to occur during adolescence (see Gillespie, *Dynamics*, 183; James, *Religious Experience*, 199). On the other hand, some scholars have claimed that religious conversion is a primarily an adult phenomenon (see Conn, *Christian Conversion*, 197, 286; Fowler, *Becoming Adult*, 116–20; *Stages of Faith*, 282; Hiltner, "Theology of Conversion," 35).

46. Gillespie, *Dynamics*, 60.

47. Ibid., 64–65.

48. Ibid., 132–40. See Erikson, *Childhood and Society*, 247–74.

with the self, others, the environment, and the divine. Gillespie argues that there are essential relationships between religious conversion experience and the identity crisis/formation experience of the person: 1) both experiences are means of radical personal change, which affects the self, ideology, behavior, and ego process at the core of a person's being; 2) both experiences have common functions in areas of ego strength genesis, identity formation, ego processes, ideological satisfactions, and role experimentation; 3) both experiences exhibit dynamic similarities in the general feeling tones, construction/content of the crises, decisions, and resultant functions of integration and congruity; and 4) both experiences promote personal need satisfaction, problem-solving, and maturation during difficult times of questing.[49] Gillespie notes that religious conversion fosters a deep, integrating effect and influence on personal attitudes, values, and feelings about oneself; likewise, personal identity formation includes feelings of wholeness and sameness in individuals.[50] As a result, Gillespie asserts that religious conversion is a particular kind of "identity forming experience."

In a related vein, James W. Fowler has examined the interrelatedness between the conversion experience and the process of faith development of the person. Fowler defines conversion as "a significant recentering of one's previous conscious or unconscious images of value and power and the conscious adoption of a new set of master stories in the commitment to reshape one's life in a new community of interpretation and action."[51] Fowler's concept of faith includes two broad dimensions: faith as a way of relating and as a way of knowing. Faith as a way of relating includes the trust, loyalty, and mutuality of the person, which is related to a sense of the self, others, and the divine. Faith as a way of knowing is an ongoing process of acting and "composing" of the known through one's life span. Fowler proposes a theory of faith development which includes a pre-stage of "undifferentiated" faith and six faith stages—1) intuitive-projective, 2) mythic-literal, 3) synthetic-conventional, 4) individuative-reflective, 5) conjunctive, and 6) universalizing.[52] Based on this theory, he shows how the faith development of the person—the "way of interpreting and relating to the ultimate

---

49. Gillespie, *Dynamics*, 191.
50. Ibid., 184.
51. Fowler, *Stages of Faith*, 281–82.
52. Ibid., 119–213; see 285–86.

conditions of existence"—influences his or her growth and transformation in a lifelong process.

From a more specific and extended view, Fowler in *Becoming Adult, Becoming Christian* understands conversion in light of the correlation of human psychological development with Christian faith development. For Fowler, religious conversion refers not simply to a single event, but "an ongoing process" in the life of the transformation of the person. More specifically, Fowler writes, "By conversion . . . I mean an *ongoing process—with . . . a series of important moments of perspective-altering convictions and illuminations—through which people (or a group) gradually bring the lived story of their lives into congruence with the core story of the Christian faith.*"[53] For Fowler, the term *self-groundedness* refers to a commitment to the establishment of one's personal destiny, in which one determines the purpose and meaning of life by oneself. In contrast, the term *vocation* indicates a process of divine calling for the person, in which one finds "a purpose for one's life that is part of the purposes of God."[54] Fowler intends to combine both the conversion experience and human development in the movement from self-groundedness toward vocation. As a consequence, Fowler contends that religious conversion involves a release from the burden of the self-groundedness of the person in making his or her own destiny; it also involves the restructuring of the growth and virtue of the person through his or her partnership with God's work in the world.[55]

Similarly, Walter Conn in *Christian Conversion: A Developmental Interpretation of Autonomy and Surrender* has elucidated the correlation between religious conversion and personal development in terms of the human drive for self-transcendence. Conn regards conversion as a personal experience of profound change—"the total reorientation of one's life"—which leads one into healthy growth, quest, and personal autonomy in a lifelong process. He suggests a threefold strategy for the study of religious conversion from a developmental perspective: 1) to explore the connection between an adequate understanding of conscience and a normative interpretation of conversion; 2) to situate the various dimensions of conversion within a pattern of personal development; and 3) to present how a critical understanding of conversion can

---

53. Fowler, *Becoming Adult*, 115.
54. Ibid., vii, 87–91.
55. Ibid., 113–15.

be grounded in a theory of self-transcendence from a developmental perspective.[56] According to Conn, religious conversion is "a special, extraordinary transformation of religious consciousness" of the person within the human developmental process.[57] Based on the work of the developmental psychologists Erik H. Erikson, Jean Piaget, Lawrence Kohlberg, James Fowler, and Robert Kegan, Conn proposes a model of personal development and self-transcendence to understand one's conversion process, which includes affective, cognitive, moral, and religious dimensions. For Conn, the person inherently has attraction to, and a need for, transcendence. Conn claims that the human drive for transcendence can be a primary motivation for religious conversion. Both religious conversion and the development of personal autonomy are commonly centered in self-transcendence. Conn asserts that religious conversion fosters "the completion of personal development toward self-transcending autonomy," which is related to the mutual interaction of justice, universalizing faith, generativity, and interindividual intimacy within the life of the convert.[58]

In sum, from the perspective of psychology of religion, conversion has been regarded as regressive psychopathology, a process of unifying the divided self, an experience of intellectual arousal and cognitive satisfaction, or a part of the positive human developmental process. On the whole, psychological studies of conversion have primarily emphasized the individual convert's inner crisis, need, and mental development/fulfillment.

These psychological studies of conversion contribute by elucidating the influence of personal factors (especially the psychological distress or crisis of the potential convert within specific personal and familial contexts) on the process of religious change. In doing so, Freudian interpretations of conversion lead us to realize the importance of childhood, the unconscious, and the possibility of pathology in the conversion experience of the person. Some psychologists (of religion) (e.g., W. James; B. J. Zinnbauer and K. I. Pargament) provide an insight into the link of the potential covert's healing of inner dividedness with his or her religious experience. Some scholars (e.g., F. Clement; S. Epstein) encourage us to pay attention to the role of human intellectual arousal

---

56. Conn, *Christian Conversion*, 1.
57. Ibid., 197.
58. Ibid., 267–68. See Conn, "Conversion," 214–15.

and cognitive satisfaction in the conversion process, while acknowledging the emotional and affective dimension of human transformation. Some psychologists (e.g., J. W. Fowler; V. B. Gillespie) compel us to explore the correlation of religious change with the human developmental process in terms of the self/person-in-relationships.

In particular, some psychologists (of religion) have assumed or preserved the existence or participation of some religious subjects—the divine (e.g., W. Conn; V. B. Gillespie; E. D. Starbuck; C. W. Stewart; C. Ullman), the sacred (e.g., A. Mahoney and K. I. Pargament; B. J. Zinnbauer and K. I. Pargament), or the Divine/God (e.g., J. W. Fowler; W. James), while exploring the correlation of religious conversion with human change. As such, they give us insights into how the potential convert's psychological distress or crisis has affected him/her to reflect on his/her past life history as well as how it has stirred his/her quests for knowing himself/herself and knowing the divine in light of the interaction of the experience of the self and the experience of the divine.

SOCIOLOGICAL STUDIES OF CONVERSION

Scholars in the field of sociology of religion have explored the impact of social and institutional factors on the conversion experiences of persons within religious communities. With respect to the complexity of the sociological studies of conversion, this section of the literature review pays attention to three main themes which are suitable for elucidating the social and communal dimensions of the human transformation process and which are beneficial for investigating the complexity and richness of religious change. These main themes are 1) conversion, deprivation, and religious affiliation, 2) conversion and social influences, and 3) conversion, member recruitment, and religious institutions.

Conversion, Deprivation, and Religious Affiliation

Sociologists have examined the role of the deprivation in the conversion process in terms of the resolution of enduring personal frustration through religious affiliation. The term *deprivation* refers to the sense of frustration, tension, disadvantage, alienation, or strain of potential converts which originates from experiences of societal inequality. *Strain theory* contends that persons engage in religious affiliations in order to satisfy conventional desires that unusual personal or collective deprivation have frustrated due to this inequality.[59] In *Religion and Society in Tension*, Charles Y. Glock and Rodney Stark assert that pre-converts "feel" deprived as a predisposing condition for conversion. Glock and Stark consider religion as a social phenomenon. In this vein, they describe conversion as a means for resolving the sense of deprivation or stress of pre-converts within their difficult social conditions in terms of the correlation between tension and religious commitment. For Glock and Stark, feelings of deprivation, as incentive for change, have tended to lead persons to participation in religious groups. These feelings of deprivation have also tended to enable persons to build new religious and social movements: "a necessary precondition for the rise of any organized social movement, whether it be religious or secular, is a situation of felt deprivation."[60] This means that deprived persons tend both to transform their unsatisfying life-styles or conditions by accepting a new ideology through religious affiliation and to deal with their felt problems by making an alliance with a supernatural force through religious commitment. In doing so, religious groups have tended to recruit these potential converts who have felt feelings of frustration, deprivation, tension, or grievance toward the social conditions of inequality. Glock and Stark note that "religious resolutions . . . are likely to compensate for feelings of deprivation rather than to eliminate its causes."[61]

In a similar vein, John Lofland and Rodney Stark in "Becoming a World-Saver: A Theory of Conversion to a Deviant Perspective" have examined how conversion experiences are related to the pre-existing strains of persons. After studying a West Coast millenarian group, Lofland and Stark find that the pre-converts perceived problems (although these problems objectively did not appear to be overly severe), and as a result, they had experienced high levels of tension over a period of time leading up to their conversions. Lofland and Stark report that a feeling of frustration or deprivation was an essential characteristic of the condition that precipitated conversion to a radical religious group/sect.[62] As a consequence, Lofland and Stark write, "For conversion a person must

---

59. Bainbridge, "Sociology," 178–81.
60. Glock and Stark, *Religion and Society*, 249.
61. Ibid.
62. Lofland and Stark, "World-Saver," 864.

experience, within a religious problem-solving perspective, enduring, acutely-felt tensions that lead him [or her] to define himself [or herself] as a religious seeker."[63] For Lofland and Stark, persons' participation in religious communities can make up for their feelings of deprivation or alienation.

Influenced by Lofland and Stark, William Bainbridge in "The Sociology of Conversion" explores the link between the enduring personal frustration and the religious affiliation of converts in the process of transformation. Bainbridge insists that strain theory would emphasize the personal needs of deprived persons to satisfy conventional social desires through the conversion experience.[64] For Bainbridge, the person experiences a sense of deprivation, which comes from comparison with other people in the society or a comparison with his or her previous situation. This means that this person is deeply frustrated with his or her life. The person becomes a religious seeker on a quest to promote a more satisfactory life. This person makes a strong commitment to the religious community and can assuage his or her feeling of deprivation or strain within a supportive religious group. As a result, Bainbridge writes, "Religion offers a way to transcend and transvalue relative deprivation. . . . In joining a religion, the person adopts an ideology about life that transforms deprivation into a virtue, or at least provides supernatural compensation for it."[65]

In a same way, Nanlai Cao agrees with other scholars' hypothesis that religious conversion is a means to resolve the feelings of deprivation, alienation, or frustration of the pre-converts within specific social contexts through religious affiliation or commitment. In "The Church as a Surrogate Family for Working Class Immigrant Chinese Youth," Cao demonstrates how persons' involvement in immigrant religious communities can make up for their feelings of frustration, deprivation, or alienation in an unfamiliar society. Cao regards a religious community (e.g., The Cantonese Church of the Lord) as "a surrogate family" for pre-converts in order to facilitate both adaptation and upward assimilation to middleclass norms in newly immigrant society (e.g., New York's Chinatown). After studying Chinese youth of working class immigrants in New York, Cao finds that the feelings of deprivation,

---

63. Ibid., 862.
64. Bainbridge, "Sociology," 178–81; see 186.
65. Ibid., 180.

strain, or tension of these marginalized Chinese youth stirred them into conversion to Christianity. Cao also finds that the ethnic church ("an Americanized, yet Chinese-led Christian church") played a vital role in fostering successful adaptation and upward assimilation to middleclass norms. It enabled the disadvantaged to overcome their difficulties and offers a caring environment to build up their confidence. As a consequence, Cao states, "The newly adopted religion becomes central in the adaptive strategy of young Chinatown Chinese in the face of socioeconomic hardship. Bound by the love of the intergenerational Chinese church family and driven by the strength of their new Christian faith, those disadvantaged immigrant youth have managed to survive the emotional and physical costs of immigration."[66]

Conversion and Social Influences

Many sociologists have explored the impact of social influences on the conversion experience in terms of interpersonal bonds and social networks. *Social influence theory* contends that persons participate in religious communities because they have formed social attachments with other members in these communities and because their attachments to nonmembers are weak.[67] In *The Social Construction of Reality*, Peter Berger and Thomas Luckmann emphasize the social and institutional dimension of religious conversion. For Berger and Luckmann, the conversion experience is centered in the social interactions of persons within the religious community. Berger and Luckmann write, "It is only within the religious community, the *ecclesia*, that the conversion can be effectively maintained as plausible. . . . It provides the indispensable plausibility structure for the new reality. . . . Saul may have become Paul in the aloneness of religious ecstasy, but he could *remain* Paul only in the context of the Christian community that recognized him as such and confirmed the 'new being' in which he now located this identity. This relationship of conversion and community is not a peculiarly Christian phenomenon."[68]

---

66. Cao, "Church," 198.
67. Bainbridge, "Sociology," 178–79.
68. Berger and Luckmann, *Social Construction*, 177–78.

In a similar way, Roger A. Straus proposes that potential converts are seekers who actively conduct their search for creative transformations within the social and institutional context of a particular group. Straus views religious conversion as "a personal and collective accomplishment," which is rooted in interpersonal interactions between the potential convert and the group members.[69] He demonstrates how religious seekers act to discover and make use of a particular means of personal transformation offered by and institutionalized within a specific community. For Straus, religious seekers actively engage in the transformation of their actions: "the way to be changed is act changed."[70] This means that during this transforming process, new converts are able "to make conversion behaviorally and experientially real to self and others, to immerse self in the world of fellow-converts, and master the specific practices institutionalized by the group for the maintenance and expansion of 'results' (the new identity, conduct, forms of subjective experience and grounds of meaning ascribed to conversion)."[71]

Like Straus, in "The Sociology of Conversion," David A. Snow and Richard Machalek elucidate the impact of social influences on the transforming experiences of converts. According to Snow and Machalek, there are three broad categories of social influences on the conversion experience: social networks, affective and intensive interaction, and role learning. Social networks are very important in explaining how people are engaged in new religious movements and organizations. Snow and Machalek have studied religious groups (e.g., Pentecostals, Evangelicals, etc.) in order to investigate the connection between social networks and the conversion experience. They find that the vast majority of group members/devotees—ranging from 59 percent to 82 percent—were recruited through social networks. The affective and intensive interaction of potential converts with other group members can function "as an information bridge, increase the credibility of appeals, and intensify the pressure to accept those appeals and corresponding practices." The process of learning roles in the religious community leads persons into cognitive and behavioral transformations.[72]

---

69. Straus, "Religious Conversion," 158; "Changing Oneself," 252–73.
70. Straus, "Religious Conversion," 163.
71. Ibid.
72. Snow and Machalek, "Sociology," 182–84.

Along the same line, Max Heirich in "Change of Heart" examines how social interaction and influence deeply affect the conversion experiences of persons in light of the correlation between the personal transformation and the social network. Heirich regards conversion as "the process of changing a sense of root reality" that provides meaning and orientation for understanding one's situation and acting in relation to it. In particular, Heirich intends to determine what specific factor has the greatest impact on the transformation experiences of converts. Heirich has studied Roman Catholic Pentecostals who received baptism and a group of non-converts who served as a matched control group. Heirich uses a broad array of indicators in order to test three factors common to sociology of conversion: stress (e.g., actively felt tension), prior socialization (e.g., the educational backgrounds of respondents or the degree of religious orientation of parents), and immediate social influence (e.g., frequent attendance with other believers at Mass). He finds that stress indicators to be no more pronounced in converts than in non-converts. He also finds that immediate interpersonal influences had more impact on the conversion experiences of respondents than personal felt tension or prior socialization. Heirich asserts that social contact is an essential factor for precipitating conversion experiences: "the process of conversion occurs through use of available social networks."[73] As a result, Heirich states that immediate social influences enable the potential convert ("a religious seeker") to stimulate a "change of heart," which involves a conscious shift in one's sense of ultimate grounding.[74]

Influenced by Lofland and Stark, Arthur L. Greil and David R. Rudy agree with other scholars' hypothesis that social influences are crucial in leading persons to conversion experiences.[75] In "Conversion to the Worldview of Alcoholics Anonymous," Greil and Rudy suggest that studies of the conversion process should pay more attention to the institutional or organizational context in which conversion occurs, while acknowledging the religious dimension of the conversion process. They

---

73. Heirich, "Change of Heart," 673. See Bainbridge, "Sociology," 187–90; Greeley, "Religious Musical Chairs," 101–26.

74. Heirich, "Change of Heart," 673–74.

75. For Lofland and Stark, becoming a convert is "coming to accept the opinions of one's friends" ("World-Saver," 871; see Kilbourne and Richardson, "Communalization," 206–12; "Paradigm Conflict," 1–21; Weininger, "Interpersonal Factor," 27–44).

Exploring Insights

describe conversion as "a radical transformation of personal identity," which is rooted in personal relationships with other members within the group.[76] For Greil and Rudy, during the conversion process, one engages in a solution to problems related to drinking, but also in the reconstruction of a personal worldview by identifying with a new ideology of a social and religious group (e.g., Alcoholics Anonymous). The central dynamic in the conversion process is rooted in one's acceptance of the opinions of other members of the community. There are similarities between the observed A.A. conversion process and the model generally described in the sociological literature on religious conversion (e.g., Lofland and Stark's model of conversion [1965]): "First, affective bonds within the group and intensive interaction with group members are necessary. Second, the likelihood is reduced that the prospective convert will interact with reference others who do not share the group's perspective. Third, the organization stresses the homogeneity of members *vis a vis* the ideology. . . . Fourth, concrete acts of commitment strengthen the loyalty of the prospective [sic] convert to the group."[77]

Similar to Greil and Rudy, in "The Spread of Religions and Macrosocial Relations," Robert L. Montgomery examines the role of the macrosocial context of potential converts in the spread of religions. Montgomery insists that religion offers important resources for the creation, consolidation, support, and strength of a society's identity. For Montgomery, the intersocietal and intergroup relations within a specific context influence the acceptance, rejection, or mixed acceptance of new religions in a given society—"Acceptance means that the introduced religion becomes part of the social identity of large numbers of people in the social unit. A rejection of the introduced religion means that it continues to be regarded primarily as 'foreign.'"[78] In some cases, the spread of a new religion is crucial both for bringing dramatic changes among numerous members of a receiving group and for providing a stronger source of resistance to outside pressures than any other available religion, especially the traditional religion. Montgomery employs the case of the Christianization of Korea to illustrate this phenomenon. Western Christianity became a very important religion in Korea during the Japanese occupation between 1910 and 1945. Because Japan had

76. Greil and Rudy, "Conversion," 6.
77. Ibid., 22.
78. Montgomery, "Spread of Religions," 38.

presented an overwhelming threat to the identity of the Korean people by forcibly imposing Japanese language and religion (e.g., "Shinto shrines"), Koreans had welcomed the Christian message advocated by the European and American missionaries. That means, as a new religion, Christianity enabled the Korean people both to resist the outside pressure of Japan and to preserve the values and the identity of Korean society.[79] As a consequence, Montgomery argues that macrosocial contexts/relations are essential in the conversions of persons or a group to a specific religion.

In a related vein, Andrew Buckser agrees with other scholars' hypothesis that social and institutional factors are crucial in leading persons to conversion experiences. In "Social Conversion and Group Definition in Jewish Copenhagen," Buckser investigates how persons convert to a specific religion (i.e., Judaism) through family relationships (e.g., intermarriage with non-Jewish persons) or social interactions with members of the community. Buckser views conversion as a social act or phenomenon in which "one enters into a set of new relationships with members of a religious community"[80] According to Buckser, as a well established minority group, the Jewish community in Copenhagen, Denmark, created a substantial institutional and cultural tradition. The Jews of this community have intermarried non-Jewish Danes at extremely high rates, although the Orthodox interpretation of Jewish law has imposed constraints on the recognition of mixed marriages. In such a situation, conversion to Judaism through intermarriage is an unavoidably communal and religious issue for this Jewish community, which usually includes tension or conflict over the nature of Jewish ethnic identity, authority, and religiosity.[81]

Buckser shows how the new convert is socialized into the specific group both by accepting the norms and beliefs of this group and by participating in the social activities and religious rituals of this group. To illustrate this process, Buckser uses the case of "marriage conversion" to Judaism in the Jewish community of Copenhagen. Anna Jensen was a Danish woman who married a Jewish man, Oskar Goldschmidt. In order to marry Oskar, Anna had attended the educational programs and rituals of this Jewish community to learn Jewish religion,

79. Ibid., 47.
80. Buckser, "Social Conversion," 69.
81. Ibid., 70–73.

Exploring Insights

ideology, and life-style for one year, together with Oskar. After successfully completing all programs, Rabbi Bent Melchior performed a conversion ceremony for Anna, at which point Anna became a Jew. The larger family and congregation members welcomed Anna to their community through intermarriage and declared her proper position in this community, even though intermarriage could be a transgression of Orthodox Jewish law. Buckser insists that Anna's marriage with Oskar had fostered extensive connections to Jewish identity ("Jewishness") and religiosity, although that process was not easy. Buckser concludes that extensive interpersonal bonds and social networks enable persons to join a specific group as well as to convert to a new religion.

Conversion, Member Recruitment, and Religious Institutions

Sociologists have examined the methods of member recruitment of religious organizations in the conversion process. David A. Snow, Louis A. Zurcher, and Sheldon Ekland-Olson suggest a microstructural approach to the recruitment process which emphasizes structural influences on recruitment strategies and patterns. They show why and how some people are recruited into particular social and religious organizations. For Snow et al., social and religious movement organization's networks function as an important determinant for recruiting new members: "recruitment cannot occur without prior contact with a recruitment agent."[82] According to Snow et al, there are four general engagement tactics that religious institutions can employ in order to recruit new members:

> (1) [The group members/agents] can channel their promotion and recruitment efforts among strangers in public places by face-to-face means; (2) They can promote via the institutionalized, mass communication mechanisms; (3) They can recruit among strangers in private places by such means as door-to-door canvassing; (4) They can promote and recruit through members' extramovement social networks.[83]

In a related vein, Rodney Stark and William S. Bainbridge account for member recruitment to cults and sects in terms of networks

---

82. Snow et al., "Social Networks," 789.
83. Ibid., 795.

of faith. In the study of religious groups (e.g., A Doomsday Group, the Ananda Commune, and the Mormons), Stark and Bainbridge find that recruitment primarily occurred in interpersonal relations between cult members and potential recruits. Religious organizations functioned as places to enable recruits to construct intensive interactions with other members. They assert that the recruitment process is centered in affective relations within specialized religious settings. As a result, Stark and Bainbridge state that "human persons desire interpersonal bonds, and they ... try to protect them from rupture" by accepting the new faith of the religious group.[84]

Similar to Stark and Bainbridge, in *Bible Believers: Fundamentalists in the Modern World*, Nancy T. Ammerman shows how a fundamentalist church has recruited new members into their community by using their own mission strategies in pluralistic American society. She describes conversion as a recruitment process—"bring them in"—in which one becomes a member in a specific congregation. For Ammerman, the term *fundamentalism* includes three characteristics: "separation from the world, dispensational premillennialism, and biblical literalism."[85] Ammerman, as a participant observer, conducts an experiential and empirical study of the fundamentalist Southside Gospel Church in Connecticut. She finds that this church emphasized separation from the world. This means that members of the congregation lived disciplined lives in which they gave up some worldly pleasures (e.g., drinking or dancing); they constantly sought God's will for their lives and maintained their religious sensibilities in everyday affairs. She also finds that the church members, as a cultural minority group in American society, had extensively used their time and energy to maintain their institutional networks as well as to extend their community by recruiting new members ("prospects"). For Ammerman, Southside Gospel Church employed systematic methods for new member recruitment which effectively motivated all church members to participate in saving souls: inviting unsaved persons ("the lost") to church worship services or activities, broadcasting the Christian message (e.g., the radio ministry, mail, or phone calls), teaching the young (e.g., Sunday School, Vacation Bible School, Southside Christian Academy, etc.), the bus ministry (i.e., the deliverance of the gospel on buses during

---

84. Stark and Bainbridge, "Networks," 1394.

85. Ammerman, *Bible Believers*, 6.

transportation of potential members), visiting prospects (i.e., a door-to-door visitation program), and encouraging the potential converts to publicly walk the aisle to facilitate "the moment of salvation" during the invitation hymn at the Sunday worship service.[86] Ammerman insists that in the recruitment process, new converts adopted the ideology of this community and reconstructed their religious identities,[87] lifestyles, and beliefs within this fundamentalist congregation. As a consequence, supporting Peter Berger's view on conservative religion as a sacred canopy, Ammerman states, "Churches like Southside provide such modern wanderers a home. They provide an all-encompassing sacred canopy in which belief is possible."[88]

In a similar way, Dean M. Kelley in *Why Conservative Churches Are Growing* delves into the correlation of strictness with religious commitment in the recruitment process. For Kelley, *strictness* refers to a "way to conserve social strength" within the religious organization.[89] Kelley catalogues three traits of the ideal-typical strict church—absolutism, conformity, and fanaticism—and contrasts them to three traits of the more lenient church—relativism, diversity, and dialogue.[90] In short, strict churches demand adherence to a distinctive faith, morality, and life-style. Kelley writes,

> Those who are serious [strict] about their faith: 1. Do not confuse it with other beliefs/loyalties/practices, or mingle them together indiscriminately. . . . 2. Make high demands of those admitted to the organization that bears the faith. . . . 3. Do not consent to, encourage, or indulge any violations of its standards of belief or behavior by its professed adherents. 4. Do not keep silent about it, apologize for it, or let it be treated as though it made no difference, or should make no difference, in their behavior or in their relationships with others.[91]

---

86. Ibid., 148–55.

87. For Ammerman, religious identities are located in the religious narratives of the specific community ("Religious Identities," 216, 223–24; "Congregational Stories," 289–301).

88. Ammerman, *Bible Believers*, 212.

89. Kelley, *Conservative Churches*, 120.

90. Ibid., 78–83.

91. Ibid., 121.

Understanding Religious Conversion

Kelley insists that the higher growth rates of the more conservative groups reflect their greater ability to present their members with "meaning," an understanding of the ultimate goals and purposes of life. For Kelley, strict churches have the organizational resources for the recruitment of potential converts and the growth of these communities. In other words, the high commitment of church members, translated into the giving of money and time, provides such groups with the material and human resources in order to carry out their mission, including recruitment of new members. Kelley suggests a strategy of member recruitment to religious organizations based on the traditional heritage of the Anabaptists and Wesleyans:

a. Be in no haste to admit members.

b. Test the readiness and preparation of would-be members.

c. Require continuing faithfulness.

d. Bear one another up in small groups.

e. Do not yield control to outsiders, nor seek to accommodate to their expectations.[92]

Influenced by Kelley, Laurence R. Iannaccone in "Why Strict Churches Are Strong" demonstrates that during the recruitment process, conservative churches encourage committed membership and demand a high level of participation. Iannaccone emphasizes the collective activities of religious institutions in order to foster both member recruitment and extended membership within groups in light of the remarkable structure for mutual aid and reinforcement. He writes, "individual members benefit both from their own religious participation and from that of others . . . a church member who attends regularly, sings wholeheartedly, greets others warmly, and testifies enthusiastically enhances not just his [or her] own spiritual life but also those of his [or her] fellow members."[93] Consequently, Iannaccone asserts that the organizational strength and resources (e.g., money and time) of strict churches enable these communities effectively to recruit new members as well as to extend successfully their groups.

---

92. Ibid., 176.

93. Iannaccone, "Strict Churches," 1185. See Olson and Perl, "Variations in Strictness and Religious Commitment," 757–64.

In conclusion, from the perspective of sociology of religion, conversion has been viewed as a resolution of enduring personal frustration or deprivation through religious affiliation, a result of interpersonal bonds and social networks, or a product of the effectiveness of institutional recruitment strategies. On the whole, sociological studies of conversion have described the converts as active religious seekers who establish relations with other persons within specialized religious settings.

These sociological studies of conversion have primarily contributed by showing the impact of social and institutional factors on the complex process of human transformation. They have effectively elucidated the interaction of the experience of the self with the experience of others in the process of the socialization or institutionalization of the person. As such, they have greatly contributed by depicting how significant other people in the religious communities/institutions have provided love, support, and belonging to make up for the potential convert's frustration with his or her deprivations in the social and cultural conditions of his or her time as well as to mold and confirm the values, expectations, and beliefs of religious groups. However, these sociological interpretations of conversion are not sufficient to investigate the potential convert's inner disconnection or struggle in his or her own mind, at which point they are inadequate to show both the interior journey toward union with the divine and the unique transformation of the individual in the process of religious conversion in terms of knowing oneself and knowing the divine.

ANTHROPOLOGICAL STUDIES OF CONVERSION

Scholars in the field of anthropology of religion have examined the role of cultural factors in the conversion process of persons or a group within specific contexts. In doing so, anthropologists have richly described the cultural context in which religious change takes place; they have tended to establish long-term relationships with persons or groups in particular cultural milieus. With respect to the complexity of the anthropological studies of conversion, this section of the literature review pays attention to three main themes because they are more beneficial for articulating the cultural dimension of the religious conversion process and for understanding better the complex phenomenon of religious change.

These main themes are 1) conversion and rationality, 2) conversion and acculturation, and 3) conversion and cultural revitalization.

Conversion and Rationality

Anthropologists have explored the impact of rationality on the conversion process within specific cultural settings. *Rationality theory*—the intellectualist model of religious change—contends that during the transition from one religious group to another, persons or groups do not "simply passively internalize symbols and meanings but actively evaluate and adjust their understanding as demands and circumstances change."[94] Based on rationality theory, Robin Horton has focused on the impact of the traditional African cosmologies on the conversion process. For Horton, *cosmology* refers to "a system of ideas about unobservable personal beings whose activities are alleged to underpin the events of the ordinary, everyday world."[95] Horton proposes a model of the African cosmology which has a two-tier structure: "In the first tier we find the lesser spirits, which are in the main concerned with the affairs of the local community and its environment—i.e., with the microcosm. In the second tier we find a supreme being concerned with the world as a whole—i.e., with the macrocosm. Just as the microcosm is part of the macrocosm, so the supreme being is defined as the ultimate controller and existential ground of the lesser spirits."[96]

Horton investigates how traditional African cosmologies affect the conversions of persons or groups to world religions (e.g., Christianity or Islam) in terms of the intellectual challenge of the encounter of the macrocosm. Drawing on numerous data of African conversions, Horton finds that the lesser spirits in the microcosm were important for Africans in order to foster the smooth running of daily village affairs and social relations. The religious concerns of Africans revolved around the explanation, prediction, and control of their concrete world (i.e., their microcosm). This means that Africans related to these lesser beings rather than the supreme being, who was not relevant to their daily lives. Horton also finds that because of increasing mobility and

---

94. Hefner, "World Building," 119.
95. Horton, "African Conversion," 101.
96. Ibid.

interaction with people from the wider social world, the Africans sought to expand their myths, rituals, and symbols in order to make sense of the new cultural situation and to reconstruct their cosmology. Horton argues that the crucial variables of religious change among indigenous peoples "are not the external influences (Islam, Christianity) but the pre-existing thought-patterns and values, and the pre-existing socioeconomic matrix."[97] He concludes that the indigenous groups were attracted to new religions according to their own needs vis-à-vis their own situation: "acceptance of Islam and Christianity is due as much to the development of the traditional cosmology in response to *other* features of the modern situation as it is to the activities of missionaries."[98]

In a related vein, Robert W. Hefner in "World Building and the Rationality of Conversion" agrees with Horton's account of African conversions because it has delineated Africans as active seekers in the process of religious change rather than as passive consumers or victims. Hefner describes conversion as a change in affiliation from one religious group to another, when an individual moves outside a restricted terrain (i.e., the microcosm) into an expanded social world (i.e., the macrocosm). Influenced by Horton, Hefner challenges the Weberian characterization of traditional religions as intellectually non-rational. According to Hefner, Max Weber has argued that traditional religions are piecemeal in their approach to problems of meaning, but world religions formulate comprehensive responses to the ethical, emotional, and intellectual challenges of human life.[99] Influenced by Weber, Clifford Geertz views world religions as more rational and universalized from a perspective of cultural relativism. Geertz insists that the primary difference between traditional and world religions is that the former are organized around a "rigidly stereotyped . . . cluttered arsenal of myth and magic," but the latter "are more abstract, more logically coherent, and more generally phrased." In other words, world religions show "greater conceptual generalization, tighter formal integration, and a more explicit sense of doctrine."[100]

Following Horton, Hefner attempts to overcome a dichotomy within the Weberian heritage between traditional religions and world

---

97. Horton, "Rationality," 221.
98. Horton, "African Conversion," 103. See Aguilar, "African Conversion," 530.
99. Hefner, "World Building," 7.
100. Geertz, "Internal Conversion," 171–72.

religions, and between the rational and the irrational. He asks: Are world religions always rational? Are traditional African religions always irrational? Hefner argues that the beliefs of traditional religions can be rational in specific cultural contexts, while acknowledging that world religions codify their doctrines more abstractly and systematically. He writes,

> Traditional [African] religions are not necessarily less rational than world religions, just narrower in focus . . . traditional religions concentrate on a smaller, more local array of problems. . . . The spirits most commonly invoked in traditional religions—ancestors, territorial guardians, nature spirits—are similarly drawn from familiar terrains. This does not mean that traditional beliefs are either irrational or even less rational than more encompassing canons. They can be entirely rational in relation to the circumstances they engage. Indeed, in a restricted social context the more universalistic dogmas of the world religions might well be meaningless.[101]

In a critically extended view, Mario I. Aguilar in "African Conversion from a World Religion" suggests an alternate approach to the study of the rationality of religious conversion. In doing so, Aguilar demonstrates a paradigm shift for the study of African conversion *from* "religious affiliation from a traditional African religious group to a world religious group" *to* "religious diversification in a specific context" in terms of reconversion to traditional practices. Aguilar agrees with Horton's model of the African cosmology for the study of conversion because it helps Africans both to explain how certain events for changes happen in their social and cultural contexts and to reconstruct new religious cosmology based on their pre-existing thought-patterns, ideologies, norms, and beliefs. According to Aguilar, Horton has focused on traditional African religious institutions that provide the foundation for the acceptance or rejection of Islam or Christianity. These local religious institutions (i.e., micro-cosmical systems) had to adapt in order to cope with macro-cosmical systems as represented by Islam and Christianity. However, Horton does not pay attention to outside forces on African conversion to Islam or Christianity (e.g., the arrival of the colonial powers, or the work of missionaries in particular geographical areas). Aguilar does not agree with Horton's view on Islam and Christianity as only

---

101. Hefner, "World Building," 20.

Exploring Insights

"catalysts—i.e., stimulators and accelerators of changes which were 'in the air' anyway"[102]—and complements Horton's perspective, by critically using Humphrey J. Fisher's approach to African conversion.[103] In that sense Aguilar explores the political and structural influences on the process of African conversion within a specific historical context. For Aguilar, Islam as an outside force enabled the Boorana people to change their cosmology and to be Muslims, because Islamic traders and clerics were present in "the markets of Isiolo, Garba Tulla, Mado Gashi, Merti and other Boorana settlements in the Waso area."[104] Aguilar asserts that "[cultural and] historical processes of [African] conversion need to be assessed not only from the point of view of one of the world religions but also in terms of the adaptability of a local religious tradition."[105]

Aguilar claims that conversions in Africa during the twentieth century cannot be simply studied in light of changes in affiliation from traditional religious groups to world religious groups. In order to illustrate a process of religious change and diversification within a social and cultural environment, Aguilar employs the case of the Waso Boorana. According to Aguilar, the Boorana people settled in the Waso area of north-eastern Kenya in the 1930s. Because of the settling of colonial administrative boundaries, they became isolated from the rest of the Boorana in northern Kenya and Ethiopia. Because of their interaction with the Somali, the Waso Boorana underwent a process of "somalisation" through which they replaced their indigenous Oromo ritual performances with Islamic practices. That is, many Boorana people had converted to Islam during colonial times (1932–62). However, after the independence of Kenya in 1963, the Waso Boorana had experienced new challenges to their own cosmology and their religious affiliation.

---

102. See Horton, "African Conversion," 104.

103. Humphrey J. Fisher does not agree with Horton's approach to African conversion that "the essential patterns of religious development in black Africa, even Christian and Islamic development, are determined by the enduring influence of a traditional cosmology" ("Juggernaut's Apologia," 153). Fisher argues that the institutions of Islam or Christianity have deeply influenced on the changes of the traditional African religious cosmology in historical contexts, based on three religious developmental stages of quarantine, mixing, and reform (ibid., 153; see "Conversion Reconsidered"). Similarly, J. D. Y. Peel comments that Horton has neglected the external influences on African conversions to Islam or Christianity from an ahistorical perspective (see "Conversion and Tradition," "History, Culture and the Comparative Method").

104. Aguilar, "African Conversion," 532.

105. Ibid., 536.

Understanding Religious Conversion

During post-colonial times (1963–92), the Waso Boorana had gradually reconverted to their traditional religion (related to both the *ayyaana*—their lesser beings/spirits—and the *Wagga*—their supreme being) and had participated in their traditional Boorana religious practices in order to reconstruct their own cosmology within a new social and cultural context, while rejecting and/or attending the Islamic or Roman Catholic rituals. Aguilar finds that the Waso Boorana responded rationally to the cultural, social, and political changes of colonial and post-colonial times in light of the adaptability of a local religious tradition in a wider world. Aguilar asserts that "religious diversification has been a sensible and rational communal response to the need to keep the Peace of the Boorana" in light of unity in diversity.[106] As a consequence, Aguilar states, "the study of conversion in Africa during the twentieth century cannot be limited to changes in religious affiliation from a local religious tradition to a world religion. African processes of conversion are fluid, and they also include processes of reconversion to religious practices socially present in the eras preceding the world religions."[107]

Conversion and Acculturation

Anthropologists have articulated the link of acculturation with the conversion experiences of persons or groups within particular contexts. *Acculturation* denotes the process of becoming adapted to a new or different culture with more or less advanced patterns in terms of cultural transition from the old context to the new context. The process of acculturation usually involves the mutual influence of different cultures through close contact. As a Christian missionary anthropologist, Alan R. Tippett has examined the role of acculturation with the conversion experiences of persons or groups in specific cultural contexts. Tippett brings his experiences in the South Pacific to a discussion of how conversion occurs in non-Western cultural surroundings (i.e., small island communities in New Guinea). He describes conversion as "a dynamic process in Christian mission" which must be intricately related to the worldview, norms, and beliefs of a new cultural group in light of the result of lasting life-change within specific environments. He deals with

---

106. Ibid.
107. Ibid., 526; see 536.

the process of the acculturation of particular group members or groups and carries out a question: "How are people (1) separated from the old context, and (2) incorporated into the new?"[108] Tippett explores the general structure of *total* group movements into Christianity. In that sense, he emphasizes *group conversion* which engages in "the process of multi-individual experience and action of a group, through its competent authority, whereby the group changes from one conceptual and behavioral context to another, within the operations of its own structure and decision-making mechanisms regardless of whether or not the external environment changes."[109] He insists, "When such group decision is specifically religious, if new elements are innovated, the group self-image may need restructuring, and a new set of norms may have to be fixed. The group may demand from each individual some ocular demonstration of separation from the old context."[110] After thoroughly reviewing his own extensive field data of the conversion process in the island world of the Pacific, Tippett schematizes a sequential stage model of the acculturation process that includes four periods and three points. In brief, Tippett's model of acculturation can be illustrated in light of "from old context (pagan) to new context (Christian)" as follows: 1) the period of awareness (a. the points of realization); 2) the period of decision making (b. the point of encounter); 3) the period of incorporation (c. the point of consummation/confirmation); 4) the period of maturity. As the conversion experience proceeds with a mobility from left to right, it passes from one unit into the next through a specific point which can be identified.[111] Tippett's model focuses on the strategies of the cultural insiders who saw the acceptance of Christianity as advantageous. This model provides a framework for understanding the dynamics of cultural transition in different and variable societies and for elucidating the stages a group goes through in the process of accepting a new religious orientation.

Like Tippett, Charles H. Kraft in "Cultural Concomitants of Higi Conversion" demonstrates the impact of cultural forces on the conversion process within a specific ethnographical setting. As an anthropologically oriented missionary, Kraft has surveyed the early period of the

108. Tippett, "Cultural Anthropology," 193.
109. Ibid., 194.
110. Ibid.
111. Ibid., 195–205; "Conversion," 206–20.

growth of Christianity among the Higi people of northeastern Nigeria. He finds that Islam was brought to the Higi area early in the nineteenth century through the conquests of the Fulani tribe. However, most of the Higi people did not convert to Islam because the Muslims in that same area were the Fulani people. The Fulani, as African warriors, had previously captured indigenous Africans and sold them into slavery. For this reason, they had traditionally become enemies of the Higi; finally, there was a strong tendency to reject Islam because of its association with the Fulani. On the other hand, within traditional Higi culture, there was another powerful tendency to respect white people based on one of their traditional proverbs—"Fear God, fear the White Man."[112] As the indigenous Higi worldview linked Whites with God rather than with man, the Higi people respected Euro-American Christian missionaries during the process of cultural and religious transformation. Moreover, the Higi people gradually reconstructed their cosmology and accepted the Christian message about God based on their pre-existing religious tradition (e.g., their concepts of the High God—*Hyelatamwe*—and household gods). Kraft asserted that the indigenous culture stimulated the Higi people to make a positive response to Christianity. He concludes that various cultural factors played an important role in fostering and eliciting conversion among the Higi people.

In a related vein, Kwai Hang Ng in "Seeking the Christian Tutelage" explores the role of cultural agency in the conversion process within a specific ethnographic setting. Ng describes a Chinese immigrant church as "a culturally embedded agency in the process of religious conversion."[113] Ng states, "the [Chinese immigrant] church as a community provides the congregants with opportunities to reinvigorate their own ethnic cultural practices on the one hand (ethnic identification), while learning American cultural values and know-how on the other (assimilation)" within a new foreign context.[114]

In a similar way, Diane Austin-Broos in "The Anthropology of Conversion" has explored the connection between cultural transformation and the conversion process within distinct ethnographical settings. Austin-Broos regards conversion as "a form of passage—a 'turning from and to'—that is neither syncretism nor absolute breach," in which

112. Kraft, "Cultural Concomitants," 434.
113. Ng, "Christian Tutelage," 212.
114. Ibid., 212.

Exploring Insights

persons engage in cultural and religious transformation within various and different times and spaces.[115] For Austin-Broos, the dynamic conversion experiences of persons or groups are centered in particular cultural and historical milieus, which include "the shifting relations between nation-states and a global economy, the new forms of identity politics within and between nations, and the increasing importance of religion in the lives of individuals."[116] Austin-Broos insists that conversion, as a cultural and religious passage, occurs in specific times and places. This cultural and religious passage enables converts to become "encultured" beings, who participate in a new form of relatedness with others (i.e., "a newly inscribed communal self"), as well as to experience a new set of embodied worldviews, identities, and beliefs.

In an extended view, Rebecca S. Norris explores the link of embodied culture and the adoption of new beliefs with the conversion experiences of persons. Norris describes conversion as a gradual process, which involves "not just adopting a set of ideas but also converting to and from an embodied worldview and identity."[117] Norris has interviewed converts at the greater Boston area in New England, who were all middle-class, in their forties, and came from Jewish or Christian backgrounds. Based on the analysis of her data from interviews, Norris presents three important consequences for achieving a better understanding of the nature of cultural and spiritual conversion in terms of embodied culture and the adoption of new beliefs:

> First, although a convert experiences conversion as a reorientation to a new religious belief system, the conversion occurs primarily because it corresponds with the convert's preexisting ideas or feelings about truth or meaning. Second, unless they are converting to a different branch of their old tradition, converts usually exhibit one of two ways of relating to the laws and rituals of their adopted religion: zealous adherence or selective performance. Third, since the worldview of the convert exists not only as abstract ideas but also as embodied reality, practicing the adopted religion requires not only the gradual assimilation of the meaning of terms and concepts based in the language and symbols of another culture, but also the performance of

---

115. Austin-Broos, "Anthropology," 1–2.
116. Ibid., 1.
117. Norris, "Converting," 171.

ritual postures and gestures requiring retraining of deep-seated somatic responses.[118]

For Norris, conversion occurs in a passage between old faiths and new faiths. Norris emphasizes religious ritual practices that help converts to deeply express their inner feelings and to gradually understand the meaning of terms, symbols, and ideologies of their adopted spiritual traditions in light of both the embodied experience and a correspondence between the outer form and the inner state. Consequently, Norris asserts that the conversion experience enables persons to participate in the process of the embodiment of culture as well as to shape a new form of worldviews, identities, and beliefs.

Conversion and Cultural Revitalization

Some anthropologists have examined the connection between the conversion experience and the revitalization of persons or groups within particular cultural environments. Anthony F. C. Wallace focuses on the link of the religious revitalization movements of persons or groups with conversion experiences within particular cultural environments. Wallace views conversion as a dynamic process of cultural renewal and revitalization in which persons engage in visions of a new way of life in order to deal with extreme stresses. For Wallace, culture, as a dynamic entity in process, contains internal mechanisms that enable it to renew itself and make itself more relevant to its current situation. Wallace describes the processes of culture change in light of deliberate intent by members of a society: "The persons involved in the process of revitalization must perceive their culture, or some major areas of it, as a system (whether accurately or not); they must feel that this cultural system is unsatisfactory; and they must innovate not merely discrete items, but a new cultural system, specifying new relationships as well as, in some cases; new traits."[119]

Wallace's theory of revitalization movements is useful for exploring the larger cultural and social process of renewal within specific contexts. Wallace defines *revitalization* as "a special kind of culture change phenomenon"; in that sense, *revitalization movements* are defined as

---

118. Ibid. See 179.
119. Wallace, "Revitalization Movements," 265.

"deliberate, conscious, organized efforts by members of a society to create a more satisfying culture."[120] For Wallace, the revitalization movement occurs in the following two conditions: high stress for individual members of the society, and disillusionment with a distorted cultural environment/*Gestalt*. Wallace contends that the structure of the revitalization process consists of five stages: 1) steady state; 2) period of individual stress; 3) period cultural distortion; 4) period of revitalization (which includes a series of functional stages of mazeway reformulation, communication, organization, adaptation, cultural transformation, and routinization); and 5) new steady state.[121]

In "Handsome Lake and the Great Revival in the West," Wallace claims that the religious revitalization movement is closely related to a prophet's revelatory visions, which provide for him (or her) satisfying relationships to the supernatural being and outline a new way of life under divine sanction. Followers achieve similar satisfaction of dependency needs in the charismatic relationship. Wallace employs the case of Handsome Lake (*Ganiodaio*), a chief in the League of the Iroquois, to illustrate this phenomenon. Handsome Lake was born in 1735 at the Seneca village of Canawaugus, New York. Because of the deaths of his wife and child around 1795, he became an alcoholic and was destitute, depressed, and near death. Thus, in 1799, Handsome Lake was very sick at the age of fifty-four. On June 15, 1799, Handsome Lake experienced a series of visions. Eight hours of his trance was mistaken for death, and preparations were made for his burial. However, he came out of the trance and reported his visions to the people. Deeply stirred by this series of visions, Handsome Lake reformed not only his own life, but also the lives of many other persons and eventually the whole Iroquois nation. Wallace asserts that the historical origin of a great proportion of religious phenomena has been in revitalization movements in light of visions of a new way of life by persons under extreme stress. As a consequence, Wallace argues that religious revitalization movements play an important role in facilitating the conversion experiences of persons or groups within cultural contexts.[122]

In a similar vein, Eldridge Cleaver in *Soul on Fire* describes his own experiences of revitalization, which can be effective in mass movements

---

120. Ibid., 264.
121. Ibid., 268.
122. Wallace, "Handsome Lake," 149–65.

of transformation. Cleaver, as a leader of the Black Panthers Party, fled the United States and settled in France with his family. After spending several expatriate years, Cleaver realized that he was no longer able to have an influence on the Black Power movement; that is, he was useless to the movement of political and social transformation. In such a situation, Cleaver lost his way and began to think of putting an end by committing suicide. One evening, he was sitting alone on the balcony of his apartment with a pistol on his lap:

> I was brooding, downcast, at the end of my rope. I looked up at the moon and saw certain shadows . . . and the shadows became a man in the moon, and I saw a profile of myself. . . . I was already upset and this scared me. . . . I saw my former heroes paraded before my eyes. Here were Fidel Castro, Mao Tse-tung, Karl Marx, [and] Frederick Engels, passing in review, each one appearing for a moment of time, and then dropping out of sight, like fallen heroes. Finally, at the end of the procession, in dazzling, shimmering light, the image of Jesus Christ appeared. That was the last straw. I just crumbled and started crying. I fell to my knees, grabbing hold of the banister; and in the midst of this shaking and crying the Lord's Prayer and the 23rd Psalm came into my mind.[123]

Cleaver's story of conversion shows how cultural symbols affect the revitalization process. Such powerful experiences during that night enabled Cleaver to participate in the process of renewal and transformation within a specific context. Cleaver describes that in his vision, Jesus looked like the traditional portrait that hung in his grandmother's kitchen. In this way, Cleaver's experience can be a good example to illustrate the renewing power of imprinted cultural symbols. Cleaver's story of conversion demonstrates that cultural symbols had powerfully remained in his inner state, although he might have explicitly ignored or rejected them. Cleaver's childhood image of Jesus, inscribed in his inner world, re-emerged at a crucial time as a symbol of healing and transformation.

In an extended view, Mary A. Reidhead and Van A. Reidhead in "From Jehovah's Witness to Benedictine Nun" elucidate the link of the revitalization movement of persons with the change of particular cultural settings. To illustrate this connection, Reidhead and Reidhead

---

123. Cleaver, *Soul on Fire*, 211.

use the case of Sylvia (from the American Midwest), who engaged in a passage into Catholicism, and ultimately Catholic monasticism, from life as a pastor among Jehovah's Witnesses. They have interviewed Sylvia from 1997 and 2000. Sylvia was born into the Jehovah's Witness culture and enculturated within its identity, worldview, and cosmology. She became a fulltime minister of Jehovah's Witness. Sylvia, as an active religious questor, yearned to be rewarded with an experience of God that would proclaim her worthiness and reward her fidelity. However, she felt that God was absent from her life; finally, this caused her much suffering (a sense of "vague restlessness"). One day, a Catholic coworker invited Sylvia to her daughter's baptism, and she participated in this Catholic ritual performance. At that time, she experienced an unexpected spiritual transformation within a different cultural setting. In Sylvia's own words: "I walked into a Catholic Church, which was taboo for me. I had no idea what Eucharistic presence was or meant. I did not know who was behind the tabernacle doors, but all of a sudden I could feel God. To this day I describe myself being as one of those stainless steel milkshake containers, cold and empty, and then being filled up with warm, fuzzy hot chocolate with marshmallows, because I felt like I was being filled."[124]

After that sacred and world-shattering event, Sylvia abandoned her cultural and social milieus of Jehovah's Witness and became a Catholic (Sylvia was baptized in April 1994). According to Reidhead and Reidhead, Catholicism opened new horizons and choices for Sylvia to express her gratitude to God, and her Jehovah's Witness upbringing scripted that she should do more than just become Catholic. Sylvia became a Benedictine nun of St. Hildegard monastery and received a new name, Sister Margaret, after canonical vows in order to construct Catholic cosmology and to make further a profound spiritual journey ("wanting to do more") in a new cultural and religious context. In that sense, Reidhead and Reidhead note, "Catholic culture provided her [Sylvia] with the option of identifying a spiritual director to guide her in the synthesizing, interpretive, meaning-making process after baptism. Her spiritual director took her to a Benedictine monastery to show her an alternative way to serve God. Her yearning to 'do more'

---

124. Reidhead and Reidhead, "Jehovah's Witness to Benedictine Nun," 185.

perhaps primed her for another religious experience that would clear up the uncertainty about what she should do."[125]

Sylvia's narrative of conversions (i.e., the first conversion from Jehovah's Witness to Roman Catholicism, and the second to Benedictine monasticism) demonstrates how the revitalization movement of persons is deeply related to the change of particular cultural and religious settings. In doing so, it shows how the cosmology, ideologies, beliefs, embodied symbols, and ritual practices of the Catholic Church and the Benedictine monastery played a preeminent role in stimulating Sylvia's movement of revitalization. As a result, Reidhead and Reidhead state, "The institutional structure—ancient ritual traditions, well-formulated theology, and local faith community of Catholicism—provided a stable environment with tools and support for Sylvia to use in reconstructing her worldview and her identity."[126]

In sum, from the perspective of anthropology of religion, conversion has been regarded as a process of rationality (i.e., the intellectual challenge of the encounter of the macrocosm), a passage of acculturation, and a movement of revitalization. On the whole, anthropologists have explored religious conversion in variety of cultural settings. Thus, they have paid attention to the contextual matrix of conversion that occurs through long-term relationships with persons or groups.

Importantly, the anthropological studies of conversion have contributed by elaborating the influence of cultural and intellectual factors on the complex process of human transformation. This means that in the emphasis on the context of acculturation or cultural revitalization of a community and of a person, they have contributed by showing the interplay of two levels of conversion—individual and communal. More specifically, the anthropological interpretations of conversion have effectively articulated how the new convert has gradually undergone cultural and intellectual changes which are related to the reconstruction of his or her religious identity, worldview, and belief in the specific cultural context. However, on the whole, these anthropological interpretations have not paid attention to the influence of psychological and religious factors on the process of religious conversion. This implies that they are not sufficient to explore the link of the potential convert's psychological distress and crisis with his or her (specific) personal and

125. Ibid., 195.
126. Ibid., 194–95.

Exploring Insights

familial contexts. Moreover, they are inadequate to articulate the role of the divine, the sacred, or God in the process of religious conversion in light of the relation between divine intervention/grace and human transformation.

THEOLOGICAL STUDIES OF CONVERSION

The study of conversion has long been a fascinating topic in the field of theology, especially in the context of Christian theology and tradition. Theologians have explored the impact of religious factors on the conversion experiences of persons or faith communities. In doing so, they have primarily emphasized the dominant influence of God on the process of human transformation. In "Conversion in Evangelistic Practice," Eddie Gibbs describes the diverse understandings of conversion among the scholars of different schools in order to identify certain theological/religious principles for the study of conversion:

1. Conversion represents a divine initiative as well as a human decision.
2. Conversion represents a long-term process as well as a one-time decision.
3. Conversion has corporate ramifications as well as an individual focus.
4. Conversion has cultural ramifications as well as a theological basis.
5. Conversion has a psychological as well as a spiritual dimension.
6. Conversion often occurs in response to invitation or even persuasion but must never be induced by manipulation.[127]

Mindful of the complexity and diversity of conversion studies undertaken by theologians, this section of the literature review focuses on four main themes because they are valuable for appreciating the religious dimension of conversion as well as for achieving an integrated understanding of the lived experience of transformation. These main themes are 1) conversion and the encounter with God; 2) conversion

---

127. Gibbs, "Conversion," 277–85.

and the Scriptures; 3) conversion and the ritual act of baptism; and 4) conversion and the reciprocity of the love of God and neighbor.

Conversion and the Encounter with God

Theologians have examined the impact of an encounter with God on the conversion experience. In "Christian Conversion," Manfred Marquardt argues that Christian conversion occurs through connection with the living God. Marquardt describes conversion as an essential part of God's saving work which involves the renewal of human beings as images of God. For Marquardt, conversion is not simply human effort to change one's life; it is a human response to an encounter with God's grace as well as human participation in the transforming work of God. Marquardt states, "Conversion is neither purely emotional nor simply a matter of human decision. It is brought forth by and grounded in God's liberating and empowering work.... Conversion is always in response to God's gracious initiative. God's prevenient and justifying grace, by enabling persons to respond freely to God's love, evokes a process of restitution of their being as images of God, of their partnership and likeness with God as loving and free agents."[128]

Similarly, Paul Tillich has demonstrated the correlation of the personal encounter and communion with "the Spiritual Presence" (i.e., God's presence) in light of estrangement, grace, and conversion. He explores how a state of estrangement can be transformed into a state of new being through God's grace. In *Systematic Theology*, Tillich views conversion as "a long process which has been going on unconsciously long before it breaks into consciousness, giving the impression of a sudden, unexpected, and overwhelming crisis."[129] He defines estrangement as 1) *unbelief* (turning away from the ground of being, God), 2) *hubris* (turning toward oneself as the center of one's self and one's world), and 3) *concupiscence* ("concupiscentia"—the unlimited desire to draw the whole of reality in one's self). For Tillich, sin refers to the state of estrangement rather than pride. Pride involves a moral quality (e.g., one's exterior wrongdoing against God), the opposite of which is humility. However, estrangement involves one's disconnection or

---

128. Marquardt, "Christian Conversion," 101.
129. Tillich, *Systematic Theology*, vol. 3, 219.

broken relationship with oneself, with others, and with the divine.¹³⁰ This estrangement is related to human ontological anxiety (a sense of "nonbeing"), which threatens the self-affirmation of the person. For Tillich, experiencing conversion means overcoming existential anxiety and promoting a relationship with the self, others, and God. Tillich describes "four principles determining the New Being as process" for fostering one's spiritual transformation and maturity through the personal encounter and communion with the Spiritual Presence: 1) the principle of awareness, 2) the principle of freedom, 3) the principle of relatedness in the state of reconciliation of the self, and 4) the principle of self-transcendence in the direction of the Ultimate with participation in the holy.¹³¹

Tillich emphasizes the interplay of one's disconnection, God's grace, and one's conversion in light of a change from the state of estrangement to the state of new being. He insists that during the encounter and communion with the Spiritual Presence, God's grace enables the person to overcome a state of estrangement and to enter into a state of new being. In that sense, Tillich focuses on one's courage for accepting the transforming power of God's grace. He writes, "[God's] grace strikes us when we are in great pain and restlessness. It strikes us when we walk through the dark valley of a meaningless and empty life. It strikes us when we feel that our separation is deeper than usual, because we have violated another life, a life which we loved, or from which we were estranged. It strikes us when our disgust for our own being, our indifference, our weakness, our hostility, and our lack of direction and composure have become intolerable to us."¹³²

Tillich depicts God's grace as a wave of light breaking into the darkness of persons, as if a voice were saying: "*You are accepted*, accepted by that which greater than you, and the name of which you do not know. Do not ask for the name now; perhaps you will find it later. Do not try to do anything now; perhaps later you will do much. Do not seek for anything; do not perform anything; do not intend anything. *Simply accept the fact that you are accepted!* If that happens to us, we experience grace."¹³³

130. Ibid., vol. 2, 47–55.
131. Ibid., vol. 3, 231–36.
132. Tillich, *Essential Tillich*, 201.
133. Ibid.

In a related vein, from a Jewish perspective, Abraham J. Heschel in *Who Is Man?* explores the impact of divine intervention on the transformation of the person in light of "God's commitment" to the human being. Heschel points out the sense of meaninglessness of the modern human being which involves the feeling of "the absence of being" or "the fear of non-being."[134] For Heschel, this sense of meaninglessness or absence of the person inherently occurs in his or her turning away from God and turning toward his or her own world: "the tragedy of modern man is that he thinks alone. He broods about his own affairs rather than thinking for all being. He has moved out of the realm of God's creation into the realm of man's manipulation."[135] According to Heschel, in the context of human disconnection to the divine, God (who is the origin of "ultimate meaning of existence") intervenes into the life of the person in order to recover and re-establish the relationship with the person. Within this divine intervention, the person enters into the process of turning toward God in which he or she experiences "a feeling of absolute dependence" upon the divine presence. In consideration of God's commitment to human life, Heschel emphasizes the continuous life of the transformation of the person: "whereas ontology asks about *being as being*, theology asks about *being as creation*, about being as a divine act. From the perspective of *continuous creation*, there is no being as being; there is only *continuous coming-into-being*. Being is both action and event."[136] Consequently, Heschel states,

> God . . . enters a direct relationship with man, namely, *a covenant*, to which not only man but also God is committed. In his ultimate confrontation and crises the biblical man knows not only God's eternal mercy and justice but also *God's commitment to man*. . . . Essential to biblical religion is the *awareness of God's interest in man*, the awareness of a covenant, of a responsibility that lies on Him as well as on us. . . . God is a partner and a partisan in man's struggle for justice, peace, love, and beauty, and it is because of His being in need of man that He entered a covenant with him for all time, a mutual bond embracing God and man, a relationship to which God, not alone man, is committed.[137]

---

134. Heschel, *Who Is Man?*, 51.

135. Ibid., 76.

136. Ibid., 71.

137. Ibid., 74–75. In the same way, Janet Aviad in *Return to Judaism* explores the religious factor—one's experience of the "sacred" or "totally other"—in the conversion

Exploring Insights

In a similar way, Emilie Griffin in *Turning: Reflections on the Experience of Conversion* deals with the link of the experience of the power of God's grace with the conversion process. For Griffin, conversion begins with a restlessness of the human heart which can find no resting place on earth. In that sense, Griffin considers conversion as a process of "turning" which one engages in an inner change and peace in oneself. Griffin insists that Christian conversion involves a "turning over of one's life and energies to God"; it is a continuing revelation and a transforming force.[138] Griffin employs her own case of Christian conversion to illustrate this phenomenon:

> When I first began to experience the power of God in my own life, I could hardly believe it. . . . [God] spoke no louder than a whisper, but I heard [God's voice]. And each time that I heard [God's voice], and [accepted God's intervention], a change occurred, the opening of a door I had not guessed was there. Each step, each crossing of a doorway was made with great uncertainty, my doubts mingling with my faith. But with each step, my strength and my conviction grew; I felt myself on sounder

---

(*teshuvah*) process of secular Jews to Orthodox Judaism. For Aviad, new converts—*baalei teshuvah*—depicted their "overwhelming sense of the sacred that seemed to press in upon them, a sort of oceanic consciousness they linked with God" (82; see ix, 13, 81, 84). In a related vein, from an Islamic perspective, J. Dudley Woodberry in "Conversion in Islam" examines the link of divine guidance (*huda*) with actual Islamizing process in terms of conversion to the Muslim faith. In other words, Woodberry pays attention to the divine involvement in the religious change of the person (or the group) (ibid., 27). According to Woodberry, conversion to the Muslim faith involves the process of "*repentance (tawba), faith (iman), submission (islam),* and their vocal *confession (shahada)*" (34; see 26–35, 40).

Meanwhile, Paul G. Hiebert in "Conversion in Hinduism and Buddhism" deals with the divine role in the conversion experiences of Hindus and Buddhists (especially *Mahayana* Buddhists), although Hinduism and Buddhism tend to emphasize less the divine intervention in the process of human change than Judaism, Christianity, or Islam. Hiebert insists that Hindu conversion involves an evolutionary progression of beliefs that lead a person to self-realization (ibid., 10–12). For Hiebert, there are various types of Buddhism (e.g., *Theravada, Mahayana,* and *Tibetan* Buddhism) in which each has different beliefs or *dharma* about the path to salvation and the nature of conversion in light of conversion to the Buddhist belief or living (ibid., 6–19). Consequently, Hiebert asserts that Hinduism and Buddhism have religious goals, namely release from the karmic cycles of rebirth, although their paths of religious change or enlightenment are different and unique. He concludes, "In both religions, conversion is a process, a series of steps involving changes in belief and practice. In both it is also a social matter, an entry into (or rejection of) a religious social order" (ibid., 21).

138. Griffin, *Turning*, 15.

ground. Something was happening in my life, which I could recognize but which I could not yet name. It was conversion.[139]

For Griffin, Christian conversion is not a "once and for all event," but a process of turning in which one experiences the saving power of God's grace. This implies that the experience of transformation is "ever-present in the Christian life." *This* Christian life of the convert occurs in the encounter with God, which can be powerful and changing for the person over a long lifetime.[140]

Similarly, Thomas C. Oden explores the impact of the transforming power of God's grace on the spiritual transformation of the person. Oden argues that God's grace is the sole basis for both one's new life and spiritual vitality. *This* grace is "God's way of empowering the bound will and healing the suffering spirit."[141] He notes, "Grace is the favor shown by God to sinners. It is the divine goodwill offered to those who neither inherently deserve nor can ever hope to earn it. It is the divine disposition to work in our hearts, wills, and actions, so as actively to communicate God's self-giving love for humanity (Rom 3:24; 6:1; Eph 1:7; 2:5–8)."[142]

As recent scholars of conversion, Gordon T. Smith and William J. Abraham agree with that the consideration of one's encounter with God is essential for a more appropriate understanding of Christian conversion. In *Beginning Well: Christian Conversion and Authentic Transformation*, Smith demonstrates that conversion is essentially centered in an encounter with the living God. Smith views conversion as "the human response to the saving work of God through Christ" in which one enters into a redemptive relationship with God in terms of the unity of God's salvation.[143] Smith emphasizes "the priority of God's initiative and the unilateral character of God's salvation" in the conversion experience of persons. In that sense, each Christian conversion represents "a story of God's grace." For Smith, the conversion experience enables the person not merely to expedite a release from sinful predicament—guilt,

---

139. Ibid.

140. Ibid., 24. See Gaventa, *Darkness to Light*, 151; Hindsley, "Monastic Conversion," 31; Lacan, "Conversion and Grace," 79–90, 118; Peace, *Conversion*, 85; Witherup, *Conversion*, 107–10.

141. Oden, *Transforming Power*, 15.

142. Ibid., 33.

143. Smith, *Beginning Well*, 16.

bondage and alienation; it enables the person to experience spiritual transformation. Smith states, "The goal of our conversion is a transformed humanity. We seek to be what we were created to be—fully human, transformed into the image of Jesus Christ. Through conversion, the Spirit of Christ enables us to be like himself that we might be fully ourselves. Christ is the head of a new humanity, true humanity infused with divine grace; and it is this humanity, with Christ as its head, for which we long. When we identify with Christ and live in gracious union with him, we become all we were created to be."[144]

In a related vein, Abraham in "The Epistemology of Conversion" explores the impact of divine action on the conversion experience. Abraham describes Christian conversion as "not simply some emotional exercise or event" but a "turning in repentance and faith to the God of Jesus Christ announced in the gospel."[145] Abraham asserts that "to be born again, to receive the witness of the Holy Spirit, to be justified, to be sanctified, and the like," is to be subject to *divine action* in light of the experience of God's transforming power. This divine action is directed to the change and healing of the human condition. It involves divine salvation brought about by the Holy Spirit which relates to matter of coming to know the truth about oneself and about God.[146]

Conversion and the Scriptures

Theologians and biblical scholars have elucidated the correlation between the Scriptures and the conversion experience of the person or the faith community. In doing so, they have studied the Bible to discover the meaning, motif, and the pattern of conversion experience among the diverse scriptural approaches. For example, George E. Morris explores the meaning of Christian conversion from a biblical perspective. According to Morris, Christian understanding of conversion derives mainly from three biblical words: the Old Testament Hebrew word *shûv*, and the New Testament Greek words *epistrephein* and *metanoein*. The word *shûv* means "to return" or "turn back" which appears over one thousand times in the Old Testament. *Shûv* is not merely turning from

---

144. Ibid., 26.
145. Abraham, "Epistemology," 184.
146. Ibid., 184. See Callen, "Mutuality Model," 145–48, 154–58.

Understanding Religious Conversion

one thing to another or from one direction to another. Rather, it must be understood in a covenantal context: conversion means "turning back" to God and the covenant previously established between God and Israel. The Greek word *epistrephein* means "to turn" or "turn around"; it denotes movements, turnings, or changes of place in both the transitive and the intransitive senses. The Greek word *metanoein* refers to "repent" or "change one's mind."[147] Morris summarizes the meanings of biblical conversion:

> 1. Biblical conversion signifies a turning from sin and a turning to God . . . 2. Biblical conversion is a fundamental reorientation of the whole person, a reorientation which requires concrete obedience . . . 3. This reorientation is both personal and communal, and not one without the other. The personal and social sides of turning to God must be held together . . . 4. Biblical conversion is not viewed as a single act but a lifelong process, a participation in a historic movement. It has a past, present, and future focus . . . 5. From beginning to end biblical conversion is response to the initiative of God. It is an act of the human being which is possible only because of a previous act of God.[148]

In a similar way, Ronald D. Witherup in *Conversion in the New Testament* examines how the Bible depicts the conversion experiences of persons. According to Witherup, both the Hebrew *shûv* and the Greek *epistrephō* basically refer to "to turn, return, or turn back."[149] In that sense, the basic meaning of conversion is "turning" in the Old and New Testament: "As in the OT, the root idea is clearly a turning. There is always movement in conversion. There is no room for the status quo, for lack of change. Conversion always involves a turning, whether a turning *from* something or someone or *to* something or someone. . . . The general NT sense of conversion is turning (*epistrephō*). It involves turning away from sin, evil, or godlessness and turning toward God, Jesus, and a righteous life."[150]

---

147. Morris, *Mystery and Meaning*, 32–35. See Barclay, *Turning*, 21–25; Conn, "Conversion," 214–15; Finn, *Death to Rebirth*, 21–30; Gaiser, "Biblical Theology," 93–94; Johnson and Malony, *Christian Conversion*, 77–80; Kasdorf, *Christian Conversion*, 41 53; Peace, *Conversion*, 346 53; Tillich, *Systematic Theology*, vol. 3, 219; Wells, *Turning*, 30–33.

148. Morris, *Mystery and Meaning*, 37.

149. Witherup, *Conversion*, 19.

150. Ibid., 21.

Exploring Insights

Witherup characterizes Christian conversion in the New Testament as follows: 1) Christian conversion occurs through an *act of God*; 2) in keeping with all of God's activity, conversion entails an element of *mystery* which is related to an intensely spiritual experience (beyond rational explanation); 3) because of its complexity, conversion is related to a variety of other *biblical themes*—sin, forgiveness, repentance, salvation, justification, baptism, faith, and the Holy Spirit. The total picture of conversion is reflected in the larger process of sanctification and salvation of God's people; 4) the root notion of conversion in the Bible is *change*, which involves turning *from* sin, death, and darkness *to* grace, new life, and light; 5) conversion is directly related to the revelation of *the kingdom of God*. As such, it is an eschatological reality, a foretaste of the new life which is to come; 6) as a *christological* reality, conversion is incorporation into the body of Christ and an intimate personal knowledge of Jesus Christ as Risen Lord and Savior; 7) the conversion experience is relational—it brings one into new relationships with God and with other human beings; 8) the message of conversion is both *externally* directed for bringing new people into the church community (evangelization) and *internally* directed to those who are already members of this community; 9) most conversions appear to be a *process* on some line of continuum, although some conversions are dramatic and single events which profoundly change a person's direction in life; 10) as soil needs to be fertilized and watered for plants to be fruitful, persons who seek ongoing conversion in life need to be prepared for God's grace; 11) ongoing Christian conversion leads one to an experience of *newness* in which one engages in the continual revitalization of faith; 12) conversion is the holistic action of God's love which sanctifies the *whole person*—the mind, the body, the heart, and the spirit; 13) authentic Christian conversion involves both attitudinal and behavioral changes in life—it is not separate from concrete actions which mirror the changed internal reality; 14) conversion is accompanied by concrete *symbolic gestures* (e.g., a cleaning water ritual) which symbolizes the change; and 15) because conversion is so often a profound existential change in life, it is natural for God's people to have the urge to spread the "good news"—"to give *testimony* to others and consequently to evangelize."[151]

---

151. Ibid., 107–10.

In a related vein, Beverly R. Gaventa shows how the Bible variously describes the form of conversion experiences. Gaventa suggests that there are at least three types of conversion ("personal change") in the Bible: 1) *Alternation* is change that grows from an individual's past behavior in light of the logical consequence of previous choices. 2) *Pendulum-like conversion* is a radical change that involves rejecting past convictions and affiliations in order to affirm new commitments and a new identity. 3) *Transformation* is also a radical change in which the past is not rejected but reinterpreted and reconstructed as part of a new understanding of God and the world; this transformation is the dominant understanding of conversion both in the Hebrew Scriptures and in the New Testament.[152] For Gaventa, the common denominator in all three categories of conversion is *change* that is opposed to maintaining the status quo. In that sense, Christian conversion always involves movement from one dimension to another. Gaventa uses the story of the Ethiopian eunuch (Acts 8:26–39) as an example of alternation. She points out "the imaginary of birth from above and new life found in the Gospel of John" as an example of pendulum-like conversion. Gaventa employs Paul's own self-description in his letters (e.g., Rom 9:1–5; Gal 1:11–12) as evidence of transformation. Gaventa concludes that all of these cases demonstrate the nature of Christian conversion—the dramatic change—which God's power has acted in the lives of God's people.[153]

Similar to Gaventa, Frederick J. Gaiser in "A Biblical Theology of Conversion" emphasizes the transforming dimension of the conversion experience in the Bible. Gaiser views conversion as "life transformation" which is closely related to "a call to return, promising a restoration of the original intimate relationship between God and humanity experienced in creation."[154] For Gaiser, God's transformation of all things—the heavens and the earth, humans and all creatures—is at the core of biblical theology. This transforming work of God provides the framework for understanding biblical conversion. The theological context of biblical conversion is rooted in God's involvement in the world as

---

152. Gaventa, *Darkness to Light*, 10–12; "Conversion," 41–43, 53–54.

153. Gaventa, *Darkness to Light*, 148–49; "Conversion," 53–54. See Witherup, *Conversion*, 5–6.

154. Gaiser, "Biblical Theology," 107.

Exploring Insights

creator, redeemer, as well as convicting and guiding Spirit. As a consequence, Gaiser writes,

> Studies show that this structure of transformation permeates the entire Old Testament. Nor is it left behind in the movement to the New Testament—the title of which is a Christian confession that the decisive transformation or conversion of the world has taken place. Jesus' parables expound the decisive move from old to new. The Johannine literature represents the work of Christ as bringing "new birth," as a passing from death to life and from darkness to light. The concept of a radical transformation effected by the revelation of God in Christ is the foundation of Pauline theology. From the beginning of the biblical literature to the end it provides the theological norm and center by which the traditional accounts of conversion are measured and understood.[155]

From an extended view, Gordon T. Smith shows how the New Testament describes human change and transformation related to the mercy and goodness of God. After reviewing the conversion stories of the Synoptic Gospels (i.e., Matthew, Mark, and Luke), Smith states,

> In the Synoptic Gospels conversion comes in response to an encounter with Jesus Christ . . . that is characterized by belief and repentance. . . . We can follow Christ only when we turn from ourselves and from all that might keep us from a full and radical commitment to him. . . . When we turn to Christ, we enter his "kingdom," which means that we come under his reign or authority (Mark 1:14–15). Further, conversion includes accepting the call of God to serve him—to participate in his kingdom purposes. And when we come to Christ we come "home." We find joy and rest for our souls, as though we were lost children being received once more into the arms of a father. Finally, this act of coming to Christ is marked by baptism, which in some significant way symbolizes all of these components or conversion.[156]

Smith delves into four different models of conversion in the New Testament (i.e., the Synoptic Gospels, the book of Acts, the letters of Paul, and the Gospel of John). Smith discovers that the New Testament calls for and assumes a conversion to Jesus Christ in terms of a human response to an encounter with Jesus Christ. From a critical and

---

155. Ibid., 95.
156. Smith, *Beginning Well*, 112–13.

integrative view of four models, Smith concludes that Christian conversion in the New Testament includes seven distinct but inseparable elements: 1) belief in Jesus Christ, 2) repentance, 3) trust in Christ Jesus, 4) transfer of allegiance, 5) baptism, 6) reception of the gift of the Spirit, and 7) incorporation into congregational life.[157]

From a narrow and extended view, some scholars have intensively studied specific book(s) in the New Testament in order to establish a pattern or paradigm of biblical conversion. In *Conversion in the New Testament: Paul and the Twelve*, Richard V. Peace examines the New Testament's portrayal of conversion by illustrating the conversion experiences of Paul in Acts and Jesus' disciples in Gospel of Mark. Peace suggests a core pattern of Paul's conversion which includes a three-part movement of insight, turning, and transformation:

> First, there was *insight*. . . . [Paul] saw that in persecuting the Christian church he had been persecuting Jesus. . . . In other words, Paul discovered that he was not working for God . . . but against God. This is the personal context within which Paul was converted. Second, there was the *turning*. This also had two parts: a turning *from* and a turning *to*. He turned from persecuting the church to joining the church. He turned from opposing Jesus to following Jesus. Third, there was the *transformation* that flowed from Paul's response to Jesus. . . . His first response is to be baptized, to align himself with the church, and to preach the good news about Jesus. He also accepts his commission to be a witness of who Jesus is to all people. He is, in other words, transformed from a zealous Pharisee into a zealous apostle. Henceforth his life takes a radically new direction.[158]

Peace uses this pattern of Paul's conversion as the guiding criteria for analyzing the conversion experience of the Twelve as found in Mark, though he also contrasts Paul's conversion as a dramatic/sudden change with the Twelve's conversion as a nurtured/gradual change. Moreover, Peace hopes that this pattern will be a normative one in order to better understand Christian conversion experiences: Christian conversion "involves new insight into God, new turning toward God, and a new life lived in response to God. It involves seeing oneself in the light of God's truth, embracing a new relationship to God, and living this out

---

157. Ibid., 125; see 108–24.
158. Peace, *Conversion*, 25–26.

within the community of God's people as a servant and witness to all people."[159]

Similarly, in *The Paradigm of Conversion in Luke*, Fernando Mendez-Moratalla establishes a consistent and systemic account of conversion in the Gospel of Luke. Mendez-Moratalla insists that conversion is a major theme in Luke's theological enterprise which emphasizes the work of God's salvation. In that sense, he studies different yet interrelated conversion narratives in Luke: conversion in the preaching of John the Baptist (Luke 3:1–17), the conversion of Levi (5:27–32), the conversion of a woman of the city, a parable of conversion—the lost son (15:11–32), the conversion of Zacchaueus (19:1–10), the conversion of the criminal (23:39–43), and the non-conversion of a ruler (18:18–30). After analyzing these conversion stories in the Third Gospel, Mendez-Moratalla proposes a *Lukan paradigm* showing conversion as the result of 1) divine initiative 2) involving conflict, because 3) it is offered to sinners, 4) as involving repentance, 5) proper use of wealth/possessions, 6) forgiveness, 7) table-fellowship and joy, 8) role reversal, 9) a climactic pronouncement, and 10) christological emphasis—the activity of Jesus as savior.[160]

Conversion and the Ritual Act of Baptism

Scholars have examined the interconnection between baptism and conversion. For example, William Barclay in *Turning to God* elucidates the link of baptism with the conversion experience of the person within the early church community. For Barclay, the early church usually demanded the new convert to be baptized through the public ritual practice. Barclay writes,

> Baptism was a perfectly deliberate publicizing of a far-reaching act of decision. It was a deliberate action in which a man [or woman] left one religion to enter another, in which he [or she] said farewell to one way of life and committed himself [or herself] to another. Baptism was something which marked a clean cut and a definite dividing-line in life. It was the public confession of a radical change which a man [or woman] had

---

159. Ibid., 101.
160. Mendez-Moratalla, *Paradigm of Conversion*, 216–22.

deliberately chosen and to which he [or she] pledged himself [or herself].[161]

Barclay asserts that baptism is a gift of the Holy Spirit for the new convert. *This* baptism is consistently connected with repentance through which one experiences the forgiveness of sins; namely, the sacrament of baptism leads the convert to experience the physical and spiritual cleaning or freedom from his or her sinful conditions.[162]

Influenced by Barclay, George E. Morris in *The Mystery and Meaning of Christian Conversion* probes the role of Christian baptism in the conversion process within the Christian community. Morris views Christian baptism as "a kind of seal or symbol of the new relationship with God which comes as a gift of the Holy Spirit and through which one is initiated into the fellowship of the church."[163] Morris employs his own case of baptism in order to illustrate an intimate connection between the liturgical act and the spiritual transformation of the person in light of Christian pilgrimage. Morris was baptized by Rev. Herndon Shepherd of a United Methodist church in the southwestern mountains of Virginia, when he was in high school. That means, during the sacrament of baptism, he was immersed in a small river in the hills of Southern Appalachia, since immersion was the most popular mode practiced in that area. Morris experienced something unusual that happened in the process of his baptism:

> This [baptism] was a great experience for me, and it did in fact signal the beginning of a new life and a new relationship. On that same Sunday I was received into the membership of the church.... There was a basic change of attitude; that is, I wanted to love people. There were also concrete acts of compassion and witness. I remember telling my mother that I was both surprised and somewhat confused by this new and mysterious compassion that made me want to reach out to people.... No one had to force me to pray, study scripture, and attend church. I wanted to! In only a short time I had read the entire New Testament.

---

161. Barclay, *Turning*, 51.

162. Ibid., 51–52. From a Jewish perspective, Aharon Lichtenstein insists that the potential convert to Judaism requires to participate in the ritual procedure in the Jewish community as well as to confess the personal experience of God—"The *ger* is born both as a servant of God and as a citizen of the nation [*Keneset Yisrael*]" ("On Conversion," 8).

163. Morris, *Mystery and Meaning*, 6.

Exploring Insights

> Though I often found the readings terribly confusing, nevertheless, at times glimmers came through and I learned to expect God's divine disclosure through the scriptures. My participation in the local church helped me understand that I was more than a solitary individual interested only in my own well-being that I could contribute to the well-being and enrichment of others.[164]

Morris characterizes Christian baptism presented in the New Testament: Christian baptism is the mark of incorporation within the Body of Christ—"by one Spirit we were all baptized into one Body." It is the mark of purification, cleansing from the old sins, and justification in the name of the Lord Jesus. Baptism is also the mark of the new covenant; it is initiation into the realm of the Spirit. Moreover, it means a close union with Christ that the believer is a participant in his death and resurrection.

In particular, Morris contends that infant baptism is valid for those who are born to Christian homes and nurtured in the Christian community. He states, "Infant baptism is a symbol of justification by faith. It symbolizes the fact that faith is a response to God's saving activity. It is a powerful recognition that God has accepted us even when we are weak, helpless infants."[165] As a consequence, Morris affirms that Christian baptism, whether infant, youth, or adult, occurs through God's initiative action; it is indispensable to the spiritual transformation of the person within the Christian community, in which the convert engages in new relationships with others and shares a common life and ministry.

Similar to Morris, Cedric B. Johnson and H. Newton Malony explores the influence of baptism on one's conversion process. According to Johnson and Malony, the early Church community expected the new convert to enter into the Christian life of repentance, faith, baptism, and fellowship. In the early church, *repentance* (*metanoia*) was the first demand made of a potential convert, who involved a profound change, especially a turning from sin. *Faith* was the second demand of a potential convert, who involved a turning or surrender to God. In the life of faith, the convert engages in a total commitment to the will of God. In the early Church, *baptism* by immersion in water was the third response demanded from the convert (Acts 8:38–39). Through the sacrament of baptism, the person united to Jesus Christ by faith and became part of

---

164. Ibid.
165. Ibid., 140.

his body ("spiritual union")—"For in the one Spirit we were all baptized into one body" (1 Cor 12:13a). *This* water baptism was only a part of the person's conversion in that it pointed to a faith and repentance that had *already* occurred. Moreover, baptism was a visible means that the convert identified with the body of believers, the church—that is, Christian baptism enabled the person both to overcome radical individualism and to incorporate into *Christian fellowship*.[166]

Likewise, Thomas M. Finn in *From Death to Rebirth: Ritual and Conversion in Antiquity* articulates the link of Christian baptism with one's conversion process. Finn considers conversion as a change or transformation which depends on the intersection between the divine and the human. According to Finn, the earliest Christian baptism was performed "in the name of Jesus (Christ)." The earliest Christians, especially Paul and his heirs, developed a telling way of expressing the relationship between death, resurrection, and baptism. Finn argues that conversion is embedded in a complex and richly articulated ritual process of baptism. The new life of the convert can be symbolized by the baptismal rite: "Conversion is seeing; seeing is the result of baptism; baptism is enlightenment."[167] Christian baptism is a passage from death to life which could be portrayed in the image of the baptismal font as tomb. The baptizand is buried in the baptismal water just as Christ was buried in the tomb; then is raised from the water, as Christ was risen from the tomb. That is, through the ritual act of baptism, the person engages in the life of rebirth and transformation.[168]

Donald L. Gelpi, as a Catholic theologian, has probed the impact of baptism in Christianity on the conversion experience. Gelpi regards Christian conversion as an "initial transition from unbelief to belief, from sin to the obedience of faith."[169] Gelpi insists that the ritual act of baptism "seals" the faith of the convert in the twofold sense: 1) it is a public certification that the baptized person "belongs to God" and that he or she has nothing to fear on the last day; 2) it is a public and official

---

166. Johnson and Malony, *Christian Conversion*, 80–85. See Markham, *Rewired*, 196–97; Nissiotis, "Conversion and the Church," 264; Wells, *Turning*, 44–46; Witherup, *Conversion*, 59.

167. Finn, *Death to Rebirth*, 256.

168. Ibid., 255–57. See Hudson, "Catholic View," 117–19.

169. Gelpi, *Conversion Experience*, 101.

sign of the new covenant between God and the convert.[170] For Gelpi, the blessing of the baptismal water recalls a series of water images from the Bible in order to illumine the meaning of the ritual within the faith community:

> The waters of creation recall that Jesus begins the new creation and that the gift of the Breath re-creates those who believe in him. The waters of the flood and the waters of the Exodus call attention to the saving effects of baptism: it purifies from sin; it effects a new liberation by sealing and completing the conversion of the candidates; and it, like the first Exodus, seals the new covenant between them and God. The waters of the Jordan remind the community that Christian baptism draws one into Jesus' own baptismal experience and messianic commissioning. The water from the side of the crucified Christ teaches that both the passion and the resurrection mediate the gift of the baptismal Breath. Finally, the command of the risen Christ to baptize all nations reaffirms the apostolic mission of the church, which the rite of baptism prolongs.[171]

Similar to Gelpi, Peter Toon delves into the connection with Christian baptism and the regeneration experience of the person. Toon views conversion as "born again" which emphasizes the new rebirth in terms of personal regeneration. He understands sacraments as symbolic actions given to the church by its head, Jesus Christ. For Toon, baptism is the first sacrament: it unites a person to Christ and the church community. Baptism, as a divine instrument, enables the person to enter into the change of life by experiencing 1) God's forgiveness, 2) regeneration, and 3) justification to the soul. Toon surveys Christian baptism as depicted in the New Testament:

> First, the rite [of baptism] was seen as intimately related to the work of God within the believer in terms of forgiveness and justification. . . . Baptism was administered to them, thereby portraying that God alone is the author and giver of salvation. Second, baptism was a once-for-all rite of entry into God's people; it was not to be repeated at a future date. . . . Third, baptism signified and symbolized incorporation into Christ and into his body (Rom 6:1–14; Gal 3:26–27). To be baptized was therefore

---

170. Gelpi, *Charism and Sacrament*, 132.
171. Gelpi, *Conversion Experience*, 149.

a synonym for being a Christian, a justified sinner, a born-again believer, and a child of God.[172]

Toon employs a doctrine of Christian baptism in the Roman Catholic Church in order to understand better the subject of baptism and regeneration ("The Dogmatic Constitution on the Church" in the Second Vatican Council): "Incorporated into the Church by baptism, the faithful are appointed by their baptismal character to Christian religious worship; reborn as sons of God, they must profess before men the faith they have received from God through the Church. By the sacrament of confirmation they are more perfectly bound to the Church and are endowed with the special strength of the Holy Spirit. Hence they are, as true witnesses of Christ, more strictly obliged to spread the faith by word and deed."[173]

As recent scholars of conversion, Gordon T. Smith and Roger E. Olson agree with other scholars' argument that baptism plays an essential role in facilitating the transforming experience of the new convert. Smith investigates the impact of sacramental and symbolic actions on the conversion experience of persons within the Christian community. Smith argues that "to be human is to use symbols"; namely, human persons use symbols to capture their identity, their important relationships, and even their deepest spiritual commitments. These sacramental and symbolic actions are essential elements for the conversion experience of new believers, because these external ritual actions enable participants to express what is happening to them internally. While stressing the formative and transforming power of the liturgy, Smith writes, "[Sacramental and] symbolic actions . . . are essential means by which religious change is experienced and expressed. Indeed, a formal religious rite or symbolic action allows sacred reality to be present and immediate. This sacred reality is no longer merely a past event, but a past event that is present to us. The [religious] rite enables the present to be sanctified by the past. 'Through its rites' . . . 'faith reactivates the sources of salvation.'"[174]

According to Smith, the sacrament of baptism played a crucial and indispensable role in fostering the conversion experience of persons in

---

172. Toon, *Born Again*, 65.
173. Ibid., 111–12.
174. Smith, *Beginning Well*, 181.

Exploring Insights

the early faith community as portrayed in the New Testament, especially in the Synoptic Gospels, Acts, Paul's letters, and the Gospel of John. That means that baptism was an integral component of the experience of coming to Christ and incorporation into the early Christian community. Smith argues that like the times of the early church, the sacramental and symbolic actions of the contemporary Christian community not only bring new converts to the presence of God, but also help them enter into a mature and dynamic Christian life as participants in the community of faith. Smith concludes, "Baptism . . . is an ideal way to sacramentalize the inner reality of faith and repentance. It speaks of repentance and the forgiveness of sins; it calls forth our faith and our resolve to live in loyal identification with Christ. It is personal but also communal, indicating our personal commitments but also our common commitments as the community of faith."[175]

Likewise, Olson elucidates how baptism in Christianity is profoundly related to conversion in light of the transforming work of God. Olson describes conversion as a "fulfillment of baptism with personal repentance and faith."[176] For Olson, Christian baptism is rooted in a specific act of God in the life of a follower of Jesus Christ. It is a visible means of God's grace which leads the convert into a life of Christian discipleship to Jesus Christ as well as an act of commitment to the Christian community. The rite of baptism is a symbol of entrance into the body of Christ; it is not salvific but an "outward sign of an inward work" through which one engages in the life of transformation and regeneration. Olson asserts that baptism is the universal rite of initiation into the Christian church. The vast majority of Christian traditions initiate children or converts into the church by means of water—either immersion into water, sprinkling of water on the head, or effusion (pouring) of water over the person being baptized. Most churches baptize in the name of the Father, Son, and Holy Spirit. In particular, most reformed evangelicals have retained that Christian conversion as a process begins

---

175. Ibid., 188–89; see *Transforming Conversion*, 139–56. See also Campbell, "Conversion and Baptism," 161. Scholars have examined how the whole Christian community affects the experience of conversion. Mark McVann views conversion as "an act of the self made possible by the experience of such human community" ("Conversion and Community," 77). The experience of conversion flows from community and returns to it to enrich it and be enriched by it (76–77; see McKnight, *Turning*, 5; Markham, *Rewired*, 197; Zehnder, *Theology of Religious Change*, 118–39).

176. Olson, *Westminster Handbook*, 162.

with infant baptism; that is, "baptism initiates a child into the covenant between God and the church; it parallels the rite of circumcision in the covenant between God and Israel."[177]

Conversion and the Reciprocity of the Love of God and Neighbor

Theologians and biblical scholars have explored the symbiotic relation between love of God and love of neighbor in the conversion process. For example, Nikos A. Nissiotis explores the link between the convert's return to God and to the church community. Nissiotis views conversion as "a process of continuous personal change and growth with and for the other members of the community."[178] For Nissiotis, the person is converted only by and in the community of the Holy Spirit through which he or she is converted to God: "Conversion does not mean withdrawing from the world, but rather engaging converted people and the whole Church in a more dynamic and creative relationship with it. Conversion is not meant to be individual, but rather ecclesial in the sense that it is a cosmic event realized through persons who are members of a world-wide community."[179]

Karl Rahner emphasizes both the personal and the communal dimension of Christian conversion. For Rahner, Christian conversion is experienced as the gift of God's grace and as human radical response to God's calling in everyday life. Rahner states,

> Conversion is hope as trusting oneself to the unexpected, uncharted way into the open and incalculable future in which God comes. . . . It is love for the neighbor, because only in conjunction with this can God really be loved, and without that love no one really knows with genuine personal knowledge who God is. It means standing firm and grasping the unique situation which is only found at this particular moment "today," not soothing oneself with the idea that it will come again, that the chance of salvation is "always" available. It is the sober realization that every conversion is only a beginning and that the rest of daily fidelity, the conversion which can only be carried out in whole lifetime, has still to come.[180]

177. Ibid., 162; see 153, 260–70.
178. Nissiotis, "Conversion and the Church," 262.
179. Ibid., 268.
180. Rahner, "Conversion," 206.

Likewise, Gustavo Gutierrez in "A Spirituality of Liberation" deals with how conversion to God is related to conversion to the neighbor. For Gutierrez, a spirituality of liberation is centered on both turning to God and turning to the neighbor. The convert's spiritual life cannot apart from the historical and social context: "Our conversion to the Lord implies this conversion to the neighbor. . . . Conversion means a radical transformation of ourselves; it means thinking, feeling, and living as Christ—present in exploited and alienated man. To be converted is to commit oneself to the process of the liberation of the poor and oppressed, to commit oneself lucidly, realistically, and concretely. It means to commit oneself not only generously, but also with an analysis of the situation and a strategy of action."[181]

Similar to Gutierrez, Ronald D. Witherup explores the link of turning toward God with turning toward others in the conversion experience. Witherup describes conversion as "not a single event but an *ongoing process*" which takes place in the context of *relationship*.[182] He emphasizes that Christian conversion brings one into a new relationship with God and with other human beings. For Witherup, God calls people into a relationship with God, a relationship that also has implications for living with other people. The relationality of Christian conversion is bi-directional, being both vertical and horizontal which enables the person into both a new spiritual journey for union with God and a new participation in the context of Christian community. Witherup writes, "Conversion involves both *internal* (attitudinal) and *external* (behavioral) changes in life. Authentic Christian conversion is never divorced from concrete actions which mirror the changed internal reality. Conversion thus always leads to some aspect of social responsibility and justice."[183]

In a related vein, William Barclay describes the Christian convert's life of "togetherness" both with God and with other people. Barclay argues that Christian conversion unites the convert to his or her community members as well as to God: "Conversion is not only conversion

---

181. Gutierrez, "Spirituality," 309. See McKnight, *Turning*, 127–29.

182. Witherup, *Conversion*, 17–18.

183. Ibid., 110. See Barth, "Awakening," 38–40; Castro, "Conversion," 355; Dubay, *Deep Conversion*, 31–32; Häring, "Characteristics of Conversion," 217–18; Kamaleson, "Call," 450–52; Kasdorf, *Christian Conversion*, 96; Lonergan, "Theology," 13; McVann, "Conversion and Community," 76–77; Morris, *Mystery and Meaning*, 133–38; Niebuhr, "Graces," 29.

towards a certain kind of [individual] life; it is conversion into a fellowship. And that is precisely where the Church comes into the [group] picture. The convert becomes a child of God and a member of God's family, which is the Church. . . . [Christian] conversion means entry into a life of togetherness, both with God and with man."[184] Barclay insists that the togetherness of the converted life is exemplified in four directions: 1) it is exemplified by *eating together*. At the early time of the Christian church, "the weekly Love Feast" (the *Agape*), as a sacrament, is not simply a symbolic meal but a real meal which all congregation shared it in order to closely link to one another in the love of Jesus Christ; 2) it is exemplified by *praying together*. The convert entered into a life of prayer in which he or she sought to experience the presence of God and depended on the guidance of God; 3) it is exemplified by *the sharing of the common things of life*. The convert of the early church entered into fellowship which issued in practical and sacrificial aid to those who were in need (e.g., the case of Barnabas, Acts 4:36–37); 4) it was exemplified by *worshipping together*. The attendance at the worship of the church is essential for the convert in order to share the sense of joy with other believers within the love of God.[185]

In a same way, Barry L. Callen examines the new convert's life both in God and in God's people. Callen insists that during the process of spiritual transformation, the convert actively responds to God's calling and he or she participates with other believers in God's mission to the world in terms of new life in Christ and in Christ's community. He notes, "True conversion is more than turning away from sin and toward God. It is turning toward a new creation that is far more than an individualistic avoidance of hell. Conversion is being turned to God and God's church, the new-creation community in which the Spirit dwells, through which the Spirit ministers, and into which the Spirit places each new believer with Spirit-gifts designed to build up the body of Christ."[186]

In conclusion, there are various understandings of religious change in the field of theology of conversion. Conversion has been understood as a result of an encounter with God, a turning from godlessness to God

---

184. Barclay, *Turning*, 71.

185. Ibid., 71–78.

186. Callen, "Mutuality Model," 158. See Marquardt, "Christian Conversion," 107–10.

Exploring Insights

transformation portrayed in the Bible, a change through ritual act of baptism within the Christian community, and a consequence through the mutual interaction between love of God and love of neighbor. On the whole, theological studies of conversion have primarily focused on the efficacy of the transforming power of God's grace in the process of human transformation.

Indeed, the theological studies of conversion have contributed by demonstrating the impact of religious factors on the process of religious change. They have primarily elucidated how divine intervention or grace has affected the human transformation. In doing so, they have contributed by showing how God is communicated with the potential convert by means of the authoritative word of the Scriptures as well as how the ritual performance of Christian baptism has affected the process of spiritual change of the person. Furthermore, in the emphasis on the interplay of turning to God and turning to others, these theological interpretations of conversion have contributed by articulating how the new convert has moved into loving relationships with oneself, others, and God; that is, how this convert has engaged in both the service of God (i.e., Christian living in solitude) and the service of neighbors (i.e., Christian living in community). However, on the whole, these theological interpretations of conversion have not paid attention to the impact of personal, social, and cultural factors on the process of human transformation. As such, in order to foster a better understanding of religious conversion, the theological studies of conversion need to respect more human science perspectives of human transformation, while acknowledging the influence of the transforming power of the divine on the process of religious change.

LEWIS RAMBO'S MODEL OF RELIGIOUS CONVERSION

This section of the literature review addresses Rambo's model of religious conversion. From a perspective that integrates psychology, sociology, anthropology, and religion, Rambo describes the central meaning of conversion as "change," which refers to "turning from and to new religious groups, ways of life, systems of belief, and modes of relating to a deity or the nature of reality."[187] For Rambo, religious conversion involves the complicated and multi-faceted process of religious change that brings about a total transformation of the person in "a dynamic force field" including people, events, ideologies, institutions, expectations, experiences, and orientations.[188] While commenting on the limitation and isolation of examining conversion from the perspective of one specific discipline (much like tracks of a metropolitan train yard running parallel to each other), Rambo tries to describe the entire train yard to us—and to do so in a way that affirms the "perspective of the 'other.'" He explains the complexity and diversity of a "converting process" from the interdisciplinary perspective as follows:

> Conversion is paradoxical. It is elusive. It is inclusive. It destroys and it saves. Conversion is sudden and it is gradual. It is created totally by the action of God, and it is created totally by the action of humans. Conversion is personal and communal, private and public. It is both passive and active. It is a retreat from the world. It is a resolution of conflict and an empowerment to go into the world and to confront, if not create, conflict. Conversion is an event and a process. It is an ending and a beginning. It is final and open-ended. Conversion leaves us devastated—and transformed.[189]

Rambo offers six motifs of conversion, based on John Lofland and Norman Skonovd's theory of "conversion motifs" as follows: 1) The *intellectual* motif refers to the person's search for knowledge about religious or spiritual issues via books, television, articles, lectures, and other media, prior to active participation in religious rituals and organizations; 2) The *mystical* motif generally pertains to "a sudden and traumatic burst of insight, induced by visions, voices, or other paranormal experiences" (e.g., the case of Saul of Tarsus); 3) The *experimental* motif involves active exploration of religious options. The potential convert has a "show me" mentality, essentially saying, "I'll pursue this possibility and see what spiritual benefits it may provide to me"; 4) The

---

187. Rambo, *Religious Conversion*, 3.

188. Ibid., 5; "Conversion," 49, 60; Rambo and Farhadian, "Converting," 24.

189. Rambo, *Religious Conversion*, 176. Rambo prefers to use the progressive word *converting* rather than the noun word *conversion*: "Perhaps the word *converting* better captures the phenomenology of the process. But, for readability, I employ the noun form conversion, although it implies a static phenomenon" (ibid., 7; see Rambo and Farhadian, "Converting," 23).

affectional motif stresses "interpersonal bonds as an important factor in the conversion process," which includes the direct, personal experiences of being loved, nurtured, and affirmed by a group and its leaders; 5) The *revivalism* motif is related to "crowd conformity to induce behavior." Individuals are emotionally aroused and new behaviors and beliefs are promoted by the revival meetings; and 6) The *coercive* motif refers to a level of intense pressure exerted on the person to participate, conform, and confess (e.g., "brainwashing," "thought reform," or "programming"). Deprivation of food and sleep, fear, physical torture, and other forms of psychological terror may render the person unable to resist the pressure to surrender to the group's ideology and submissive life-style, and may also be deployed to gain control over the person's life.[190]

Rambo highlights the study of personal, social, cultural, and religious dimensions of conversion to gain an integrated understanding of conversion. While emphasizing an interdisciplinary approach to religious change, he presents a systemic stage model of conversion which includes context, crisis, quest, encounter, interaction, commitment, and consequences.[191] Rambo's model of conversion is "not only multidimensional and historical but also *process oriented*."[192] This means that his systemic stage model is in contrast to a sequential (stepwise) stage model. Rambo eschews a strict step-by-step model because the process of conversion is one in which multiple factors interact simultaneously and cumulatively over time. In other words, his systemic stage model is not simply linear but interconnected, and there is a sometimes a "spiraling effect"—a going back and forth among stages. The summary of each of the seven stages is listed as follows:

Stage 1: Context—The Ecology of the Conversion Process

Context is the ecology in which conversion takes place. This context includes a panorama of conflicting, confluent, and dialectical factors that both promote and constrain the process of conversion.[193] Conversion happens within a specific context, and context affects the nature and

190. Rambo, *Religious Conversion*, 14–16.
191. Ibid., 7–18, 165–70.
192. Ibid., 17.
193. Ibid., 20, 164.

process of conversion. According to Rambo, there is not a "split," but a strong interaction between the person and the environment. Indeed, people shape their political, religious, economic, social, and cultural worlds. Conversely, people are influenced by the socialization processes of the wider world. The networks of relationships and the cumulative effects of education, training, and institutional structures all affect the potential convert.[194]

Context includes *marcrocontext* and *microcontext*. Macrocontext refers to "the total environment," including political systems, religious organizations, relevant ecological considerations, transnational corporations, and economic systems. Microcontext is the more immediate world of a person's family, friends, ethnic group, religious community, and neighborhood. These forces of the immediate world are essential to the creation of a sense of identity and belonging, and to the shaping a person's thoughts, feelings, and actions.[195] According to Rambo, microcontext and macrocontext are knit together in numerous ways. While some elements of the microcontext confirm and facilitate the larger context (e.g., when a religious organization reinforces patriotic values), other elements prohibit and seek to change the macrocontext (e.g., when a group challenges prevailing political values). Rambo demonstrates that persons, communities, ethnic groups, and nations are situated within and shaped by various superstructures and infrastructures, which affect the content and form of conversion and resistance. Congruence and conflict come together in fascinating ways to either foster or repress the onset of the crisis stage.[196]

Stage 2: Crisis—Catalyst for Change

Crisis refers to a disorientation or disruption in the world of the potential convert caused by the interaction of external and internal forces. It involves the felt frustration of individuals that prepares them for conversion. Rambo notes that preceding conversion, the crisis may be "religious, political, psychological, or cultural in origin."[197] Crisis in life may trigger the search for new religious options. This implies that the

194. Ibid., 165.
195. Ibid., 21–22; "Conversion," 52.
196. Rambo, *Religious Conversion*, 22, 42–43.
197. Ibid., 44.

Exploring Insights

crisis stage causes a series of disruptions to a person's sense of self, and also undermines his or her fundamental orientation to life, raising deep questions about existence. For Rambo, the crisis may serve as the initial trigger of conversion, and may also be a major force in an ongoing process of conversion. The cumulative effect of the crises can result in fostering a conversion process.[198]

The crisis stage includes two broad sets of factors. The first set stresses the nature of the crisis, which involves the intensity (degree of severity), duration (length of time), and scope (whether it is internal or external to the person) of the crisis. The second set is comprised of catalysts for conversion. Rambo describes catalysts for conversion in terms of different categories: "mystical experience," "near-death experience," "illness and healing," "the question, Is that all there is?" (i.e., a growing sense of dissatisfaction with life), "desire for transcendence," "altered states of consciousness" (e.g., higher state of consciousness without the use of drugs), "protean selfhood" (e.g., a search for meaning and for a more stable sense of self), "pathology" (e.g., emotional illness), "apostasy" (i.e., leaving a religious tradition), and "externally stimulated" forces (e.g., colonial powers or the activity of missionaries/advocates).[199]

The degree of flexibility, resilience, and creativity of the crisis needs to be considered. According to Rambo, much of the literature in the human sciences has emphasized social disintegration, political oppression, or something very dramatic as instigating crises. Some cultures, societies, persons and religions are able to withstand a severe crisis and adapt to it in a productive manner, while others are more fragile, and may be rendered vulnerable to outside influence.[200] Crises of transition may give rise to great openness to religious options that were ignored or rejected previously. In any case, the crisis will "more than likely stimulate activity to relieve the discomfort, resolve the discord, and remove the sense of tension. For many [potential converts], this activity can be identified as a [religious] quest."[201]

---

198. Ibid., 46–48.
199. Ibid., 46, 48–55
200. Ibid., 46–47; "Conversion," 53; Rambo and Farhadian, "Converting," 25–26.
201. Rambo, *Religious Conversion*, 55.

Stage 3: Quest—Active Search

Quest refers to the "active search" of the potential convert, who seeks solutions to his or her problems and strives to find meaning, purpose, and transcendence in life. The quest stage encompasses different ways in which persons respond to crises, and the ways in which persons orient themselves to life, especially the religious life.[202] The quest stage stresses the active nature of the potential convert's engagement with his or her predicament. Rambo's discussion of the quest stage begins with the assumption that potential converts actively seek to maximize meaning and purpose in life, to erase ignorance, and to resolve inconsistency. During the times of quest, this active search becomes compelling; potential converts look for resources that offer growth and development in order to "fill the void," solve the problem, or enrich life.[203]

Rambo identifies three important factors in exploring the quest stage of his model: 1) *Response style* describes whether a person responds actively or passively to conversion; 2) *Structural availability* refers to the freedom of a person or persons to move from previous emotional, intellectual, and religious institutions, commitments, and obligations into new options; 3) Assessing *motivational structures* emphasizes the following question: What motivated a person to convert? Typically, human motivations are complex, involving emotional, intellectual and religious features.[204] For Rambo, assessing motivational structures is another way of examining the degree of a person's active quest for religious change or passive vulnerability to religious advocates. Rambo offers six basic motivations that may stimulate an individual or group to seek religious change: the need to experience pleasure and avoid pain; the need for a conceptual system; the need to enhance self-esteem; and the need to establish and maintain relationships; the need to obtain a sense of power; the need to experience transcendence.[205] For Rambo, the order and intensity of these motivations will vary among people as well as within an individual at different times and in different circumstances. These motivations in the quest stage extend throughout

---

202. Rambo and Farhadian, "Converting," 27.

203. Rambo, *Religious Conversion*, 56.

204. Ibid., 56, 60; "Conversion," 53; Rambo and Farhadian, "Converting," 27.

205. Rambo, *Religious Conversion*, 63–64; Rambo and Farhadian, "Converting," 28.

the next encounter and interaction stages as sources of attraction to a new religious orientation, and ultimately into the commitment stage as reasons to solidify one's commitment.[206]

The potential convert continually engages in the process of world construction and reconstruction in order to generate meaning and purpose in life, to maintain psychic equilibrium, and to assure continuity. For Rambo, the quest stage/motif highlights the potential convert as actively seeking something "more" in religious life. This questing for something more or something better than one's present situation may involve seeking new ways of coping with life's problems, seeking new beliefs to transform the potential convert, and seeking new emotional experiences in a connection to the divine and other persons.[207]

Stage 4: Encounter—Advocate and Potential Convert in Contact

Encounter refers to the contact between the advocate (proselytizer) and the potential convert (active seeker), who relate dialectically to one another. This encounter stage brings potential converts who are in crisis and searching for new (religious) options together with advocates (e.g., missionaries) who are seeking to provide the questors with a new orientation. The encounter stage might be seen as "the vortex of the dynamic force field" in which conversion takes place.[208]

For Rambo, there are three major components of the encounter stage: the advocate, the potential convert, and the setting of the encounter. During this encounter stage, advocates and potential converts mutually influence one another in specific contexts. The outcome of the encounter can range from total rejection at one end of the spectrum to complete acceptance at the other. The constellation of events that may transpire between the two poles of rejection and acceptance is ferociously complex in specific conditions.[209]

Rambo notes that the advocate is often persistent and creative. For Rambo, the advocate's strategy is important in that the scope, goals, and methods of conversion necessarily shape both the advocate's tactics and

---

206. Rambo, *Religious Conversion*, 63–65; "Conversion," 54.
207. Rambo, *Religious Conversion*, 56, 166; Kahn and Greene, "Conversion Whole," 235.
208. Rambo, *Religious Conversion*, 87, 167.
209. Ibid., 66, 87, 100; "Conversion," 54.

the potential convert's experiences. The advocate's missionary strategy includes four main elements: the degree of proselytizing, the strategic style, the mode of contact, and the benefits of conversion. *The degree of proselytizing* refers to the extent to which a religious organization is seeking to reach out and incorporate new members. There are two different *strategic styles*. In *diffuse (systems-oriented) strategy*, the advocate tends to circulate widely within a community, seeks to persuade large numbers of persons (especially community leaders), and thus transforms a whole village. In *Concentrated (personalistic) strategy*, the advocate tends to focus upon particular individuals who are marginal to their community. The advocate's actual *mode of contact* with potential converts stresses the following questions: Is the contact public (e.g., "mass rallies" or "revival meetings") or private (e.g., direct-mail contact)? Is it personal (i.e., "face-to-face forms of contact") or impersonal (e.g., media such as television radio, or etc)? The religious community can usually provide *the benefits of conversion* to the potential convert: a system of meaning (e.g., a comprehensive, coherent, and compelling cognitive framework), emotional gratifications (e.g., a sense of belonging, relief of guilt, or development of new relationships), new techniques for living, charismatic leadership, and (access to) power (e.g., experiencing the external and/or internal influence of the divine; experiencing a healing power of the divine).[210]

Rambo asserts that the motivations and adaptations of both religious advocates (missionaries) and potential converts (active agents) for conversion are not "unidirectional," but "dialectic" for engaging new options. In this encounter stage, for example, the missionary as an advocate wants to be effective, and therefore assesses the situation and modifies strategies and tactics in order to be more successful in particular settings. This missionary makes specific changes in order to adapt himself or herself to a specific context (e.g., tolerance, translation, assimilation, Christianization, acculturation, and/or incorporation). Simultaneously, the receptive potential convert confronts the new belief, practice, or religious group or tradition. This potential convert as an active agent seeks out what it is that he or she wants and rejecting what he or she does not desire. Like the missionary, the potential convert undergoes specific transformations in order to adapt himself or

---

210. Rambo, *Religious Conversion*, 76–86; "Conversion," 54–56; Kahn and Greene, "Conversion Whole," 235–36; Rambo and Farhadian, "Converting," 28–29.

Exploring Insights

herself to a specific condition (e.g., cultural oscillation, scrutinization, combination, indigenization, and/or retroversion).[211]

Rambo notes that the setting of the encounter between the advocate and the potential convert provides important background for facilitating religious conversion. Religious group members try to gather at public locations in order to seek encounters with potential converts in *a public setting* (e.g., the university campus meeting). The use of huge public gatherings, by charismatic persons (e.g., Billy Graham), may affect the potential to create a sense of transcendence and may also help the person feel a part of someone/Someone (e.g., the divine) much greater than himself or herself. On the other hand, personal one-on-one encounters may provide private intimacy in *a personal setting* that facilitates the conversion process (e.g., Mormons' mission strategy—"going door-to-door").[212]

Stage 5: Interaction—The Matrix of Change

Interaction has to do with a more intensive and extended exchange/interchange between the advocate and the potential convert in the religious community. In this interaction stage, the potential convert chooses to continue the contact with the advocate and become more involved in a specific religious group, while the advocate works to sustain the interplay with the goal of persuading the person to convert. If the potential convert continues with the religious group after the initial encounter, the interaction intensifies. Here he or she learns more about the teachings, life-style, and expectations of the religious community, and is provided with opportunities, both formal and informal, to become more fully incorporated into it.[213]

For Rambo, the key conceptual element of the interaction stage is encapsulation. Encapsulation refers to "the creation of an environment in which communication and social interaction are controlled in order to allow the potential convert to experience the new religious ideas."[214] Based on Arthur L. Greil and David R. Rudy's encapsulation theory,

---

211. Rambo, *Religious Conversion*, 97–101.

212. Rambo and Farhadian, "Converting," 29.

213. Rambo, *Religious Conversion*, 102; "Conversion," 56; Rambo and Farhadian, "Converting," 29.

214. Kahn and Greene, "Conversion Whole," 236.

Rambo describes three types of encapsulation in the interaction stage: physical, social, and ideological. These three varieties of encapsulation overlap and reinforce one another. *Physical encapsulation* may be achieved by taking people into remote areas where communications can be monitored, so that no sources of information are available to the potential convert. *Social encapsulation* means "directing the potential convert into life-style patterns that limit significant contact with 'outsiders.'" *Ideological encapsulation* involves the use of a worldview and belief system that "inoculates" the adherent against alternative or competitive systems of belief.[215]

Rambo notes that when a sphere of influence has been established by encapsulation, the four dimensions of interaction—relationships, rituals, rhetoric, and roles—are deployed in the conversion process. *Relationships* create and consolidate emotional bonds to the religious community. In many cases, establishing a new kinship and friendship networks forms the foundation upon which a new perspective or way of life is built. *Rituals* enable the potential convert to experience the religious dimension of the conversion process (e.g., something "more"). Through singing, recitation of Scriptures, and prayer in religious communities, ritual actions consolidate persons and groups and instill "a deeper sense of belonging." *Rhetoric* provides the potential convert with a new system of interpretation ("the language of transformation") relevant not only to the religious sphere of life but also, in some cases, to be totality of a person's life. It helps the converting person utilize new language and metaphors in a specific religious group that serve as "a vehicle for the transformation of consciousness" (e.g., for Christians, "sinner" and "God's grace"). *Roles* provide new expectations of behaviors consonant with the potential convert's ascribed status within the group. Playing a role in a public religious setting enables the potential convert to experience and act out a new way of life, frequently with a sense of mission.[216]

---

215. Rambo, *Religious Conversion*, 105–6; "Conversion," 57.

216. Rambo, *Religious Conversion*, 107–23, 167–68; Kahn and Greene, "Conversion Whole," 236; Rambo and Farhadian, "Converting," 30–31.

Stage 6: Commitment—The Consummation and Consolidation of Transformation

Commitment is the consummation of the conversion process. In this commitment stage, the potential convert decides to affiliate with the new religious community. He or she undertakes a series of actions which solidify a new spiritual orientation and incorporate its meaning into daily life.[217]

Rambo identifies five common elements of the commitment stage: decision making, rituals, surrender, testimony, and motivational reformulation. *Decision making* usually involves an intense reflection and confrontation with the self. This commitment decision is often dramatized and commemorated with a public demonstration of the convert's choice to be a valid member of a faith community. *Rituals* are important for their symbolic enactment of the commitment decision, and typically involve a symbolic repudiation of the old self and an embracing of a new identity ("bridge burning events"). Commitment rituals (e.g., baptism) are powerful in that they not only provide a kind of ultimate transformation for a person's experience of the conversion process, but also provide a means by which to consolidate his or her beliefs and involvement in a faith group.[218] The experience of *surrender* is, for many converts, "the turning point away from the old life and the beginning of a new life, produced not by one's own controlling volition but by the power of God's grace."[219] This experience of surrender empowers the convert with a sense of connection with the divine and the religious community. *Testimony* is the narrative witness of a person's life before and after conversion. The public aspect of testimony consolidates the person's commitment to the group, serves as a potent reminder of the community's basic values and goals, and links the convert's personal story with the group's story. *Motivational reformulation* means that the initial motivations of the convert for interacting with the group are further transformed both in the process of his or her public testimony, manifested in language transformation and biographical

---

217. Rambo, *Religious Conversion*, 124, 168.

218. Ibid., 124, 170; Kahn and Greene, "Conversion Whole," 236; Rambo and Farhadian, Converting," 32.

219. Rambo, *Religious Conversion*, 132.

reconstruction, and in the process of his or her personal development and spiritual growth in the faith community.[220]

Stage 7: Consequences—The Effects of Converting Process

Consequences refer to the cumulative effects of the converting process over time when experiences, identities, and commitments are consolidated. In this stage, the convert is constantly assessing the effects of the new religious option and deciding whether the new religion is relevant or viable. For Rambo, the consequences of conversion are determined "in part by the nature, intensity, and duration of the conversion and the response to conversion in a person's or a group's context."[221] Rambo agrees with many contemporary scholars' argument that authentic conversion means "an ongoing process of transformation" through life. Rambo suggests five elements to the exploration of consequences: the role of personal/social bias in assessment (e.g., the particular religious community's or academic discipline's criteria for evaluating conversion), general observations, socio-cultural and historical consequences, psychological consequences, and theological consequences of conversion.[222] This means that to make a careful assessment of the consequences of conversion is to transcend "parochial denominational perspectives" that have dominated past scholarship, and to offer a way of bringing the human sciences and religious studies together.

Influenced by Donald J. Gelpi's theory of conversion, Rambo notes that the nature of the consequences of conversion includes affective, intellectual, ethical, sociopolitical, historical, and religious dimensions.[223] After having met about two hundred religious converts over twelve years, he especially clarifies the theological consequences that have been reported by these converts as follows: a sense of relationship with God, a sense of relief from guilt/sin, a sense of mission and a reason for living, a sense of belonging in a new community, a new sense of meaning and order in life, a sense of wholeness and peace, and a sense of God's presence in a spiritual journey to transformation. For Rambo, the

---

220. Ibid., 132, 139 41, 168 69; Rambo, "Psychology of conversion," 173; Kahn and Greene, "Conversion Whole," 237; Rambo and Farhadian, "Converting," 31, 137.

221. Rambo, *Religious Conversion*, 144.

222. Ibid., 142.

223. Ibid., 146–54.

initial change of the converting person is the first step in a long process and pilgrimage. More profound changes may continue for months, and even years, after the initial conversion takes place.[224]

SUMMARY

Due to the diversity and complexity of the phenomenon of religious conversion, scholars have provided diverse accounts of the conversion experience. Psychologists have viewed conversion as a regressive and pathological phenomenon, a movement of transition from the divided self to the integrated self, an experience of epistemic exploration and cognitive satisfaction, or a process of the positive human development. Sociologists have regarded conversion as the resolution of the potential convert's frustration or deprivation by way of religious affiliation, the result of social attachments or interactions with other members within religious communities, or a product of the effectiveness of member recruitment strategies of particular social and religious organizations. Anthropologists have considered conversion as a process of the intellectual challenge of the encounter within specific cultural settings (i.e., rationality), a passage of cultural transition from the old context to the new context (i.e., acculturation), or a movement of cultural renewal and revitalization. Theologians have understood conversion as a result of the personal encounter or communion with God, a turning toward the work of God's salvation depicted in the Scriptures, an experience of the new rebirth or regeneration through ritual performance of baptism within the faith community, and a continuous transformation through Christian life in prayer in God and Christian life in action for others. Significantly, there is no common theoretical definition of conversion. This means that previous studies have tended to lead the reader to a one-dimensional interpretation of religious conversion and have examined this dynamic process from the perspective of one theoretical discipline. They have not critically integrated religious and social science perspectives for understanding religious conversion. Thus, there is a great demand for more critical and mutually-informing conversation among theological and social scientific studies of conversion.

---

224. Ibid., 146, 160–62.

Understanding Religious Conversion

In order to understand the complexity and richness of the phenomenon of religious change, Rambo invites the perspectives of psychology, sociology, anthropology, and religious studies into critical and mutually-informing conversation and presents a model of religious conversion that is composed of context, crisis, quest, encounter, interaction, commitment, and consequences. His model helps us explore the complicated and multi-faceted elements of human religious change, and thus demonstrate the benefits of constructing an interdisciplinary approach to the process of human transformation.

3

Illustrating the Case of St. Augustine
His Main Life History and Thought

[As "the first modern man," Augustine] came to exercise pervasive influence not only on contemporaries but also on the West since his time. . . . 1. The theology and philosophy of the medieval schoolmen and of the creators of medieval universities were rooted in Augustinian ideas of the relation between faith and reason. . . . 2. The aspirations of all western mystics have never escaped his influence, above all because of the centrality of the love of God in his thinking. . . . 3. The Reformation found its mainspring in criticizing medieval Catholic piety as resting more on human effort than on divine grace. The Counter-Reformation replied that one can affirm the sovereignty of God's grace without also denying the freedom of the will and the moral value ("merit") of good conduct. 4. The eighteenth century found itself passionately divided between those who asserted the perfectibility of man and those who saw human nature as held down by a dead weight of personal and collective egotism; in other words by what Augustine called "original sin." 5. In reaction against the Enlightenment the Romantic movement identified the heart of religion with feeling rather than with the conclusions of intellectual arguments . . . [Augustine] pioneered a highly positive evaluation of human feelings. . . . 6. He was the most acute of Christian Platonists and did much to lay the foundations for the synthesis between Christianity and classical

Understanding Religious Conversion

> theism stemming from Plato and Aristotle. . . . 7. He saw . . . that issues of supreme importance are raised by the problem of the relation of words to the reality. . . . He was a pioneer in the critical study of non-verbal communication.
>
> —Henry Chadwick[1]

THIS CHAPTER DESCRIBES THE case of St. Augustine's conversion experience in order to illustrate the process of religious change. More specifically, it presents a sufficient account of Augustine's main life history (354–430 A.D.) and some of his basic thought to create a better understanding of the process of his conversion. This account helps us to appreciate that Augustine's conversion experience occurred in his lifelong process of transformation.

Over the past 1,600 years, Augustine has been influential for religious people in stimulating a deep spiritual pilgrimage. This study portrays Augustine's specific life events based on the changes of localities and the chronological order of his lifetime, consisting of the following three sections: 1) before his conversion to Christianity, 2) his conversion to Christianity in the summer of 386, and 3) after his conversion to Christianity.[2] In conjunction with this description of Augustine's life history, this study intends to articulate some aspects of Augustine's thought in order to establish a more accurate understanding of the process of his conversion. Broadly, Augustine had shifted from Manichaeism to skepticism, from skepticism to Neoplatonism, and from Neoplatonism to Christianity. The main themes of his thought, which are deeply related to Augustinian spirituality, are 1) God and the soul, 2) sin and God's grace, 3) creation, time, and eternity, 4) the unity of the love of God and love of neighbor—contemplation and action, and 5) the Christian church and baptism.

---

1. Chadwick, *Augustine*, 1–3.

2. I agree with some historians' statement that the conversion process is different under different times and particular historical contexts (see MacMullen, *Christianizing*, 3–5, 56–57, 123–24) while I also agree that the conversion process includes the universal dimension of change—the common ground of human transformation.

BEFORE AUGUSTINE'S CONVERSION TO CHRISTIANITY

This section of the chapter provides an account of Augustine's life history before his conversion to Christianity (354–386). The exploration of Augustine's first thirty-two years of his life helps us to establish a better understanding of his conversion experience in the Milanese garden in the summer of 386. This section includes the following mains themes: 1) Thagaste: the early years (354–370), 2) Carthage: Manichaeism and common/unlawful marriage (*concubinage*) (371–374), 3) From Carthage to home and back (375–383), and 4) Rome and Milan: skepticism and Neoplatonism (383–386).

Thagaste: The Early Years (354–370)

Augustine was born at Thagaste, a Roman provincial town in North Africa (modern Souk Ahras in Algeria), on November 13, 354 (*b. vita.* 1.6; *ep.* 126.7; Possidius, *v. Aug.* 1).[3] According to Augustine, his Father, Patricius, was an African pagan, but was baptized on his deathbed, when Augustine was about seventeen (*conf.* 2.3.6, 3.4.7, 9.9.22). Although his father was not wealthy, Patricius owned some property and was a town councilor of modest means (2.3.5; Possidius, *v. Aug.* 1). He was an affective man, but hot-tempered (*conf.* 9.9.19). In Augustine's words, his mother, Monica, was an ardent Christian whose devotion to Augustine would play a critical role in his later spiritual life (9.8.17). She was a mild and patient woman, but strong-willed (9.9.19–21). Augustine had a brother (Navigius), a sister (Perpetua, who later became superior of a monastery of women at Hippo), and perhaps other siblings.[4] Like many other fourth-century converts (e.g., Bishop Ambrose), Augustine started life as a catechumen (1.11.17).[5] His mother tried to raise him as an attentive Christian: Augustine drank in the name of Christ with

---

3. Thagaste (or Tagaste) was a small town in the eastern part of Numidia about fifty miles southeast of Hippo Regius and about a hundred and fifty miles southwest of Carthage.

4. Bonner, *St. Augustine*, 38–41; Bourke, *Augustine's Quest*, 1–3.

5. According to Henry Chadwick, "Catechumens [within the Christian tradition] were sanctified by the sign of the cross, prayer invoking the protection of God and the child's guardian angel, laying on the hands, and salt placed on the tongue as an act of exorcism" ("Introduction and Notes," 13).

his mother's milk (1.6.7). He grew up a devout Christian, though his mother delayed his baptism. More specifically, when Augustine suffered from serious illness—"pressure on the chest suddenly made hot with fever and almost at death's door"—in his childhood, his mother Monica hastily made arrangements for her son to be baptized in the sacrament of salvation before his death. However, this sacrament of baptism was postponed because Augustine suddenly recovered his physical health. Later Augustine expressed his dissatisfaction with the decision of his mother for postponing his baptism and for her potential permissiveness regarding his youthful sensuality (1.11.17–18).[6]

In school, Augustine was a brilliant student who rapidly advanced to the highest levels of academic success, although his recollection of early boyhood was closely related to the painful memory of his schooling: "I was beaten . . . [and] compelled to follow [the laborious courses] by an increase of the toil and sorrow" (1.9.14). Both Patricius and Monica were eagerly ambitious for their son. They recognized Augustine's superior gifts and sought to give him an opportunity to develop them. After completing Augustine's elementary training in Thagaste, they sent their son, at fifteen, to school at a neighboring town, Madauros, in order to learn literature and oratory (369–370). At the age of sixteen, Augustine's study was interrupted, and he was called home because of his family's lack of funds (2.3.5–6): "Augustine was back again at Thagaste. . . . This was a miserable year, marked by a disquieting act of vandalism, and overshadowed by the sudden onslaught on an ambitious boy, who had hitherto been under constant pressure to succeed at school, of a belated adolescence."[7]

During his adolescence, Augustine's life was extremely turbulent. He amused himself by delving into sensual pleasures of all kinds, despite his parents' efforts to occupy him with schooling. For example, the sixteen year-old Augustine and some friends stole "a huge load of pears" and then, instead of eating these pears, they threw them to the pigs (2.4.9). Upon later describing this pear-theft event, Augustine severely reproached himself for what he considered a senseless and vicious act—"my pleasure was not in the pears; it was in the crime itself,

---

6. Clark, *Augustine*, 1–2. In the time of Augustine, Christians were often baptized after adolescence so that the sins of their youth might be forgiven by baptism (ibid., 1–2).

7. Brown, *Augustine*, 26.

Illustrating the Case of St. Augustine

done in association with a sinful group"—in terms of sin, wickedness, and inappropriate human friendship of a peer group (2.5.10–2.9.17).

Carthage: Manichaeism and Common/Unlawful Marriage (371–374)

In 371, Augustine (who was seventeen years old) went to Carthage in order to continue his study, especially rhetoric, with the financial support of his friends and relatives (e.g., Romanianus). Carthage was the biggest city in North Africa (the second greatest city of the Western Roman Empire), which was an important place of politics, education, and culture in the Roman world. Augustine described this city as "a cauldron of illicit loves" which leapt and boiled around him (*conf.* 3.1.1).[8] He sought "an object for [his] love" and was captivated by theatrical shows (3.1.1–3.2.2). However, his ingrained habit of religious practice prompted Augustine to attend the Mass of the Catechumens in the Christian community, where it seems, he met and fell in love with a young (freedwoman or lower-class) woman. He lived with this woman (whose name was not known for certain) for fifteen years;[9] his son, Adeodatus ("Given by God," perhaps a common name in North Africa), whom he dearly loved, was born in 371 (4.2.2).[10]

---

8. Ibid., 26–27.

9. Peter Brown writes, "In all probability [Augustine's unnamed woman] had been a good Catholic throughout her life" (*Augustine*, 80; see Finn, *Death to Rebirth*, 216; Wills, *Saint Augustine*, 16, 41–42).

10. See Bourke, *Augustine's Quest*, 15–16; Finn, *Death to Rebirth*, 216; O'Donnell, *Augustine*, 38–39, 58; Wills, *Saint Augustine*, 16–18. In the milieu of Augustine's age, marriage was strictly regulated under Roman law, which was concerned with controlling citizenship rights. It was forbidden between certain classes, and some groups of people were not permitted to marry at all. As such, concubinage (*concubinatus*) was regarded as an alternate form for monogamous/stable relationship and as a respectable solution for conflicts within concrete human conditions (Power, "Concubine," 222). It was common that bishops in late antiquity decided it would be impossible to forbid Communion to anyone faithful to one partner in such a relationship (Hippolytus, *apost. const.* 16.23; Leo I, *ep.* 167). In both church and state law, concubinage constituted a gray area and was very often assimilated to marriage in practical situations (Power, *Veiled Desire*, 104; "Concubine," 222). In light of Roman social history, recent scholarship has emphasized the blurred boundary between legal marriage and long-term concubinage, taking seriously Augustine's perception of his partnership as a marriage (*conf.* 6.12.22; O'Connell, "Sexuality," 78–81; O'Donnell, *Augustine: Confessions*, vol. 2, 377; Power, "Concubine," 223).

During his study of rhetoric, the young Augustine was quiet, but was the top student in his class (3.3.6). At the age of eighteen/nineteen, as part of his rhetoric curriculum, Augustine read Cicero's *Hortensius*,[11] which led him into an arduous quest for truth and philosophy (*conf.* 3.4.8; *sol.* 1.10.17). However, *Hortensius* failed to grip him entirely, because this book did not contain the Christian belief or message (which was related to "the name of Christ") (*conf.* 3.4.7–8). For this reason, Augustine (re)turned his attention from *Hortensius* to the Christian Scriptures but was disappointed with the Bible; that is, the literary quality of the early Latin version of the Bible appeared to him unsophisticated and "unworthy in comparison with the dignity of Cicero" (3.5.9).

In order to find spiritual and intellectual comfort, he gave his allegiance to Manichaeism, which was basically composed by the syncretistic and dualistic system (e.g., Light and Darkness or Good and Evil). Manichaeism incorporated elements from Zoroastrianism, Buddhism, Judaism, and Christianity because each was recognized as a preparatory step in the universal message that Mani (216–217) proclaimed. Based on Persian dualism, Mani's conception of the relation between spirit and matter, and of salvation, in many ways resembled those of Gnosticism.[12] Thus, the Manichean mythology was a radically dualistic cosmology denigrating the material world. The Manicheans explained the existence of evil by positing a conflict between God, the cause of all good, and matter, the source of evil. The origin of the material world was attributed to an evil creator, whose power was perpetually at war with that of a good creator who was not responsible for the evil in the world. Human beings were viewed as caught up in this inter-cosmic conflict between the power of the good creator and the power of the evil creator; as such, human persons were not responsible for their evil deeds. The Manichees identified human salvation as the liberation of light trapped within their material bodies, which was achieved by extreme ascetic rejection of all that belongs to the material sphere, especially the physical appetites and desires. In this vein, the Manichees repudiated parts of the Bible, especially the books of the Old Testament

---

11. Cicero wrote *Hortensius* in 45 B.C. near the end of his life, which is lost except for quotations (many in Augustine's works). In this book, Cicero rebutted Hortensius' opinion that philosophical study has no social utility and does not contribute to human happiness. As book ten of *Confessions* points out, Augustine was affected by Cicero's analysis of the sources of happiness (Chadwick, "Introduction and Notes," 39).

12. Walker, *History*, 98–99.

because they conceived the God of the Old Testament as a corporeal or material substance; they also considered the Old Testament as the story of the evil power's reign over this world. The membership of the Manichean party was in two classes: the "Elect" practiced their full austerities; and the "Hearers" accepted Manichean teachings, but with much less strictness of practice. Manichaeism was widespread in the Roman Empire, especially in the fourth and fifth centuries when it grew rapidly. Its influence lasted until the late Middle Ages. As such, Augustine became a Manichee (i.e., a hearer) and adhered to the religious and philosophical sect with much emphasis on magic and numerology for nine years. He took cover within Manichaean dualism in order to explain conveniently both the origin of evil and the utter goodness of God. He viewed God as an extended, and infinitely diffused, material substance (3.6.10–3.7.14, 7.5.7).[13]

From Carthage to Home and Back (375–383)

After finishing his study in Carthage, Augustine, as an ardent Manichee and a newly minded rhetorician, returned to his home town, Thagaste, with his unmarried wife and his son in order to open a school of grammar and rhetoric in 375. He then proceeded to attempt to convert his Christian friends to Manichaeism (*conf.* 3.11.19). At that time, after the death of his father Patricius in 371, his mother Monica turned all of her attention to Augustine: "As mothers do, she [Monica] loved to have me [Augustine] with her, but much more than most mothers" (5.8.15). However, Monica was deeply disappointed that her son made an unlawful marriage and embraced Manichaeism against traditional Christian belief. She expelled him from home. She had bitterly wept and had prayed daily for her son's salvation that he might become again a Christian (3.11.19). Eventually, Monica had a vision that she should take her son back; her vision was based on both the inspiration of her own dream about the future of Augustine—"Her vision was of herself standing on a rule made of wood. . . . When she looked, she saw me standing beside her on the same rule" (3.11.19)—and the advice of a provincial bishop to whom she had tearfully lamented her wayward

13. Bonner, *St Augustine*, 157–92; Bourke, *Augustine's Quest*, 17–23; Brown, *Augustine*, 35–49; Markus, "Life," 503; McGinn and McGinn, *Christian Mystics*, 153; Walker, *History*, 98–99.

son—"Go away from me: as you live, it cannot be that the son of these tears should perish" (3.12.21).

In the meantime, Augustine, the young Manichee, met his Christian friend in 376. He realized that this unnamed friend was arranged to be baptized before death because his friend suffered from a serious illness. Augustine met his friend and mocked him, who did faithfully receive the sacrament of Christian baptism. As such his friend was upset; a few days later, his friend died when Augustine was absent (4.4.8).[14] When he heard of the death of his unnamed friend, Augustine was very shocked and shameful, and decided to leave his town: "My home town became a torture to me; my father's house a strange world of unhappiness; all that I had shared with him was without him transformed into a cruel torment. My eyes looked for him everywhere, and he was not there . . . I fled from my home town, for my eyes sought for him less in a place where they were not accompanied to see him. And so from the town of Thagaste I came to Carthage" (4.4.9; 4.7.12).

In the same year, 376, Augustine (who was twenty-two years old) returned to Carthage and, as a great scholar, he taught rhetoric until age twenty-nine. He made many friends in the process of striking success of study and teaching, including Vindicianus (a current proconsul of Africa), Nebridius (who later became a crucial member of the lay monastery), Flaccianus (a future proconsul of Africa), and Alypius (who was a student of Augustine and later became a closest friend).[15] He participated in the oratorical contest of Carthage and was crowned for a theatrical poem (4.2.3, 4.3.5). Augustine published a well-received book, *On the Beautiful and the Fitting* (380/381), which was dedicated to Hierius the Syrian, a contemporary orator in Rome. Augustine admired him for his reputation and wanted to be known by him (4.13.20–4.14.21). However, the Manichean dogma gradually ceased to satisfy Augustine's sharp intellect and the deep religious issues that were tormenting him. His Manichean associates urged him to meet the highly respected Manichaean bishop, Faustus (who was a leading thinker and apologist in their religious sect), when their bishop arrived in Carthage. In their meeting, Faustus could not answer the questions Augustine posed, and he lacked the wide-ranging quality of liberal learning that the young intellectual expected. With this feeling of

14. Brown, *Augustine*, 53; Wills, *Saint Augustine*, 30–32.
15. Clark, *Augustine*, 3.

disenchantment, Augustine lost all respect for Manichaeism: "After he [Faustus] had clearly showed his lack of training in liberal arts in which I had supposed him to be highly qualified, I began to lose all hope that he would be able to analyze and resolve the difficulties which disturbed me" (5.7.12). The inadequacy of Faustus' answers to Augustine's questions led a young Augustine to remain outwardly a Manichee but to become now inwardly a skeptic (5.3.3–5.7.13).[16] In addition to his intellectual and religious frustration within the Manichaean sect, the rowdiness of Augustine's students in Carthage led this young teacher of the liberal arts into a more unendurably feeling of disenchantment (5.8.14). Augustine became despondent, restless, and decided to move to Rome. His mother, Monica, vehemently opposed her son's departure to a far-away, remote place. But in fall 383, Augustine was able to set sail for Rome after deceiving his mother in a rather heartless fashion, by declaring that his intention was only to take leave of a friend. While Monica returned to a little oratory, dedicated to St. Cyprian, to pray, Augustine escaped by ship in the night, leaving his mother to her lamentations: "When morning came, [Monica] was crazed with grief, and with recriminations and groans. . . . These agonies proved that there survived in her the remnants of Eve, seeking with groaning for the child she had brought forth in sorrow (Gen 3:16). And yet after accusing me of deception and cruelty, she turned again to pray for me and to go back to her usual home. Meanwhile I came to Rome" (*conf.* 5.8.15).[17]

Rome and Milan: Skepticism and Neoplatonism (383–386)

In the same year, 383, Augustine arrived in Rome within the hospitality of his Manichaean patrons, although he had no enthusiasm in his mind for Manichaeism. He fell gravely ill on arrival but he did not arrange to receive any Christian rite of baptism (*conf.* 5.9.16).[18] After recovering his health, he became a professor of rhetoric in Rome. Augustine realized that his students committed no acts of vandalism, but they did intend to avoid paying their tuition: they clubbed together and transferred to another teacher just as the fee came due (5.12.22). In early autumn 384,

---

16. Bourke, *Augustine's Quest*, 35–38.

17. Ibid., 39–40; Bonner, *St. Augustine*, 69–70; O'Donnell, *Augustine: Confessions*, vol. 1, 52.

18. Bonner, *St. Augustine*, 70.

Augustine moved to Milan, the Western capital of the Roman Empire, by the aid of his Manichean friends. Symmachus especially, as a prominent Manichee and a powerful prefect of Rome, helped Augustine to acquire a government appointment as the municipal chair of rhetoric in Milan (5.13.23).[19]

Through the circle of intellectuals of Milan, Augustine found the books of Neoplatonists (e.g., Plotinus and Porphyry), which disabused him of his Manichaean materialism.[20] He was inspired by these Neoplatonic books that God, as spirit, is the incorruptible, infinite, and eternal creator of all that exists, and that evil, far from being a substance, is the absence or privation of being. In addition, Augustine learned from these books that the Divine was buried deep within him, awaiting only discovery that he sought by introspection (7.10.16).[21] However, Augustine later realized and recalled that the books of Neoplatonists did not include the name of Jesus Christ, that is, the Platonic philosophers had no knowledge of the Word's taking flesh and dying for human sin (7.21.27).

While living in Milan, Augustine was significantly influenced by Bishop Ambrose, who was a Roman aristocrat.[22] Along with his read-

---

19. Bourke, *Augustine's Quest*, 41–42; Brown, *Augustine*, 55–61.

20. Brown, *Augustine*, 82–95; Harrison, *Augustine's Early Theology*, 27–31; O'Donnell, *Augustine*, 122–23; O'Meara, *Young Augustine*, 139–53. Neoplatonism was a pantheistic and mystical interpretation of Platonic thoughts. It was founded by Ammonius Saccas in Alexandria and was developed by Plotinus (205–270), who settled in Rome about 244; the leadership of Neoplatonism was passed from Plotinus to Porphyry (233–304). For Neoplatonists, God is simple, all-perfect, and absolute existence, from whom the lower existences come. God is the One, above the duality implied in thought, and from God the Nous emanates. From the Nous the world-soul derives being, and from that individual souls. From the world-soul the realm of matter comes. Each stage is inferior in the amount of being it possesses to the one above reaching in gradations from God to matter. Neoplatonists viewed salvation as "a rising of the soul to God in mystic contemplation, the end of which was union with the divine"; the morals of Neoplatonism, like those of later Greek philosophy generally, were ascetic (Walker, *History*, 98; see Chadwick, *Augustine*, 17–24; Harrison, *Augustine's Early Theology*, 77–79).

21. O'Donnell, *Augustine: Confessions*, vol. 1, 89–90.

22. In the fourth century, there was doctrinal turmoil that embroiled not only Cyril of Jerusalem—he was exiled three times—but also Christian emperors, leaders, thinkers, and lay people from west Gaul all the way to East Syria. The cause of this turmoil was a divisive question in a religious controversy: "In what sense is Christ, the son of God, divine?" There was an answer at the Council of Nicaea in 325: "as son of God, Christ is what his Father is, divine in nature; Son and Father are consubstantial" (Finn,

ings of the Neoplatonic books, he listened to the preaching of Bishop Ambrose. Based on his own exegetical rule of "the letter kills, but the Spirit gives life" (2 Cor 3:6), Bishop Ambrose allegorically explained many sections of the Bible, instead of interpreting its texts merely literally. Augustine gradually found himself becoming interested in the content as well as the rhetoric technique of his sermons (*conf.* 5.13.23–5.14.24).[23] In particular, through Ambrose's gifted interpretation of the Bible, Augustine began to recognize a greater depth and wisdom in Christian doctrine or belief than he had previously supposed (5.13.23). Ambrose, as a Christian and a Neoplatonist mentor, had affected Augustine to turn away from Manichaeism and toward Christianity. However, in line with the teaching of the Academics, Augustine remained skeptical about the possibility of finding any truth. As such he decided to become again a catechumen and to just remain in the status of catechumen within the Christian community of Milan (5.14.25).

About this time, Augustine's mother, Monica, came to Milan. She was happy because her son was no longer a Manichean, although Augustine was not yet a baptized Christian believer (6.1.1). She regularly attended the Mass of the church and sincerely followed Bishop Ambrose's spiritual guidance about the African religious practices (6.2.2).[24] In particular, Monica helped her bishop, when he had defended the church against the Roman army during the time of religious controversy against the Arians (9.7.15).

Death to Rebirth, 213–14). However, this answer provoked more tumult than the question had, pitting anti-Nicene Christians, customarily called Arians, and Nicene Christians against each other (214–15). In 374, the death of the Arian bishop, Auxentius, led the Milanese into seeking a successor of the New Basilica (Milan's cathedral). The two factions, the Arians and Nicene Christians, were soon in bitter struggle as to the theological complexion of the successor. As such Ambrose, the young governor of the province, entered the New Basilica to quiet the throng. The cry of a child was raised, "Ambrose for Bishop," at which point the congregation regarded this voice as a divine command. Ambrose was elected bishop of Milan, although he was a just catechumen. Shortly after, Ambrose was baptized by Simplicianus, his father and spiritual mentor, on November 30, 374. Strongly attached to the Nicene faith, Ambrose made no compromise with the Arians, and resisted all their attempts to secure places of worship in Milan. At that time, the Arians were aided by the Empress Justina, mother of the youthful Valentinian II (Bourke, *Augustine's Quest*, 44, 83; McLynn, "Ambrose," 17–19; Sun, *Time and Eternity*, 228; Walker, *History*, 128–29).

23. Bourke, *Augustine's Quest*, 50–51; Brown, *Augustine*, 74–77; O'Donnell, *Augustine*, 54–55; O'Meara, *Young Augustine*, 109–24.

24. Bourke, *Augustine's Quest*, 45; O'Donnell, *Augustine*, 150.

Meanwhile, Monica found that Augustine was still living with his unmarried wife and his son, Adeodatus. Monica persuaded Augustine to dismiss his "unlawful" wife because she was a hindrance both to her son's lawful marriage with a woman of a higher class and to her son's ambitions for pubic office: "In a small provincial town in Africa, the only alternative to a career that took him far away from his background, was poverty and boredom; and the only chance of permanent success, an alliance with those great families, who, in distant Rome and Milan, controlled the destinies of men of talent from the provinces."[25] Augustine discharged his unmarried wife, whereby she returned to North Africa and vowed herself to continence (6.15.25).[26] Her departure plunged Augustine to the depths of misery, although his son Adeodatus remained with him in Milan (6.15.25).[27] Augustine was engaged to a young Milanese heiress—who was twelve years old—and, by Roman law, had to wait two years to marry her. Because Augustine was unable to maintain continence, he procured another woman (6.15.25).[28]

Although Augustine was intellectually convinced of the truth of Christianity, he still held back from seeking baptism. During the period of his existential despair (the summer of 386), Augustine, as Ambrose once had done, put himself in the hands of Simplicianus, who was a convert from Paganism and now a celebrated priest, in order to consult

---

25. Brown, *Augustine*, 52.

26. Chadwick, *Augustine*, 15–16; O'Donnell, *Augustine: Confessions*, vol. 2, 383–85.

27. There are diverse opinions about Augustine's dismissal of his unmarried wife. A strong tradition has argued that Monica must take the blame for engineering this dismissal in her motherly project to get Augustine married and baptized, but the snobbery of the Milanese has also been blamed (Brown, *Augustine*, 51–52, 79–81). More recently Augustine has been held responsible for his own decisions (Power, *Veiled Desire*, 104). Some scholars do not even perceive it as a problem, understanding his action simply as the natural decision of an elite man within the milieu of his age, when a permanent marriage with a lower-class woman would prevent the attainment of his ambitions for public office (E. A. Clark, "Asceticism," 68; O'Meara, *Young Augustine*, 123; Quinn, *Companion*, 326). Certainly, many bishops and ascetic teachers would have seen the dismissal of a concubine and a legitimate betrothal as a moral as well as a political step upward (Brown, *Augustine*, 79; see Hippolytus, *apost. const.* 16.23; Leo I, *ep.* 167; Power, "Concubine," 222). In his own later sermons, Augustine, as Bishop of Hippo, was against concubines for the married, or for those who took them cynically as a stopgap before marriage (*s.* 224.3).

28. See Bonner, *St. Augustine*, 78–79; Bourke, *Augustine's Quest*, 51–52; Plumer, "Book Six," 104–5; Vaught, *Journey*, 152–53.

with his spiritual mentor about his troubles.[29] Simplicianus recounted for Augustine the conversion story of Marius Victorinus, who was born in Africa and became a famous orator in Rome. Although Victorinus was an ardent and venerable Neoplatonist philosopher, he publicly confessed his Christian faith and received the sacrament of baptism within the Christian community in 355. Consequently, he resigned his professorship in Rome because of the edict of the emperor Julian (8.5.10).[30] Augustine knew Victorinus' work and could not miss the parallels in his own life (8.1.1–8.5.10).[31] Shortly thereafter, Augustine (and Alypius) received a surprise visit of Ponticianus who was an African and did hold high office in the court. By chance Ponticianus found a book of the letters of the apostle Paul on the table which Augustine had been reading.[32] As a baptized Christian believer, Ponticianus encouraged Augustine in his study of the Bible. Augustine (and Alypius) heard several more conversion stories from Ponticianus, including the story of Antony the Egyptian monk who was a pioneer of desert monasticism, and the stories of two friends of the Emperor who immediately adopted the ascetic life (8.6.14–15).[33] These conversion stories led Augustine into the depths of the restlessness of his heart: "The arguments

29. Simplicianus, as a senior priest, moved from Rome to Milan in order to baptize Ambrose, who was a governor but was unpredictably appointed as a bishop of Milan in 374. "In Rome Simplicianus knew Marius Victorinus, a rhetorician of African origin, who embodied the ideal of high culture, writing (extant) books on grammar, rhetoric, and dialectic, translating some of Aristotle's logic, and presenting to Latin readers works by Porphyry and Plotinus. Victorinus read Neoplatonism into the prologue to St John's gospel, and could count himself a Christian fellow-traveller" (Chadwick, "Introduction and Notes," 134). Simplicianus became a successor of Ambrose as bishop of Milan in 397 and died in 400 (ibid., 133).

30. Julian's edict of June 17, 362 was based on the presupposition that pagan literature and pagan religion are indissoluble. Many Christians (e.g., Gregory of Nazianzus) resented it. In *City of God*, Augustine regarded this edict as "an act of persecuting intolerance" (*civ. Dei* 18.52) (Chadwick, "Introduction and Notes," 139–40).

31. Bourke, *Augustine's Quest*, 59–61; O'Donnell, *Augustine*, 59; Wills, *Saint Augustine*, 44–45.

32. While writing book eight of his *Confessions*, Augustine cited the letters of the Apostle Paul, especially *Romans*. The identifiable citations of Romans in book eight make a pattern as follows: 1) *conf.* 8.1.2—Rom 1:21–22; 2) *conf.* 8.5.11—Rom 7:17; 3) *conf.* 8.5.12—Rom 7:22–25; 4) *conf.* 8.10.22—Rom 7:17, 20; 5) *conf.* 8.12. 29—Rom 13:13–14; and 6) *conf.* 8.12.30—Rom.14:1 (see O'Donnell, *Augustine: Confessions*, vol. 3, 3).

33. Bourke, *Augustine's Quest*, 62–63; Brown, *Augustine*, 99; Finn, *Death to Rebirth*, 220.

were exhausted and all had been refuted. The only thing left to it was a mute trembling, and as if it were facing death it was terrified of being restrained from the treadmill of habit by which it suffered 'sickness unto death'" (8.7.18; see 8.8.19).

AUGUSTINE'S CONVERSION TO CHRISTIANITY IN THE SUMMER OF 386

This section of the chapter presents an account of Augustine's conversion to Christianity in the summer of 386. Augustine himself portrayed his own conversion experience in a garden of Milan (*conf.* 8.8.19, 8.11.27, 8.12.28–30). In the agony of his internal warfare, he had painfully experienced a cleft between his ideals and his conduct (8.5.10).[34] One day in the late summer of 386, he rushed into the garden and threw himself down under a certain tree because his self-condemnation and internal tension became unendurable. Here Augustine prayed to God, "Grant me chastity and continence, but not yet" (8.7.17). In the midst of his violent turmoil in which his divided will struggled against itself, Augustine heard a divine voice and command—"Pick up and read, pick up and read"—through the chanting of a neighboring child and read the letter of the apostle Paul—"Let us live honorably as in the day. . . . Put on the Lord Jesus Christ, and make no provision for the flesh, to gratify its desires" (Rom 13:13–14). While reading the Bible, Augustine had experienced the intervention and revelation of the divine in his mind and his life. This garden experience transformed him. A light of confidence shone in his heart and the darkness of uncertainty vanished (8.12.28–29). Shortly after, like Augustine, Alypius read the letter of Paul (i.e., Rom 14:1) and also converted to God (8.12.30). From the garden Augustine and Alypius came to Monica and told her what had happened to them. She was filled with joy (8.12.30).

This garden experience at Milan enabled Augustine to make a new decision for reorganizing the rest of his lifetime. Augustine made up his mind both to give up his ambition for success in this world and to stand firmly upon the rule of Christian faith. Thus, Augustine resigned his

---

34. Augustine used Paul's Epistle to the Galatians 5:17 in order to portray his conflict between two wills: "For what the flesh desires is opposed to the Spirit, and what the Spirit desires is opposed to the flesh; for these are opposed to each other, to prevent you from doing what you want."

professorship of rhetoric, renounced his legal betrothal with a young rich heiress for acquiring a higher status in Roman society (e.g., a governor of a province), and engaged in the life of asceticism and celibacy in the Christian community (8.12.30).[35]

Augustine's description of his garden experience at Milan in the summer of 386 is essential for understanding his conversion to God—"You converted me to yourself" (*convertisti enim me ad te*) (8.12.30).[36] About a decade later, Augustine wrote the *Confessions* (397–401 A.D.), which was a spiritual autobiography of his ongoing-progress of transformation. This book lays out the narrative of his conversion—from birth to baptism. Augustine's garden experience at Milan represents the moment of decision for his new life. The preceding thirty-two years of his life had led up to this garden experience. Along with his conversion to Christianity, Augustine became a great *converting* person and had engaged in other decisive events for his remaining forty-four years (e.g., his baptism in 387).[37]

AFTER AUGUSTINE'S CONVERSION TO CHRISTIANITY

This section of the chapter describes Augustine's life history after his conversion to Christianity (386–430). His garden experience enabled the convert Augustine to find a new way of Christian living in solitude and community for the rest of his life. This section consists of three main themes: 1) Cassiciacum, Milan, Ostia, and Rome: the communal life, Christian baptism, and the mystical vision (386–388), 2) Carthage and Thagaste: the monastic life as a layperson (388–391), and 3) Hippo Regius: the monastic life and church ministry as a monk and a priest/bishop (391–430).

---

35. Bonner, *St. Augustine*, 87–92; Bourke, *Augustine's Quest*, 63–67; Brown, *Augustine*, 96–102; Harrison, *Augustine's Early Theology*, 20; Lancel, *Saint Augustine*, 95–98; O'Donnell, *Augustine: Confessions*, vol. 3, 55–71; Wills, *Saint Augustine*, 45–47.

36. O'Donnell, *Augustine: Confessions*, vol. 1, 102.

37. Finn, *Death to Rebirth*, 221.

Cassiciacum, Milan, Ostia, and Rome: The Communal Life, Christian Baptism, and the Mystical Vision (386–388)

After his conversion to Christianity, Augustine retreated to the country estate of his fellow professor, Verecundus, at Cassiciacum (now Casago Brianza), while accompanied by his mother, son, brother, two cousins, his closest friend Alypius, and other friends (*conf.* 9.2.2–3).[38] During his stay at Cassiciacum, Augustine suffered from a serious infection in his lungs, and now he resigned his professorship of rhetoric: "During that summer in consequence of too heavy a teaching load in literary studies, my lungs had begun to weaken. Breathing became difficult. Pains on the chest were symptoms of the lesion, and deprived me of power to speak clearly or for any length of time; ... it was virtually enforcing the necessity of resigning the burden of my teaching responsibility" (9.2.4).

After recovering his health, Augustine, as a Christianized Neoplatonist, earnestly participated in philosophical discussions with his friends. More specifically, he held extended discussions with his circle of intelligent colleagues about the possibility of arriving at truth, the happy life and the knowledge of God, providence and the problem of evil, the quest for God, and the immortality of the soul. Based on these philosophical and religious discussions, Augustine wrote some of his early works: *Against the Skeptics* (386); *On the Happy Life* (386) in which he contended that wisdom is a certain spiritual "measure" that corresponds exactly to the soul's needs, and that the true knowledge of God is wisdom and happiness—the human soul desires happiness which can be attained only in the possession of God; *On Order* (386), his first written struggle with the problem of evil, in which Augustine insisted that the divine order is achieved through the spiritual and intellectual discipline which leads to the knowledge of self and of the spiritual world, and that 1) nothing can exist outside the divine order, 2) evil does not have its source within this order, and 3) divine justice does not permit evil to escape order, but calls it to a proper ordering; *The Soliloquies* (386–387), a personal dialogic monologue, in which he earnestly sought for knowing both God and the soul; *On the Immortality of the Soul* (386–387) in which he argued that the soul is unchangeable

---

38. According to Vernon J. Bourke, Augustine lived together at Cassiciacum with at least eight others: "his mother, Monnica; his son, Adeodatus; his brother, Navigius; two cousins, Lastidianus and Rusticus; two pupils, Licentius and Trygetius; and Alypius" (*Augustine's Quest*, 70).

and immortal. Besides these works, Augustine began to write *On Music* (387–391) and later completed it in Africa. In this work, Augustine understood music as a discipline that is related to the preparation for describing and understanding the nature of the unseen.[39] As such, here Augustine had gradually developed his statement of the twofold object of philosophy, which emphasized the interaction between God and human soul:

> To philosophy pertains a twofold question: the first treats of the soul; the second, of God. The first makes us know ourselves; the second, our origin. The former is the more delightful to us; the latter, more precious. The former makes us fit for a happy life; the latter renders us happy. . . . This is the order of wisdom's branches of study by which one becomes competent to grasp the order of things and to discern two worlds and the very Author of the universe, of whom the soul has no knowledge save to know how it knows Him not. (*ord.* 2.18.47; see *sol.* 1.2.7, 2.1.1; Plotinus, *enn.* 1.6.9)

Consistent with (his conversion experience in Milan) and his healing experience in Cassiciacum, Augustine was strongly determined to receive Christian baptism. He wrote a letter to Bishop Ambrose of Milan about his baptism and asked which specific part of the Bible was appropriate for preparing his baptism. Ambrose encouraged him to become a baptized Christian and recommended him to read the prophet Isaiah. Several months later, Augustine, as a catechumen, returned to Milan to participate in the Milanese baptismal liturgy (*conf.* 9.5.13).[40] On the night of April 24–25, 387 (at the Easter Vigil), Augustine was baptized, along with Adeodatus and Alypius, by Bishop Ambrose at the baptistery of the Milanese cathedral (9.6.14). As later Possidius (who was Augustine's biographer) notes, "Straightway, established in the Catholic faith, an ardent desire was awakened in [Augustine] to perfect himself in religion, and so with the coming of the holy days of Easter he received the water of baptism. And thus it happened that by divine grace he received through the great and illustrious prelate Ambrose the salutary doctrine of the Catholic Church and the divine Sacraments" (Possidius, *v. Aug.* 1). Augustine rejoiced in the presence of God and

---

39. See Bourke, *Augustine's Quest*, 70–78; Brown, *Augustine*, 108–16; Clark, *Augustine*, 8; Markus, "Life," 498; Sun, *Time and Eternity*, 239–40.

40. Bonner, *St. Augustine*, 94–95.

celebrated his sacrament of baptism with his mother, his friends, and church members.[41]

Not long after his baptism, Augustine made up his mind to go back to North Africa with his mother, Adeodatus, Navigius, Alypius, and his other faithful friends (e.g., Evodius) in order to establish a new monastic lay community (9.8.17). When they arrived at Ostia on the Tiber (which was far removed from crowds), they rested themselves to rehabilitate their strength for a long voyage to North Africa. On a beautiful day, Augustine and his mother, Monica, were standing, leaning out of a window of the house overlooking a garden; then they profoundly and honestly talked about spiritual pilgrimage in this world, related to issues of Christian lives of past, present, and future. During this conversation, they were deeply immersed into themselves; they felt the intervention of the divine within themselves and experienced the steadfast love of God. This means that Augustine and his mother shared a mystic/ecstatic experience of union with God at Ostia (9.10.23–26).

However, a few days later, Monica fell sick of fever. Monica realized that she would not recover from her serious illness and requested that her sons (Augustine and Navigius) bury her body at Ostia, although she previously intended to be entombed next to her husband's tomb in her hometown (9.11.27–28). Monica died: "On the ninth day of her illness, when she was aged 56, and I was 33, this religious and devout soul was released from the body" (9.11.28). Augustine deeply lamented his mother's death (9.12.29). Monica was buried at Ostia (9.12.32–9.13.37).[42] Around this time, the plan of Augustine and his friends for returning to North Africa was delayed for a year. Although the precise reason for this delay was not clear, it was related to the unexpected death of Monica[43] and a blockade of the Mediterranean:

---

41. Bourke, *Augustine's Quest*, 81–83; Brown, *Augustine*, 117–18; Finn, *Death to Rebirth*, 221–31; O'Donnell, *Augustine*, 59–61.

42. Augustine describes Monica's life, especially the story of her death, as found in *Confessions* 9.8.17–9.13.37. This story of the death of Monica is one of the noblest monuments of ancient Christian literature. Medieval pilgrims recorded the epitaph on Monica's tomb at Ostia, which was placed early in the fifth century by Anicius Aucherius Bassus, consul in 431. In the summer of 1945, the tomb of Monica was discovered when some young people were digging a hole in a small courtyard beside the church of Santa Aurea at Ostia in order to plant a post for their basketball game (Brown, *Augustine*, 121–24; Lancel, *Saint Augustine*, 119; Sun, *Time and Eternity*, 241).

43. Bourke, *Augustine's Quest*, 90.

> Monica's death seems to have altered his plans and delayed his return for a year . . . from certain words of Augustine, it seems to have been due to the unsettled conditions brought about by the rebellion of Maximus, the military governor of Britain, who had been raised to the purple by his soldiery in the spring of 385 and had established himself in Gaul after the assassination of the Emperor Gratian on 25 August of the same year. In 387 Maximus' armies drove the young emperor Valentinian from Italy; his fleet controlled the sea, while Gildo, the Count of Africa, was on friendly terms with him. In these circumstances, Augustine may well have deemed it prudent to remain in Italy until the political situation should become more settled, or at least a little clearer.[44]

Augustine and his followers went to Rome and lived together. During this period, Augustine held philosophical and religious conversations with his friends and recovered his strength. As a newly baptized Christian, Augustine met church leaders of Rome and learned the main doctrines of Christianity and the sacraments of the Roman churches. At the same time, he also contacted his former Manichean friends and patrons of Rome in order to refute their claims of Manichaeism and to encourage them to be converted toward Christianity: "Augustine felt that there was no hurry about starting the journey. He hardly knew the Rome of the Christians. During his earlier period of teaching there, he had lived and worked with his fellow Manicheans. Now he had an opportunity to learn the doctrines and practices of the Church of Christ in the Eternal City. At this time, Augustine looked forward to a quiet life of monastic retirement and study."[45]

During his stay in Rome, as a newly baptized Christian, Augustine continuously repudiated Manichean teachings about God and the human person and wrote some of his early works: *The Greatness of the Soul* (387–388), proposed as the record of a dialogue between Augustine and his friend Evodius, in which Augustine demonstrated the soul's greatness which culminates in the three levels of moral purification, of the soul's gazing upon the truth, and of its contemplative vision of the truth; *On the Catholic and the Manichean Ways of Life* (387–389), his first response undertaken directly against Manichaeism, in which he had attempted to defend the Old Testament, to show the

44. Bonner, *St. Augustine*, 104–5.
45. Bourke, *Augustine's Quest*, 90.

superiority of Christian asceticism than Manichean asceticism, and to attack the high claims made by the Manichees for continence. Besides these works, Augustine began to write *On Genesis against the Manichees* (388–389/390), the first of many works of scriptural exegesis, in which Augustine rejected the Manichean negative attitude on the Old Testament and achieved his literal interpretation of the words of Genesis consonant with Christian faith. He also began to write *On Free Will* (388–395), which he later completed in Africa.[46] After the defeat of Maximus' armies on August 28, 388, Augustine finally set sail for North Africa with his son, brother, and friends with the hope of pursuing a monastic life.[47]

Carthage and Thagaste: The Monastic Life as a Layperson (388–391)

Circa the autumn of 388, Augustine (now a mature middle-aged adult) arrived at Carthage, North Africa, after having lived in Italy for five years. During his stay in Carthage, Augustine met his former pupils and devout Christian leaders of Carthage (e.g., Aurelius, deacon and future bishop of Carthage). In particular, Augustine encountered Eulogius, his former student and now a teacher of rhetoric; Eulogius shared his unusual dream which was related to a vision for Augustine—Augustine's role in and his impact on the churches of North Africa in the future. When Eulogius was preparing a portion of Cicero to read with his pupils on the following day, he was baffled by a difficult passage. In the same night, during his sleep, Eulogius dreamed that Augustine, his former teacher, appeared to him and extraordinarily instructed him on how to understand the difficult part.[48]

Not long after his arrival at Carthage, Augustine went to his hometown, Thagaste, with his son Adeodatus, his friend Alypius, Evodius, and other friends. Augustine sold most of the family property to help the poor, but held his former house at Thagaste in order to found a lay Christian monastery (Possidius, *v. Aug.* 3; see *ep.* 126.7; *s.* 355.2). At that time, Augustine knew two forms of monastic life: "the solitary hermitage of the desert anchorites and the community life of the cenobites

---

46. Bonner, *St. Augustine*, 105, 135; Bourke, *Augustine's Quest*, 91–105; Clark, *Augustine*, 9–10; Sun, *Time and Eternity*, 242.

47. Bonner, *St. Augustine*, 105–6; Bourke, *Augustine's Quest*, 105.

48. Bonner, *St. Augustine*, 106; Bourke, *Augustine's Quest*, 106–7.

whom he had visited in Milan and Rome";[49] he chose the latter. Within this little monastic community, Augustine kept a form of shared life with other members and continued his studies and meditation (much as at Cassiciacum) with the circle of intelligent, resourceful, and devoted colleagues. He wrote some of his early works: *On the Teacher* (389) in which he insisted that human persons need to use signs in order to teach any reality to other persons, and that the reality to which the sign refers is known not through the sign itself but through consulting the "inner teacher," Christ; *On the True Religion* (389–390), Augustine's last work prior to his priestly ordination, which was dedicated to his friend and former patron, Romanianus. From a perspective of Christian Neoplatonism, it was apparently intended to wean Romanianus from the Manichaeism toward a contemplative mode of Christianity. Besides these works, Augustine finished *On Genesis against the Manichees* (388–389/390).[50]

Meanwhile, Augustine lost his son, Adeodatus, who was born in Carthage in 372 and was baptized with his father, Augustine, and Alypius by bishop Ambrose of Milan in 387. Adeodatus had participated in the philosophical conversations at Cassiciacum; he returned to Thagaste with Augustine and was superbly educated both in the Scriptures and in Virgil, and had some knowledge of Punic. Augustine's *On the Teacher* (389) was proposed as the record of a conversation between Adeodatus and Augustine. Because Adeodatus was so brilliant, Augustine was greatly satisfied; but the youthful Adeodatus died around 389 (*conf.* 9.6.14).[51]

Augustine also lost his close and valued friend, Nebridius, who was born near Carthage and had "enthusiasm for the truth and for wisdom" (6.10.17). Nebridius, as a Manichee, followed Augustine to Milan (6.10.17, 7.2.3.) but became a baptized Christian soon after Augustine. He returned to Africa with Augustine and sincerely served God and God's people. Nebridius died around 390 (9.3.6–9.4.7). Such deaths of Adeodatus and Nebridius led Augustine into the depths of sorrow and agony; Augustine was no longer content to "live sweetly

---

49. Bourke, *Augustine's Quest*, 108.

50. Bonner, *St. Augustine*, 106–9; Bourke, *Augustine's Quest*, 107–22; Brown, *Augustine*, 125–27; Clark, *Augustine*, 10; Markus, "Life," 499; Sun, *Time and Eternity*, 242–43.

51. Fitzgerald, "Adeodatus," 7; Lancel, *Saint Augustine*, 140–43.

with the mind" (*ep*.10.1).⁵² During the past several years, Augustine had experienced tremendous and tragic losses, including those of his loving family members (e.g., separation with his unmarried wife, the deaths of Monica and Adeodatus) and his faithful friends (e.g., the deaths of Nebridius and Verecundus). That meant that he needed both to reestablish his monastic community in a new locality (with an established rule) and to find new members for his religious group. Thus, Augustine went to Hippo Regius (near modern Bone in Algeria) in early 391.⁵³

Hippo Regius: The Monastic Life and Church Ministry as a Monk and Priest/Bishop (391–430)

At the age of thirty-seven, Augustine arrived at Hippo Regius, a coastal town some fifty miles from Thagaste, in order to extend his project of the Christian monastery. A long time later, Augustine recalled the goal of his visit during his preaching: "I, whom by God's grace you see before you as your bishop, came to this city as a young man; many of you know that. I was looking for a place to establish a monastery, and live there with my brothers" (*s*. 355.2). By chance he participated in the worship service of the cathedral of Hippo. Surprisingly, Augustine was appointed as a priest under pressure of Bishop Valerius and his congregation, although he vehemently resisted against this appointment: "I was caught, I was made a priest" (*s*. 355.2). That means that Augustine forcibly became an assistant for the aged and Greek-speaking bishop, Valerius; this bishop had long desired to have a priest who could preach to the people in fluent Latin. Now Valerius had secured Augustine and encouraged him to do so.⁵⁴ Later Possidius, Augustine's biographer, described this scene in which Augustine was seized for the office of presbyter:

> Now at this time the holy Valerius was bishop in the Catholic church at Hippo. But owing to the increasing demands of ecclesiastical duty, he addressed the people of God and exhorted them to provide and ordain a presbyter for the city. . . . So they laid hands on [Augustine] and, as is the custom in such cases,

---

52. Quoted in Brown, *Augustine*, 128.

53. Brown, *Augustine*, 129–30; Walker, *History*, 162.

54. Bonner, *St. Augustine*, 114; Brown, *Augustine*, 131–32; Lancel, *Saint Augustine*, 150–52; O'Donnell, *Augustine*, 24–25; Walker, *History*, 162.

> brought him to the bishop to be ordained, for all with common consent desired that this should be done and accomplished; and they demanded it with great zeal and clamor, while he [Augustine] wept freely. (Possidius, *v. Aug.* 4)

Augustine realized that he had no way to avoid the command of God's church. Accordingly, he received his ordination as priest of the church of Hippo. Augustine requested of Valerius 1) that he needed to leave the church of Hippo for six months in order to acquire more meditation and study of the Scriptures to enable his task of ministering to God's people (*ep.* 21.1–6), and 2) that he needed to reconstruct a monastic community at a new place, Hippo. Augustine's requests were permitted by Bishop Valerius; Valerius provided a garden (close to the cathedral) to Augustine and his friends for building a monastery (*s.* 355.2). Augustine gradually became a priest of profound convictions, who put his experience and idea at the service of the church of Hippo. Bishop Valerius strongly supported Augustine to be an able priest. He gave opportunities to Augustine (the 'priest') for preaching to the congregation in the cathedral of Hippo, although these practices were unusual in the tradition of the African church: "It was not the custom in Africa for bishops to allow presbyters to preach before them."[55] Not a long time after, Augustine became a famous preacher and an influential church leader in Africa, at which point he was invited to deliver a sermon in the presence of the assembled bishops in the African Council at Hippo in 393. Based on this sermon, he published *On the Faith and the Creed*.[56]

During the time of his priesthood, Augustine had primarily struggled against the Manichean heresy. He was involved in public disputation with the Manichee, Fortunatus in 392 at the baths of Sossius, which resulted in the ruin of Fortunatus' reputation and his departure from the city to hide his humiliation. As such, Augustine produced *Debate with Fortunatus the Manichee* (392). At that time, Augustine completed one of his anti-Manichean works, *On Free Will*. In this essay, Augustine repudiated the Manichean doctrine that evil (*malum*)

---

55. Bonner, *St. Augustine*, 114. Possidius states, "He [Bishop Valerius] gave his presbyter [Augustine] the right of preaching the Gospel in his presence in the church and very frequently of holding public discussions—contrary to the practice and custom of the African churches" (*v. Aug.* 5).

56. Bonner, *St. Augustine*, 115; Bourke, *Augustine's Quest*, 126; Brown, *Augustine*, 133–35; Clark, *Augustine*, 11; Sun, *Time and Eternity*, 246.

has a real existence, independent of good; then he argued that evil had no origin other than the freely exercised choice of the will. He wrote another anti-Manichean work, *On the Usefulness of Belief* (391–392) which was addressed to his friend, Honoratus, whom Augustine had himself persuaded to become a Manichee, and whom he now wished to lead back from Manichean error to Christian truth. Besides these works, Augustine produced *On Two Souls, Against the Manicheans* (391–392/3). In this book, he rejected the Manichaean belief that there were two warring souls in every human being—one emanating from the principle of good (or light) and the other from evil (or matter), and that wrongdoing was not the responsibility of the individual, but the action of the evil soul. Augustine also began to work *The Literal Meaning of Genesis* (393–426), which was not completed.

In 395, Augustine became a coadjutor bishop of Hippo Regius with the strong demand and support of Bishop Valerius, although his nomination of the coadjutor bishop was not quite in conformity with ecclesiastical norms of the Council of Nicaea in 325 (Possidius, *v. Aug.* 8).[57] After the death of Valerius, Augustine, who was forty-two years old, succeeded Valerius as bishop of Hippo in 396 (*ep.* 31.1–9; *v. Aug.* 8). However, Bishop Megalius of Calama, along with some others, was more aware of Augustine the Manichee than of Augustine the (Catholic) Christian, although Bishop Aurelius of Carthage, the episcopal primate, was affirmative. In fact, some were not convinced of the sincerity of Augustine's conversion.[58] For this reason, Augustine, as a bishop, wrote *Confessions* (397–401) to demonstrate the truth of his conversion to God and the church community as well as to guide God's people into the proper Christian living before God (*retr.* 2.6.1). He noted, "This I desire to do, in my heart before you [God] in confession, but before many witnesses with my pen" (*conf.* 10.1.1). About this time, Augustine also wrote *Miscellany of Eighty-Three Questions* (388–396), which was a collection of answers to questions that had been submitted to him by his congregation concerning Christian living and church ministry.

---

57. Bonner, *St. Augustine*, 119–20; Bourke, *Augustine's Quest*, 136–37; Clark, *Augustine*, 11; Lancel, *Saint Augustine*, 182–85. The eight canon of the Council of Nicaea in 325 forbade that two bishops were simultaneously appointed in one diocese. Later Bishop Augustine regretted his ordination as auxiliary bishop of Hippo against the edict of the Council of Nicaea; so he supported this edict in his ministry of the church.

58. Clark, *Augustine*, 11.

Illustrating the Case of St. Augustine

In the earlier part of his episcopate, up to about 405 A.D., Bishop Augustine had continuously engaged in public disputation with the Manichean scholars and had written some polemical works. More specifically, Augustine wrote *On Continence* (395–396) in which he refuted the Manichean notion of the human person as composed of two antagonistic substances—the flesh and the spirit; he argued that both the flesh (the body) and the spirit (the soul) are created by a good God and are therefore good in themselves, and that the human person is the "whole" unity of the body and soul. He also published *Against the Epistle of Manichaeus Called Fundamental* (396–397) in which he began by recalling his nine years with Mani's followers and then explained why he turned to Christianity. Augustine produced *On the Nature of the Good* (396–398/399) in which he described God as supreme good and all other beings as hierarchically arranged according to their own innate goodness; this God is the author of all those goods. At that time, Augustine had a public controversy with the Manichean bishop, Faustus, who only accepted parts of Christian Scriptures (e.g., the New Testament), and who viewed the deity of the Old Testament as a wicked and corporeal substance. As such, Augustine wrote *Reply to Faustus the Manichean* (397/398–400) in which he primarily defended the unity of the two Testaments, the Old Testament fulfilled in the New Testament. In 404, Augustine held another public debate with Felix, the Manichaean leader (an "Elect") who eventually agreed to become a Christian at the close of the debate. As such he produced *Against Felix, a Manichee*.

Indeed, Augustine had further developed his understanding of the nature of God and nature of good and evil during his debates with the Manichees and his polemical writings. Influenced by Christian Neoplatonism, Augustine discovered the most fundamental problem of the Manichean account of God, namely, God's materiality must imply God's divisibility. Augustine described his mystical experience of union with God on the basis of Neoplatonic three-stage pattern: the first stage is an initial withdrawal from the sense world; the second is an interior movement into the depths of the soul; the third is a movement above the soul to a vision of God (*conf.* 7.10.16).[59] Importantly, this experience of his soul's journey to God enabled Augustine to establish a new account of

---

59. Ibid., 108–19; Harrison, *Augustine's Early Theology*, 27–31; MacDonald, "Divine Nature," 85–96; McGinn and McGinn, *Christian Mystics*, 154–55; O'Meara, *Young Augustine*, 125–53.

God—the Spirit—as indivisible, immaterial, infinite, invisibly present, and the source of all existence in contrast to the Manichaean materialistic dualism. It also enabled Augustine to realize that the Divine could be found in his inner self (*conf.* 7.1.1–2, 7.5.7, 7.10.16, 7.20.26; *c. ep. Man.* 15.20).[60] As such, Augustine firmly rejected Manichaean teaching that there were two creators: an evil god who was the source of material reality and a good god who created the spiritual world. For Augustine, God was the sole author and creator of all that exists and all that exists must be, in so far as it is of divine creation, good (*conf.* 13.20.28, 13.28.43).

While repudiating the Manichaean doctrine that evil has a real existence, Augustine demonstrated that evil has no "substance," but is merely a privation of Good (*privatio boni*) (*conf.* 7.5.7; *civ. Dei* 14.11; *c. Jul. imp.* 3.206; *retr.* 1.8.1).[61] Evil results from the distortion of the power given by the creator; it is a subversion or corruption of the good created order. For Augustine, the Manichaean negative view of matter and the body is wholly mistaken. Augustine insisted that both matter and the body are God's creations and therefore good (see *conf.* 13.28.43); they only become evil when the human soul chooses (by his or her free will) what God has forbidden. In doing so, Augustine refuted the Manichaean view that the human person has two opposed souls—one good and the other evil, and that the person is not responsible for his or her evil deeds (see *duab. an.* 1.1). Further, he argued that the Manichaean habit of only accepting those parts of Scripture (e.g., the New Testament), which suited them, was wrong and unsatisfactory.[62]

Along with his understanding of the nature of the divine as well as the nature of good and evil, Augustine had formulated his concept of the human person. For Augustine, a human being is seen to be not primarily a "natural" creature but a being created in the image of God (*div. qu.* 51.1–4; *Trin.* 14.16.22, 14.19.25). The human being is originally made good and upright, possessed of free will, endowed with the possibility of not sinning and of immortality (*corrept.* 33; *Simpl.* 1.2.18). Augustine insisted that a human being is "a rational soul having a body" (*Jo. ev. tr.* 19.5.15). In this vein, he described human nature as a substantial unity of soul and body, the inner and outer aspects of the person,

---

60. Ayres and Barnes, "God," 384–86; Markus, "Life," 503.

61. Bonner, *St. Augustine*, 115, 135; Gilson, *Christian Philosophy*, 144; Gonzáez, *Christian Thought*, 41–42; Harrison, *Augustine's Early Theology*, 32, 49.

62. Bonner, *St. Augustine*, 116, 136, 193–236.

respectively: "If, again, we were so to define man as to say, Man is a rational substance consisting of mind and body, then without doubt man has a soul that is not body, and a body that is not soul" (*Trin.* 15.7.11; see *b. vita* 2.7; *ep.* 116.2.4; *Trin.* 11.5.8, 15.11.20).[63] There was no discord in human nature. The human being was happy and in communion with God (*civ. Dei* 14.26).

Augustine asserted that the soul is a creature of God. The unitary human soul is not divine but created "out of nothing" (*ex nihilo*) (*conf.* 12.7.7; *civ. Dei* 14.11; *Gn. litt.* 7.1.1–7.4.6, 10.2.3). The human soul is neither an emanation from God, nor is the soul co-eternal with God. Against the Manichees, he argued that the human soul only has its total existence from God who is the source of all life (*duab. an.* 1.1). For Augustine, the human soul is "a certain kind of substance, sharing in reason, fitted to rule the body" (*quant.* 13.22). The soul is not like bodily being; it does not have length, breadth, or depth. Nor is there more in larger parts and less in smaller parts, but rather the soul is whole wherever it is. In other words, the soul is immaterial/incorporeal and "above" the material reality of the body. This soul serves as a pointer to the nature of God. Yet, it is still mutable and serves only to reveal the incomparable and infinitely surpassing reality and "light" of the divine (*conf.* 12.17.24; *ep.* 166.2.4).[64]

Augustine emphasized the mediating position of the soul between God and the body as found in his conception of the vertical order of being. He elaborated that the incorruptible, inviolable, and immutable was better than the corruptible, violable, and mutable, and that God cannot be changed in any way (*conf.* 7.1.1). For Augustine, everything other than God is subject to change, with bodies changing in place and time and souls changing only in time. Therefore, the absolutely immutable God stands at the top and bodies that change in time and place are at the bottom, but souls which change only in time occupy the middle position so that they can either turn to God for their happiness or to bodies in sin (*ep.* 18.2; *Trin.* 11.5.8).[65] In this sense, Augustine stated, "The soul . . . is more excellent than the body, but God, the author and

---

63. Teske, "Augustine's Theory," 116; "Soul," 807–12. According to Augustine, the nature of the human being is "good"; this human nature "may spring either a good or an evil will" (*ench.*15).

64. Teske, "Augustine's Theory," 117–22.

65. Ibid., 116–17.

creator of each, is more excellent than both soul and body" (*Simpl.* 1.2.18). In Augustine's view of existence and reality, there is nothing closer to God than the human rational soul, which is the image of God (*civ. Dei* 11.26).[66]

Augustine contended that the human soul was originally made in the image of the triune God: "We resemble the divine Trinity in that we exist; we know that we exist, and we are glad of this existence and this knowledge" (*civ. Dei* 11.26). Following this image of the triune God in human nature, Augustine presented a relationship between God and the soul. For Augustine, God is the creative ground of the world in terms of love. As such, this God is Being itself ("Truth itself") who is identical with the source of all existence and reality. The human soul exists only by participation in Being itself; the soul enters into the divine—loving ground of Being: "If I do not abide in [God], I can do nothing" (*conf.* 7.11.17; see 10.1.1; *ord.* 2.19.51; *Gn. litt.* 12.26.53–12.28.56; *ep.* 92.3).

For Augustine, the human search for God—the ascent of the soul to God—is essential for true happiness. True happiness is found in the enjoyment of the presence of God who is the Truth itself. A happy life rejoices in God and for God (*conf.* 10. 1.1, 10.22.32; 10.23.33). According to Augustine, "to possess God" (*capax Dei*) means "not to be without God" (*b. vita.* 3.21).[67] The great dignity of the human soul is that it is able to possess God—the highest nature—by worshiping God who has made the soul in God's image (*Trin.* 14.4.6, 14.8.11, 14.12.15; *civ. Dei* 10.1–3).

Consistent with his conceiving of the relationship between God and the soul, Augustine had also developed his idea of creation, time, and eternity during his controversies with Manichees and his polemical writings against Manichaeism. While acknowledging that God's creations are inherently good, Augustine believed that "in the beginning God made heaven and earth" (*conf.* 12.13.16; see Gen 1:1). He clearly proclaimed God as "Creator of all things"—*Deus Creator omnium* (*conf.* 11.27.35; see 11.12.14).[68] Augustine formulated the doctrine of creation "out of nothing" (*ex nihilo*), when he explored the relation of God to the world. Nothing precedes creation not even matter or what the Greeks

---

66. Clark, *Augustine*, 30–33; Gilson, *Christian Philosophy*, 217–19.

67. Babcock, "Cupiditas and Caritas," 17–26.

68. Clark, *Augustine*, 34–35; Gonzáez, *Christian Thought*, 38–39; Harrison, *Augustine's Early Theology*, 74–77, 94.

Illustrating the Case of St. Augustine

called *hyle*; this creation is made without aid of an independent substance (*Gn. litt.* 1.1.1–1.15.29; *civ. Dei* 12.1).[69]

Augustine regarded time as a creature of God: "There was . . . no time when you had not made something, because you made time itself" (*conf.* 11.14.17; see 11.13.16, 11.30.40; *Gn. litt.* 5.5.12).[70] The question how time was before creation is meaningless, because time is created with the world. Time is not coeternal with God since God is permanent (*conf.* 11.14.17, 11.10.12). For Augustine, time has a beginning and an end (11.11.13, 12.33.48); that is, it is the form of the finitude of things, as space is also. Time is mutable and temporal (11.14.17); it is not an objective reality in the sense in which a thing is.[71]

For Augustine, there is only one world process. Augustine rejected the Greek concept, held by Aristotle and the Stoics, which asserts that the world is cyclical—there are cycles of birth and rebirth that repeat themselves infinitely (11.11.13, 11.13.16, 11.14.17). For Augustine, the Greek view of cyclicism threatens the unique particularity of Christ's absolutely efficacious death and resurrection, because it lumps the repetition of particulars with the recurrence of types: "For 'Christ died once for all for our sins'; and in rising from the dead he is never to die again: he is no longer under the sway of death. And after the resurrection 'we shall be with the Lord for ever'" (*civ. Dei* 12.14).

Augustine repudiated the definition that identifies time with the bodily or celestial motions more generally: such motions take place in time, but are not time itself (*conf.* 11.23.30, 11.24.31, 11.26.33). Time is not dependent on physical movement (e.g., the story of Joshua [Josh 10:12–13] about the movement of heavenly/celestial bodies—"the sun stopped but time went on" [*conf.* 11.23.30]). Augustine also discarded the notion that we normally measure time by time itself—a longer time by comparison with shorter ones (11.15.18, 11.26.33). Moreover, he disagreed with the customary way of speaking of time that there are "three times," past, present, and future (11.17.22, 11.14.17).

Augustine portrayed time as distension in the mind (*distentio animi*). Augustine's account of time is affected by the Neoplatonist Plotinus. The term "distension" (*distentio*) literally means a spreading out. In that sense, Plotinus viewed time as a spreading out (*diastasis*) of life,

---

69. Knuuttila, "Time and Creation," 103.
70. Clark, *Augustine*, 35; Gilson, *Christian Philosophy*, 145, 189.
71. Knuuttila, "Time and Creation," 103–4; Tillich, *Christian Thought*, 117.

which is implied that the life of the soul in a movement of passage from one way of life to another (Plotinus, *enn.* 3.7.11–13). Augustine's famous remark of time as an extension in the mind (e.g., *conf.* 11.20.26) has its parallel in Plotinus' account of it as the life of the soul.[72] Augustine held that time itself is neither a corollary nor an antecedent measure of external regularities, but an internal regulation which the mind itself imposes on phenomena (*conf.* 11.28.37–38). While he paid attention to the present state of time (11.15.20–11.21.27), Augustine emphasized that time is nothing more than an extension of mind/the soul (11.26.33, 11.21.27); past, present, and future are simply three states of mind—these three mental states could all exist at once as *distentio* in the mind (11.20.26, 11.26.33, 11.27.36, 11.28.37–38).[73] Augustine wrote,

> That is why I have come to think that time is a simply a distention. But of what is it a distention? I do not know, but it would be surprising if it is not that of the mind itself (*conf.* 11.26.33). . . . What is by now evident and clear is that neither future nor past exists, and it is inexact language to speak of three times—past, present, and future. Perhaps it would be exact to say: there are three times, a present of things past, a present of things present, a present of things to come. In the soul there are these three aspects of time, and I do not see them anywhere else. The present considering the past is the memory, the present considering the present is immediate awareness, the present considering the future is expectation (11.20.26)

Augustine had further developed his concept of time in his meditation and studies of the Bible, especially Paul's letters. Augustine's remark of time in *conf.* 11.29.39 is affected by St. Paul's language of "being stretched" (Phil 3:12–14), which is linked with the thought of Plotinus that "multiplicity is a falling away from The Unity [the One]" and is extended in a scattering—"there is nothing to bind part to part" (*enn.* 6.6.1; see 6.7.1–42).[74] For Augustine, the experience of the spreading out of the soul in successiveness and in diverse directions is a painful

---

72. Chadwick, "Introduction and Notes," 240; González, *Christian Thought*, 40–41; Knuuttila, "Time and Creation," 109–13; O'Connell, *St. Augustine's Confessions*, 139–42; Sorabji, "Time," 218, 232.

73. Gilson, *Christian Philosophy*, 194–95; O'Connell, *St. Augustine's Confessions*, 140–41; Sorabji, "Time," 212–15; Sun, *Time and Eternity*, 73–88; Vaught, *Access*, 135–36.

74. Chadwick, "Introduction and Notes," 240.

and anxious experience. This implies that the soul's existence in time, its immersion in "action," is evidence of its "fallen" state. For this reason, Augustine spoke of the salvation of the soul as deliverance from the time of the fallen state to God's eternity.[75]

For Augustine, the term *eternal* signifies what is without beginning or end; it is properly predicated of God. Augustine insisted that eternity is before and after a definite beginning and a definite end (*en. Ps.* 134.6), whereas time has this beginning and end. Eternity involves timelessness and changelessness; it is something beyond all the categories (*conf.* 11.13.36). For Augustine, the eternal is always immutable and unchangeable (11.14.17; *en. Ps.* 134.6); the eternal is only present (*conf.* 11.11.13).[76]

Augustine emphasized that eternity is simultaneously *copresent* with the whole of time, measuring every interval, departed, eventuating, and projected. All temporal intervals take their origin from an eternity; this non-successive eternity sets and sustains them on their successive course of time (11.11.13). The intuition of eternity does not retro-see the past or foresee the future, but strictly sees the whole expanse of time (*civ. Dei* 11.21). For Augustine, God's eternity involves a wholly all-at-once duration, without temporal parts or variation (*conf.* 11.13.16; *en. Ps.* 101.2.8). This God's ever-standing eternity is complete in itself, needing no temporal augmentation (*s.* 225.2).[77] Augustine noted, "Your 'years' are 'one day' (Ps 89:4; 2 Pet 3:8), and your 'day' is not any and every day but Today, because your Today does not yield to a tomorrow, nor did it follow on a yesterday. Your Today is eternity" (*conf.* 11.13.16).

Significantly, Augustine paid attention to the linkage between eternity and time. He focused on Christ the mediator, who has bridged a gap between the eternal and the temporal, and who has liberated human beings from the time of the fallen state (*conf.* 11.29.39). The sacrifice of Jesus Christ on Calvary put death to death (*en. Ps.* 148.8; *s.* 125.6); in this Jesus Christ, the human beings are lifted up to the changeless years of eternity (*en. Ps.* 101.1.12–14, 101.2.14).

---

75. Ibid. See O'Connell, *St. Augustine's Confessions*, 142.

76. Knuuttila, "Time and Creation," 106; MacDonald, "Divine Nature," 96–101; Tillich, *Christian Thought*, 118–19.

77. Quinn, "Eternity," 318.

Through Jesus Christ, malign temporality is conquered, empowering the new person to overcome the manyness of time—the soul's being "stretched out" in time to its endless and restless desire—through union with the eternal One (*conf.* 11.29.39). In other words, through his death, this mediator has enabled the human soul to enter into the way of salvation from the distraction, dissipation, dispersion of time to a contemplative eternity (*en. Ps.* 148.8). As Augustine and Monica rose to a mystical encounter with God in the beatific vision at Ostia (9.10.23–26), a participant of God's eternity becomes union with Wisdom and is enrapt in divine joy.[78] Consequently, Augustine confessed, "'Because your mercy is more than lives' (Ps 62:4), see how my life is a distension in several directions. . . . You are my eternal Father, but I am scattered in times whose order I do not understand. The storms of incoherent events tear to pieces my thoughts, the inmost entails of my soul, until that day, when, purified and molten by the fire of your love, I flow together to merge into you" (11.29.39).

Although Augustine was primarily involved in his disputation with the Manichees at the period of his priesthood and his early episcopate, he had also engaged in his vehement controversy with the Donatists. Augustine was confronted with Donatism not long after his ordination to the priesthood in the cathedral church of Hippo Regius in 391. At that time, Donatism was widespread in northern Africa; Hippo was within an area in which Donatists were in the majority and Catholics in a position of weakness. Two major issues between Augustine and the Donatists were ecclesiology and the nature of baptism.[79] These two issues were deeply rooted in the conditions of Diocletian persecution (303–304 A.D.) against Christians in the Roman Empire: "It was a time of fearful persecution. As in the days of Decius there were many martyrs, and many who 'lapsed.' . . . The severity of the persecution varied with the attitude of the magistrates by whom its penalties were enforced. Cruel in Italy, North Africa, and the Orient, the friendly

---

78. Ibid., 320. For Augustine, clock time is physical time, which tends to repeat itself. However, the meaning of time is the *kairos*, which involves the historical moment; it is the qualitative characteristic of time; divine revelation unveils the meaning of sacred history in terms of the link of time with eternity (Tillich, *Christian Thought*, 118; see Quinn, "Time," 837).

79. Markus, "Life," 503.

'Caesar,' Constantius Chlorus, made apparent compliance in Gaul and Britain by destroying church edifices."[80]

This Diocletian persecution had led to a schism in Christianity; so the unity of the church was threatened. In particular, the African churches were divided. There were more and less rigorous factions, fanatics and prudent compromisers, in many churches. Clergy who handed over copies of the Scriptures to the authorities were generally regarded as apostates. However, there was a wide range of attitudes toward "collaborators," or those who had failed to make a sufficiently determined stand in resistance. A disputed election of a bishop at Carthage formally culminated the schism between the two factions. The Donatist party charged that the ordination of Caecilian, the new bishop of Carthage in 311, was invalid because he had surrendered copies of the Scriptures in the recent persecution. As such this party chose a counter-bishop, Majorinus in 316. Majorinus was able to be a successor of the bishop Donatus, from whom the schismatics received the name Donatists. The Donatist churches grew rapidly, claiming to be the only true church possessed of a clergy free from deadly sins—apostasy—and of the only valid sacraments. For Donatists, if the priest was guilty of sin which was related to handing over the Scriptures to be burnt, he could not administer a sacrament, for his sin had destroyed his sacerdotal character—he had lost the Holy Spirit and, hence, the ability to baptize. Consequently, those whom he baptized had to be rebaptized; Donatists routinely rebaptized converts from Catholic churches.[81]

In the context of the serious division between Catholic and Donatist parties, as a priest and a bishop, Augustine was involved in the conciliatory action to deal with the African church's troubles. In doings so, Augustine wrote *Psalm against the Donatists* (393–394) in which he accounted for the origin and progress of the schism within the African church, disagreed with the Donatist practice of rebaptizing Catholics who came over to their party, and charged the Donatist party because they were the ones who lacked charity and broke church unity. Augustine also produced *On Baptism, against the Donatists* (400–401). In this work, he dealt with two major issues: ecclesiology and the nature of baptism. Whereas the Donatist party described the church as a

---

80. Walker, *History*, 100.

81. Bonner, *St. Augustine*, 137; Chadwick, *Augustine*, 75–77; Clark, *Augustine*, 80–81; O'Donnell, *Augustine*, 13–15; Walker, *History*, 106.

community of the sanctified or the pure, Augustine depicted the church as a mixed community of saints and sinners—the mixture of good and evil—and advocated an invisible church as an area of God's action in the world (the city of God) which was not always conterminous with the institutional church. As such, he refuted the Donatist argument that a cleric (who separated himself from the church through apostasy) lost the Holy Spirit and, hence, the ability to baptize; consequently, those (who were baptized by this cleric) had to be rebaptized. While emphasizing baptism as the sacrament of the remission of sins, Augustine argued that the sins of the minister could not be an impediment to the grace of God because this grace did not belong to him or even to the church but to God—(Christian baptism through the grace of God was valid and effective; that is, it was unnecessary for rebaptizing, although it was performed by the sinful minister).

Augustine published *The Unity of the Church* (401–405) in which he charged the sectarianism and exclusivism of the Donatists, who did not maintain communion with overseas churches; he characterized the Christian church as the body of Christ united in love to its head and emphasized the universal church based on ecclesial unity. In addition, Augustine continuously wrote anti-Donatist works, including *To the Letters of Petilian, the Donatist* (401–405) in which he repudiated the Donatist belief that only their baptism was valid, that is, Catholic baptism was invalid because Catholics were heretics; *To Cresconius, a Donatist Grammarian* (405–406) in which he carefully argued against Donatist rebaptism and defended Catholic baptism; he insisted that the minister, pious or sinful, was only an instrument by which Christ forgave sins; *Against the Donatists* (411–412) in which he argued that the Donatist bishops had misinterpreted the Scriptures by ignoring verses about the universal spread of the church; then he invited them to return to the true Christian church in unity and peace.

In 411, Augustine took a leading part in the conference at Carthage in the hope of healing the division between Catholics and Donatists (*ep.* 22.1.2). In 418, Augustine had a public disputation with Emeritus, the Donatist bishop of Caesarea (the modern Cherchel, in Algeria), which he had visited on behalf of the bishop of Rome. As such, he produced *Proceedings with Emeritus* (418) in which he challenged Emeritus' obduracy in remaining in the Donatist party and appealed to Emeritus to imitate Christ most humble.

Indeed, Augustine had developed his concept of the sacrament of Christian baptism during the anti-Donatist controversy. Augustine continuously argued that sacraments are the work of God, not of human persons. That means that the true administrator of the sacraments is not the priest but Christ. The priest is only an agent or instrument through whom Christ chooses to work; thus the validity of the sacraments cannot be destroyed by the character of the priest. Augustine insisted that the purity of the minister was irrelevant; it was the purity and power of Christ that made baptism effective. Like water passing through a stone irrigation channel, the power of Christ passes through a sinful minister unpolluted and bears fruit in the recipient (*bapt.* 3.10.15; *Jo. ev. tr.* 5.15). Therefore, baptism does not need to be repeated for (re)entering the Christian Church (*bapt.* 1.4.5; *Jo. ev. tr.* 6.15).[82]

In Augustine's view, Christian baptism is interrelated to the communion of the church. Augustine emphasized the centrality of the presence of the Spirit of holiness in the community of the baptized. The Holy Spirit enters with his gift of *caritas* into the baptized soul, thus making the soul a dwelling of the Trinity (Rom 5:5). For Augustine, baptism is an indelible seal by which a person is marked as belonging to the flock of Christ: "You . . . are sheep belonging to Christ, [and] you bear the Lord's mark in the sacrament which you have received" (*ep.* 173.3). Augustine considered baptism both the sacrament of the remission of sins and the rebirth for the newness of life: "We thank God, who gave his Church such a gift. Here you are; you are going to come to the holy font, you will be washed in saving baptism, you will be renewed in *the bath of rebirth* (Titus 3:5), you will be without any sin at all as you come up from that bath" (*s.* 213.9; see *f. et op.* 20.36).

In the time of Augustine, while candidates would receive baptism, it was normally administered at Easter because "the greater joy of the feast attracts them" (*s.* 210.2). Easter not only celebrated the passing over of Christ from death to life (*s.* 103.6); it also implied that "this passing from death to life is . . . wrought in us by faith, which we have for the pardon of our sins and the hope of eternal life, when we love God and our neighbour. . . . According to this faith and hope and love, by which we have begun to be 'under grace,' we are already dead together

---

82. Bonner, *St. Augustine*, 138, 237–75; Bourke, *Augustine's Quest*, 138–74; Lancel, *Saint Augustine*, 271–86; Markus, "Life," 504; Tillich, *Christian Thought*, 131; Walker, *History*, 106.

with Christ, and buried together with Him by baptism into death; as the apostle hath said, 'Our old man is crucified with Him'" (*ep.* 55.2.3).

During the rite of baptism, the water of the font was sanctified by the name of Christ and the sign of the cross (*Jo. ev. tr.* 118.5; *s.* 229A.1). Candidates stripped off their clothes and entered the font one by one; that is, they had to step down into the font because "the Lord's Passion demands the humble person" (*s.* 125.6). There they would stand waist-deep in the water. They were "consecrated in the words of the gospel" in the name of the Father, and of the Son, and of the Holy Spirit (*bapt.* 3.14.19, 6.25.46; *ep.* 23.4). After these rites, the newly baptized donned new robes made of white linen (*s.* 260C.7; see 120, 223). Then they offered each other the kiss of peace—"Peace be with you" (*s.* 227, 229.3). Finally, the newly baptized were invited to Communion—the sacrament of the Lord's Table (*s.* 272; see 227, 229.1–3, 229A.1–3). For Augustine, the baptized person who partakes of communion really receives the body and the blood of Christ, not in the sense of physically eating them, but rather in the sense that, by eating the elements of bread and wine, one becomes a partaker of the body and blood of Christ (*s.* 227, 229.2, 229A.1–3, 272).[83]

For Augustine, sacraments include all the holy usages and rites of the church. They are the visible signs of the sacred things that they signify. Baptism and the Lord's Supper are pre-eminently sacraments. By the sacraments the church is knit together.[84] Furthermore, the sacraments are necessary for salvation: "The churches of Christ maintain it to be an inherent principle, that without baptism and partaking of the Supper of the Lord it is impossible for any man to attain either to the kingdom of God or to salvation and everlasting life" (*pecc. mer.* 1.34).

Along with his formulation of view on Christian communion through the practice of the sacrament of baptism, Augustine had also developed his concept of ecclesiology during the anti-Donatist controversy. He strongly emphasized the unity and universality of the church, animated by the Holy Spirit, against all separatist movements, especially the sectarianism of the Donatist party. For Augustine, the activity of the

---

83. Clark, *Augustine*, 71, 73–79, 100; Gonzáez, *Christian Thought*, 51–53; Harmless, "Baptism," 85–87; Lohse, *Christian Doctrine*, 136–41.

84. Walker, *History*, 166.

Holy Spirit unites the church (*ex. Gal.* 13).⁸⁵ The church as a whole, the church in heaven and on earth, is the temple of God (*ench.* 56).

This expression of the church as the temple of God indicates a relationship between God and the community of the faithful, thus referring to the presence of God in human beings. There is no perfect identity between the church on earth and the community of saints, but the saints reign already now with Christ. In this sense, the church is already the reign of Christ, the heavenly kingdom or the body of Christ (*civ. Dei* 20.9).

For Augustine, all the members have to be united with the universal body of the church: "You are the body of Christ and members" (1 Cor 12:27). These members cannot live outside this body of the church, because whoever is an enemy of unity is an enemy of love. Love is a gift of the Holy Spirit, and the Spirit is present only in this love. As such the members of the church possess Christ (*Christum habere*) only by love; this does not imply that prayers, baptism, Eucharist, forgiveness of sins, fasting, and special charisms are without value, but they are not decisive for possessing Christ (*s.* 90.5–6; *ep. Jo.* 3.3–5).⁸⁶

In this sense, Augustine affirmed that love is the principle that unites the church. The spirit of love is embodied in the church as the unity of peace—the re-establishment of the original divine unity that is disrupted in the sinful state of existence; it is something that can be found only in the church. For this reason, Augustine adopted the view of Cyprian that "salvation . . . is not without the Church," namely, there is no "salvation outside the Church" (*nulla salus extra ecclesiam*) (*bapt.* 4.17.25; see 3.16.21). Salvation is impossible without the inpouring of *agape*, that grace given like a fluid into the hearts of human persons.⁸⁷

Augustine's doctrine of the church is deeply rooted in a notion that the body of Christ is constituted by communion. The unity of the church depends on one's understanding of the nature of membership in the church. Augustine insisted that sacraments are essential for communion of the church. The church is primarily the active gathering of new humankind into communion with Christ, who is "Head of the Church." God did not wish the only Son to remain alone; God adopted us as children in order to be brothers and sisters for the Son (*en. Ps.*

---

85. Van Bavel, "Church," 169, 171.
86. Ibid., 171–74.
87. Tillich, *Christian Thought*, 132.

49.2; *ep. Jo.* 8.14). Christ, as the head of the church, acts in the sacraments of the church; all sacraments are his property (*Cresc.* 2.21.26).[88] From the moment that human persons follow Jesus in faith, hope, and love, communion with Christ comes into existence.

Consistent with his debates with the Manichees and the Donatists, Augustine had engaged in another difficult controversy with the Arians. There was a long disputation about the issue of the divine Trinity within Christian churches. More specifically, in the East, Origen's theological influence was dominant. Origen had presented opposing senses of God's trinitarian nature in the Eastern churches. That means that he had taught the eternal generation of the Son; but at the same time he identified the Son as a second God and a creature. About 320, these Origen's teachings caused an actual controversy between Arius and his bishop Alexander in Alexandria. Arius, a follower of Origen, contended that Christ was a created being. For Arius, the Son was not of the substance of God, but was made like other creatures of "nothing." Thus, the Son was not eternal, although He was both the first-born of creatures and the agent in fashioning the world. Arius contended that Christ was God in a certain sense, but a lower God, in no way one with the Father in essence or eternity. In the Incarnation, this Logos entered a human body, taking the place of the human reasoning spirit. From Arius' view, Christ was neither fully God nor fully man, but a third reality (*tertium quid*) between. On the other hand, Bishop Alexander was influenced by the other side of Origen's teaching. For Alexander, the Son was eternal, like in essence to the Father, and wholly uncreated. Meanwhile, in order to promote the unity of the church, the Council of Nicaea was held in May, 325; it rejected the presentation of the Arians. This Council of Nicaea emphasized the unity of substance between Christ and the Father; it confirmed that the Son was eternal, "begotten, not made," and "of one essence (*homoousion*) with the Father."[89]

In the context of the conflict of Nicene Christians and Arians, Bishop Augustine (who had followed Athanasius, Basil of Caesarea, Gregory of Nyssa, Gregory Nazianzen, Hilary of Poitiers, and Ambrose of Milan) supported the Creed of the Council of Nicaea and repudiated the Arian account of the Trinity that limits simplicity or Godhead to one of the three persons. As such, he wrote *On Faith and the Creed*

88. Van Bavel, "Church," 170.
89. Walker, *History*, 76, 107–11.

(393) in which he was concerned with issues of trinitarian doctrine and refuted the Arian idea of the inferiority of Christ to the Father; as such, he employed certain images of the trinitarian plurality (spring and river, root, trunk and branches of a tree) found in early writers like Tertullian. Augustine also produced *On the Holy Trinity* (399–419/422) in which he paid attention to both the divine unity and the full equality of the "persons," whereas Origen and Arius taught the subordination of the Son and Spirit to the Father. More specifically, Augustine articulated that there is so great an equality in the Trinity, that not only the Father is not greater than the Son, but neither are the Father and the Son together greater than the Holy Spirit. He refuted Eastern remains of subordinationism that the Father is the sole source of all and that the Holy Spirit proceeds from the Father alone. Along with his polemical works, Augustine was involved in an actual debate with the veteran anti-Nicene campaigner Maximinus in Hippo who arrived in Africa with the army under the command of the Goth, Count Sigiswulf (although he was not a Goth himself). Based on this disputation, Augustine published *Debate with Maximinus, an Arian Bishop* (427/428) in which he rejected Maximinus' statement that the Father alone is the true, the "great" God because only the Father is "incomparable, immense, infinite, unborn, and invisible"; he argued that the Son is as invisible as the Father is. Besides these works, the aged Augustine produced *Against Maximinus, an Arian* (428) in which he replied to Maximinus' lengthy speech because Augustine did not have enough opportunity to answer to Maximinus' questions during their former debate; here Augustine was better able to articulate the nature of God's trinity.

Indeed, Augustine had developed his understanding of God, especially God's trinitarian nature, during his anti-Arian controversies and writings. He emphasized the same unity of substance and the same quality of the Trinity (*Trin.* 6.3.4–6.7.9). For Augustine, God is simple, absolute being, as distinguished from all created things, which are manifold and variable. God is the basis and source of all that exists. Augustine argued that "the Father, Son, and Holy Spirit, of one and the same substance, God the creator, the Omnipotent Trinity, work indivisibly" (*Trin.* 4.21) and that "the Father, Son, and Holy Spirit, one God, alone, great, omnipotent, good, just, merciful, Creator of all things visible and invisible" (*Trin.* 7.6.12). For Augustine, the Father and Son and Spirit are not separate things, although they are distinct and "other" to each other. He described the three trinitarian persons as equally simple and as all being life itself: yet they are neither three Gods, nor three Goods, but one God because of the generative order that links them together (*conf.* 13.11.12; 9.1.1).

For Augustine, the divine Trinity could be depicted as "God one in three and three in one" (*Una trinitas et trina unitas*) (*conf.* 12.7.7). This God, or this Good, is simple, and what is begotten (not "created") by the Good is equally simple. Thus, the Father begets the Son, but this is the generation of a simple being by a simple being, and thus the two are co-eternal, simple, and immutable. The Spirit is also simple, begotten of the other two, and together these three are one God (*civ. Dei* 11. 24; *div. qu.* 50; *Trin.* 6.5.7). The triune God is the "one eternal and true reality," from who "flows" all good; this triune God is "eternal, immortal, incorruptible, unchangeable, living, wise, powerful, beautiful, just, good, blessed, spirit" (*Trin.* 15.5.8).[90]

In his doctrine of the Trinity Augustine emphasized not only the oneness of the divine essence but also the union of the divine persons in love (Matt 22:37–40; *Trin.* 6.5.7). Love is the essence of the Godhead, and accounts for both the unity of substance and the Trinity of persons. The Father, the Son, and the Holy Spirit are bound together by—"are found in"—this love (*Trin.* 9.2.2). Augustine gives his preference to a triad in which the Father is represented by memory (*memoria*), the Son by understanding/intelligence (*intelligentia*), and the Spirit by will (*voluntas*) (*Trin.* 10.11.17–18). Later, the Council of Constantinople (381) condemned Arianism. Augustine's concept of tribune God, the unity and equality of the persons, was acknowledged at the Third Council of Toledo (589) in Spain, as a part of the so-called Nicene Creed; it has spread over the West. To this day, there is a dividing issue of the understanding of Father, the Son, the Holy Spirit between the Greek and Latin churches.[91]

In the later part of his episcopate, especially after 411, Bishop Augustine had primarily engaged in vehement controversies with the Pelagians (although he was involved in the disputation with the Donatists and Arians). Pelagius was a British (or Irish) monk of high learning and great moral earnestness, who had settled in Rome about 400. Pelagius

---

90. Ayres and Barnes, "God," 385, 389; Gilson, *Christian Philosophy*, 223–24; Lancel, *Saint Augustine*, 377–87; Walker, *History*, 163.

91. Bonner, *St. Augustine*, 141; Walker, *History*, 163–64.

Illustrating the Case of St. Augustine

and his disciples practiced extreme ascetic living and sought stricter ethical standards in Rome. After the sack of Rome by the army of Alaric the Goth in 410, Pelagius and his follower Caelestius departed to Carthage in North Africa. At first, Augustine sympathized with the Pelagian movement, which preached "authentic Christianity" to Christians who bore the name "Christian" but who were not living up to the moral demands of the faith. However, gradually, Augustine confronted a deep theological gap between the Pelagians and himself, as he established the link between the supremacy of God's grace and human sin.[92] For Pelagians, the human being is capable of holiness through a combination of natural endowments and personal efforts.[93] Indeed, Pelagius held to the freedom of the human will; so his position had well expressed his motto, "If I ought, I can." Based on the popular Stoic ethics, Pelagius denied any original sin inherited from Adam and believed therefore that children are innocent. He affirmed that human death is not a result of the fall, but a natural event and that all human beings have the power not to sin.[94]

However, Augustine repudiated the Pelagian position as denying original sin, rejecting salvation by infused grace, and affirming human power to live without sin. Based on his own religious experience (e.g., the garden experience [*conf.* 8.12.28-30]), Augustine believed that he had been saved by irresistible divine grace from sins that he could never have overcome by his own strength. In that sense, Augustine placed all his emphasis on the helplessness of the human being to do any good whatsoever without the grace of God, and upon the disastrous consequences of Adam's sin for his posterity unless cleansed by baptism.[95]

In a context of the doctrinal conflict between Pelagius and Augustine, Pelagius journeyed to the East and his follower Caelestius remained in Carthage and sought to be ordained a presbyter by Bishop Aurelius. At that time, Bishop Aurelius received from Paulinus, a deacon of Milan and Ambrose's biographer, a letter accusing Caelestius of six errors: "(1) Adam was made mortal and would have died whether

---

92. Chadwick, *Augustine*, 108–11; Lancel, *Saint Augustine*, 325–34; Markus, "Life," 504.

93. Bonner, *St. Augustine*, 140.

94. Tillich, *History*, 123–24; Walker, *History*, 168.

95. Bonner, *St. Augustine*, 138–40, 352–93; Brown, *Augustine*, 340–53; Clark, *Augustine*, 45–48; Walker, *History*, 168–69.

he had sinned or had not sinned. (2) The sin of Adam injured himself alone, and not the human race. (3) New-born children are in that state in which Adam was before his fall. (4) Neither by the death and sin of Adam does the whole race die, nor by the resurrection of Christ does the whole race rise. (5) The law leads to the kingdom of heaven as well as the Gospel. (6) Even before the coming of the Lord there were men without sin."[96]

As such in 411, an advisory synod in Carthage rejected Caelestius' ordination. In 416, two North African synods—one for its local district in Carthage and the other for Numidia in Mileve—condemned the Pelagian opinions; then Pope Innocent I (402–417) confirmed the decision of these African synods. In May 418, the Council in Carthage continuously held Augustine's position that Adam became mortal by sin, that children should be baptized for the remission of original sin, that grace was necessary for right living, and that sinlessness is impossible in this life. Moved by the actions of this Council, the new Pope Zosimus issued a circular letter condemning Pelagius and Caelestius. After the death of Augustine, in 431, the Third Council in Ephesus officially rejected Pelagianism in the West and East.[97]

While involving in his controversy with the Pelagians, Augustine had composed his anti-Pelagian works. For example, he wrote *On the Merits and Remission of Sins, and on the Baptism of Infants* (411–412) in which he repudiated the teaching of Caelestius, who denied any transmission of original sin from Adam, while approving of infant baptism, not for the remission of sin but to make infants inheritors of the kingdom of heaven; Augustine insisted that Adam's sin caused the necessity of infant baptism, and that no one has ever lived or will live in the present world without sin; that is, baptism is necessary for people of all ages for the forgiveness of sins. Augustine also published *On Nature and Grace* (413–415) and *On the Grace of Christ and Original Sin* (418) in which he argued that human nature, created sound, has been disordered by sin, which could be purified by Christian baptism through divine grace—the grace of Christ. Augustine produced *The Enchiridion* (421–422), which was written for a layman, Laurentius, who had asked

---

96. Walker, *History*, 169. See *gr. et pecc. or.* 1.36, 2.2.

97. Bonner, *St. Augustine*, 312–51; Bourke, *Augustine's Quest*, 175–200; Lancel, *Saint Augustine*, 331–43; Lohse, *Christian Doctrine*, 110–22; Markus, "Life," 504; Sun, *Time and Eternity*, 264–68; Walker, *History*, 169–70, 135–36.

Augustine for a handbook explaining some basics of Christian faith. Augustine contended that true wisdom is not simply knowledge of the basics of what Christians believe, but a way of life—the worship of God—in which one involves faith in what is presented for Christian belief, and the ordering of hopes and loves to reflect this faith. The aged Augustine wrote two treaties: *On Grace and Free Will* (426/427) and *On Rebuke and Grace* (426/427), addressed to the monks of Hadrumetum, in which he insisted that free choice of the will or good was impossible unless aided by divine grace, and that admonition is justified in the case of a Christian who had fallen into sin. Along with these works, Augustine had a long confrontation with Julian of Eclanum, the Pelagian bishop, who disagreed with Augustine's concept of original sin and held that Adam was created mortal, with an intellect like that of his descendants. As such, Augustine published *Against Julian, an Unfinished Book* (428–430) in which he argued that the superiority of Adam's unvitiated created nature made his fall the greater and the more disastrous; it brought death, spiritual and physical, on him and his progeny.

During his long debates with the Pelagians and his polemical writings, Augustine had formulated the doctrine of original sin and God's grace, which dominated Western theology for over a thousand years. Augustine argued that the sin of Adam and Eve ("the first human beings") affected their human nature in such a way that it must be inherited to their children (*Gn. litt.* 10.11.18). For Augustine, Adam, the first man, was originally created good but he was corrupted by sin. Adam fell into a state of total and hopeless ruin, of which the proper ending is eternal death (*civ. Dei* 14.15). This sin and its consequences involved all the human race (*civ. Dei* 13.14; *pecc. mer.* 1.10). Augustine contended that the soul of the infant is guilty; the sin of the infant is real (not just sins by analogy) and is transmitted by way of propagation/generation (*pecc. mer.* 1.2, 1.8–10; see Rom 5:12).[98] Augustine wrote, "If Adam had not fallen from you, there would not have flowed from his loins that salty sea-water the human race—deeply inquisitive, like a sea in a stormy swell, restlessly unstable" (*conf.* 13.20.28). For this reason, for Augustine, baptism is the necessary means of salvation for all humankind, including infants (*pecc. mer.* 1.70).[99]

---

98. Mann, "Augustine," 81–82; González, *Christian Thought*, 43–46.
99. Holt, "Original Sin," 608.

Augustine struggled to unite the spiritual character of sin in everybody with the hereditary character of sin that derives from Adam. Original sin is something that happens in the spiritual dimension of the person, but it is also bodily. For Augustine, sin (*peccatum*) refers to the willful misdirection of the love that is fundamental to the life of the soul. It is deeply rooted in the human being's turning away from God: "Sin . . . is a disorder and a perversion in the human being—that is, a turning away from the creator, who is more excellent, and a turning to created things, which are inferior" (*Simpl.* 1.2.18).[100] As such sin is not simply moral failure; it is not even disobedience. Disobedience is not the cause of sin, but a consequence. The cause of sin is turning away from God—the highest good (*nat. et gr.* 33). The immediate consequence of human turning away from the highest good is the loss of this good. This means that the fallen human being is excluded from God—the divine loving ground of being: "For wherever the human soul turns itself, other than to you, it is fixed in sorrows . . . [the soul] rush[es] towards non-being" (*conf.* 4.10.15; see *ench.* 2).[101] The loss of the highest good is the essential and existential punishment to the human being—the death of both the soul and the body; so the human being "has become like nothingness" (*civ. Dei* 13.2; 14.15).

Augustine paid attention to the first death of the human soul and body. For Augustine, Adam, the first man, opted to be apart from God (*Gn. litt.* 11.42.59; *div. qu.* 51.1). Indeed, Adam forsook God, and was then forsaken by God: "The soul [of Adam] . . . was not first forsaken by God, so that it forsook him as a result; it first forsook, and as a result it was forsaken" (*civ. Dei* 13.15); "so he [Adam] was dead in spirit, of his own will; but doomed, against his will, to die in body; forsaking eternal life, he was condemned also to eternal death, unless he should be set free by grace" (*civ. Dei* 14.15).

Augustine argued that the natural state of the human, created good (*ench.* 15) and disordered by sin, can only be restored by the redemptive action of God in Christ (*civ. Dei* 14.11; *ep.* 145.1–3; *Gn. litt.* 10.11.19; *Trin.* 13). For Augustine, human sin is "eradicated not by the removal of some natural substance which had accrued to the original, or by the removal of any part of it, but by the healing and restoration of the original which had been corrupted and debased" (*civ. Dei* 14.11).

100. Lohse, *Christian Doctrine*, 114; Mann, "Augustine," 80.
101. Tillich, *Christian Thought*, 125–28.

In this vein, human weaknesses or unhappiness, which is related to punishment for sin, can be cured by God's healing (*civ. Dei* 15.6). Healing begins when the human being turns to God through Jesus Christ. Augustine had accepted the Incarnate Christ as the mediator between God and humanity in order to strongly experience the saving power of God (*conf.* 7.18–19, 7.21.2; *ench.* 108; *pecc. mer.* 1.18, 1.33, 1.62).[102] To restore loving relationships between God and the human, Christ became flesh: "Christ Jesus, the Son of God, is both God and man" (*ench.* 35; see *ench.* 108; *en. Ps.* 148.8; *s.* 125.6).

As a divine and human mediator, the Incarnate Christ wished to bring eternal peace to humankind and to restore true freedom (*libertas*) (Col 1:19–22; 1 John 4:9; *civ. Dei* 14.11; *corrept.* 2). Augustine contended that the punishment of sin has been turned by the great and wonderful grace of the Savior to a good use and to the promotion of righteousness (*civ. Dei* 13.4). He noted, "From the misuse of free will there started a chain of disasters: mankind is led from that original perversion, a kind of corruption at the root, right up to the disaster of the second death, which has no end. Only those who are set free through God's grace escape from this calamitous sequence" (*civ. Dei* 13.14).

For Augustine, grace (*gratia*) refers to the divine operation in humans through which we are moved to know and love God (*corrept.* 3; *ep.* 166.2.5; *nat. et gr.* 4, 34): "This grace . . . is hiddenly bestowed in human hearts by the Divine gift" (*praed. sanct.* 13).[103] Augustine insisted that the soul has a longing for the restoration of the first good nature of Adam and Eve before the fall, even if it is in the fallen state. The restoration of the soul can be actualized in the loving grace of God: "Little by little, Lord, with a most gentle and merciful hand you touched and calmed my heart" (*conf.* 6.5.7). Augustine believed that God's grace restores and reactivates the interior spiritual senses of the human beings that were originally intended to lead us to God before being wounded by sin.[104] Thus, God's grace acts to counter the damage which sin has done to human nature, by cooperating with the good that remains in human nature—in order to make the human completely good again (*nat. et gr.* 4, 34).

---

102. See Harrison, *Augustine's Early Theology*, 32–34, 37, 252–54; McGinn and McGinn, *Christian Mystics*, 156.

103. See Burns, "Grace," 391.

104. Ibid., 398; McGinn and McGinn, *Christian Mystics*, 166–67.

Understanding Religious Conversion

Augustine asserted that God's grace transforms the human image of God into Christ-likeness. At this point, free choice (*liberum arbitrium*) is also transformed (*nat. et gr.* 81); it becomes a spiritual freedom (a *libertas*), whereby one spontaneously chooses to do God's will with delight (*ench.* 32; *nat. et gr.* 67; *c. Jul. imp.* 6.11). Within the Incarnated Christ, God's grace means the divine presence in the world upon which the creatures' own operations are totally dependent. Through God's grace, the healing of the human soul and body involves a turning from the restless desires of the heart to God, the source of existence and reality. God's grace, as the infusion of love by the Holy Spirit, frees the enslaved will to choose that which is pleasing to God, "not only in order that they may know, by the manifestation of that grace, what should be done, but moreover in order that, by its enabling, they may do with love what they know" (*corrept.* 3).

As early noted, for Augustine, God's grace is irresistible.[105] The effect of this saving grace is twofold: 1) Faith is instilled—"The faith by which we are Christians is the gift of God" (*praed. sanct.* 3; see 39), and 2) sins, both original and personal, are forgiven at baptism (*pecc. mer.* 1.34, 1.39, 1.70). Grace is given by God (*ench.* 107; *nat. et gr.* 4); it is given to everybody who becomes a Christian through the sacrament of baptism. The forgiveness of sins happens in baptism and is received by faith.[106] In that sense, Augustine confessed, "I will love you, Lord, and I will give thanks and confession to your name because you have forgiven me such great evils and my nefarious deeds. I attribute to your grace and mercy that you have melted away my sins away like ice" (*conf.* 2.7.15).

Consistent with the formulation of his doctrine of original sin and God's grace, Augustine had developed his concept of infant baptism during the controversy with the Pelagians. As noted earlier, Caelestius, one of Pelagius' disciples, claimed "that Adam's sin injured only Adam himself, and not the human race; and that infants at their birth are in the same state that Adam was in before his transgression" (*gr. et pecc. or.* 2.2; see 1.36; 2.3–4). In this vein, the Pelagians refused "to believe that in infants original sin is remitted through baptism, for they contend that no such original sin exists at all in people by birth" (*pecc. mer.* 1.9).

---

105. Gilson, *Christian Philosophy*, 153–56; Gonzáez, *Christian Thought*, 46–47.
106. Tillich, *Christian Thought*, 129; Walker, *History*, 165.

However, Augustine did not agree with the Pelagians' claims about infant sinlessness. For Augustine, such claims implicitly denied that Jesus had saved infants, for if they were truly sinless, then there would be nothing for him to save them from (*s.* 174.7; *gr. et pecc. or.* 2.33). Augustine was convinced that the church's practice of infant baptism had been handed down from Jesus and the apostles (*pecc. mer.* 1.39). He argued that the Christian church has been accustomed to baptize truly "infants for the remission of sins—not, indeed, sins which they have committed by imitation owing to the example of the first sinner, but sins which they have contracted by their very birth, owing to the corruption of their origin" (*gr. et pecc. or.* 2.17). Through the sacrament of baptism, infants came to enjoy the "benefits of the Mediator"; they were delivered from evil, reconciled with God, enlightened by the Spirit, and incorporated into the body of Christ, the church (*pecc. mer.* 1.18, 1.26, 1.33, 1.35, 1.39, 1.70).[107]

Meanwhile, as a monk and priest/bishop of Hippo, Augustine reorganized and managed the monastery in a more specific fashion with established rules (Possidius, *v. Aug.* 5), which was influenced by the spirit and actions of the apostolic community at Jerusalem as described in the Acts of the Apostles: "When they had prayed . . . they were filled with the Holy spirit. . . . Now the whole group of those who believed were of one heart and soul. . . . There was not a needy person among them, for as many as owned lands or houses sold them and brought the proceeds of what was sold. They laid it at the apostles' feet, and it was distributed to each as any had need" (Acts 4:31–35). Following the community rule of one mind and one heart in the one Christ, Augustine's monastic group settled down to a life of prayer, scripture reading, (philosophical and theological) discussion, and writing (Possidius, *v. Aug.* 5).[108] Later Augustine's monastic community had produced many devoted Christian believers (who had distinguished talents) and important church leaders of Africa (who had strongly supported Bishop Augustine's anti-heretical controversies):

> Here [at Hippo, Augustine] established a new community. He was joined by some of his friends from Thagaste, including Evodius and Severus, while new recruits subsequently came

---

107. Harmless, "Baptism," 89–90.

108. Bourke, *Augustine's Quest*, 126–27; Clark, *Augustine*, 88–92; Harrison, *Augustine*, 182–87; Lancel, *Saint Augustine*, 224–32; Lawless, "Rules," 739–40.

forward: Possidius, the future bishop of Calama and Augustine's biographer; Profuturus, afterwards bishop of Cirta; Urban, the future bishop of Sicca; and Peregrinus, who was to preside over the church of Thenae. It is possible that a written rule was provided. . . . The little band of friends who for nearly three years had followed a common way of life at Thagaste was transformed into a regular religious community.[109]

As one of the members of the monastery and one of Augustine's closest friends, Alypius was faithfully at the side of Augustine throughout his lifetime. Born in Thagaste (*conf.* 6.7.11), Alypius was a student of Augustine (6.7.11), and became a Manichee with him (6.7.12). Augustine admired his integrity (6.10.16) and treated him as a "heart's brother" (9.4.7). Alypius was baptized with Augustine and Adeodatus by Bishop Ambrose of Milan on April 24–25, 387 (9.6.14), and participated in the discussions at Cassiciacum (9.4.8). He returned to Africa and engaged in a monastic life with Augustine and others at Thagaste and then at Hippo. He was appointed as bishop of Thagaste in 394 and cooperated with Augustine in order to serve and guide effectively the African church. As such Alypius was one of seven Catholic bishops at the conference of 411 with the Donatists and he played an important part in the Pelagian controversies.[110]

While engaging in both his monastic life and his pastoral ministry (including his long controversies with the Manichees, Donatists, Arians, and Pelagians), Augustine had developed his understanding of the unity of the love of God and love of neighbor—contemplation and action. Love (caritas) is one of the central subjects of Augustine's thought. According to Augustine, love is a movement, an inclination, or a striving (*div. qu.* 35.1). Human beings live on the basis of this love. Love is a force of the soul and the life; it determines life in a good or evil way. This love flows from the dynamism of the will, which becomes concrete through the loved object (*ord.* 2.18.48). Augustine elucidated that love is a gift of God; it endows the human will with a new desire, a striving for divine truth, wisdom, and justice. God has loved us first (1 John 4:19; *s.* 34.2), as appears from the sending of his incarnate Son as well

---

109. Bonner, *St. Augustine*, 113–14. See Possidius, *v. Aug.* 11; Bourke, *Augustine's Quest*, 126–28; Brown, *Augustine*, 136–37; Clark, *Augustine*, 11. For thirty-five years, Augustine remained bishop of Hippo and changed the bishop's residence into a monastic household for clerics.

110. Fitzgerald, "Alypius," 16–17.

as from the gift of the Holy Spirit (see 1 John 4:9). He asserted that "the love of God has been poured into our hearts through the Holy Spirit which has been given to us" (*amare deum de deo*) (*s.* 34.3; Rom 5:5).[111]

Throughout his life, Augustine had reflected on the role of love in the path to God—"love is the soul's weight" (*conf.* 13.9.10). By means of the gift of divine love of *caritas*—the God-centered love—one has the power to ascend to God, while through the self-centered love of *cupiditas* one flees from God (*div. qu.* 36.1–4).[112] God's love of *caritas* enters into human hearts by means of the Holy Spirit rather than that of the human free will. It enables human beings to receive a new knowledge of God in faith; it also enables us to experience a new impetus of desire—a longing for God that always pursues the ineffable God (*en. Ps.* 104.3). Through this love of *caritas*, our likeness to God is growing—the greater our likeness to God, the more our love will increase, and the more clearly we will perceive God, for "God is love" (1 John 4:8). The more we perceive God, the better we become aware of his ineffability and incomprehensibility: "The closer you come to his likeness, the more progress you make in charity, and the more sensitive to God you become" (*en. Ps.* 99.5).

For Augustine, the authenticity of the love of God is only tested by the love of neighbor. The human being's capacity to love God comes only from God, and with this love we should love the neighbor (*s.* 265.9; *Trin.* 15.17.31, 15.18.32). God's self-revelation as love becomes for us an appeal, a demand, and a commandment to love our neighbors as God loves them (*ep. Jo.* 8.4; *ex. Gal.* 45; *s.* 350.2). Indeed, it is impossible to love God without loving our neighbors (*div. qu.* 36.4; *f. et op.* 16.27–30). Augustine relied strongly on biblical arguments for his position (e.g., Matt 5:23–24, 1 John 4:20). That means that his argument was derived not only from the revelation in St. John's Epistle that God is Love (1 John 4:8), but also from Christ's assurance that human beings are specially loved by God (*doc. Chr.* 1.27.28). In order to experience the love of God, one must begin by loving one's neighbor. Although the love of God comes first in the order of commanding (*ordo praecipiendi*), the love of neighbor comes first in the order of performing (*ordo faciendi*)

---

111. Van Bavel, "Love," 514–15.

112. Babcock, "Cupiditas and Caritas," 31–34; McGinn and McGinn, *Christian Mystics*, 161–62.

(*Jo. ev. tr.* 17.8; *s.* 265.9).[113] Augustine contended that one, who loves one's brother or sister, loves God because one loves love itself, which is of God, and is God (*Trin.* 8.8.12).

For Augustine, the reason for the incarnation of the Son of God is the revelation of God's love for the human being (John 1:14, 3:16).[114] Augustine insisted that Jesus Christ "came in the flesh to gather in one" through love; as such, if one does not possess this love, one denies Christ's incarnation (*ep. Jo.* 6.13–7.2). The experience of and participation in Christ involves charity for others. He stated, "In Christ, you have it all. Do you want to love your God? You have in Christ, *In the beginning was the Word, and the Word was with God, and the Word was God* (John 1:1). Do you want to love a neighbor? You have in Christ, *And the Word was made flesh and dwelt among us* (John 1:14)" (*s.* 261. 8).

Augustine used the terms *uti* and *frui*, which could be considered a proper pair, in order to discuss a relationship between love for God and love for neighbor. In *On Christian Teaching*, he defined theses words: "Enjoyment [*frui*], after all, consists in clinging to something lovingly for its own sake, while use [*uti*] consists in referring what has come your way to what your love aims at obtaining, provided, that is, it deserves to be loved" (1.4.4). *Frui* is love in an absolute way—the love of enjoyment; *uti* is love in a relative way—the love of use. Augustine raised a provocative question: "whether human beings ought to regard themselves as things to be enjoyed, or to be used, or both" (*doc. Chr.* 1.22.20). Augustine basically answered that only God can be *enjoyed* (i.e., loved) as an absolute end, whereas finite things must always be *used* as vehicles to God's love, or *enjoyed* for God's sake (*doc. Chr.* 1.23.22, 1.33.36–37). More specifically, he clarified these notions when responding to the following questions: 1) Is the human being to be an object of *frui*? To this Augustine immediately answers no, not here on earth. 2) Is the human being to be an object of *uti*? To this Augustine immediately answers yes, here on earth. 3) Is the human being to be an object of both *frui* and *uti*? Augustine's final answer is yes: Human beings are to be objects of *uti* and we are also to be objects of *frui* in the proper sense of the term, but this is a heavenly not an earthly *frui*, and it is *frui* "in God" because God alone, and not other human beings, brings human life to full supreme happiness (*doc. Chr.* 1.22.20–1.34.38; *civ.*

---

113. See Van Bavel, "Love," 512–13.

114. Ibid., 510.

Dei 19.13, 19.17).[115] Human beings are allowed to love created things, especially our neighbor, but we have to love them in relation to the Creator; so it is no longer cupidity/desire (*cupiditas*) but love (*caritas*) (*Trin.* 9.8.13). Augustine stated, "The peace of the Heavenly City [the city of God] is a perfectly ordered and perfectly harmonious fellowship in the enjoyment of God, and a mutual fellowship in God; the peace of the whole universe is the tranquility of order—and order is the arrangement of things equal and unequal in a pattern which assigns to each its proper position" (*civ. Dei* 19.13).

From Augustine's mature spiritual and theological perspective, the reciprocity of love of God and neighbor is essential for the proper relationship between contemplation and action. Based on the primacy of love of God and neighbor in the Bible (e.g., Matt 22:37–40), Augustine constantly confronted with a following issue during his lifetime: To what extent can "the inner life of the spirit" (i.e., a life of prayer/solitude) be harmonized with "an active apostolate and the performance of charitable works" (i.e., a life of community/social engagement)? Indeed, Augustine had struggled to reconcile his early and continuing preference for the contemplative life with the many duties surrounding his priesthood, and later, his episcopacy (*epp.* 10.1–3, 21.1–6, 48.1–4).[116] Although he designated contemplation as the "better part" (*melior pars*, e.g., the story of Martha and Mary [Luke 10:38–42]), this did not imply that action is bad, but only that it must give way to something more perfect (*s.* 103.5–6). Augustine intended to establish a more refined ideal of Christian charity that fully integrates the love of God and neighbor, and thereby upholds both precepts of the Great Commandment (*civ. Dei* 19.19; *Trin.* 8.8.12).

Augustine sought to harmonize these seemingly disparate but mutually enriching dimensions of Christian living—contemplation and action. According to Augustine, "faith cannot save without good works" for others, that is, faith "*works by charity*" (*f. et op.* 16.27). This implies that the necessity of love (*necessitas caritatis*) demands a willing acceptance of our social engagement and ecclesiastical obligation, while the love of truth (*caritas veritatis*) seeks the "sanctified leisure" (*otium sanctum*) of contemplation (*civ. Dei* 19.19). In other words, "no one has a right to lead a life of contemplation to the neglect of temporal

---

115. Canning, "Uti/frui," 860; Sun, *Time and Eternity*, 178–80.
116. Torchia, "Contemplation and Action," 233–35.

responsibilities, but no one should be so immersed in active service as to relinquish the delight of truth (*veritatis delectatio*) completely."[117] In effect, the good of the earthly city deserves our attention as we patiently anticipate the realization of the heavenly city (*civ. Dei* 11.1, 14.28, 18.2, 19.13–19).

Throughout his long episcopate, in addition to his duties as bishop of Hippo, Augustine worked and wrote for the benefit of the whole church of God. In particular, he spent much of his time to participate, vigorously and powerfully, in debates with the Manichees, Donatists, Arians, and Pelagians for defending and reestablishing essential elements of Christian teaching and doctrine (e.g., the concepts of God and the soul, sin and God's grace, the Christian community and the sacrament of baptism, the unity of love of God and neighbor, etc). As such, Augustine courageously faced the political and cultural challenges of his times. On August 24, 410, Rome, the former capital of the Roman Empire, was taken by the army of Alaric the Goth. Many pagans criticized Christianity, contending that Rome had been preserved inviolate while she worshipped the old gods, but that Rome had fallen to barbarians after adopting Christianity. Many Christians were anxious about this tragedy and had fundamental questions about the meaning of this terrifying portent. In order both to defend Christianity against pagans and to comfort God's people within the depths of disturbance, Augustine composed a majestic work, *City of God* (413–426/427); it has been valuable in the study of Augustine's thought.[118] On September 26, 426, Augustine nominated Eraclius (or Heraclius) to succeed him as bishop of Hippo with the acceptance of his whole congregation and retreated for his health for a while (*ep.* 213.1–7). About this time, he

---

117. Ibid., 233.

118. Bonner, *St. Augustine*, 140; Chadwick, *Augustine*, 96–106; Clark, *Augustine*, 94–107; Harrison, *Augustine*, 194–221; Lancel, *Saint Augustine*, 391–412. *City of God* consists of the twenty-two books that are divided by two main parts: 1) Books 1–10 are a refutation of the "false teachings" of the pagans; 2) Books 11–22 are a "demonstration and defense" of the truth of Christian faith. Augustine distinguished *the heavenly city* from *the earthly city*. For Augustine, the heavenly city is directed by God-centered love and acquiesces in divine revelation and instruction. In contrast, the earthly city is guided by self-love and lives according to what Scripture calls the flesh (*civ. Dei* 11.1; 14.28; 18.2; 19.13–19; see Fortin, "City of God," 196–202).

Illustrating the Case of St. Augustine

began to write *The Retractions* in order to list and review all his works (except his Epistles and Sermons); he completed it in 427 (*v. Aug.* 28).[119]

In 429, Gaiseric and his Vandals landed in North Africa. Before this Vandal army raided the rich eastern provinces of Africa, a number of bishops appealed to Augustine to take refuge, with regard to the proper conduct of a bishop in the event of hostile attack. In particular, Bishop Honoratus of Thiabe quoted the words of the Gospel—"When they persecute you in one town, flee to the next" (Matt 10:23)—to persuade Augustine and to justify flight in the face of persecution. Augustine held strongly to the traditional African view that it was the duty of a bishop to remain among his flock for as long as anyone had need of him, while quoting words of the Gospel: "I am the good shepherd. The good shepherd lays down his life for the sheep. The hired hand, who is not the shepherd and does not own the sheep, sees the wolf coming and leaves the sheep and runs away" (John 10:11–12) (*ep.* 228.1–6).[120] Augustine sent a pastoral letter for the African churches in order to deliver advice on the withdrawal of bishops from the churches at the approach of the Vandals: "There were circumstances when flight was justified: when, as in the case of St Athanasius, the bishop was the sole object of attack and his sacred ministry could be discharged by others, or if all the inhabitants of a spot had fled, so that there was nothing to be gained by the clergy remaining. But if the laity remain, and the danger to clergy and laity is the same, then the laity must not be deserted in their time of need."[121]

Indeed, Augustine managed to pass his message onto the African churches and stood firmly by his pastoral responsibilities, ideals, and Christian beliefs while other bishops were driven from their churches and provinces by the Vandal invaders: "With the approach of the enemy, people will flock to the churches, some seeking to be baptized, some to be reconciled, others to be absolved. If the clergy have gone, they will depart unregenerate and absolved. Accordingly, the clergy must remain. If their blood is shed, they will have their reward like the martyrs, for having laid down their life for the people committed to their charge."[122]

---

119. Bonner, *St. Augustine*, 153; Brown, *Augustine*, 411.
120. Bonner, *St. Augustine*, 152–54; Brown, *Augustine*, 428–29.
121. Bonner, *St. Augustine*, 154. See *ep.* 228.2, 228.6; Possidius, *v. Aug.* 30.
122. Bonner, *St. Augustine*, 154–55. See *ep.* 228.8–9.

In the time of this calamity, the aged Bishop Augustine was bitterly grieved in his heart. He had only one prayer to God: "either that He [God] may be pleased to free this city which is surrounded by the foe, or if something else seems good in His sight that He make His servants brave for enduring His will, or at least that He may take me from this world unto Himself" (Possidius, *v. Aug.* 29).[123] The presence of the savage army of Vandals around the city wall did not alter Augustine's ministry, writing, and his spiritual way of life: "Until he [Augustine] fell ill with his last sickness, he continued to preach to the people, and with the Vandals at the gate, he continued writing the great reply to Julian of Eclanum, the last and most formidable of the Pelagian controversialists."[124]

Augustine's friends and followers joined Augustine in offering up the same prayer, although they had been lamenting the calamities that had overtaken them. After three months of the siege of Hippo by the Vandals, old Bishop Augustine became sick with a high fever (*v. Aug.* 29). During the last ten days of his illness, he had prayed to God and had meditated on penitential Psalms of David with abundant tears. At the age of seventy-six, he died in peace on August 28, 430 (*v. Aug.* 31). After the death of Augustine, the siege of Hippo lasted eleven months; it was sacked by the Vandals and was burned and destroyed by them in July 431, but Augustine's library was fortunately preserved by Possidius (*v. Aug.* 29, 31).[125] On August 28 every year the Christian church celebrates the heroic virtues of this bishop and theologian, who celebrated in his *Confessions* the steadfast love of God as source of the salvation of all God's creatures.[126] *Confessions* has remained influential for millions of religious people who have humbly agreed with Bishop Augustine's faithful statement—"You stir man to take pleasure in praising you,

---

123. Bonner, *St. Augustine*, 153–54; Brown, *Augustine*, 429.

124. Bonner, *St. Augustine*, 154. See *v. Aug.* 31.

125. Bonner, *St. Augustine*, 153–56; Brown, *Augustine*, 436–37; O'Donnell, *Augustine*, 315–16; Harrison, *Augustine*, 221–22. Possidius was one of members of Augustine's monastery at Hippo (*v. Aug.* 15) and later became bishop of Calama in 397. When the Vandal army besieged Hippo in 429, he remained there with Augustine; after the death of Augustine and the sack of Hippo by Vandals, Possidius, as Augustine's biographer, published a book, *The Life of Augustine*. He later recalled his loving relationship with Augustine for almost forty years (*v. Aug.* 31; see Vessey, "Possidius," 668).

126. Clark, *Augustine*, 12.

because you have made us for yourself, and our heart is restless until it rests in you" (*conf.* 1.1.1).

SUMMARY

The case of Augustine's conversion experience enables us to understand the impact of personal, social, cultural, and religious factors on the process of religious conversion. The sufficient account of Augustine's main life history helps us establish a better account of his transformational process. This means that it leads us to realize that Augustine's conversion experience was the sum of what happened in his life before, during, and after his conversion to Christianity in the summer of 386. Following the specific changes of localities and the chronological order of his life history, Augustine's main life-changing experiences are presented: 1) his experiences of beatings at school and parents' laughing/God's silence about them (*conf.* 1.9.14–15), 2) the pear-stealing episode (2.4.9–2.6.12), 3) the death of his unnamed friend (4.4.7–9), 4) the failure of Faustus to address the objections of Augustine to Manichean cosmology (5.6.10–5.7.13), 5) his escape from his mother through an act of deception (5.8.15), 6) his dismissal of his unmarried wife (6.15.25), 7) the relationships with his spiritual mentors (e.g., Christian Platonist Simplicianus [8.5.10]) and his friends (e.g., Alypius [8.9.27–8.12.30, 9.6.14]), 8) the famous garden experience (8.12.28–30), 9) his baptism by Bishop Ambrose (9.6.14), 10) the mystical vision he and his mother shared at Ostia (9.10.23–26), 11) his monastic life and church ministry as a monk-priest/bishop of Hippo Regius (Possidius, *v. Aug.* 4, 5, 7, 8), and 12) his last ecclesiastical struggle for defending his flock and church during the blockade of Hippo by the Vandal army (*v. Aug.* 29, 30, 31).

Along with knowing Augustine's life history, the exploration of some of his basic thought helps us to promote a more appropriate understanding of the process of his conversion. Augustine's thought was deeply rooted in his transformation from Manichaeism, through skepticism and Neoplatonism, to Christianity, which pivoted on his life-changing events. It was related to the social, cultural, historical, political, and religious environments of his time. Especially, his main thought—God and the soul; sin and God's grace; creation, time, and eternity; the unity of the love of God and love of neighbor; the Christian church and baptism—was more developed within his numerous and vigorous debates with the Manichees, Donatists, Arians, and Pelagians.

4

Getting Insights
Critical Search for Interpretations of Augustine's Conversion

> The *Confessions* . . . makes an implicit claim as a meta-narrative of conversion. It is not only Augustine's story but the stories of Victorinus, Ponticianus, the two courtiers at Trier, Antony of Egypt, Monnica, and as I am inclined to think, the mother of Adeodatus. There are as many kinds of conversion narratives in the *Confessions* as there are people who are converted. To avert that any one of these conversion stories is the most fitting representation of Christian conversion in the *Confessions* is simply misleading.
>
> —F. B. A. Asiedu[1]

THIS CHAPTER ATTEMPTS TO get insights through critical search for interpretations of Augustine's conversion from psychological, sociological, anthropological, and theological perspectives. While retrieving the contours of the interpretations of religious conversion in chapter 2, this chapter moves to examine the key contributions and limitations of the previous studies of Augustine's conversion, at which point it attempts to deepen the basic ideas of the interpretations of Augustine's conversion

---

1. Asiedu, "Example of a Woman," 305.

as well as to investigate the most salient or essential elements of interpretations of his lived experience of transformation. Then it presents specific interdisciplinary questions that intend to extend critically the contributions of the literature by bringing together various disciplines.

PSYCHOLOGICAL STUDIES OF AUGUSTINE'S CONVERSION

Psychologists (of religion) have explored the impact of personal factors on Augustine's conversion experience. There are different interpretations of the phenomenon of Augustine's religious change among the scholars of different schools. Mindful of the complexity and diversity of the psychological studies of Augustine's conversion, this section of the literature review focuses on three main themes because they are valid for appreciating the personal dimension of religious change and because they are helpful to achieve an integrated understanding of Augustine's conversion narrative. These main themes are 1) Augustine's conversion and regressive psychopathology, 2) Augustine's conversion, crisis, and the unification of his divided self, and 3) Augustine's conversion and his mental development.

Augustine's Conversion and Regressive Psychopathology

Freudian scholars have primarily interpreted Augustine's conversion experience in light of the oedipal conflict, self-reproach, and a sense of guilt. As noted earlier, Sigmund Freud considers religious conversion as a matter of surrendering to the father's or Father's will within the context of the Oedipus complex (which is inherently accompanied by emotional illness and pathological regression).[2] Freud insists that the human sense of guilt is rooted in the Oedipus complex of one's childhood in light of the structure of mind of id, ego, super-ego: "man's sense of guilt springs from the Oedipus complex."[3] He notes,

> Clearly the repression of the Oedipus complex was no easy task. The child's parents, and especially his father, were perceived as the obstacle to a realization of his Oedipus wishes; so his

---

2. Freud, "Religious Experience," 245–46; *Ego and the Id*, 22–31, 48–49.
3. Freud, *Civilization*, 93; see 94–95; *Ego and the Id*, 30.

infantile ego fortified itself for the carrying out of the repression by erecting this same obstacle within itself. It borrowed strength to do this, so to speak, from the father, and this loan was an extraordinarily momentous act. The super-ego retains the character of the father, while the more powerful the Oedipus complex was and the more rapidly it succumbed to repression (under the influence of authority, religious teaching, schooling and reading), the stricter will be the domination of the super-ego over the ego later on—in the form of conscious or perhaps of an unconscious sense of guilt.[4]

In "Mourning and Melancholia," Freud discusses the symptomatology of melancholia, and contends that in melancholia, the lost object is internalized and the rage against the lost object is therefore self-directed. This, in Freud's view, explains why the melancholic person engages in exaggerated self-reproach.[5] Endorsing Freud's concepts of religious conversion, oedipal complex, and melancholia, Freudian psychologists have argued that Augustine's conversion experience is in part an effort to resolve his oedipal conflict which involves his self-reproach and oedipal anxieties. As such, they have predominantly viewed Augustine's *Confessions* as a record of a pathological personality. In doing so, they are concerned with the oedipal issues of Augustine, which focus on his ambivalent relationships with his father (Patricius) and with his mother (Monica) (in terms of triadic relationships between parents and child), and on relational issues of difference, power, competition, and sexuality.

Influenced by Freud, E. R. Dodds in "Augustine's *Confessions*: A Study of Spiritual Maladjustment" interprets Augustine's conversion experience in light of the oedipal complex, self-reproach, and a sense of guilt. Dodds describes Augustine's disrupted mental status as at war within himself, acknowledging William James' idea of the divided self. For Dodds, Augustine's sick soul or dividedness is "the recurrent ground-theme of the *Confessions*" which is rooted in his oedipal complex and his sense of wrongness before the divine and others. In that sense, Dodds depicts Augustine's *Confessions* as an introspective autobiography, which indicates "the intimate record of a neurotic conflict."[6]

---

4. Freud, *Ego and the Id*, 30; see 48–49.
5. Freud, "Mourning and Melancholia," 243–51.
6. Dodds, "Augustine's *Confessions*," 44.

Understanding Religious Conversion

In his understanding of the *Confessions*, Dodds is more concerned with *Augustine the man* rather than *Augustine the saint* or *Augustine the theologian*. As such he writes,

> With the theological and devotional content of the *Confessions* the present paper is not concerned. It is addressed to the ordinary reader; and its purpose will have been attained if it convinces him that the humanity revealed in the *Confessions* is neither irrelevant to the saint's achievement nor limited in its tragic appeal by the unfamiliarity of its setting. . . . Just as we do not face the surgeon's knife unless there be something seriously amiss with our bodies, so no man faces the anguish of self-analysis unless there be grave trouble in his soul. Every introspective autobiography represents an act of spiritual surgery, and its *raison d'etre* is a condition of spiritual maladjustment which must be laid bare before it can be fully dealt with.[7]

Within a Freudian psychosexual framework of the Oedipus complex, Dodds asserts that the origins of Augustine's self-condemnation and his neurotic conflict were rooted in the circumstances of his early childhood. For Dodds, the self-reproach and pathological conflict of the early Augustine had inherently influenced the formation of the young and adult Augustine's basic thought.[8] Dodds states,

> The origins of the conflict are to be looked for in Augustine's family history. His mother, Monica, was a pious countrywoman who had been reared by an old nurse in a tradition of fervent Catholicism, at a time when paganism was still in the ascendant in Roman Africa. . . . While still in her teens this devout and sensitive child was given in marriage to a small country squire named Patricius, a pagan by tradition and temperament if not also by confession. . . . Monica suffered much in the early years of her married life. . . . Of this ill-assorted union Augustine was the fruit. It was his tragic destiny to combine in a small and sickly body the warring souls of both his parents and fastidious intellect which served each soul in turn.[9]

---

7. Ibid., 44.

8. In particular, Dodds pays attention to the role of Monica in the formation of Augustine's personality, his life-style, and his thought. For Dodds, the factor of Augustine's relationship to his mother Monica does not assure psychological well-being (ibid., 48).

9. Ibid., 44–45.

Importantly, Dodds views Augustine's conversion more as a suppression than a resolution of his neurotic conflict, whereas James regards his conversion as a transformative process of unifying his divided self.[10] In this way, Dodds contends that the adult (or the saint) Augustine's condition of spiritual maladjustment emerged from his earlier familial conflict; his spiritual maladjustment, as founded in his introspective autobiography itself, showed evidence of the un-resolving or continuing neurotic conflict until his adulthood. Although Dodds admires Augustine's impressive capacities for self-analysis and for employing words in order to communicate his subjective experiences with precision and depth of understanding,[11] he negatively concludes,

> In that moment in the garden—did the old Adam really die? Was the conflict never renewed?. . . . The immediate consequence of the decision was . . . a sense of happiness and a return to normal mental activity. . . . Nevertheless it is difficult to believe that the Augustine of later years—the bishop who forbade any woman to set foot in his palace, the theologian who defended the use of coercion in religious schisms, the moralist who thought it folly to weep for the death of a friend, the ascetic who boasted that he had learned to swallow his food as though it were physic (*Epp.* 93, 204; *Conf.* IV., 7 [12], X., 31 [44])—it is difficult to believe that this man had found within the Church the true mental balance which he had failed to achieve outside it.[12]

Similarly, Charles Kligerman describes Augustine's conversion and his life story within a classical psychoanalytic framework of the Oedipus complex. According to Kligerman, Augustine's conversion emerged from an abnormal identification with the mother and a passive feminine attitude to the father displaced to God.[13] Kligerman regards Augustine's *Confessions* as a psychiatric personal history without the contaminating presence of an interviewer. For Kligerman, the *Confessions* shows vividly how desperately Augustine struggled for his manhood; this book is analogous to the free association in psychoanalytic treatment in which Augustine was "emotionally labile and [spoke]

---

10. See James, *Religious Experience*, 171–76.
11. Dodds, "Augustine's *Confessions*," 54.
12. Ibid., 53.
13. Kligerman, "Psychological Study," 108.

from the heart in a rhapsodic fashion."[14] Kligerman notes that Augustine suffered from unresolved oedipal conflicts. Like Dodds, Kligerman insists that Augustine's psychopathological conflict was rooted in his earlier family environment. In particular, the religious difference between Patricius and Monica led to profound parental conflict in the family which had affected Augustine's personality and his mental development. He writes,

> His father, Patricius, a civil servant of the Roman state, was a sort of magistrate or tax collector—and a pagan. The mother, Monica, later St. Monica, was a devout Christian from a Christian family. This religious difference led to intense parental conflict which was decisive for Augustine's entire development. . . . In the childish imagination of Augustine, Patricius represented the power and prestige of Rome, paganism, the religion of the ruling class, and masculinity. Monica represented Africa, the mother country, whose great city was Carthage, Christianity, then more prevalent among the lower classes, and femininity. His boyhood dreams of glory must have been associated with following in his father's footsteps leading him to Rome—magnificent center of the universe. Carthage was great, but it was not Rome; Africans were provincials.[15]

Indeed, Kligerman views Monica's influence on the construction of Augustine's psychic development negatively, whereas Augustine himself praises her piety and gives her a great deal of positive credit in the *Confessions*. Kligerman pays attention to Augustine's problematic relationship with his mother in light of Augustine's oedipal conflict, especially his unhealthy identification with his mother. He states,

> Often frigid, but passively compliant, such women are extremely frustrating to their husbands. Monica had a hostile attitude toward sexuality but submitted dutifully to her unfaithful husband. . . . Emotionally alienated from her husband [Monica] had grown especially close to her oldest son and pinned her hopes on him. Augustine tells us how she daily wept over him, praying for his soul. It is not hard to detect an erotic quality in such behavior. Frigid hypermoral women frequently find concealed incestuous gratification in such stormy emotional scenes with their sons. For him it must have been extremely seductive yet

---

14. Ibid., 99, 102.
15. Ibid., 98, 104.

frustrating process, and sheds light on the turbulence of his adolescence. Augustine was a typically overstimulated child, culminating in a character type who seeks constantly to master his overwhelming tension and never finds adequate discharge—hence his violent emotionality and passionate fervor.[16]

In consideration of Augustine's oedipal situation, Kligerman asserts that Augustine was deeply attached to his mother and viewed his father as a rival for his mother's affections. Importantly, the oedipal Augustine could not resolve his psychosexual conflict in the normal way, through positive identification with his father, because his mother, Monica who disappointed in her marital relation, "turned her love to her eldest son in an engulfing type of seductiveness."[17] As such, Augustine was unable to form a normal identification with his father; while receiving confusing signals from his mother—both attraction and repulsion—Augustine's only choice was to develop an abnormal identification with her. For Kligerman, Augustine's abnormal identification with his mother was reflected in his conversion to her religious faith; during the conversion to his mother's religion, Augustine identified with God in the passive way that a male, deprived of his masculinity by an overpowering mother, was forced to relate to a father-figure. In this sense, while viewing Augustine's conversion as an act of submission to a super-ego God, Kligerman states,

> Augustine regarded this voice of a child as the voice of God. Probably it was his own voice projected and perceived in hallucinatory fashion. Since Augustine retreated from incestuous attachment to a mother identification, then redoubled his masculine strivings, during the height of his tension when the ego was especially weak, he resorted to projection and regression to a pregenital level. Thus it is the voice of a *boy or girl*—it does not matter. "Take up and read" repeated his childhood technique of appeasing his elders; by study he averted cruel punishment. His earliest prayers to God were that he might not be beaten at school. Thus "take up and read" was one of the first external voices of a harsh punitive authority introjected as *superego*. Under its prodding, Augustine made up his mind.[18]

16. Ibid., 98, 101.
17. Ibid., 104.
18. Ibid., 107.

Consequently, Kligerman contends that Augustine's conversion was rooted in his oedipal conflict, which did not deploy his healthy identification with his mother. For Kligerman, Augustine did not successfully resolve his oedipal conflict throughout his life. In other words, Augustine's oedipal conflict kept plaguing him to the end of his days; as such, Augustine's resort to religion is nothing more than a futile effort in order to externalize his psychosexual conflicts associated with an emotionally charged oedipal situation.[19]

Like Dodds and Kligerman, David Bakan and James E. Dittes agree with the idea that Augustine's conversion experience is an effort to resolve his oedipal conflict. From a classical psychoanalytic point of view, Bakan in "Some Thoughts on Reading Augustine's *Confessions*" examines Augustine's conversion and his life story in light of the Oedipus complex, the unentailment of the self, and a sense of guilt/reproach. Bakan views Augustine's *Confessions* as an autobiography in which he struggled to separate himself from life; in other words, in the *Confessions*, Augustine vividly showed a "vaulting struggle to identify the limited ego with all of the grandness and timelessness which he attributes to God."[20] In this vein, Bakan characterizes Augustine's writing as *reproach*:

> [Augustine] reproaches his contemporaries. He reproaches himself, and there are veiled reproaches to his father and even to his mother. He brings himself to the reproach of God, particularly in connection with the discussion of the problem of good and evil in the world, the implicit reproach of God for having made him with certain imperatives, especially the sexual imperative, but then always falls short of asserting the reproach against God. He almost reproaches God, and then substitutes devotional discourse for what might have been reproach.[21]

In consideration of Augustine's reproach, Bakan asserts that Augustine attempted to make himself to be totally "unentailed," remote, or alienated from all existence. According to Bakan, Augustine was one of the vainest of persons because he so sought to concern himself only with himself. From a Freudian perspective, Bakan tends to pathologize Augustine's conversion and his life story in terms of oedipal conflict and

---

19. Ibid., 108.
20. Bakan, "Some Thoughts," 150.
21. Ibid., 149.

infantile immaturity. In doing so, similar to Kligerman, he emphasizes Augustine's "compulsive sexuality."[22] For Bakan, the oedipal elements in Augustine are "patent." Significantly, these oedipal and immature elements of Augustine's psyche were deeply related to his understanding of religiosity (which had later profoundly affected the formation of Western religiousness and its culture). As a result, Bakan concludes,

> [Augustine's] severe distinction of lust from affective involvement is in itself indicative of immaturity; and it is perhaps one of the unfortunate things of the history of Western culture, that this particular immaturity should have been made one of the foundation tenets of the world's religiosity. He is critical of his sexual activities because he sees them as expressions of habit, compulsion, flesh, and lust. However, instead of attempting to move in the direction of being able to enlarge his love, he moves, rather, in the reverse direction, of alienating himself from any real love.[23]

In the same way, James E. Dittes interprets Augustine's conversion and his life story in light of his oedipal complex and his psychological bondage to his mother. Like Dodds and Kligerman, Dittes contends that Augustine's internal conflicts were deeply rooted in his earlier familial environment that had stirred Augustine's oedipal conflict and guilt feelings. In doing so, Dittes focuses on Augustine's attachment to his mother, Monica, who had captured her little son away from any relation with his father, Patricius. He writes,

> Augustine shared with Joseph of Egypt and with Freud of Vienna the fate of being the first-born son of a young woman and of an older and aloof father. Monica seems especially to have hovered and fawned over Augustine.... If she suffered so much emotional deprivation in her own marriage... she sought great gratification from her young son, in their earlier years together, as well as in the later years, when she was capable of moving in on Augustine's household, of forcing him to send away the mother of his child (VI, 15), of sabotaging his marriage plans at least twice (II, 3; VI, 13) and later of sharing a mutual mystical experience in which it is difficult to avoid hearing erotic overtones (IX, 10).[24]

---

22. Ibid., 150–51.
23. Ibid., 150.
24. Dittes, "Continuities," 133.

Dittes asserts that the little Augustine raised by such an insistent mother developed a strong attachment and dependence upon her.²⁵ In such a situation, for Dittes, Augustine was unprepared for the rugged life of school and the world of other boys. He tended to have shrunk, virtually as a cowering "mama's boy," from the sternness of teachers, and from the shenanigans of fellow students.

Similar to Bakan, Dittes points out the immature personality of Augustine as found in the *Confessions*: "In a number of ways, Augustine seems preoccupied with himself, in a way appropriate for an infant, and relatively unconcerned with the welfare of circumstances and persons beyond himself, except as they affect him."²⁶ As such, Dittes illustrates a case of Augustine's "apparent coldhearted dismissal of the mother of his child" in order to elucidate Augustine's abnormal personality. He claims that "she [the mother of Adeodatus] apparently suffered genuine distress (VI, 15), but Augustine seems heedless of her—he never even mentions her name—and remains preoccupied with his own feelings of deprivation."²⁷

Like Kligerman and Bakan, Dittes argues that Augustine did not resolve his oedipal conflicts in the normal way, through positive identification with his father, Patricius. In consideration of the dynamics of the oedipal situation, he contends that Augustine suffered the misfortune of having *won* the oedipal conflict with his father because his father died when he was sixteen. The death of his father led the adolescent and young Augustine to establish more submission and dependency upon his mother, Monica. Dittes notes, "After years of the most vigorous assertion of his independence, Augustine submitted. He surrendered to his mother, and to her church and to her wishes. He abandoned masculine sexuality. He abandoned all active personal striving, including his vocational roles and aspirations. He abandoned those things which his

---

25. Like Dittes, Paul W. Pruyser emphasizes Augustine's attachment to his mother throughout his lifetime: "In these *Confessions* there is great emphasis on his relation to the mother with a concomitant neglect of the relations to father, son, siblings, and concubine. Little is said about the impact of father's death, if any, on the boy Augustine" ("Psychological Examination," 287). Although he attempts to minimize a tendency toward infantilizing or pathologizing Augustine and his life, Pruyser insists that Augustine never fully renounced his attachment to his mother and never completely identified with his father (ibid., 288).

26. Dittes, "Continuities," 133.

27. Ibid., 134.

father particularly endorsed and represented. He abandoned, in short, the effort to be a father [for Adeodatus]. Instead he became an obedient son [for Monica]."[28]

Although Dittes acknowledges that during his early and mid-thirties, Augustine's life and thought underwent radical transition, he asserts that there was still the impact of ongoing unresolved oedipal conflicts on the adult Augustine's life. In this sense, Dittes supports the traditional Freudian interpretation that Augustine's oedipal problems forced him to relate to God in the same passive way that he related to Monica. Concerned with the interconnection between Augustine's personal history, his unresolved psychological conflicts, and his theological views, Dittes places Augustine's relations with the divine in terms of the Oedipus complex: "If Augustine's neo-Platonic understanding of God and the God and the world is monistic, it may not be too facetious to say that it is also mom-istic."[29] For Dittes, Augustine's persistent adult oedipal conflicts had affected his teaching on creation and sovereignty, the problem of evil, original sin and grace, predestination, redemption, church authority and the sacraments, and his dealings with the Manichees, Donatists, and Pelagians.[30]

In a related vein, Paul Rigby in "Paul Ricoeur, Freudianism, and Augustine's *Confessions*" explores Augustine's conversion and his life story in light of the Oedipus complex and the recognition of fatherhood. For Rigby, Augustine's conversion was closely linked to his proper identification with his father, Patricius, in the oedipal situation. Acknowledging that a Freudian reading of religion is "the necessary deconstructive moment in the modern appropriation of such classical religious texts as the *Confessions*," Rigby recasts the psychological study of Augustine as an instance of the constructive dialogue between Freudianism and religion proposed by Paul Ricoeur.[31] For Rigby, the *Confessions* revealed two Augustines and two theologies: "one neu-

28. Ibid., 137.
29. Ibid., 138.
30. Ibid., 132-33, 138-40.

31. Rigby, "Paul Ricoeur," 93-95. According to Rigby, Ricoeur's hermeneutical method for a constructive conversation between Freudianism and religion "enables us to find in the *Confessions* the arduous path which the individual, the Christian churches, and culture must follow to arrive at an articulation of Christianity credible among the human sciences and to enter into dialogue with a God who is more than a necessary illusion" (ibid., 95).

rotic with a theology satisfying wish-fulfillment; the other transformed beyond the reach of Freudianism by the figures of the Spirit."[32] This implies that the outcome of Augustine's oedipal conflicts is neurotic as well as non-neurotic.

Previous scholars interpreting Augustine's conversion and his *Confessions* in a classical Freudian approach—Dodds, Kligerman, Bakan, and Dittes—have examined how Augustine's mother (Monica) had influenced the formation of the personality, thought, and religiosity of her son. They have argued that Augustine *did not resolve* his oedipal conflicts; that is, he could not normally identify with his father (Patricius) because his mother had frozen Patricius out of her affections and because she had seductively controlled Augustine and determined to have her son all for herself. As such, they have emphasized Patricius' inability to be an effective father, a positive role model, for his son. However, Rigby provocatively examines how Augustine's father had affected the construction of the personality, thought, and religiosity of his son. He contends that Augustine *did resolve* his oedipal conflicts in the appropriate, prescribed way through positive identification with his father. For Rigby, Patricius was not a weak or ineffective father for his son. Rather, Patricius limited his fatherhood to procreation which was related to a narrow biological view of the father-son relationship that does not take seriously the personhood of the other.

Significantly, Rigby challenges us to reconsider the psychological influence of Patricius on Augustine, and to look at Patricius' possible influence on his son's understanding of the divine and religiosity. For Rigby, after Patricius' baptism, Augustine did not condemn his father but accepted him: "Augustine's portrait of his father is no longer antagonistic after Patricius' baptism.... At the end of Book IX Augustine recognizes before God, without antagonism or remorse, his dead father."[33] In this sense, concerned with the neurotic aspect of Augustine's oedipal conflict, Rigby emphasizes the non-neurotic outcome of his oedipal conflict. This implies that Augustine recognized Patricius as a mortal father whom it is no longer necessary to kill and thereby renounced the megalomania of his own omnipotent desire. While advancing Peter Brown's idea of a complimentary process in Augustine's relations with

---

32. Ibid.
33. Ibid., 99.

Monica,[34] Rigby emphasizes the two dimensions of the successful resolution of Augustine's oedipal conflicts which were related to that "with Patricius the move is from rejection to acceptance; with Monica it is from idealization to ordinariness."[35]

Importantly, Rigby argues that Augustine developed the grounds for a deeper view of fatherhood during and after observing his father's baptism into the Christian church. For Rigby, while repudiating the fatherhood of "contingency and caprice of bodily desire," Augustine affirmed his father (Patricius), who became not an individual father but an actual member of "the ethical life of the [Christian] community."[36] This affirmation led Augustine to recognize the fatherhood of the divine. For Rigby, Augustine rejected the idea that God was father by virtue of the procreative role. Rather, he understood God as father who was a God of gratuitous act of liberation: "God as father is a figure modeled on salvation, on a new creation: he is in the future; he is not an ancestor connected with kinship or begetting; he is not caught in the immediacy of life. He is a figure of transformation offering the possibility of mutual recognition between himself and his children."[37] As a result, Rigby points out that Augustine constructed a positive identification with his father (Patricius) and with his "God father," although Augustine did not achieve a wholly healthy resolution of his oedipal conflicts. Through this constructive identification with his father, as both human and divine, Augustine actually deepened prevailing cultural and theological understandings of fatherhood.

As noted above, Freudian scholars have emphasized the oedipal conflict and a sense of guilt in the interpretation of Augustine's conversion experience. They have described Augustine's *Confessions* as a record of regressive psychopathology. In doing so, they contribute by elucidating Augustine's endless self-reproaches, his oedipal anxieties, his oedipal guilt, and his obsessive personality within Augustine's relationships with his father (Patricius) and with his mother (Monica) in light of triadic relationships between parents and child. As such, Freudian studies of Augustine's conversion have focused on the importance

---

34. For Brown, after the death of Monica, the adult Augustine had recollected and re-established his relations with his mother (*Augustine*, 157–58).

35. Rigby, "Paul Ricoeur," 99.

36. Ibid., 105–6.

37. Ibid., 108.

of childhood, the unconscious, and the possibility of pathology in Augustine's conversion experience. They provide us with insights into the link between the young Augustine's psychological crisis/distress and his early familial environments when interpreting the first stages of his conversion process.

However, Freudian interpretations of Augustine's conversion have tended to reduce all of Augustine's mental processes to psychopathological processes without adequate historical facts about his childhood experiences,[38] because they have explained Augustine's personality and his conversion in light of a model of a person derived from the study of psychopathology. More specifically, Freudian scholars have too much depended on Freud's concept of the Oedipus complex as a primary explanatory principle of Augustine's conversion, his thought, or his life history.[39] As such, they have guided readers to interpret Augustine's conversion as a regressive, disintegrative, and pathological phenomenon which was inherently related to his expression of emotional illness and neurotic conflict. In doing so, they have overemphasized the issues of Augustine's sexual conflict in light of the oedipal complex and anxiety, at which point they are more concerned with the regressive and pathological dimension of Augustine's conversion than the developmental and progressive dimension of his conversion.

    38. As noted earlier, Freudian scholars—E. R. Dodds, C. Kligerman, D. Bakan, and J. E. Dittes—insist that Augustine's guilt feelings and neurotic behaviors were rooted in the intractable and inevitable contrariety of having a pagan father and a Christian mother in light of Freud's concept of the Oedipus complex within the psychosexual framework. However, Lawrence Daly claims that Freudian scholars have tended to distort historical facts because they do not present sufficient evidence of fundamental hostility between Augustine's father and his mother ("Psychohistory," 245–49; see Fredriksen, "Augustine and His Analyst," 209–14; O'Meara, *Young Augustine*, 213). For Daly, the classical psychoanalytic approach has relied too much on Freud's concept of the Oedipus complex as the single explanatory principle of Augustine's behaviors in his lifetime (ibid., 250; see "Augustine's *Confessions*," 185–86).

    39. As discussed earlier, Freudian scholars have argued that Augustine's (thought or) theology is rooted in and is a response to his oedipal conflict (see Bakan, "Some Thoughts," 150–51; Dittes, "Continuities," 138–40). In this study, basically, I agree with that the early Augustine's inner conflict within his familial context might have affected the formation of his personality and thought. However, as noted in chapter 3, we need to remind that Augustine had moved from Manichaeism, through skepticism and Neoplatonism, to Christianity. This implies that the formation of Augustine's thought/theology is not simply located in a response to his early experience of oedipal conflict, but an evolving process of his faith and knowledge which are profoundly related to the social, cultural, historical, political, and religious contexts of his time.

Moreover, Freudian scholars have exclusively examined Augustine's personality and his experiences with reference to a particular period in childhood (the "oedipal" period). For this reason, they have neglected the exploration of the influences of Augustine's experiences and events that occurred before or after that time. They have also tended to have a muted appreciation of the ongoing interaction between Augustine and others/(Other) after his childhood. This implies that Freudian interpretations are not sufficient for explaining the life-long effects of conversion on Augustine's relationships with himself, others, and the divine for facilitating psychological development and spiritual maturity.

Augustine's Conversion, Crisis, and the Unification of His Divided Self

Psychologists of religion have viewed Augustine's conversion as a progressive and regenerative phenomenon that resolves an emotional crisis through the unification of the divided self. They suggest that Augustine's conversion occurred during and after a period of stress, despair, and even crisis. For example, William James proposes Augustine's conversion as "a classic example" of religious change. James characterizes Augustine as a morbid-minded person. More specifically, he elaborates on Augustine in light of "the psychological basis of the twice-born character" which "seems to be a certain discordancy heterogeneity in the native temperament of the subject, an incompletely unified moral and intellectual constitution."[40]

From a perspective of psychology of religion, James views Augustine's conversion as a psychological process of unifying his divided self. For James, during this unifying process, Augustine's interior world was a battle-ground for what he felt "to be two deadly hostile selves, one actual, the other ideal" in light of self-loathing and self-despair.[41] As such, James depicts Augustine as a sick soul and introduces him as the first of several typical cases of discordant personality, with melancholy in the form of self-condemnation and sense of sin:

---

40. James, *Religious Experience*, 167–68.
41. Ibid., 171.

> You all remember his half-pagan, half-Christian bringing up at [Thagaste and in] Carthage, his emigration to Rome and Milan, his adoption of Manicheism and subsequent skepticism, and his restless search for truth and purity of life; and finally how, distracted by the struggle between the two souls in his breast, and ashamed of his own weakness of will, when so may others whom he knew and knew of had thrown off the shackles of sensuality and dedicated themselves to chastity and the higher life, he heard a voice in the garden say, "*Sume, lege*" (take and read), and opening the Bible at random, saw the text, "not in chambering and wantonness," etc., which seemed directly sent to his address, and laid the inner storm to rest forever. Augustine's psychological genius has given an account of the trouble of having a divided self which has never been surpassed.[42]

For James, Augustine's conversion involved an interior transformation from the divided self to the integration of the self in relation to his experience with the divine ("a More"). This means that Augustine's conversion experience enabled him to enter into a (psychological) process for remedying his inner incompleteness and for reducing his inner discord; that is, during his transformation process, Augustine shifted from the state of storm, stress, and inconsistency to the state of firmness, stability, and equilibrium.

James contributes by advancing the approach of psychology of religion to Augustine's conversion as a conflict resolution in his profound experience of interior transformation ("twice born") through his inner communion with the Other. Consequently, he notes,

> Saint Augustine . . . emerged into the smooth waters of inner unity and peace, and I shall next ask you to consider more closely some of the peculiarities of the process of unification. . . . It brings a characteristic sort of relief; and never such extreme relief as when it is cast into the religious mould. Happiness! [H]appiness! [R]eligion is only one of the ways in which men gain that gift. Easily, permanently, and successfully, it often transforms the most intolerable misery into the profoundest and most enduring happiness.[43]

As contemporary scholars of Augustine's religious change, W. Paul Elledge and Donald Capps basically agree with the statement

---

42. Ibid., 171–72.
43. Ibid., 175.

that Augustine's conversion is an effort to resolve the dividedness of his self through the experience of the divine. From an extended way, in "Embracing Augustine," Elledge views Augustine's conversion as a transforming process for unifying his divided self, for reconciling to his previous disrupted relationships with others (e.g., Monica and his unnamed friend), and for embracing the divine. He accepts James' argument that conversion is a satisfactory response to the threat of the disintegration of the inner self, while acknowledging the Freudian interpretation that conversion was in part an effort to resolve an oedipal conflict. Based on these Jamesian and Freudian legacies, he hypothesizes that conversion partially results from the operation of unconscious forces in combination with manipulation by other persons. Following James, Elledge characterizes Augustine as a classic incarnation of the divided will.[44] He insists that Augustine's conversion experience enabled him to change a sense of his diffusion, division and fragmentation into a sense of his order and integration, wholeness and inner harmony.[45] Elledge notes, "On this complex identity, conversion works to revolutionize and stabilize, radically to alter and quietly to preserve established life patterns in slightly readjusted modes. The process of conversion takes Augustine from restraint through renunciation and release into a repossession which includes an escape hatch, i.e., from the closed embrace of mundane attachments into God's open one that neither empties itself nor ceases by its openness to embrace."[46]

Elledge proposes the embrace motif to link Augustine's relations with Monica and his unnamed friend to the conversion experience. For Elledge, the word *embrace* captures the very ambivalent nature of Augustine's relationships with others. Elledge insists that in Augustine's case, to be embraced means, by and large, to be held back, restrained, and controlled; accordingly, embraces are imprisoning and emasculating. Yet, not to be embraced means to be ignored, abandoned, and betrayed. Whether tendered or withheld, invited or rejected, embraces are not simply experiences of joy; rather, they are associated, in Augustine's own experiences, with pain and wounding. For Elledge, Augustine wrestled with his two life-shaping embraces—one with his mother; one with his unnamed friend—before engaging in his final struggle with

---

44. Elledge, "Augustine," 81.
45. Ibid., 74. See Allison, "Empirical Studies," 24.
46. Elledge, "Augustine," 81–82.

and his surrender to God's embrace.[47] Elledge reads Augustine's conversion experience as developing from earlier vexed relationships, particularly those with his mother Monica and the unnamed friend, and as reflecting the reconciling transformation, or sublimation of these relationships. These relations involve two major figures in his garden experience (*conf.* 8.7.16–8.12.30): Continence, the woman who beckons to him from across the garden, and Alypius, Augustine's lifelong friend. Elledge demonstrates dynamic parallels between Monica and Continence; and between the unnamed friend, whose death caused Augustine tormenting grief (4.4.7–9), and Alypius, who was with him throughout his conversion experience (8.8.19–8.12.30).

Like David Burrell, Elledge describes Monica's prominent role in Augustine's conversion process positively, although he comments that Monica, in part, functions as "manipulating and controlling" within the mother-son relationship. For Elledge, Monica's tears for Augustine (3.11.19–3.12.21) simultaneously beckon and chastise, summon and ward off, invite a consoling embrace and dare one to try it. They did "recreate [her] son, make him anew"; accordingly, her tears led Augustine to "become spiritually engendering, ontologically regenerative."[48] In this sense, Elledge regards Monica's dream of the wooden rule (3.11.19) as a revelation of Augustine's surrender to "an embracing merger," which will undo all the estrangements, large and small, that have occurred between them, in one massive capitulation. He also considers Monica's dream of the wooden rule as an invitation to Augustine to the Christian faith of his mother: "That Augustine *will* join his mother [and] will embrace her faith."[49]

Elledge emphasizes a dynamic link between the mother-son relationship and the God-self relationship in terms of the embrace motif, although the God-self relationship is not merely reducible to the mother-son relationship. For Elledge, Augustine came to God in and through Monica, and her embrace served as a mediating channel to God and God's embrace. As such, Augustine's conversion experience was engaged in not only reconciliation to his mother, but also reconciliation to God. Elledge writes, "Augustine salvages something of his identity and autonomy by moving *through* Monican arms that contain,

---

47. Ibid., 75–81.
48. Ibid., 78. See Fenn, "Magic," 81.
49. Elledge, "Augustine," 78.

Getting Insights

extend, and point to seek the God beyond mortal fastening. The Monican embrace finally serves as a kind of conduit or channel, containing the son passing through her and even directing him, but unable to hold except in passage, possessing and surrendering at the same time."[50] Consequently, Elledge asserts that Augustine's conversion is a satisfactory response in order to integrate his divided self, to overcome his earlier vexed relationships with others, and to embrace the divine in light of repairing fragmented wholeness and becoming "a Romantic."[51]

From a more specific and extended view, Donald Capps takes up William James' observation that Augustine is a classic example of the discordant personality or divided self, and employs E. R. Dodds' article on Augustine's "spiritual maladjustment"—in order to explore the psychological bases, especially parental, for Augustine's discordant personality and to evaluate the effectiveness of Augustine's efforts to overcome the discordancy through his personal religious conversion. Like James, Capps characterizes Augustine in light of the psychological basis of the twice-born character. This implies that Augustine's early personality was discordant and heterogeneous in his native temperament, "an incompletely unified moral and intellectual constitution."[52] Capps explains this heterogeneous personality as "the result of the inheritance of the traits of character of incompatible and antagonistic ancestors" that are supposed to be preserved alongside each other.[53] For Capps, Augustine's emotional distress played an important role "in precipitating [his] mental rearrangements" through the resolution of his self's dividedness. Following James, Capps identifies the characteristic of Augustine's conversion as "hope, happiness, security, and resolve."[54]

Importantly, Capps asks why Augustine's self was disrupted and how his personality became "heterogeneous," commenting that James did not sufficiently speculate the cause of Augustine's divided self. Capps

---

50. Ibid., 86.

51. Elledge says, "If to be a 'Romantic,' means to be a man acutely aware of being caught in an existence that denies him the fullness for which he craves, to feel that he is defined by his tension toward something else, by his capacity for faith, for hope, for longing, to think of himself as a wanderer seeking a country that is always distant, but made ever-present to him by the quality of the love [and/or imagination] that 'groans' for it, then Augustine has imperceptibly become a 'Romantic'" (ibid., 87).

52. Capps, "Divided Self," 552.

53. Ibid., 553–54. See James, *Religious Experience*, 169.

54. Capps, "Divided Self," 558–59.

agrees with Dodds' statement that the origins of Augustine's divided self are to be looked for in his family history.[55] In other words, the division of Augustine's self was due to the fact that he was raised by parents of very different personalities and conflicting worldviews: "Augustine had the misfortune to be the fruit of 'this ill-assorted union. . . . It was his tragic destiny to combine in a small and sickly body the warring souls of both his parents and a fastidious intellect which served each soul in turn."[56]

In fact, for Capps, Augustine underwent "the warring souls of both his parents" until his religious experience in a garden of Milan.[57] Through this personal religious experience in Milan, Augustine resolved his heterogeneous conflicts of two souls, thus, he unified his wavering and divided self. As a result, he asserts that Augustine's conversion is a valuable response in order to overcome his discordancy through his personal religious experience.

As noted above, Jamesian scholars have regarded Augustine's conversion experience as a satisfactory and positive response to the state of his tension and inner conflict. In doing so, they contribute to understanding the process of Augustine's conversion by advancing their psychological approaches to Augustine's conversion as a conflict resolution in his profound experience of interior transformation ("twice born") through his inner embrace with the divine, which entails a process of unifying his divided self.

As such, when we attempt to understand Augustine's conversion, these Jamesian studies encourage us to look at how Augustine's conversion experience was involved in a (psychological) process to overcome his inner discord or division (the sickness of the soul); that is, during his transforming process, how Augustine moved from a state of storm, stress, and inconsistency to a state of firmness, stability, and equilibrium. In particular, while preserving the existence or activity of the religious subject—the divine, the sacred, or God—in the process of human transformation, these studies provide us with insights into how Augustine's psychological distress or crisis had compelled him to think about what was the real problem in his life as well as to enter into his

---

55. Ibid., 551–52, 559. See Dodds, "Augustine's *Confessions*," 44–45.
56. Capps, "Divided Self," 561.
57. Ibid., 560–64.

quests for knowing himself and knowing the divine in light of the interaction of the experience of the self and the experience of the divine.

Augustine's Conversion and His Mental Development

Post-Freudian scholars have primarily examined Augustine's conversion experience in light of the process of self-becoming through his mental development and progressive maturity.[58] In doing so, they have emphasized pre-oedipal experiences, shame, and narcissism to interpret Augustine's conversion experience. Post-Freudian interpretations explain Augustine's *Confessions* as a record of the process of self-becoming through developmental and progressive maturity rather than a record of the pathological personality.

Paula Fredriksen significantly suggests that scholars should interpret the themes of the pre-oedipal years in Augustine's *Confessions*.[59] In other words, while repudiating Freudian studies of the *Confessions*, Fredriksen proposes a narcissistic interpretation of Augustine partly as an alternative to Freudian Oedipal interpretations with respect to

---

58. As post-Freudian psychoanalysts, Donald W. Winnicott and Heinz Kohut reject Freud's drive/instinct model by using a relational understanding of human development. Winnicott and Kohut move psychoanalytic thinking and practice from a "one-person psychology," which focuses on the internal, unconscious life of the isolated individual, toward a "two-person psychology" in which a person's internal world is always understood to be a reaction to current relational experience (e.g., one's interaction with a mother or with an analyst) (Schlauch, *Faithful Companioning*, 72; see 55–72). Both Winnicott and Kohut emphasize the pre-oedipal line of human development—the interdependent mother-infant dyad.

59. From a psychological and historical perspective, Paula Fredriksen gives an insight into the exploration of Augustine's conversion experience in light of narcissistic personality and human development, and leads us to examine the sufficient historical data for facilitating a more accurate and coherent explanation of Augustine's conversion (see "Augustine and His Analyst," 224). Like Fredriksen, some scholars— P. Brown, L. J. Daly, M. R. Miles, and D. Jonte-Pace—spell out and emphasize the psychological variables at work in Augustine's conversion process. These scholars have examined the historical facts or circumstances of Augustine's conversion in the fourth century as well as the source of religious experience in the relationship between infant and mother or the pre-oedipal dynamics of the infantile psyche. This means that during the description of Augustine's conversion, they have paid attention to the emotional/affective dimension as well as the intellectual/cognitive dimension (see Brown, *Augustine*, 163; Daly, "Augustine's *Confessions*," 196). In this way, Daly claims that Augustine's conversion is neither a neurotic product in the classical Freudian perspective nor "an idiosyncratic process" in the perspective of traditional historians (ibid., 192).

the historical evidence. She hypothesizes that "Augustine manifests the conflicts of the narcissistic personality."[60] While emphasizing Monica's relentless pursuit of her son (which she accepts as historically true) in light of the mother-son relationship, Fredriksen characterizes Augustine as a narcissist, who deeply experienced an inability to achieve true object-love and a crushing need for the approval of others. For Fredriksen, Augustine underwent a "troubled separation/individuation process."[61] Fredriksen pays attention to Augustine's narcissism, which is related to Augustine's attitudes toward sexuality. She asserts that in the matter of sexuality, Augustine came to critique his own narcissism; he came to "see sex as pure narcissistic gratification, self-serving *cupiditas*."[62] Consequently, Fredriksen notes, "He cannot truly love; his assessment of the nature of sexual love is shaped by his experience of only enjoying a narcissistic gratification from the person loving him."[63]

By accepting and advancing Paula Fredriksen's preeminent suggestion of a narcissistic reading of the *Confessions*, Donald Capps has interpreted Augustine's conversion in the *Confessions* in terms of the pre-oedipal experiences, self-reproach, narcissistic injury, and a sense of shame. Capps in "Parabolic Events in Augustine's Autobiography" describes Augustine's conversion experience as a process of self-disclosure or self-becoming, which indicates a sign of developmental and progressive maturity.[64] For Capps, shame is related to the whole self whereas guilt is related to the acts of transgression: "Guilt can be externalized, while shame is totally self-involving."[65]

---

60. Fredriksen, "Augustine and His Analyst," 219.
61. Ibid., 220–21.
62. Ibid., 221.
63. Ibid., 222.
64. Capps, "Parabolic Events," 260–69.
65. Ibid., 264. See *Depleted Self*, 74–76; "Self-Reproach," 585.

Getting Insights

Influenced by Heinz Kohut's self psychology,[66] Capps characterizes shame as a sense of inner isolation or "tragic estrangement."[67] For Capps, shame or narcissistic injury is rooted in a lack of parental empathy toward a child; it involves one's experience of disconnection with oneself, others, and the divine. Indeed, shame is a threat to one's basic disposition of trust and it constricts the shamed person within the "narrow life-world." Capps notes, "Shame is a response to our failure to live up an ideal that we have held for ourselves and that shame is therefore the experience of a self-deficiency. Even where this ideal was implanted originally by a parent, it is now self-owned, and thus the shame is a reaction to the failure to live up to one's own self-ideals. We are disappointed in ourselves. We have once again let ourselves down, and we are puzzled and angry at ourselves: 'Why do I do this to myself?'"[68]

Capps asserts that the shame experience could be a seed of "disenchantment" with the world. This means, this shame experience is profoundly alienating; it determines that the shamed person will never return to the place or setting where this shameful experience occurred: "Shame experiences are strangely out of place."[69] For Capps, as a shamed person tends to hide from others, he or she also tends to hide from God. However, this shamed person could be healed in empathic relationships with the divine and with others.[70] This implies that overcoming one's shame experiences means re-establishing one's relationships with the divine and others.

Capps states that in Augustine's case, his self-reproach was rooted in the dynamics of his shameful events over his lifetime. Unlike Freudian

---

66. Heinz Kohut defines *the self* as an enduring personality structure, which serves as "a center of initiative and recipient of impressions" as well as "the center of the individual's psychological universe" (*Restoration*, 99, 311; see 93–139). According to Kohut, "*selfobjects* are which we experience as part of our self" (Kohut and Wolf, "Disorders of the Self," 414). For Kohut, the self-selfobject relationship determines the health and vitality of the self. Selfhood means essentially being-in-relationship (*Analysis Cure*, 50, 61). Kohut describes his concept of *selfobject experience* by using the three narcissistic transferences of *mirroring* (the need for acknowledgement and acceptance), *idealizing* (the need to admire and merge with an omnipotent selfobject), and *twinship/merger* (the need to feel a degree of alikeness with other people) (192–207; see *Restoration*, 37–56, 105–25).

67. Capps, *Depleted Self*, 71–84.

68. Ibid., 72.

69. Ibid., 77; see "Scourge of Shame," 79.

70. Capps, *Depleted Self*, 27–37, 86–100; "Parabolic Events," 266–69.

psychologists who have viewed Augustine's conversion experience as an excessive preoccupation with guilt, and therefore as evidence of an obsessional personality structure, Capps understands his conversion as a progressive and mature process in light of the dynamics of shame. For Capps, in the *Confessions*, Augustine's self-reproach is the effect of his decision to expose the shameful state of his inner self to the divine and to his readers.[71]

Capps asserts that in his *Confessions*, Augustine's self-disclosure is central for understanding the process of his transformation experience. For Capps, there are five self-disclosive events of Augustine in the *Confessions*: "a) the pear-stealing episode, b) the death of Augustine's unnamed friend, c) his escape from his mother through an act of deception, d) the famous garden experience, and e) the mystical vision he and his mother shared shortly before her death."[72] These episodes basically demonstrate that Augustine had struggled with his profound sense of shame. In recollecting these experiences, Augustine came face to face with his shameful self. This process of his self-examination was painful but absolutely necessary in order to re-experience his shame through memory and narrative and to open himself to God and to his readers. For Capps, during the description of his main life history, Augustine raised a critical autobiographical question, "What has become of me?" Augustine's answer was something like this: "I am becoming a person who, in disclosing shame, is open to God."[73] More specifically, Capps writes,

> Augustine understands that to hide himself from God, out of a sense of shame and exposure, is *to hide God from himself*. . . . While Adams sought to hide his shame from God, Augustine dares to reveal his shame through his *Confessions* because he perceives that, through such self-disclosure, *God* will appear to *him*. The problem with concealing one's shame is not that one thereby hides from God, but that one hides God from oneself. By forcing himself to confront his shame, Augustine opens himself to the presence of God [and to his readers].[74]

---

71. Capps, "Parabolic Events," 263.
72. Ibid., 262.
73. Ibid., 262, 268.
74. Ibid., 267–68.

In consideration of Augustine's shame and his self-disclosure, Capps portrays Augustine as a "transformed narcissist." Whereas Freudian psychologists are concerned with oedipal issues, which focus on the ambivalent relationships between mother, father, and child, and on issues of difference, power, competition, and sexuality, Capps emphasizes pre-oedipal issues, which involve the more primitive or primordial relationship between mother and child, and center around the child's needs for emphatic response.[75] Following Kohut's view, Capps describes that the narcissist is manifestly unable to respond to demands for a change from narcissism to object love. He characterizes "untransformed narcissism" which involves "an inability to relate to the external world, a tendency toward emotional isolation and a resistance to the claims of others."[76] For Capps, there are the two crucial elements of a narcissistic structure: "a grandiose self image . . . and a powerfully idealized parent image."[77] Capps insists that one's transformation of narcissism usually occurs in the middle of adulthood. During the process of this transformation, the narcissism of exhibitionism and grandiose fantasies is replaced with a more mature narcissism, which consists of the following basic features: 1) personal creativity; 2) empathy;[78] 3) acknowledgement of the finitude of the self; 4) capacity for humor; and 5) wisdom.

From a self psychological perspective, Capps attempts to show "a narcissistic reading of the *Confessions*"—in order to articulate Augustine's struggles with his sense of self-depletion, shame, and narcissistic injury. He notes that "Augustine presents himself in the *Confessions* as a self-acknowledged narcissist."[79] Whereas Freudian psychologist Paul Rigby focuses on Augustine's relationships with his father (Patricius) in light of the oedipal conflict and guilt, Capps emphasizes more

---

75. Capps, "Augustine as Narcissist," 121.

76. Ibid., 126.

77. Ibid., 123.

78. Heinz Kohut describes empathy as "vicarious introspection," which is "the capacity to think and feel oneself into the inner life of another person. It is our lifelong ability to experience what another person experiences, though usually, and appropriately, to an attenuated degree" (*Analysis Cure*, 82; Lee and Martin, *Psychotherapy*, 105–17).

79. Capps, "Augustine as Narcissist," 121.

Augustine's relationship with his mother (Monica) in light of shame and narcissistic personality.[80] In doing so, he points out,

> [The *Confessions*] provides the basic rationale for Augustine's autobiographical project, includes patent narcissistic themes, including the powerfully idealized parental image (God as one who sees our innermost thoughts and feelings but who is also loved and longed for); renunciation of the grandiose self ("I am a thing displeasing to myself"); and narcissistic injury in the form of shame ("the abyss of man's conscience lies naked" and "I feel shame for myself"). A combination of interpretive methods could thus be employed to explore the claim that Augustine is a narcissistic personality.[81]

According to Capps, it is not difficult to find evidence of Augustine's narcissistic characteristics in the *Confessions*. Indeed, Augustine's personal stories with others (e.g., the pear-stealing episode, his jocular behavior prior to his unnamed friend's death, or the dismissal of his common-law wife), which had preceded his garden experience in 386, were inherently narcissistic; these narratives commonly consisted of "experiences involving narcissistic injury, or threats to personal self-esteem" through humiliation, disapproval, and embarrassment. For Capps, the transformations of Augustine's narcissistic injury occurred in his middle of adulthood when he engaged in writing the *Confessions*.[82]

As a result, Capps asserts that Augustine's conversion was "a life-changing event" in light of self-reproach, shame, and the transformation of narcissism.[83] For Capps, Augustine's conversion experience led him to overcome the immobilizing and despiriting influence of the shame, which was reflective of his earlier isolated life-style. Further, it enabled Augustine to make constructive use of his shame for his new life in relationship with the divine and others (although he might not become "an unambiguously transformed narcissist").[84]

As self psychological scholars, Volney Gay, Andrés G. Niño, and Sandra L. Dixon basically support and advance the idea that Augustine's conversion experience is a transformative process of self-exposure or

---

80. Ibid., 123; see "Self-Reproach," 589.
81. Capps, "Augustine as Narcissist," 123.
82. Ibid., 121–27.
83. Capps, "Self-Reproach," 586.
84. Capps, "Augustine as Narcissist," 125–27.

self-becoming, which involves a progressive maturity by overcoming a sense of shame and narcissistic injury (self-isolation) and by establishing empathic relationships with others and the divine (self-esteem). In "Augustine: The Reader as Selfobject," Gay focuses on pre-oedipal experiences/anxieties, shame, and narcissism to interpret Augustine's conversion experience.[85] According to Gay, there are two types of anxieties: 1) oedipal anxieties are reflected in "triadic relationships between distinct actors: mother, father, and child," which involve issues of difference, power, and competition; in contrast, 2) pre-oedipal anxieties are deeply related to the dyadic relationship between mother and child, which involve the child's need for empathic response in the form of assurance, reassurance, and positive approval. In other words, whereas oedipal anxieties have symbolically to do with fear of external attacks on one's body, particularly treasured body parts like the eyes and the genitals ("castration anxiety"), pre-oedipal anxieties emerge as internal attacks upon the self through unbearable feelings of worthlessness, which has the effect of dissolving or hopelessly fragmenting the inner self ("fragmentation anxiety"—the fear of going to be pieces).[86] Gay repudiates Freudian oedipal interpretations of the *Confessions*, which have overemphasized issues of sexual conflict in light of the oedipal complex and anxiety. However, like Capps, Gay pays attention to the psychological importance to Augustine's purpose and his act of writing the *Confessions*. He regards Augustine's *Confessions* as "a *covert* plea for selfobject relationships" with both God and his human readers, which involves a need for affectionate resonance from God and his readers as well as a lament and protest over their absence and loss.[87]

From a Kohutian perspective, Gay looks at how Augustine had tried to overcome his shame experiences and pre-oedipal anxieties in the *Confessions*; in this vein, he raises a question, "How could [Augustine] control himself and how channel his skills in ways that would restrain himself and keep his feet on the ground?"[88] Gay contends that Augustine's unending self-analysis and his unending complaints

---

85. According to Gay, "pre-oedipal theory systematically investigates the pathways that lead from relatively diffused, partial selves, to an adult sense of continuity and coherence" ("Augustine," 70).

86. Ibid., 65–67. See Kohut, *Restoration*, 104.

87. Gay, "Augustine," 65, 69.

88. Ibid., 69.

about his moral failings derived from his repression of selfobject needs. However, for Gay, during the writing of the *Confessions*, Augustine confronted his narcissistic injuries and his pre-oedipal anxieties and struggled with his sense of self-fragmentation; as such, he made a decision to open his painful conditions of incoherence and he remarkably moved himself to be related to the divine (the Selfobject) and others (selfobjects). Consequently, Gay writes, "An extraordinarily talented boy [Augustine] searched for other persons whom he could idealize and then trust with that task. In Kohut's terms, he needed to find suitable selfobjects. Hence he looked to Faustus, then Ambrose, and finally God, the most ideal of fathers. If it is God, not I, who commands such powers, then surely God will hear my confession, 'because you first willed that I should confess to you, O Lord my God. For you are gracious, your mercy endures for ever.'"[89]

In the same way, within the framework of Heinz Kohut's self psychology, Andrés G. Niño in "Restoration of the Self: A Therapeutic Paradigm from Augustine's *Confessions*" depicts Augustine's conversion experience as a process of self-becoming in terms of a transcending self, empathic relationships, and transformed narcissism.[90] Niño agrees with Peter Brown's view that "the writing of the *Confessions* was an act of therapy of [self-examination]."[91] As such, he states, "Augustine's personal story has been recognized as a pioneering self-analysis and a forerunner of modern psychology and existentialism. . . . The *Confessions*, written ten years after Augustine's conversion, documents a revision of his life at a critical juncture in the form of a dialogue between the self, God, and the reader."[92] This means that the *Confessions* contains Augustine's relational dialogue between Augustine and God, and between Augustine and his readers—an appeal for an empathic response from God and human readers.[93] Importantly, Niño focuses on the psychological and transcendental dimensions of the restoration of the self which relates to a human need for the inner experience of the divine: "Transcending one's self through a relation to that Being constitutes an-

89. Ibid.

90. Niño, "Restoration," 9.

91. Brown, *Augustine*, 158. See Weintraub, *Value of the Individual*, 26.

92. Niño, "Restoration," 9.

93. Ibid., 16. See Capps, "Parabolic Events," 268; Gay, "Augustine," 65, 69; TeSelle, "Augustine as Client," 93; Weintraub, *Value of the Individual*, 22.

other dimension of human experience with a potential for cohesiveness at various levels of personality functioning."[94] In consideration of the transcending self and transformed narcissism, Niño asserts that during his conversion experience, Augustine was involved in the process of restoration, though not completed, which was relevant to a movement from a sense of emptiness and fragmentation to a sense of coherence and meaning: "By reconstructing and organizing the narrative of his own experience [in the *Confessions*], he sets the foundations for a new ideal of personality that includes individuality, introspection, and the capacity for transcendence.... Throughout *Confessions*, we see Augustine gradually making the move from living by the pleasure principle, a man enjoying 'a truant's freedom' (III, 3), to participating in a deeper dimension of life which happened because he yearned for both the truth and a new way of being."[95]

In a more advanced way, Sandra L. Dixon in *Augustine: The Scattered and Gathered Self* describes Augustine's conversion story in light of shame and narcissism—"Shame appears to be a large part of this representation of the moment of his conversion."[96] Dixon regards Augustine's conversion as "change" which involves the unity of the scattered self as well as the healing of the narcissistic injury ("damaged grandiosity").[97] For Dixon, through this process of change, Augustine's self was integrated or gathered; it "allows him to find stability and continuity in his life."[98] Dixon considers Augustine's experiences of floggings at school in his boyhood (and his parents' lack of sympathy) as the origins of his shame and narcissistic injury. She emphasizes the influence of Augustine's experiences of beatings, damaged grandiosity, and a sense of deep shame on his personality and mental development.[99]

Dixon asserts that Augustine's sense of shame and damaged grandiosity led to a lack of coherence for himself and for others in which he felt sorrow, hostility, and coldness. She uses the metaphor of a vertical split in the psyche to interpret Augustine's personality and life story. For Dixon, the word *split* refers to "a strong division" of the person;

---

94. Niño, "Restoration," 9.
95. Ibid., 9, 12.
96. Dixon, *Augustine*, 133.
97. Ibid., 121.
98. Ibid. See Browning, "Psychoanalytic Interpretation," 142.
99. Dixon, *Augustine*, 56; see 54–57, 131–32.

the *vertical split* indicates "a division in the person's consciousness."[100] This vertical split appears most distinctly in persons who in one way or another lead a double life. In consideration of the concept of the vertical split, Dixon depicts Augustine as a shamed person who has a fragmented inner self and has an inability to relate to the divine and others.

While acknowledging Kohut's concept of *many-ness* (the fragmented self) and *one-ness* (the cohesive self), Dixon pays attention to Augustine's use of the symbolism of *the many* and *the One*, which he drew from both Neoplatonic and biblical sources, and in particular on his specification of it in his image of the "scattered and gathered self" in the *Confessions*.[101] For Dixon, the theme of the scattered self and the many focuses on the status of the self in isolation or estrangement. This implies that an isolated person in his or her earthly life is scattered among other persons in light of the fragmentation of the soul. On the other hand, the theme of the gathered self and the One emphasizes the status of the self in relation to the divine and others. This implies that a relational person is (or relational persons are) gathered toward the divine in light of the unity of the soul (or souls) for inner healing. Using this theme of the many (*many-ness*) and the One (*one-ness*), Dixon describes Augustine's transforming process which moves from self-isolation or self-reproach to self-relation or self-esteem.[102] In emphasizing Augustine's theme of the many and the One, Dixon suggests a psychological study of mysticism which illustrates Augustine's religious experience:

> A person who has had a mystical experience, whatever one may believe about the divinity or humanity of its source, would come away from the experience with a very strong magnet for idealizing. . . . Augustine's experience with Monica at Ostia can thus be seen to have reinforced the shift in his self from reliance on grandiosity to reliance on the idealizing pole of the unconscious core of his being. This interpretation in no way precludes the possibility that they did touch in a moment of total absorption "eternal wisdom which abides beyond all things." The mystics' claims that such experience strengthens the psyche could

---

100. Ibid., 122.
101. Ibid., 24–37.
102. Ibid., 135.

be understood in part through the psychological concept of idealizing.[103]

As a result, Dixon concludes that Augustine's conversion in book eight of the *Confessions* and his mystical experience with his mother at Ostia in book nine did not result in regression from adulthood, as some Freudian psychological interpreters would have it. Rather, these experiences enabled Augustine to overcome his inner division (his vertical split) and his narcissistic injury, to maintain an effectively changed balance between grandiosity and idealization, and to establish a new life in relation to the divine and others.

Similarly, from an object relations perspective,[104] William B. Parsons in "St. Augustine: 'Common Man' or 'Intuitive Psychologist'?" elaborates on Augustine's conversion as a process for healing through self-exposure and self-examination in light of transformed relation, the changed representation of God, and enhanced creativity. He portrays Augustine as "a 'great man,' an intuitive psychologist who fashioned a religious therapeutic system."[105] In consideration of Capps' concepts of shame and self-disclosure, Parsons asserts that Augustine came to be transformed by exposing himself toward God: "The process of disclo-

---

103. Ibid., 160.

104. *Object Relations Theory* is a strand of post-Freudian psychoanalytic theory, which explores the nature and origins of interpersonal relationships or "object relations" rather than instinctual drives. An "object" is the other, that is, a person from the external environment that is internally and psychologically significant to the person. In this vein, object relations refers to the feelings, images, memories, and attitudes that have something to do with a "relationship" with this or that object, usually with significant caretakers or persons in one's life. Object relations theory places an emphasis than did Freud on the influence of early relationships with primary caregivers on personality formation as well as adult interpersonal experiences (Clair, *Human Relationships*, 7; Greenberg and Mitchell, *Object Relations*, 13–14; Hamilton, *Self and Others*, 13). In object relations theory, the term *transition* refers to a state of changing (Horton, *Solace*, 18). According to Donald Winnicott, the term *transitional space* refers to "an intermediate area of *experiencing*" that exists between subjectivity and objectivity, between fantasy and reality, between the internal and the external, and between "me" and "not-me (*Playing and Reality*, 2–3, 107). Based on Winnicott's concept of transitional space, Paul Pruyser positions the "illusionistic world" between the autistic world and the realistic world (*Play*, 64–65). The term *illusion* is derived from the Latin *ludere*, which means to play (ibid., 68, 165). For Pruyser, religion is a kind of "illusion processing" in the illusionistic world in which one may develop one's capacity for play, creativity, imagination and symbolization. Through creative play in the illusionistic world, one may experience the holy or the mystery (ibid., 152–78).

105. Parsons, "St. Augustine," 156.

sure... is not merely the guilty confession of one tempted by instinctual demands yet fearful of super-ego condemnation. For Augustine, one *becomes* oneself by speaking to God.... This speaking or confessing entailed not simply a recognition of one's past but an active catharsis of it."[106] Following Peter Brown's understanding of the *Confessions*, Parsons views Augustine's *Confessions* as a therapy, which involves "a turning about of the heart, a purging of the inner eye."[107] In that sense, he states, "the aim of this catharsis [through the therapy] was not to abandon strong feeling or even repress them, but rather to transform them, to direct them more profitably through insight into their nature. In this context, then, confession becomes an earnest attempt to be healed through a process of self-exposure and self-examination in which one can isolate elements of recollection, insight, catharsis, renunciation/structure building and sublimation."[108]

Like Woollcott and Niño, Parsons emphasizes the creative dimension of Augustine's conversion rather than the regressive psychopathological dimension. For Parsons, Augustine had reconstructed and transformed his earlier conflicts into his strengths in adulthood. In other words, Augustine felt inner conflicts, but he used his Christian beliefs to investigate his conflicts, not defend against them. Parsons writes, "The resolution of unconscious intrapsychic conflict following religious conversion results in a shift in psychic economy with resultant greater unity and integration, and with the subsequent sense of liberation and may lead to more creative endeavor in gifted persons."[109]

For Parsons, Augustine's conversion must be qualified with respect to the issue of the therapeutic use of his beliefs and religion which

106. Ibid., 171.

107. Ibid. Brown states, "The writing of the *Confessions* was an act of therapy of [self-examination]" (*Augustine*, 158).

108. Parsons, "St. Augustine," 171.

109. Ibid., 177. See Woollcott, "Creativity and Religious Experience," 279–80. Although he is not primarily a post-Freudian, but a Freudian, Philip Woollcott attempts to surpass a Freudian tendency toward infantilizing and pathologizing Augustine and his life. Woollcott analyzes Augustine, found in the *Confessions*, focusing upon his creative abilities to resolve inner conflicts. He views Augustine's continuing childhood tension from his oedipal conflicts as a force for his creative breakthrough and change in adulthood rather than a decisive factor of his regressive pathology (ibid., 283). For Woollcott, Augustine's creative conversion enabled him to feel a sense of liberation as well as to establish his "great theological works and the writing of his *Confessions*" (ibid., 280–82).

relates to the highly elaborated intellectual aspect of Augustine's God Representation (God as "inner physician," etc.). Parsons casts doubt on Freud's assertion that the God Representation of all individuals is based solely on the Oedipus complex and subject to the return of the repressed. Influenced by Ana-Maria Rizzuto, Parsons regards the God Representation as "a 'work of art' overdetermined on a variety of levels, being influenced by culture at large, incorporating sexual and non-sexual elements, pre-oedipal as well as oedipal developmental considerations, representational/ideational components, and subject to the 'evolution' implied in the epigenetic view of the life-cycle."[110] According to Parsons, in the Freudian perspective, Ambrose was "at best nothing more than a consolation for Augustine's masculine narcissism after the fact of conversion." Unlike the classical psychological interpretation, Parsons emphasizes the preeminent role of Ambrose in Augustine's transforming process, especially in the new formation of his God representation. Parsons writes, "Ambrose was to serve as a [transference-] Father figure for Augustine, being able to secure his trust and hence easing of the unconscious ambivalence he felt toward Patricius. Further, Ambrose provided a kind of 'fatherly sponsor' for Augustine's emerging Christian identity. At the same time, Ambrose was to function as the mediator of new ideas that would radically alter Augustine's world views."[111] In consideration of the role of Ambrose, Parsons insists that through this conversion process, Augustine's God representations were positively changed *from* harsh, critical, and judging *to* forgiving, guiding, and healing; Augustine had eventually restored his sense of "basic trust" and his cohesiveness of the self.

Significantly, Parsons repudiates the Freudian view of Augustine's conversion to Christianity that "[Augustine's] Christianity was that of the common-man, i.e., born out of a need to escape from the hard truths of reality, based on the dynamics of the Oedipus complex and subject

---

110. Parsons, "St. Augustine," 173. See Rizzuto, *Birth*, 46. Ana-Maria Rizzuto contends that psychologically speaking, "God is a special [or illusory] transitional object" (ibid., 178). For Rizzuto, *the God representation*, like an image of mother or father, is a kind of transitional creation in transitional space (ibid., 177). The studies of the God Representation have contributed to understand not only the religious sphere of human affairs, but also the psychic life of all persons through their status as psychological objects within the representational world.

111. Parsons, "St. Augustine," 174.

to the enduring cycle of repetition and the return of the repressed."[112] From an object relations perspective, Parsons asserts that Augustine's conversion should be understood as a healing process through self-examination with respect to the interplay of transformed relation, the reconstructed representation of God, and enhanced creativity. He concludes,

> Augustine's conversion became the occasion through which he could start on the path to a new, *transformed* relation to his "Father." ... One could almost speak of Augustine's God Representation as displaying elements of the "wished-for" father: one who "punishes," yet does so out of love; who guides, leads, finds and forms in his image the lost and despondent "son." In return, Augustine is able to start putting aside his ambivalence by learning to "forgive" his Father, hence re-instituting the trust and love that characterizes a healthy, father/son relationship.... The benefits of such a "conversion" gave rise in Augustine to enhanced creativity.[113]

In a related vein, Kim Paffenroth in "Book Nine: The Emotional Heart of the *Confessions*" characterizes Augustine's conversion as change and continuity in light of his ability to relate to himself and others. Paffenroth emphasizes conversion to continuity rather than a simply static conversion itself. According to Paffenroth, "conversion is not the climatic, most difficult, or most important step: reconciling one's postconversion self with one's preconversion self is the real challenge, and the real measure of personal success, psychological integration, and new spiritual health."[114] Agreeing with Margaret R. Miles' evaluation of the *Confessions*, Paffenroth depicts Augustine's *Confessions* as "therapeutic [work] in a deep and ancient sense—diagnosis and healing of a sick and broken human nature."[115] While acknowledging "Augustine's *crisis* conversion"—his own spiritual death and rebirth within his relationships with the divine—in book eight of the *Confessions*, Paffenroth elucidates Augustine's transformative process in book nine, which in-

---

112. Ibid., 165.

113. Ibid., 177.

114. Paffenroth, "Book Nine," 152.

115. Ibid., 138. Miles insists, "The *Confessions* is primarily therapy in the Platonic sense of a methodical conversion from a 'misidentification of reality,' to recognition of the reality, the patterns of behavior, that has been implicitly but identified within one's most intimate and pressing experience" ("Infancy," 351).

volves his reconciling relationships with himself and others. In doing so, he examines how Augustine presents his friends, family, and the Manichees in his final autobiographical book nine in light of resolutions of distorted relationships with others and within himself. As such, he pays attention to the process of reconciling Augustine's postconversion self with his preconversion self. Whereas describing Augustine's preconversion self "as divided, conflicted, [and] alienated" in terms of a being split, Paffenroth describes Augustine's postconversion self as integrated, unified, and reconstructed in terms of a being in relationship.[116] While regarding book nine as "the real climax of *Confessions*," Paffenroth asserts that Augustine entered into his healing process, by speaking of his attitude toward their past sinful lives and selves; indeed, he resolved all his deep interpersonal issues with father, mother, friends, and even the Manichees.[117] This implies that Augustine coped with his painful past; he became a better adjusted, more faithful, or more normal person in light of the process of the constant reinvention of Augustine himself. As a result, Paffenroth insists that Augustine moved *from* the state of an injured narcissist who was unable to relate to others ("discontinuity") *to* the state of a transformed or retrieved narcissist who was able to relate to others ("continuity"): "Augustine has now learned how to love properly."[118] He notes,

> Augustine is not finally [an injured] narcissist, for he concludes and climaxes the autobiographical part of *Confessions* not with a story about himself, but with . . . stories about others. . . . [More specifically] in the profundity of his heart Augustine held a story which was not only his own but that of Monica, of Adeodatus, of Alypius, of Simplicianus, of Ambrose, of Nebridius, of Romanianus, [and] of the host of friends who had shared his experiences. . . . Augustine seems to have made a large amount of room for the other characters, and he treats them with concern and interest that goes beyond their effect on him or their place in his life. . . . Augustine's attachment and loyalty to his friends, his appreciation and love for his parents, and finally this even more difficult attitude of forgiveness and hope toward the Manichees together go a long way toward such a reconciliation.[119]

116. Paffenroth, "Book Nine," 147–53.
117. Ibid., 138; see 147, 150, 151.
118. Ibid., 147.
119. Ibid., 146, 150, 152.

As noted above, post-Freudian psychologists have viewed Augustine's conversion as an earnest effort to be healed through a process of self-exposure and self-examination, to overcome a sense of shame and pre-oedipal anxieties (self-isolation), and to promote loving relationships with others and the divine (self-esteem). In doing so, they contribute to an understanding of Augustine's *Confessions* as a record of the transformative process of self-becoming through developmental and progressive maturity rather than a record of abnormal and regressive psychopathology. Post-Freudian interpretations provide us insights into the interaction between Augustine's psychological development and his ongoing relationships with others/Other in the process of his conversion.

In sum, there is no common psychological definition of Augustine's conversion. Augustine's conversion has been regarded as regressive psychopathology, a process of unifying his divided self, or a part of his mental developmental process. On the whole, psychological studies of Augustine's conversion have primarily focused on his inner crisis, need, and mental development.

More specifically, Freudian scholars—D. Bakan; J. E. Dittes; E. R. Dodds; C. Kligerman; P. W. Pruyser; P. Rigby—have described Augustine's endless self-reproaches, his oedipal anxieties, his oedipal guilt, and his obsessive personality within Augustine's relationships with his father (Patricius) and with his mother (Monica) in light of triadic relationships between parents and child. They lead us to realize the importance of childhood, the unconscious, and the possibility of pathology in Augustine's conversion experience. Jamesian scholars—D. Capps; W. P. Elledge; W. James—have elucidated the correlation between one's emotional crisis, the unification of the divided self, and religious change in light of a progressive and regenerative phenomenon of Augustine's conversion. They help us to look at how Augustine's conversion resulted in conflict resolution through his inner transforming experience ("twice born") which was deeply related to the experience of the divine ("a More"). Post-Freudian scholars—D. Capps; S. L. Dixon; V. Gay; A. G. Niño; K. Paffenroth; W. B. Parsons—have emphasized Augustine's pre-oedipal experiences, his sense of shame, and his transformation of narcissism to interpret his conversion experience. They guide us to recognize that Augustine's conversion experience was not simply a single event, but a process of self-disclosure or self-becoming, which

Getting Insights

indicated a sign of developmental and progressive maturity rather than a sign of regressive pathology.

As such, these psychological studies of Augustine's conversion contribute by articulating the impact of personal factors (especially Augustine's psychological crisis) on the process of religious change. This means that they lead us to look at how the young Augustine's psychological distress was deeply related to his early traumatic injuries ("empathic failure" or "internalized bad object") within the specific personal and familial contexts of his childhood (e.g., his experiences of floggings at school and parents' mocking at his stripes/God's silence about it [*conf.* 1.9.14–15; *civ. Dei* 21.14]). In this way, some scholars encourage us to investigate how Augustine's early traumatic injuries had negatively influenced the formation of both his self-image and his representation of God (as scourging or indifferent [e.g., *conf.* 1.9.14, 3.3.5]) in light of the correlation of a deep sense of self-reproach, inability to love others/Other, and suffering.[120]

While acknowledging the link between the young Augustine's psychological crisis and his early personal and familial environments, Jamesian and Post-Freudian scholars provide us with insights that Augustine's expression of psychological distress (e.g., *conf.* 8.5.10) was not simply a negative symptom of pathology, fragmentation, or estrangement; rather, for Augustine, it could be a painful yet meaningful movement to think about what was the real problem in his life as well as what was the real cause of his sense of dividedness and restlessness in his mind.

Apparently, some psychological (or psychology of religious) studies of Augustine's conversion also contribute by assuming the presence or activity of the religious subject—the divine, the sacred, or the Divine/God—in the process of his transformation (e.g., D. Capps; S. L. Dixon; W. P. Elledge; V. Gay; W. James; A. G. Niño; W. B. Parsons) (although they have not investigated, primarily and explicitly, the influence of religious factors [e.g., the transforming power of God's grace] on the process of Augustine's spiritual change). They give us insights into how Augustine's sense of inner division and restlessness had affected himself to recollect and reflect upon his life history as well as how it had stirred himself to enter into his search for knowledge of the self and the

---

120. See Capps, "Augustine as Narcissist," "Scourge of Shame," "Vicious Cycle"; Dixon, *Augustine*; Dodds, "Augustine's *Confessions*"; Ferrari, "Boyhood Beatings."

Understanding Religious Conversion

knowledge of the divine in light of the correlation between the experience of the self and the experience of the divine. This means that they lead us to pay attention to the process of Augustine's inner transformation from the divided self to the integration of the self in relation to his deep experience with the divine, the sacred, or God.

However, psychological interpretations of Augustine's conversion almost exclusively focus on the personal factors in the process of his transformation. As such, psychological studies of Augustine and his conversion have not paid attention to the social and cultural conditions of intellectual climate of Late Antiquity.[121] In order to facilitate a better understanding of Augustine's conversion, the psychological studies need to respect more social, cultural, and religious/theological approaches to human transformation, while acknowledging the influence of personal factors on the process of human change.

SOCIOLOGICAL STUDIES OF AUGUSTINE'S CONVERSION

Scholars have explored the impact of social and institutional factors on the conversion process of Augustine within Christian communities (although most of them are not primarily sociologists in the field of sociology of religion but Augustinian scholars). This section of the literature review focuses on two main themes which are suitable for articulating the social and communal dimensions of the religious conversion process and which are preeminent for establishing a richer and more accurate perception of Augustine's lived experience of change. These main themes are 1) the influence of others' conversion stories on Augustine's conversion, and 2) Augustine's conversion, interpersonal bonds, and the Christian community.

The Influence of Others' Conversion Stories on Augustine's Conversion

Scholars have examined the impact of the conversion stories of other people on Augustine's conversion process. For example, William J.

---

121. See Daly, "Psychohistory," 249.

Getting Insights

O'Brien explores the correlation of Augustine's conversion narrative with others' conversion stories. O'Brien focuses on the stories within the conversion narrative: "Simplicianus' story about Victorinus; Ponticianus' story about Antony; and Ponticianus' story about two of his friends who happened upon Antony's life story—*a story within a story.*"[122] According to O'Brien, the first storyteller, Simplicianus (who was a philosophical and spiritual mentor of Ambrose, the bishop of Milan) told Augustine the story of Victorinus. Victorinus was identified as a professor of rhetoric in Rome and he translated some books of the Platonists (which had affected Augustine's life and thought). But later, Victorinus, who was an old man and learned in all the liberal sciences, was drawn toward Christian conversion through his study of the Holy Scriptures and Christian literature. As a result of his attentive reading, Victorinus was determined to declare publicly his conversion to Christianity and his salvation in the Christian community, for he was "seized by the fear that Christ might deny him before the holy angels if he was too faint-hearted to acknowledge Christ before men."[123] O'Brien insists that this story of Victorinus' conversion stirred in Augustine's heart a desire to follow his example of humility; further, it enabled Augustine to pay attention to his state of bondage of the will, especially his inner division, which he had not noticed before.[124]

According to O'Brien, at the time of Augustine's experience of his inner division of the will, Ponticianus, a high court official and a Christian, came to Augustine. When Ponticianus found that Augustine was reading Paul's epistles, he was moved to tell Augustine about conversion stories of his friends, who had been deeply influenced by the story of Antony, the Egyptian monk. If Simplicianus' story about Victorinus' conversion occasioned for Augustine an inner division, then Ponticianus' story about his friends' conversions compelled Augustine to acknowledge the roots of his inner conflict. In this way, O'Brien writes, "As it was a fellow rhetorician's story [of Victorinus] which brought Augustine to the realization of the tug exerted by his own past, so he

---

122. O'Brien, "Approach," 49. In a same way, Wills claims that a series of the conversion accounts of other people did "form a kind of drumbeat leading up to Augustine's own conversion" to Christianity in the garden in Milan (*Saint Augustine*, 45; see *Augustine's Conversion*, 53–8, 101–5, 112–13, 118–19).

123. O'Brien, "Approach," 49. See Vaught, *Encounters*, 72.

124. O'Brien, "Approach," 49–50.

indicates it was the story of a fellow countryman from Africa named Ponticianus which brought him to the brink of conversion."[125]

O'Brien asserts that after listening to Ponticianus' story about his friends' conversions, Augustine, in turmoil, now retreated with Alypius to a Milanese garden in order to ponder the meaning of others' conversion stories. While weeping in his agony, he withdrew from Alypius and heard the voice of a child saying, "Take it and read, take it and read." Augustine understood this voice as "a divine command," and he opened his book of Scripture and read it; finally, he converted to Christianity.[126]

Importantly, in the case of Augustine's conversion, O'Brien emphasizes the structural importance of the story within the story because he is convinced that Augustine meant for his story to be for his reader as effective as others' stories have been for him. Consequently, O'Brien states, "Suppose there is another story within Augustine's story of his conversion that his reader may have heard before, a story which, if remembered, would increase the impact of Augustine's account immeasurably."[127]

Likewise, E. Ann Matter in "Conversion(s) in the *Confessiones*" elucidates how others' conversion stories affected Augustine's spiritual change in light of the interlocking stories of conversion in the *Confessions*. While commenting on Arthur D. Nock's concept of conversion, Matter understands Augustine's conversion as a "gradual progression" in which his narrative was deeply related to others' stories.[128] She notes, "The story of the *Confessiones* cannot be told with the vocabulary of Nock's idea of conversion, because the striking flexibility and sense of progression documented in Augustine's account of the search for ultimate truth does not accord with Nock's idea of the 'sudden moment of truth.'"[129] Employing the metaphor of "a Chinese [or Korean] box of stories of conversion,"[130] Matter attempts to explore Augustine's conversion narrative within others' conversion stories. She writes, "To proceed

---

125. Ibid., 50.
126. Ibid., 51–52.
127. Ibid., 53.
128. Matter, "Conversion(s)," 26. See Stark, "Dynamics," 45; cf. Nock, *Conversion*, 7.
129. Matter, "Conversion(s)," 26.
130. *This* Chinese or Korean box is formulated by the ongoing-containing structure of a smaller box within a bigger box. See Vaught, *Encounters*, 82–83.

Getting Insights

chronologically: Antony was moved by a chance encounter with the Gospel of Matthew, the young men at Trier by the story of Antony, Ponticianus by the experience of these friends, Augustine by the narrative of Ponticianus. The cumulative weight of precedents seems a more important part of the story than the idea of a 'sudden dramatic moment.'"[131] More specifically, Matter describes the "interlocking stories of the conversion" of Antony, Ponticianus' two friends, Ponticianus, and Augustine as follows: as found in book eight of the *Confessions*, before his conversion to Christianity, Augustine was unable to conceive of a spiritual substance and was unable to relinquish his sensual gratifications. At that time, Augustine met a fellow North African, Ponticianus, who had a position in the Emperor's court. Ponticianus told a series of conversion stories that fitted together neatly: the first was the story of Antony, who was a monk of Egypt, and of the "flocks of monasteries" that had grown up from Antony's example (*conf.* 8.6.14–15). Then Ponticianus told Augustine how the conversion story of Antony had influenced two of his friends. Ponticianus' two friends (who were imperial officials) had gone to Trier with the royal court. One evening, while wandering in the gardens close to the city walls, they came upon "a certain house, where lived certain servants of God, poor in spirit, of whom is the kingdom of heaven" (8.6.15). There they found a book of the life of Antony. After reading this book, they had been influenced by the life of Antony and then decided to give up their imperial posts and to enter into the monastic community. Because of their example, Ponticianus himself decided to be baptized a Christian. After hearing the conversion stories of Ponticianus and his two friends, Augustine was disgusted with himself. He reflected that after reading Cicero's *Hortensius* at the age of nineteen, he had made little progress in resolving his spiritual quest for the Truth. Instead, Augustine had pursued his worldly career, satisfied his earthly needs, and dabbled in a variety of religious and philosophical groups such as Manichaeism, astrology, or Neoplatonism. In the depth of his anguish, he rushed into the garden. There Augustine heard a divine voice and read one of Paul's Epistles. He finally dedicated himself to God and engaged in the celibate and monastic life ("a life of ascetic renunciation of the flesh").[132] Consequently, Matter asserts that there is an analogous relation between Augustine's

---

131. Matter, "Conversion(s)," 25.
132. Ibid., 24–26. See Elledge, "Augustine," 82; Stark, "Dynamics," 49, 51.

conversion narrative and others' conversion stories. This implies that we need to examine the conversion stories of other people in order to understand "the special quality" of the conversion story of Augustine in the *Confessions*.

Like Matter, Frederick Van Fleteren probes how Augustine's conversion narrative is related to the conversion stories of other persons in the *Confessions*. Van Fleteren regards Augustine's conversion to Christianity as "a radical change" in which Augustine committed himself to a new life.[133] According to Van Fleteren, there are no fewer than twelve various conversion stories in the *Confessions*: 1) Augustine's reading of the *Hortensius* (*conf.* 3.4.7–8); 2) the first conversion of Alypius, from the Carthaginian circus (4.7.11–12); 3) the final conversion of Augustine from astrology (7.6.8–10); 4) the intellectual conversion of Augustine (7.9.13–7.21.27); 5) the conversion of Victorinus (8.2.3–5); 6) Augustine's conversion from the story of Ponticianus (8.6.14–16); 7) the conversion story told by Ponticianus (8.6.15); 8) the conversion of Antony (8.6.14, 8.12.29); 9) Augustine's own conversion (8.8.19, 8.11.27; 8.12.28–30); 10) Alypius' conversion (8.12.30); 11) the conversion of Monica from wine-bibbing (9.8.19); and 12) the vision at Ostia (9.10.23–26).[134] Van Fleteren claims that in the *Confessions*, Augustine depicted others' conversion stories in order to help the reader to understand better his own conversion narrative. More specifically, Van Fleteren notes,

> The similarities between Augustine's own conversion and the conversions of others afford us a further insight into Augustine's conversion; the deeper meaning of what is merely mentioned in the description of the scene in the garden becomes clearer when compared to the other stories. Thus, the literary structure of the conversion passages is identified as a *Formgeschichte*. This is not to say that a conversion in the garden in Milan did not take place; but it is to say that Augustine interpreted other lives in terms of his own.[135]

According to Van Fleteren, this *Formgeschichte* as a structure of the conversion story/history consists of the following three distinguished yet mutually-informing moments: "(1) the events leading up to

---

133. Van Fleteren, "Augustine's Theory," 73.
134. Ibid., 65–66.
135. Ibid., 73.

the conversion; (2) the moment of conversion itself; (3) the short and long term effects of the conversion."¹³⁶ While emphasizing this literary structure within conversion stories, Van Fleteren delves into the radical changes of the converts, including Augustine and others, as founded in the *Confessions*: for example, the conversion of Victorinus enabled him to confess publicly his faith of Jesus Christ before the members of the Christian community (although his public confession caused to be left his professorship of rhetoric in the context of the persecution of Christianity within the Roman Empire) (*conf.* 8.2.5);¹³⁷ the conversion of Antony involved a change to the life of a hermit (8.6.14); the conversions of the friends of Ponticianus encouraged them to enter into a movement from secular service for the empire to the service of God (8.6.15); the conversion of Augustine stirred him to resign the chair of rhetoric, to engage in a celibate life, and to reject any desire for worldly gain (8.12.30).¹³⁸ Significantly, Van Fleteren understands Augustine's spiritual change within the context of others' transformative stories. As a result, he concludes that the conversion stories of other people played an important role in the process of Augustine's transformation.

Augustine's Conversion, Interpersonal Bonds, and the Christian Community

Scholars have explored the link of Augustine's conversion experience of his intimate interactions with his intimate interactions with other people and his participation in Christian communities. For example, Garry Wills examines the role of Augustine's affective bonds and his intensive encounters with others in the experience of his transformation in light of a network of friendships. Wills views Augustine's conversion as a process that was inherently related to the "continuity" of change in his life development.¹³⁹ According to Wills, Augustine came to

---

136. Ibid.

137. According to Harmless, Victorinus had retired from public life when Julian the Apostate had banned Christians from holding such prestigious teaching posts. In the midst of persecution, Victorinus had kept the following moral and faithful position: "throw off all delay; profess the Christian faith; remember the Last Judgment; abandon ambition, even at the cost of retirement" (*Augustine*, 92).

138. Van Fleteren, "Augustine's Theory," 70–71.

139. Wills, *Augustine's Conversion*, 5–6, 20.

Understanding Religious Conversion

Simplicianus when he was in the depth of his spiritual struggle against his desire for "lust" and his worldly ambition for a successful career. Simplicianus expertly diagnosed Augustine's needs and appropriately provided the moral and spiritual guidance for the young Augustine.[140] As such, Wills describes how Simplicianus had specifically cared for Augustine as follows:

> Simplician . . . helped in the four crucial ways. First, he regularly [met] Augustine. . . . Simplician was a sympathetic interlocutor who "by asking questions like a student became the teacher of those he asked." . . . Augustine corresponded with him later, calling him "Father." . . . A second service was Simplician's recommendation to read the letters of Paul, which engaged Augustine at levels Isaiah could not, at that time, reach. [Augustine] was reading Paul on the day of his conversion. A third service was the introduction of Augustine to a flourishing Christian Neoplatonism in Milan. Simplician had been a friend of Marius Victorinus, the translator of Plotinus. . . . As the center of the Neoplatonist circle in Milan, he was familiar with Mallius Theodore, to whom Augustine would dedicate one of his earliest works. A last kindness he did Augustine was to tell him pointed stories of others' conversions. Augustine . . . appreciated it.[141]

Wills contends that, like Simplicianus, Ponticianus led Augustine to be changed when Augustine had lost his way in spiritual darkness. He guided Augustine to think about the correlation between Christian life in solitude and Christian life in community by illustrating the ascetic life of Antony in the desert ("the single excellence of hermits") as well as the life of Ponticianus' two friends (and their two affianced women) in the monastic community ("'flocks' [*greges*] of monastic saints"). For Wills, eventually, Ponticianus challenged Augustine to enter into the interior journey for God in the garden of Milan and to engage in Christian life in community.[142]

Importantly, from the viewpoint of Augustine's conversion as a process, Wills claims that Augustine became a Christian in the summer of 386, but that his life of conversion did not "end in the garden in Milan."[143] After his garden experience, Augustine involved membership

---

140. Ibid., 111–13.
141. Wills, *Saint Augustine*, 44–45.
142. Wills, *Augustine's Conversion*, 117–19.
143. Ibid., 6.

in a community of learned celibates. As such, Wills illustrates the friendship of Verecundus for Augustine and his fellows. Verecundus provided his villa of Cassiciacum to Augustine and his fellows in order to support them while they engaged in philosophical and religious discussions and to establish their continuous spiritual journey for God and community (even though he could not join this group because of his tie to a wife).[144] Wills insists that the monastic and communal life of Augustine and his followers at Cassiciacum was deeply influenced by the example of the ascetic life of Ponticianus' four friends at Trier. Acknowledging the communal aspect of human sin and redemption within the Christian community, Wills pays attention to Augustine's ongoing spiritual life with other people in the Christian group.[145] More specifically, he notes,

> Augustine is setting up a network of friendships that will correspond to the network of friendship exemplified in Pontician's immediately following and crucial account of the four friends in Trier. Augustine's final struggle in the garden, when he separates himself even from his closest friend Alypius, may give the impression that his conversion was an entirely private and single action. But he means to show that grace acts within the social framework. Even sin came into the world by a perverse social sense, the *socialis necessitudo* that made Adam retain his solidarity with Eve. Redemption also has a communal aspect. The generosity of Verecundus, based on his sense of duty to his friends, is a happier kind of *socialis necessitudo*, which will be continued when he offers his villa at Cassiciacum to the community of his friends.[146]

---

144. Ibid., 117.

145. Ibid., 117–19. See Harrison, *Augustine*, 162–67; Martin, *Restless Heart*, 46–47; McMahon, *Medieval Meditative Ascent*, 129–42. John F. Monagle insists that the theme of Christian friendship is essential for Augustine spiritual life. According to Monagle, Augustine used the Cicero's concept of *amicitia* (friendship) to convey the meaning of friendship that signifies a human "bond which unites two or more persons in mutual sympathy" ("Friendship," 81). However, after his conversion to Christianity, Augustine became more convinced that "no true and virtuous friendship can exist unless it is rooted in the common love of God" (85; see *s*. 361.1). Monagle claims that for Augustine, God is the source and the reference of Christian friendship (85; see *civ. Dei* 13. 24; Lienhard, "Friendship," 372–73; Paffenroth, "God in the Friend," 131–33). For Monagle, Augustine's concept of Christian friendship involves "Christian, fraternal charity" in light of the love of God and neighbor (86, 92).

146. Wills, *Augustine's Conversion*, 117.

Wills asserts that for Augustine, the Christian life "was not a matter of his single salvation but of a philosophical [and spiritual] discipline jointly pursued with others."[147] Augustine did finally bring together the partners he needed to pursue the Christian life in community at Cassiciacum and Hippo. Consequently, Wills remarks that Augustine's continuous interactions with other people played an important role in establishing "drumbeat" directing of his own conversion to Christianity in the Milanese garden as well as his participation in the Christian community.

Along the same line, Carl G. Vaught probes how Augustine's interpersonal bonds and his participation in Christian communities deeply affected the process of his conversion in terms of correlation between personal transformation and a web of Christian friendships. Vaught contends that Augustine's Christian conversion of book eight is interwoven with two themes: 1) becoming a Christian and 2) the emergence of a Christian community.[148] In the time of his hesitation to become a Christian, surprisingly, Augustine experienced loving care and support from other important persons: for example, 1) Bishop *Ambrose* of Milan helped Augustine to overcome the impact of Manichaean heritage on his thought and belief in which Augustine could not "conceive of spiritual substance that transcends the distinction between Good and Evil."[149] Ambrose's sermons, which reflected Christianized Neoplatonism, especially encouraged the intellect Augustine to make an inner journey toward union with the Truth in light of the relation between God and the soul; 2) *Simplicianus* became a spiritual mentor for Augustine, as he was a spiritual father for Ambrose. Simplicianus, as a Christian Platonist, had been a servant of Christ for many years.[150] Augustine wanted to talk with Simplicianus about more personal and existential issues than he had ever been able to talk publicly with Ambrose; importantly, he met Simplicianus because he was "a Christian"

---

147. Ibid., 118.

148. Vaught, *Encounters*, 67.

149. Ibid., 57.

150. Vaught depicts, "Simplicianus is a Christian Neoplatonist, who approves the introduction of God and his Word in the Neoplatonic writings. However, he is also a humble follower of Christ, opposing other philosophers who focus only on the physical world, and diverging from proud Neoplatonists who neglect the pathway that leads to God" (ibid., 72; see O'Donnell, *Augustine: Confessions*, vol. 3, 6–7, 13–15).

rather than "a Neoplatonist."[151] Throughout their meetings, Simplicianus illustrated how he himself moved from paganism to Christianity; then he advised Augustine how to deal with his spiritual abyss and existential predicament and how to follow Christ's example of humility. (As such, Simplicianus told the story of Victorinus' transformation—a role model of Christian humility through dedication to Jesus Christ.);[152] 3) At the time of his visit, *Ponticianus* realized that Augustine had read the letters of Paul and that he had seriously struggled with his own spiritual and existential problems rather than his philosophical and intellectual reflections. Ponticianus came closer to Augustine's heart, not only by informing him of the life of Antony in the desert, but also by telling him a story about himself and his friends, who were members of the emperor's court that Augustine aspired to join. Like Ambrose and Simplicianus, Ponticianus led Augustine to become a Christian; that is, he encouraged Augustine to engage in a turning toward God and to embrace the humility of the cross in light of the radical reorientation of the will.[153]

Vaught asserts that with this loving care and support from other significant persons (i.e., Ambrose, Simplicianus, and Ponticianus), Augustine converted to Christianity in the garden of Milan.[154] Vaught emphasizes that during and after Augustine's conversion to Christianity, Alypius and Monica were changed ("converted") *together*. This means that Alypius, who was present with Augustine in the garden, also cast himself to Christ and overcame his weakness of will through faith in God.[155] After hearing what had happened to Augustine and Alypius in

151. Vaught, *Encounters*, 72. See Starnes, *Augustine's Conversion*, 217.
152. Vaught, *Encounters*, 69–74.
153. Ibid., 79–81.
154. Ibid., 90–99.
155. Vaught insists that although the conversion of Alypius was derivative on the experience of Augustine, both conversions displayed their uniqueness, and each conversion reflected the character of the one who underwent it. Vaught notes, "In the case of Alypius, fallenness expresses itself in weakness rather than in self-accentuation; in the case of Augustine, this same predicament expresses itself in erotic power rather than humility. However, in both instances, the grace of God inverts the structure of the soul. The transformation of Alypius differs from the conversion of Augustine, but each has an internal structure that mirrors the other: the weakness of Alypius becomes the strength to accept a divine gift, and the strength of Augustine becomes the weakness to embrace his limitations. The same inversion that has transformed Augustine transforms Alypius as well; and when this occurs, the internal structure of their separate

the garden, Monica leaped for joy at the good news of their conversions. While she praised God for accomplishing more than she could ever ask or think, Monica abandoned her own worldly ambition and desire for her son Augustine to achieve professional success by marrying a Roman heiress. As such, Vaught claims that the transformations of Augustine, Alypius, and Monica in the summer of 386 enabled them to become real "friends" in faith in God and to establish "a new kind of community" in light of interaction with companions and a web of Christian friendship.[156] More specifically, Vaught writes,

> When Augustine reads a passage from the book of Romans in the garden in Milan, he not only trembles at the voice of God, but also finds the deliverance he seeks while his friend, Alypius, is sitting beside him (8.12.30). From this experience, a Christian community emerges (8.12.30); and the structure it exhibits not only overcomes the philosophical isolation of the Neoplatonic vision, but also expresses the new creation that God generates within Augustine's soul. . . . [This] new kind of community . . . is not a collection of role players like the adolescent community with which Augustine begins, nor is it a negative community in which participants become isolated from one another. Rather, it includes an indefinite number of individuals that are (finite-infinite) images of one another in relation to God. . . . Augustine, Alypius, Monica, and other members of this new community are identical in certain respects, but also different. The transforming Word of God that the Bible makes accessible does not cancel their differences; for though it is rich enough to individuate them, it also gives them common ground in relation to God.[157]

Vaught insists that for Augustine, Christian friendship is a crucial factor in this new community as found in the *Confessions*. According to Vaught, this Christian friendship presupposes that those who have stood alone before God stand together.[158] In that sense, Vaught points

---

experiences binds them together" (ibid., 101).

156. Ibid., 100–103. See *conf.* 8.12.30.

157. Vaught, *Encounters*, 65, 102.

158. Vaught writes, "Unlike Plato, who holds the community together with a noble lie, and unlike Hobbes, Rousseau, and Locke, who bind it together with a social contract, Augustine suggests that communities arise naturally when separate individuals are oriented positively toward the same object. Thus, he suggests that the love of God binds Augustine, Alypius, and Monica together, where they turn away from merely finite objects of affection, and where they are oriented toward what is infinite in its

Getting Insights

out that the pear-stealing episode, as described in book two, led from a positive community of friends to a negative community of isolated individuals. By contrast, Christian conversions, as portrayed in book eight, led "from individuating experiences with God to a community that not only holds its members apart, but also binds them together."[159]

Significantly, in the view of Christian friendship, Vaught pays attention to the communal dimension of the Ostia vision in which Augustine and his mother a shared mystical experience (*conf.* 9.10.23–26) (while acknowledging the personal dimension of spiritual experience). Augustine and Monica were bound together by the fact that they became the members of the new spiritual community in faith in Christ ("putting on Christ"), that is, they celebrated their citizenship in the City of God ("a foretaste of eternal life").[160] Vaught notes, "Experiences like this [Ostia vision of Augustine and his mother] are rare in mystical literature; for moments of mystical ecstasy often obliterate the individuals who engage in them, and usually involve a single individual the exclusion of a larger community. However, in this case, Augustine describes a shared mystical experience that mirrors the structure of the Christian community, and within which individuals stand alone together in the presence and absence of God."[161] As a result, Vaught asserts that other significant people (i.e., Ambrose, Simplicianus, and Ponticianus) played a pivotal role in the process of Augustine's conversion. These persons helped Augustine when he underwent his spiritual abyss and existential predicament. Augustine overcame his hesitation of becoming a Christian when he converted to God in the Milanese garden. During and after Augustine's conversion to Christianity, Alypius and Monica were transformed together; finally, Augustine and his fellows engaged in the new Christian community, which was rooted in the web of Christian friendship.

Similar to Vaught, Mary J. Kreidler elaborates on how Augustine's continuous interactions with other people influenced his conversion to Christianity as well as his participation within the Christian community. She regards Augustine's conversion experience as "a life-process" of change during which he engaged in Christian life of humility and

---

own right" (ibid., 103).

159. Ibid.
160. Ibid., 105–6, 124–29.
161. Ibid., 128.

199

community.¹⁶² In line with Wills and Vaught, Kreidler contends that Simplicianus and Ponticianus guided Augustine to enter into "a movement away from the intellectual pride" of the young philosopher who saw himself as the source of his own wisdom and virtue "to an experience of the humility of the Incarnate Christ as model and healer."¹⁶³ For Kreidler, within the context of the loving care and support by other people, Augustine finally converted to Christianity.

Kreidler claims that Augustine's conversion in the Milanese garden did not remain the alienated experience of an individual. Augustine's conversion experience enabled him to accept "the humble servant Christ" and to become a "humble Christian" for others. While emphasizing the link between Augustine's conversion and his solidarity in the church community, Kreidler writes, "Augustine's conversion . . . took place within an ecclesial community. . . . [As such] Augustine's understanding of community [did] undergo a *metanoia*. That *metanoia* center[ed] in a growing understanding of unity and a perception of community as a corporate entity."¹⁶⁴

Importantly, Kreidler pays attention to Augustine's spiritual life and his pastoral ministry as a priest and a bishop at Hippo based on the interaction of humility and community. For Kreidler, there is the interrelatedness between Augustine's garden experience and his pastoral ministry ("the life of charity of the humble Christian") in terms of the personal transformation and the network of Christian friendships. Clearly, Kreidler points out that after his conversion to Christianity, Augustine became involved in a strong solidarity with others: "ministry for [priest and bishop] Augustine begins with solidarity not superiority."¹⁶⁵ That means that Augustine's life of charity began with his identification with "the humble Incarnate Christ" as well as his identification with his brothers and sisters as sinners in a process of ongoing change.

As a result, Kreidler asserts that significant other people (i.e., Simplicianus and Ponticianus) provided their care and support to Augustine to place himself in the humble Incarnate Christ. Augustine's

---

162. Kreidler, "Conversion," 515, 520.

163. Ibid., 511–13. Kreidler notes, "In the *Confessions* Augustine consistently contrasts pride and humility. Pride is the characteristic of the unconverted Augustine while humility is the possession of the incarnate Christ" (ibid., 511).

164. Ibid., 515.

165. Ibid., 513; see 510.

conversion enabled him to facilitate a corporate sense of his own identity as a member of the church community. That is, his garden experience led him to bind together his brothers and sisters within Christian community: "It is [Augustine's] conversion that understands that love makes [the] solidarity of [his] relationship with others possible in the community of the Church and religious communities that model that Church for the rest of the Body."[166] While agreeing with Zumkeller's idea that Augustine's pastoral activity began with his service of love to the Church community, Kreidler concludes that Augustine's conversion experience brought him out of his own narrow world to an awareness of and presence to a larger world that demanded "a humble love which stands in solidarity with all the members of the Body, [the Church community]."[167]

In a related vein, Alan Kreider in *The Change of Conversion and the Origin of Christendom* examines the relation between the conversion experience of the person and the resocialization process within the church community. Kreider emphasizes the corporate dimension of conversion in the context of the early Christian church in light of conversion and solidarity. In doing so, he pays attention to the stories of early Christian converts and examines the processes by which they became Christian. Kreider views Christian conversion as a "journey" of change in which the convert involves the transformation "not just of belief but also of belonging and behavior."[168] Influenced by William Harmless, Kreider formulates the journey of conversion in the context of the early church (which was fully developed in the fourth century) by using the following four stages of resocialization: 1) evangelization, 2) the catechumenate, 3) enlightenment, and 4) mystagogy.[169] Agreeing

166. Ibid., 520; see 518.
167. Ibid., 519–20. See Zumkeller, *Augustine's Ideal*, 198–99.
168. Kreider, *Change*, xv; see xiv, 109.

169. According to Kreider, the journey of conversion in the context of the early church consisted of the four stages of resocialization: 1) the stage of *evangelization* involved "contact between Christians and a potential believer" which was informal and depended on the particular experience of each person; 2) in the stage of *the catechumenate*, church leaders examined the candidates, after which they gave potential believers their approval and admitted them to become catechumens; 3) the stage of *enlightenment* referred that when a candidate's behavior was adjudged to have changed sufficiently, he or she was admitted to be concentrated upon Christian belief. The candidates received exorcisms and other spiritual preparations culminating in the baptismal rites through which the catechumens were "born in water"; 4) the stage of

with Wayne A. Meeks' attentiveness to the convert's belonging of the community,[170] Kreider writes,

> [Early Christian] conversion involved becoming the kind of person who belonged to that kind of community. This could not happen quickly. It could come about only when candidates submitted themselves to a process of "resocialization" by which their new community superintended the transformation of their beliefs, their sense of belonging, and their patterns of behavior. No longer would they live by the values of the dominant society. A process of examination, instruction, and ritual rehabituated the candidates for conversion, re-reflexing them into the lifestyle of an alternative community.[171]

For Kreider, Augustine's conversion was one of the most famous early Christian conversion stories. Augustine's conversion involved belonging and solidarity with the Christian community in light of the resocialization into an alternative community. That means that the young Augustine eventually belonged to his mother's religion (i.e., Christianity) as well as the Roman Empire's religion (i.e., Christianity) in the late fourth century in the West. Later Bishop Augustine was being asked to attempt to foster more members of the Christian church as well as to engage in the use of religious coercion in order to defend Christianity against the Donatists and pagans and to accomplish the unity of the African church.[172]

From a more specific viewpoint about the pastoral ministry of Bishop Augustine, by using this model of the journey of conversion in the early church, Kreider distills how Augustine had attempted to urge potential believers to become a Christian as well as to establish the unity of the converted person with the converted community. As such,

---

mystagogy indicated that the catechists in the week after Easter explained the meaning of the rites of baptism and Eucharist and "experience" in which the new converts had just participated (ibid., 21–22; see 57–64).

170. Meeks characterizes early Christian conversion as "the change of primary reference groups, the resocialization into an alternative community" in light of the conversion experience and the institutionalization process (*Christian Morality*, 26). He writes, "[In the context of the early church] becoming a Christian meant something like the experience of an immigrant who leaves his or her native land and then assimilates to the culture of a new, adopted homeland. Such a transfer of allegiances and transformation of mores requires a resocialization" (ibid., 12).

171. Kreider, *Change*, 21. See Meeks, *Christian Morality*, 12.

172. Kreider, *Change*, 54–65, 70.

Getting Insights

Kreider depicts Bishop Augustine as not a simply *convert*, but a *converter* who had strongly (or rigorously) urged "the catechumens to be converted."[173] In other words, he focuses on the story of Augustine the converter in his pastoral ministry at Hippo rather than on Augustine as convert in the garden of Milan. More specifically, Kreider describes,

> Augustine was bishop of Hippo in North Africa for thirty-four years, from 396 to 430. During this time, "orthodox" Catholic Christianity decisively established itself as the religion of the imperial establishment, and through this its influence spread into every town. Augustine reflected on the results of this Christianization: "In this city there are many houses in which there is not even a single pagan, nor single house in which there is not a Christian" (s. 302.19). In this process of conversion, Augustine played a role that was vital locally, but he also left his impact upon the history of Christendom as a whole.[174]

According to Kreider, Augustine of Hippo (who wrote a book, *First Catechetical Instruction*) retained and used the model of the four stages of the conversion journey in the context of the North African church in the late fourth and early fifth centuries. In doing so, Augustine actively participated in the process of Christianization; that is, he was involved in the process of converting ("christening"/"recruiting") the catechumens into the church community through the sacrament of Christian baptism. Kreider remarks that Augustine, as a missionary pastor, was profoundly concerned that people would be converted in the fullest sense of the word. Following his predecessor Cyprian, Augustine understood his role as "an exalted one" within the process of facilitating the membership of the Christian community.[175]

As a result, Kreider asserts that Augustine's conversion was a movement of spiritual journey of change in light of the resocialization or institutionalization process within the church community. Augustine's conversion experience was deeply relevant to his personal change of belief and behavior as well as to his sense of belonging and solidarity with others in the Christian community. Further, his conversion

---

173. Ibid., 54–55, 57.

174. Ibid., 54.

175. Ibid., 54–56, 94. Kreider contends that for the early Christians, Christian baptism was a "means of entry into the Christian community" in which conversion was completed (ibid., 20).

experience stirred him to establish a new kind of Christian community with his followers and to engage in the process of converting ("resocializing") potential believers—the christening of the catechumens—into the church community (i.e., the North African church).

In conclusion, from the perspective of sociology of religion, Augustine's conversion has been viewed as a product of the effectiveness of the conversion stories of other people (on his transformation) and a change through his interpersonal bonds within Christian communities. On the whole, sociological studies of Augustine's conversion have described the young Augustine as an active religious seeker who had established relations with other persons within specialized religious settings.

The sociological studies of Augustine's conversion have primarily contributed by elucidating the impact of social and institutional factors on the complex process of his transformation. In doing so, they have effectively showed the interaction of the experience of the self with the experience of others in the process of Augustine's socialization or institutionalization. More specifically, they have demonstrated how Augustine molded and confirmed the values, expectations, and beliefs of religious groups through his interactions with significant other people and his participation in religious communities. As such, when we attempt to reinterpret Augustine's conversion, these sociological studies encourage us to realize that the conversion stories of other persons—"a story within a story"—compelled Augustine to overcome his isolated life style, to be converted to Christianity, and to follow their example of humility in faith in Christ. In doing so, they lead us to recognize that Augustine's intimate interactions with other people (e.g., Simplicianus or Ponticianus) in the Christian communities helped him to make up for his frustration with his deprivations in the social and cultural conditions of his time, as well as to foster a new ability to live together with others in the community in light of interpersonal bonds and a network of Christian friendships. However, these sociological interpretations of Augustine's conversion are not sufficient to depict deeply Augustine's inner disconnection and restlessness in his mind, or to articulate Augustine's interior journey toward union with the divine and his unique transformation in the conversion process in light of knowing himself and knowing the divine.

ANTHROPOLOGICAL STUDIES OF AUGUSTINE'S CONVERSION

Scholars have explored the impact of philosophical and cultural factors on the conversion process of Augustine in the field of the anthropology of religion (although most of them are not predominantly anthropologists but Augustinian scholars). This section of the literature review pays attention to two main themes because they are proper and beneficial for articulating the philosophical and cultural dimensions of religious conversion as well as for achieving a richer and more accurate perception of Augustine's conversion narrative. These main themes are 1) the impact of the Neoplatonic heritage on Augustine's conversion and 2) Augustine's conversion and the Christian monastic movement.

The Influence of the Neoplatonic Heritage on Augustine's Conversion

Scholars have explored the influence of Neoplatonic sources on Augustine's intellectual conversion in order to elucidate how Augustine reshaped his (personal and religious) identity, worldview, and belief through his experiences of philosophical and cultural changes. For example, Phillip Cary probes how Neoplatonism affected Augustine's inner spiritual journey toward the divine. Cary explains the nature of inwardness within the Western philosophical and cultural context (which is deeply related to Augustine's concept of interiority) as follows:

> The history of inwardness is the story of how Westerners developed the desire to see within the soul and therefore came to conceive of the soul doing what no eye ever did: turning to look within its own self.... The god's command "Know Thyself," interpreted to mean "know thy soul," stood as a motto at the head of ancient treatises on the soul, hinting at a promise of divine knowledge as the fruit of self-knowledge. Thus inwardness involves more than a conception of the self; it is concerned with the divine, the eternal, the ultimate. From its inception, inwardness meant seeking a glimpse of the soul's inner relation to its divine origin.[176]

Cary contends that the deeper dimension in Platonism was inherently linked to the soul, even if it was not originally inside it. As such,

---

176. Cary, *Augustine's Invention*, 10.

he explores how Plato's theme of *the intelligible world* was modified into Plotinus' theme of *the inner world*. Cary writes,

> It was . . . Platonism that first conceived of that deeper dimension, that other world that is more real and true than the visible, bodily world—and it is to this other world that we must look for the roots of Western inwardness. . . . Plato himself did not locate this other world in the soul but rather in what he called "the intelligible place," a realm of being whose elements are not material and therefore are not visible to the eyes of the body, but rather are "intelligible," that is, understood by the intellect alone. This is the place of Platonic Ideas or Forms. Later Platonists called it "the intelligible world." Plotinus was evidently the first to conceive of it as an *inner* world, located within the soul.[177]

In this sense, Cary elucidates how the books of Neoplatonic thinkers (e.g., Plotinus) guided Augustine to realize the incorporeal dimension of divine nature as well as to enter into an interior journey for the Truth. According to Cary, the central problem of the young Augustine's life was his intellectual problem, which was related to "how to see God."[178] In other words, influenced by Manicheism, the young Augustine thought of God as a material being. According to Cary, the young Augustine was still under the influence of Manicheism (that is, he was present with the materialist habits of thought), although he was no longer a member of the Manichean sect. For this reason, when Augustine tried to conceive of God, his mind did draw "images from the world perceived by [his] five physical senses and then [did] think that these mental images (which he call[ed] 'phantasms,' related to the Greek word from which we get 'fantasy') somehow represent God."[179] Cary points out that his intellectual and philosophical failure led him to conceive of God as taking up space: "God is present everywhere, young Augustine knows, but how? His materialistic heart can only imagine God as spread out through all the places in the universe, like water filling a sponge (7.5.7). But that means one part of God must be in one place, and another part in another place, and more of him in an elephant than in a sparrow (7.1.2)."[180]

177. Ibid., 11.
178. Cary, "Book Seven," 107–8.
179. Ibid., 109.
180. Ibid.

Cary examines how Augustine resolved his intellectual problem after his reading of Plotinian books.[181] He emphasizes the role of Plotinus in reshaping Augustine's conception of the divine nature, while acknowledging the influence of Porphyry on the reformation of Augustine's thought.[182] In particular, Cary pays attention to the conceptual structure of Plotinus' "turning into the inside," which underlies Augustine's theme of inwardness. For Cary, Plotinus emphasized that the human person "must turn inward to find [the divine] because the higher part of the soul, continually contemplating, is identical to the divine Mind. Hence turning into the soul's interior is turning to God, and self-knowledge yields knowledge of all that is divine, eternal, and ultimate."[183] Cary asserts that through the books of Plotinus (which were written with an intellectual depth and poetic beauty), Augustine had learned "the Platonist [ontological] notions of incorporeality, incorruptibility, unchangeability, and omnipresence."[184] As such, Augustine had gradually realized a pivotal way to turn into the inside, namely, to see the Good in the soul: "What is the way? And what is the means? How can one behold this extraordinary beauty which remains in the inner sanctum and will not come outside to be seen by the profane? Let him who can arise and come into the inside, leaving the sight of his eyes outside and not turning back to corporeal beauties."[185]

Augustine did think of this Plotinian call to "arise and come into the inside," where God is found. In that sense, the solution to Augustine's intellectual problem (of conceiving the nature of God) began when Augustine came to himself and turned inward, just like the Plotinian Prodigal Son.[186] This means that, admonished by the books of the Platonists to return to himself and led by God's inward help, Augustine entered his "inmost place" of the soul and found the light of eternal Truth. In doing so, by employing Plotinus' conception of integral omnipresence, Augustine felt convinced that "the divine is not spread out

181. Ibid., 112–17. See Chadwick, *Augustine*, 23; Harrison, *Augustine*, 11–15, 178; *Augustine's Early Theology*, 27–28; Kenney, "Augustine's Inner Self," 90; Lawless, *Augustine*, 35–39, 156–57.

182. Cary, "Book Seven," 113.

183. Cary, *Augustine's Invention*, 28; see 20; "Interiority," 455. See also Plotinus, *enn.* 1.6.8, 5.1.12, 5.8.11, 6.5.7, 6.9.7.

184. Cary, "Book Seven," 113.

185. Ibid., 114. 1.6.8. See *Augustine's Invention*, 9–11, 28–30.

186. Cary, "Book Seven," 114–15. See Plotinus, *enn.* 1.6.8.

part-by-part in space like water in a sponge, but is present everywhere *as a whole.*"[187] This implies that this Plotinus' conception of integral omnipresence had played a prominent role in Augustine's opening meditation on the nature of God at the beginning of *Confessions* (1.2.2–1.4.4); further, Augustine clearly expressed his newly changed understanding of the omnipresence of the divine: "God is not stretched out or poured out through space, whether finite or infinite (as if there could be more of Him in one part than in another) but is present as a whole everywhere—just like Truth, which no one in their right mind would say is partly in this place and partly in that; for after all, Truth is God."[188] As a result, Cary asserts that Neoplatonism had affected the young Augustine to overcome his materialistic thinking of God as "being a bodily thing" and to enter into his mind for his interior journey for the Truth. For Cary, Augustine's concept of inwardness is rooted in Plotinian Platonism and its doctrine of the divinity at the core of the soul. Augustine's reading of the books of Neoplatonists (especially some Plotinus' works) had guided him to achieve a deeper ontological understanding of the nature of being, namely, to establish a better conception of God's omnipresence. While emphasizing that Augustine's vision of the mind's eye gave him the solution to his problem of conceiving the nature of God, Cary concludes,

> [In the movement of turning inward ("examining the soul") and looking upward ("contemplating God")] Augustine charts a journey toward God which begins when he enters into the depths of his own self (*intravi in intima mea, conf.* 7.10.16) and reaches its destination when he looks above himself to see the light of immutable Truth (i.e., God), which is visible only to the eye of the mind. In turning inward Augustine looks first at the cognitive powers of his own soul. Ascending through these faculties, from senses through memory to intellect or mind, Augustine finally recognizes that the Truth the mind sees is above the mind itself, because Truth is immutable while the mind is not.[189]

---

187. Cary, "Book Seven," 115. See Plotinus, *enn.* 6.4.1–6.5.12.

188. Cary, "Book Seven," 115, quoted in *ep.* 118.23.

189. Cary, "Interiority," 455. See Bouyer, "Latin Fathers," 468–75; McMahon, *Medieval Meditative Ascent*, 9–10, 60–77, 152; "Book Thirteen," 212–17; Newton, "Augustine's Use," 2–4.

In the same vein, John J. O'Meara in *The Young Augustine: The Growth of St. Augustine's Mind Up to His Conversion* examines the role of Neoplatonism in Augustine's conversion in light of the ascent of the soul. In doing so, O'Meara pays attention to the intellectual and rational dimension of Augustine's transformation in terms of the submission of intellect, while acknowledging the moral and spiritual dimension of it in terms of the submission of will. Basically agreeing with Arthur D. Nock's idea about "conversion to philosophy,"[190] O'Meara contends that the search for and the acceptance of a new philosophy tend to stir persons to set up a different (or better) standard of values within the intellectual and cultural context. In that sense, he argues that Neoplatonism affected Augustine's transformation of religious identity as well as his cultural change.

According to O'Meara, Augustine was influenced by Neoplatonists (especially Plotinus and Porphyry who were related as "master and principal interpreter").[191] More specifically, O'Meara elucidates the impact of Plotinus and Porphyry on the formation of Augustine's Neoplatonic thought as follows:

> Plotinus' essay *On Beauty* informed him of a spiritual Trinity and dispelled forever his Manichean notions of a corporeal deity. Other essays of Plotinus equally dispelled his Manichean view of evil as a substance. Plotinus, moreover, summoned him from amongst the many to aspire through purgation and the higher operation of his intelligence to union with the One. [In the meanwhile] Porphyry's *Return of the Soul* also spoke to him of the Trinity and of purgation and union. Further it alone told him of the necessity of a Mediator for the many [who were

---

190. According to Nock, *conversion* to philosophy was a common thing at the time of Augustine. Nock views the philosopher as "the man able to relieve humanity of this and that failing, and his functions as reproaching and exhorting and teaching" (*Conversion*, 173). In this way, Eugene Kevane emphasizes Augustine's philosophizing process for establishing a better way of Christian life: "Augustine is promising a renewed and healed condition of philosophy, because the purgation of the pagan condition of mind and soul by the power of the new religion will brighten the vision of the inner eye" ("Christian Philosophy," 60–61).

191. O'Meara emphasizes that Augustine had been affected by both Plotinus and Porphyry (*Young Augustine*, 127–28, 131, 135, 152–53). See Chadwick, *Augustine*, 17–24; Harrison, *Augustine*, 13; *Augustine's Early Theology*, 27–28; Van Fleteren, "Ascent," 64.

incapable of raising themselves to a life of purgation and intellectual contemplation].[192]

For O'Meara, in book seven of the *Confessions*, Augustine described how the theme of the Neoplatonic ascent of the soul had really impressed him in the process of his intellectual submission to Christianity.[193] Here Augustine could reach his lofty contemplation to experience the divine, that is, he could arrive at the vision of the Good. As a result, O'Meara remarks that the new Neoplatonic knowledge of Augustine had greatly affected his conversion experience in the garden of Milan[194] (as well as his mystical experience at Ostia).[195] O'Meara concludes,

> This . . . was the stage to which the Neo-Platonist books had brought him. [Augustine] aspired to a life not only free from worldly cares and preoccupations, but given wholly to the contemplation of the immaterial One, the Good, the Father. Such a life involved an ascetic purgation of the soul of all the

---

192. O'Meara, *Young Augustine*, 153. According to O'Meara, although Porphyry helped Augustine to search for "a Mediator to lead the mass of mankind to the Father," like other Neoplatonists, he regarded Jesus as "an excellent man" and rejected the Christian belief of the Incarnate Christ who became a mediator between the divine and the human (ibid., 139–41; see Bonner, "Starting with Oneself," 165; Cary, "Book Seven," 120; Harrison, *Augustine*, 30–38; *Augustine's Early Theology*, 32–33; O'Connell, *Augustine's Confessions*, 79–80). In the context that Augustine did not discover the theme of the Incarnation in the teaching of Neoplatonists, Augustine read the Bible, especially the letters of St. Paul. Like his reading of the books of the Neoplatonists, his reading of the Epistles of Paul affected his transformation (ibid., 155–58, 191; see Cary, *Augustine's Invention*, 31; "Book Seven," 119–20; Harrison, *Augustine*, 88–93; Lancel, *Saint Augustine*, 87–88; O'Donnell, *Augustine: Confessions*, vol. 3, 3).

193. O'Meara, *Young Augustine*, 133. See 138; *conf.* 7.10.16, 7.17.23, 7.20.26.

194. O'Meara insists that while scholars have explored the impact of the Neoplatonists on Augustine and his thought, there is an enormous controversy whether Augustine was converted to Neoplatonism or Christianity (ibid., 125–27). According to O'Meara, some scholars (e.g., P. Alfaric) have supported the idea that Augustine was a Neoplatonist rather than a Christian during (and after) his garden experience in 386 (ibid., 126–27). However, acknowledging Augustine had been deeply influenced by Neoplatonism, O'Meara claims that Augustine truly became a Christian: "Augustine's conversion to Christianity was sincere and complete, due emphasis is placed on the part played in it by Neo-Platonism" (127; see 155, 165, 215–16).

195. Ibid., 205–9. Like O'Meara, scholars have claimed that the Neoplatonic theme of the ascent of the soul toward the divine affected Augustine's vision of God at Ostia (*conf.* 9.10.23–26), as it influenced his garden experience in Milan (8.12.28–29) (see Bouyer, "Latin Monasticism," 497–99; Cary, "Book Seven," 121; Lancel, *Saint Augustine*, 86; Van Fleteren, "Ascent," 64; Vaught, *Encounters*, 124–28).

unnecessary defilements which arose from its being imprisoned in the body. He could not expect that he would immediately he granted an ecstatic vision of the One; nor was it in fact granted him. He could aspire to it and make himself less worthy of it: this he attempted to do.[196]

Like O'Meara, Serge Lancel in *Saint Augustine* explores how Augustine's reading of the books of the Neoplatonists influenced the intellectual dimension of his conversion in terms of the inward turn and ascent of the soul towards the divine. For Lancel, Augustine was not able "to conceive of the incorporeal" dimension of the divine because of his old Manichean belief.[197] As such, Augustine met Bishop Ambrose of Milan who was a Christian Neoplatonist and participated in the worship service in the Milanese cathedral, at which point he heard the sermons of Ambrose:

> In May or June following the Eastertide of 386 Ambrose preached a series of sermons—including the *De Isaac* and the *De bono mortis*—in which, as in the *De Iacob*, preached previously, there is a heavy use of themes that hark back to the *Enneads* of the emperor Gallienus' favorite thinker, Plotinus, who in the middle of the third century had developed in Rome, but in Greek, an original philosophy that rethought Plato's doctrine and had made him the master of what is conveniently termed Neoplatonism.[198]

In the meantime, Augustine as a young rhetorician also participated in the Milanese circle of the intellects—the "network of intellectual relationships"—in which some members were Christians, including Ambrose, and others were pagans.[199] Within his engagement in this intellectual group, Augustine read some books of the Neoplatonists. At this point, Lancel pays attention to the role of Neoplatonists in the process of Augustine's intellectual transformation. Particularly, he emphasizes the influence of Plotinus on Augustine's intellectual conversion

---

196. O'Meara, *Young Augustine*, 138.

197. Lancel, *Saint Augustine*, 85.

198. Ibid., 82. See Cary, "Book Seven," 122; O'Connell, *Augustine's Confessions*, 64–65; Vaught, *Encounters*, 57, 146.

199. Lancel, *Saint Augustine*, 78–79, 82–83. See Chadwick, *Augustine*, 22; Brown, *Augustine*, 485–86; O'Donnell, *Augustine: Confessions*, vol. 2, 413–20; Vaught, *Encounters*, 146.

in 386, acknowledging the influence of Porphyry on him.[200] Lancel asserts that through his reading of Plotinus' books, Augustine had not received simply the intellectual information of Neoplatonism, but "had created in him the conditions for a reflective withdrawal into himself, experienced with great intensity."[201] For Lancel, in book seven of the *Confessions*, Augustine described not a single experience, but a series of "spiritual anabases" which were related to the theme of the ascent of the soul towards God ("Plotinian ecstasies"). Here Augustine accounted for his spiritual apprehension of God and the soul in light of the knowledge of the self and the knowledge of the divine. While emphasizing the impact of Neoplatonists on Augustine's (religious) life and thought, Lancel describes Augustine's continuous intellectual transformation in light of the conversion of the intellect:

> From the Neoplatonists Augustine had received not only encouragement to spiritual exercise; through them he had gained access to a philosophy which seemed able to answer many of the questions he had been asking himself for some dozen years; to be more exact, the reflective withdrawal into himself, the first condition of an "anagogic" ascent towards the divine, after that fleeting grasp of the Being, had enabled him, thanks to that illumination, to achieve a view of the world that was to become the basis of his metaphysics. Many of the articles of that philosophy, notably in its most strictly ontological aspects, would remain the fixed points in his thinking in the rest of his works, including his preaching as bishop.[202]

Importantly, Lancel insists that during his struggling toward an interior journey for the divine, Augustine overcame the Manichaean doctrine of evil, which claims a real existence, independent of good. This means that, influenced by the Neoplatonic ontological theme of the hierarchical order of being,[203] Augustine effectively resolved his problem of evil; now he understood that evil has no "substance" or ul-

---

200. Lancel, *Saint Augustine*, 84–85. See O'Connell, *Augustine's Confessions*, 73–74.

201. Lancel, *Saint Augustine*, 84.

202. Ibid., 87; see 85.

203. According to Lancel, Augustine confessed that "I beheld all things below you, and saw that it cannot be said absolutely that they exist or absolutely that they do not exist: they are, in truth, because they are from you, but they are not, because they are not what you are. For what truly exists, is that which endures immutably" (ibid., 87). See Chadwick, *Augustine*, 19; Cary, "Book Seven," 117.

timate source of its own, but it is merely a privation of good. Lancel writes,

> There is . . . between beings—the "things"—a hierarchy of well-defined ontological density starting from the Being and dependent on him. God is Supreme Good, and what is corruptible and mutable, very low down on the ontological scale, is also good, since created by God. As for evil, whose origin had obsessed Augustine for a long time, "it was not a substance, because if it were a substance, it would be good." The right question regarding evil was not, "Where does it come from?" but, "What is it?," as he would soon develop it in two of his early works. In this Augustine was reacting like a good disciple of Plotinus, but also as a listener to Ambrose, who had probably drawn his attention to the definition of evil as the deprival of good in his preaching in the spring of 386.[204]

As a result, Lancel asserts that the Neoplatonists had helped Augustine to establish a new way of understanding of the divine nature—the incorporeality and indivisibility of God—and to participate in the movement of the ascent of the soul to seek union with the divine. In other words, Augustine's reading of the Neoplatonic books had enabled him to "escape from the Manichaean errors" which were related to his conceiving of God as a material and divisible being as well as to his conceiving of evil as a substance. Lancel concludes that Neoplatonists (e.g., Plotinus) and Christian Neoplatonists (e.g., Ambrose) had played a preeminent role in Augustine's intellectual conversion.

Augustine's Conversion and the Christian Monastic Movement

Scholars have articulated the influence of the Christian monastic movement on the process of Augustine's conversion. For example, Carol Harrison examines the relation between Augustine's conversion to Christianity and his ascetic and celibate life in the context of the Christian monastic movement. Harrison depicts the link of the Christian monastic movement with the social and cultural milieu of the fourth century in the West: "Throughout the Christian Empire, and especially when persecution came to an end with the conversion of the Emperor

---

204. Lancel, *Saint Augustine*, 87. See Bonner, "Starting with Oneself," 165; Harrison, *Augustine's Early Theology*, 32; Kevane, "Christian Philosophy," 64–66.

Constantine, asceticism was linked with, and often expressed in terms of, or held to replace, martyrdom—the martyrs had been the Christian elite, those who had denied the world and battled with the forces of evil. Celibacy, asceticism, and the common life were later viewed within the same frame and motivated by the same ideals."[205]

While portraying Augustine's conversion and his life history in light of the transition from paganism to Christianity, Harrison writes,

> For Augustine lived at a time of transition—from a classical pagan past to a new Christian empire—initiated by the conversion of the Emperor Constantine to Christianity in AD 312. Of course, paganism and the thought world and social structures that went with it were not obliterated, rather there was a slow, unsteady, faltering and rather ambiguous process of confrontation, accommodation, rejection and coercion before an identifiably "Christian" culture and society founded upon a conviction that Christianity was the true philosophy and true religion, emerged.[206]

In the emphasis on the social and cultural change of the fourth century, Harrison pays attention to the impact of the ascetic life of the Egyptian Antony (who was the architect of desert monasticism) on Augustine's life of change. By the time (especially the summer of 386) that Augustine was struggling with his search for the divine, Ponticianus talked about the story of Antony, the most well-known and influential Eastern ascetic.[207] (Meanwhile, he also mentioned the Christian monastery on the outskirts of Milan, which was under the care of Bishop Ambrose.) Ponticianus told of the monastic life of his two friends who were former imperial officials. At Trier, after their reading the book on the life of the monk Antony, Ponticianus' friends "were converted on the spot, deciding to 'serve God'—in other words, become monks,

---

205. Harrison, *Augustine*, 185.

206. Ibid., xii.

207. William Harmless regards Christian Egypt as "the birthplace of monasticism" (*Desert Christians*, 17). According to Harmless, Antony (c. 254–356) has been routinely described as "the first monk" and the "father of monasticism." He was certainly a pioneer who won worldwide acclaim because of Athanasius' influential biography, the *Life of Antony* (published c. 357). Athanasius portrays Antony as an "anchorite," that is, a hermit. There is a set of seven letters ascribed to Antony, and virtually every early text passes on sayings of his or stories about him (ibid., 18; see Bouyer, "Monasticism," 308–17).

too."²⁰⁸ (When their fiancées later heard of this, they also dedicated their virginity to God.) As such, Harrison asserts that both the ascetic life of Antony and the celibate life of Ponticianus' friends had challenged Augustine to become a Christian as well as to imitate their lives. More specifically, she writes, "Augustine took Ponticianus' words to heart; they gave him an appalling vision of his own vileness from which he could not escape except by heeding them and suffering their judgement upon his own situation. The subsequent passages recount Augustine's attempt to embrace the celibate, ascetic life, and are followed by the famous conversion scene."²⁰⁹

According to Harrison, after his conversion to Christianity in 386, Augustine did not choose to pursue the "ideal of marriage," but did enter into the communal life of celibacy which would be later related to the (re)formation of Christian monasticism in the West. Prior to his baptism, Augustine came to Cassiciacum with his friends; this Christian philosophical community at Cassiciacum was "social, organizational, [and] ascetic," although it was not explicitly regarded as a Christian monastery. Harrison insists that after his baptism in 387, Augustine had planned to return to Thagaste, his hometown in North Africa, with his mother and friends to carry out their "holy enterprise" (*placitum sanctum*) (*conf.* 9.9.2), that is, to establish a Christian community there. However, because of Monica's death at the seaport of Ostia as well as a blockade of the Mediterranean, Augustine and his followers instead came to Rome for a year.²¹⁰

Harrison claims that in Rome, Augustine learned much more about Christian monasticism. The Christian monastic movement of Rome had impacted Augustine to better understand the formal structure of the Christian monastery. Harrison notes,

> Augustine spent this year in Rome, which . . . was very much at the centre of strong ascetic movements and debates in the 380s and 390s. Athanasius had spent seven years in Rome, from 339, during his second exile. Peter, his successor and brother, had also stayed in Rome after Athanasius' death, from 373 to 378. Jerome had been in Rome from 382 to 385. Evagrius of Antioch had translated the *Life of Antony* into Latin c. 370. Through

208. Harrison, *Augustine*, 179; see 178.
209. Ibid., 179.
210. Ibid., 177–79.

these channels ... Eastern monasticism influenced the emerging monastic movements of the West.[211]

During his stay in Rome, Augustine had visited a number of monasteries, at which point he was deeply impressed with the *practices* of Eastern asceticism which included "manual labour (which he regards as an Eastern tradition), the common life and sharing of possessions, chastity, the rule of the 'father' who cares for his 'sons.'"[212] Augustine was gradually aware of the forms of Christian communal life that would inform the Christian community at Thagaste and that would be later included in his *Rule* for Christian monasticism at Hippo.

According to Harrison, after learning about the Christian monastery in Rome (especially about the traditional Eastern asceticism), Augustine returned to Thagaste in 388. This implied that he began to enter into the celibate and ascetic life in North Africa. By using his family house and land, here Augustine established a Christian (philosophical) community with his friends which was called a lay monastery of *serui dei* ("servants of God"). For Harrison, there were various monastic forms in the West of the fourth century, which ranged "from house asceticism and house communities, to anchorites, wandering monks, and coenobitic monasteries, together with the thin line between ascetic and monk."[213] Harrison remarks that Augustine (and his followers) at Thagaste did not simply participate in philosophical retreat, but engaged in Christian living of celibacy and asceticism. In this community of Thagaste, Augustine was primarily concerned with Christian themes of Scripture, faith, incarnation, and the church, although he had participated in philosophical discussions with his friends.[214]

According to Harrison, in 391, Augustine moved his monastery from Thagaste to Hippo because he was unpredictably ordained as a priest of the cathedral of Hippo. He reformulated his monastery with his friends in the garden of basilica at Hippo; namely, he continued his

---

211. Ibid., 179–80. See Lawless, *Augustine*, 41–42. Harmless illustrates some figures—Athanasius (c. 295–373); Evagrius Ponticus (c. 345–399); John Cassian (d. after 435); Jerome (c. 347–c. 420)—who were deeply involved in the development of Christian monasticism; that is, who had introduced the desert spirituality of Egypt to the Lain West (*Desert Christians*, 19–20).

212. Harrison, *Augustine*, 180.

213. Ibid., 181.

214. Ibid., 180–81.

Getting Insights

monastic life in the community with the permission of Bishop Valerius.[215] This implies that as a monk (and as a priest), Augustine began life in community at Hippo and adopted the way of monastic life in which he was to remain until his death. In doing so, in order to organize and manage the lay and clerical monasteries at Hippo, Augustine had established specific rules, which were primarily influenced by the spirit and actions of the apostolic community at Jerusalem as described in Acts 4:32–35. Harrison contends that for Augustine, the first goal of the monastic life is to live together in unity, and to have "one heart and soul" directed towards God. In that sense, the essential rule of this monastic community was that "all things must be held in common, and there was given to everyone as he had need."[216] Following early African theologians' emphasis on the Christian life in community, the *Rule* of the Christian community of Hippo focuses on oneness through charity in light of "many bodies but not many minds, many bodies but not many hearts."[217]

Clearly, Harrison asserts that the relationships of members within the monastic community at Hippo were viewed as "selfless mutual service and regard."[218] Augustine regarded the ideal form of the Christian community or human society as a perfectly ordered and perfectly harmonious fellowship in the enjoyment of God and mutual fellowship in God. Within the context that emphasizes oneness, harmony, and love in the treatment of monastic life of the *Rule*, human sin was understood as a failure of the love, fellowship, and friendship which lies at the heart of the Christian community and which defines it in relation to God.[219]

As a result, Harrison states that there is a close interrelatedness between Augustine's conversion to Christianity, his life of celibacy, and Christian monasticism. This means that 1) the early Christian monastic

---

215. Ibid., 181. See *epp.* 31, 33.2; *s.* 355.2.

216. Harrison, *Augustine*, 182. See *reg.* 1.2; Possidius, *v. Aug.* 5.

217. Harrison, *Augustine*, 183. See *en. Ps.* 132.3–4; Clark, *Augustine*, 88. According to Harrison, "African theologians, such as Tertullian and Cyprian, foreshadow Augustine's emphasis on Acts 4: 32–35 and the oneness of charity expressed in the holding of goods in common in a life in community, when they speak of Christian perfection. They, and numerous witnesses before them, provide evidence for the long-standing practice of chastity in the African Church, by women (*uirgines*) and men (*spadones, continentes*), and also clergy" (*Augustine*, 185).

218. Harrison, *Augustine*, 183.

219. Ibid., 158, 191. See *civ. Dei* 19.13.

movement (i.e., the acetic life of the Egyptian Antony and the celibate life and Ponticianus' friends and their fiancées) helped Augustine to be converted to Christianity in 386 as well as to embrace a life of celibacy and asceticism; 2) during his celibate life in Rome, the traditional Eastern asceticism encouraged Augustine to learn more about the forms of Christian monasticism (e.g., the pattern of communal prayer, of manual labor, or of the authority structure); 3) Augustine's transformation in the Milanese garden as well as his learning of the practices of Eastern asceticism in Rome enabled him to engage in a more developed Christian monastic movement as well as to establish a Christian philosophical community at Cassiciacum (386), the community of *serui dei* at Thagaste (388), and the lay and then clerical monastery at Hippo (391, 395/6).[220] While paying attention to Augustine's basic rule of "one heart and mind in loving fellowship and by sharing of goods" within the Christian monasticism, Harrison concludes,

> The positive attraction of the monastic life is . . . significant: community, friendship, intellectual companionship, order—all things which the early works and the *Confessions* make clear Augustine was seeking from the beginning. The ascetic environment in North Africa, fostered by Tertullian, Cyprian, and Ambrose, the martyr ideal and the classical, contemplative, philosophical mould into which the Christian monastic ideal so easily fitted, together with Augustine's own profound personal inclination towards the values of the monastic life.[221]

In line with Harrison, George Lawless in *Augustine of Hippo and His Monastic Rule* explores the correlation of Augustine's conversion to Christianity with the Christian monastic movement. Lawless views Augustine's conversion as "a voluntary surrender of sexuality, property, and power" which will be later related to his monastic ideal of "chastity, poverty, and obedience."[222] For Lawless, Augustine's garden experience in the summer of 386 challenged him to make a decision to live as a celibate servant of God. Like Harrison, Lawless emphasizes the influence of the ascetic lives of Antony and the monks of the Egyptian desert on Augustine's transformation. For Lawless, Ponticianus' vivid account of the monastic living of Antony and his followers had guided Augus-

220. Harrison, *Augustine*, 177–93. See Van Bavel, "Introduction to the Rule," 4.
221. Harrison, *Augustine*, 193.
222. Lawless, *Augustine*, ix.

tine to stand humbly before God in the garden of Milan and to enter into the life of celibacy and asceticism.[223]

In consideration of the impact of the ascetic lives of Antony and his followers on Augustine's conversion to Christianity, Lawless pays attention to the juxtaposition of Matthew 19:21 (which moved Antony into his transformation and his monastic life in the desert) with Romans 13:13–14 (which affected Augustine's placing himself in Jesus Christ in the Milanese garden as well as his resolution to embrace the life of celibacy and asceticism).[224] More specifically, Lawless writes, "While Paul enjoins a triple injunction, Jesus' invitation to the 'rich young man' evokes a single renunciation as regards riches, property, and possessions. Juxtaposition of Matt 19:21 with Rom 13:13–14 in the *Confessions* (8. 12. 29) is a deliberate stroke of Augustine's artistry. In and of itself, of course, ascetic renunciation is valueless. 'Come, follow me' in Matt 19:21 echoes the words with which Jesus called his disciples. 'Put on the Lord Jesus Christ' of Rom 13:14 likewise insists upon this positive aspect of asceticism."[225]

Lawless asserts that at this particular time of Augustine's decision to imitate the example of Antony, that is, to follow Jesus Christ and give up his worldly career (i.e., his professorship of rhetoric), the new convert Augustine began to enter into the life of asceticism, which would later be related to his celibate and communal life with his friends at Cassiciacum and then in Rome as well as his lay or clerical monastic life at Thagaste and then at Hippo. According to Lawless, Augustine retreated with his friends to Cassiciacum during the idyllic interlude between Augustine's conversion in the Milanese garden and his baptism by Ambrose at the Easter Vigil in 387.[226] This retreat at Cassiciacum had offered an opportunity to Augustine to experience the life of community as well as the life of contemplation: "Work (both physical and intellectual), contemplation (both philosophical and Christian), prayer and serious dialogue on a variety of themes—these were the happy notes which sounded in this lovely place of retreat."[227] During these tranquil days at Cassiciacum, a monastic inclination lay dormant in Augustine's

223. Ibid., 9–10, 13, 57. See E. A. Clark, "Asceticism," 67.
224. Lawless, *Augustine*, ix, 15, 25–26.
225. Ibid., 25.
226. Ibid., 29–37.
227. Ibid., 36–37.

soul: "This monastic impulse in the young Augustine manifested itself in his indefatigable desire for God and the intensely personal character of his experiences to such a pitch that his proselytizing temperament attracted others to share their lives with him."[228]

According to Lawless, after his baptism, Augustine and his followers arrived in Rome by way of Ostia. As Harrison points out, Lawless insists that during this time in Rome, Augustine had learned the hallmarks of the Christian monastic life, which included "shared possessions, chastity, and holiness." In doing so, he was impressed with the organizational skills and practices of eastern monasticism (especially the Pachomian tradition), which included the pattern of prayer, reading of the Scriptures, manual labor, fasting, or clothing.[229]

In emphasizing Augustine's admiration of eastern monasticism, Lawless contends that the heritage of Neoplatonism had affected Augustine's understanding of the practices of eastern monks (e.g., "their contemplation of God's beauty") in Rome as well as his establishment of the Christian monasteries at Thagaste and then at Hippo.[230] While paying attention to the link of the Plotinian theme of the ascent of the soul toward the divine—"the flight of the alone to the Alone" (*enn.* 6.9.11)—with Augustine's meditation and his monastic life in light of the human desire to know God and the soul (see *reg.* 8.1; *sol.* 1.2.7, 1.13.22), Lawless states,

> The soul's activities are depicted in Plotinian terms as a seven-stage process: animation, sensation, art, virtue, tranquility, ingress, and contemplation. On Augustine's own admission, this sevenfold schema is arbitrary and breaks down further into a tripartite ascent: body—soul—God, stressing sequentially the significance of the soul to the body, to itself, and to God. Seven similar levels of ascent resemble a ladder of beauty and lend still another perspective on the soul's movement towards God.

---

228. Ibid., 34.

229. Ibid., 38–40; see "Rules," 739. According to Harmless, Pachomius (c. 292–346)—the Egyptian monk—has been viewed as the "founder of cenobitic monasticism"—that is, of monks living in organized communities. He established a remarkable confederation of monasteries in Upper Egypt and composed the first known monastic rule. Pachomius' life was celebrated in a sense of a series of biographies, composed in the 390s and preserved in Greek and Coptic. Now we have various rules, letters, and addresses attributed to Pachomius and to his successors, Theodore and Horsiesius (*Desert Christians*, 18; see Schaff, "Monasticism," 195–98).

230. Lawless, *Augustine*, 11, 35–39.

The importance of this model is equally germane to Augustine's aesthetic and ascetical theory. In the concluding chapter of his monastic *Rule* Augustine will, in fact, urge the servants of God who live in the monastery "to observe these precepts with love as lovers of spiritual beauty" [*reg.* 8.1].[231]

For Lawless, after learning Christian monasticism in Rome, Augustine returned to Thagaste in North Africa in 388. Agreeing with Peter Brown's view on Augustine's life at Thagaste, Lawless insists that the goal of the Thagaste group was not to participate in simply a philosophical retreat, but to achieve better Christian living in the lay community.[232] In 391, Augustine left Thagaste for Hippo for an interview with an aspirant to monastic life and in search of another place to found a monastery. Here Augustine was unexpectedly ordained to the presbyterate of Hippo. Augustine as a monk-priest established a lay monastery in a garden within the church property at Hippo.[233] Moreover, after ordination to episcopate, the monk-bishop Augustine also founded the clerical monastery at the "bishop's house" (as well as monasteries for women at Hippo). This means that, surprisingly, Augustine had attempted to "monasticize" the cleric—*the clericalization of the monk*—"the monk exemplifies the ideals of Acts 4:32, at the same time deepening his solidarity with Christ and his Church on their way to the Father."[234] In this process of the clericalization of the monk, about ten bishops of the African church came form Augustine's monastic community at Hippo, including Bishop Alypius and Bishop Possidius.[235] In doing so, Augustine had employed his monastic *Rule* in order to take care of his monasteries

---

231. Ibid., 39. Lawless writes, "At the heart of [Augustine's monastic] *Rule* as well as within the heart of Plotinian metaphysics one hears undertones, resonating at a still deeper level, between the one and the many, unity and multiplicity. . . . With the full force of his Trinitarian theology Augustine gradually enriches and enlarges Plotinus' concepts of unity and multiplicity. Only in the company of others could he long for, desire, search, find, and love the beauty which he established as the goal for all adherents of his monastic *Rule*" (ibid., 156–57; see Bourke, "Socio-Religious Issues," 211; Collinge, "Augustine's Theology," 60).

232. Lawless, *Augustine*, 45–54. See Brown, *Augustine*, 125–29.

233. Lawless, *Augustine*, 54, 58–59.

234. Ibid., 158; see 62.

235. Lawless notes, "Alypius . . . will become bishop of Thagaste. Possidius is destined to become bishop of Calama, as Profuturus will become bishop of Cirta. . . . 'About ten men' later become bishops in the north African Church and these, in turn, 'established monasteries'" (ibid., 60; see Zumkeller, *Augustine's Ideal*, 84).

effectively. His monastic *Rule* was primarily influenced by the apostolic Jerusalem community in which all members had attempted to become "one heart and one soul" in God. In that sense, Lawless writes, "With respect to common life, Matt 19:21 will eventually be upstaged by Augustine's decided preference for Acts 4:32-35, which had idealized the early Christian community in Jerusalem."[236]

Importantly, Lawless remarks that as a monk and a bishop, Augustine had kept a balance between the life of contemplation and the life of church ministry ("the nexus between the individual and the common good").[237] This implies that for Augustine, there was an inherent correlation between the service of God and the service of God's people in light of the interaction between his monastery and his church. Indeed, Augustine had participated in his monastic life, which was associated with the fulfillment of his pastoral ministry in the church community. Lawless writes, "As a monk-priest [and a monk-bishop], Augustine inveterately combined intellectual activity with pastoral ministry. Common life at Hippo resonated with many religious and philosophical ideals from the world of late antiquity. . . . [Augustine's] life together remained fundamentally fraternal and was inspired by the example of the apostles in the primitive Jerusalem community. Its [cultural and] social dimension was triggered as much by the requirements of Augustine's temperament as by the pastoral solicitude which was demanded by ministry in a servant-Church."[238] As a result, Lawless asserts that Augustine's conversion experience and his celibate and ascetic life were profoundly influenced by the early Christian monastic movements (i.e., the acetic life of the Egyptian Antony in the desert, the celibate life of Ponticianus' friends at Trier, and the traditional eastern asceticism in Rome, and the early Christian communal life at Jerusalem). While emphasizing the interaction of conversion to Christianity, the life of celibacy, and Christian monasticism, Lawless concludes that these early Christian monastic movements had played a pivotal role in Augustine's conversion to Christianity as well as in his foundations of the lay Christian community at Thagaste and the lay and clerical monasteries at Hippo.

236. Lawless, *Augustine*, 15; see "Rules," 739. See also Collinge, "Augustine's Theology," 56.
237. Lawless, *Augustine*, 156.
238. Ibid., 61–62.

Along the same line, Adolar Zumkeller in *Augustine's Ideal of the Religious Life* elucidates how Christian monastic movements affected Augustine's transformation in the Milanese garden as well as his Christian living through the service of God and the service of God's people. Zumkeller views Augustine's conversion as a life change which engages in the renunciation of worldly ambition and the life of celibacy and asceticism: "From the time of his conversion his only desire was to live as a 'servant of God,' i.e., a monk. As bishop, too, Augustine lived and died as 'a poor man of Christ.'"[239] Zumkeller contends that for Augustine, to be converted to Christianity meant to become a Christian, that is, to become a servant of God ("a monk") through the monastic way of life:

> To Augustine monastic profession (*professio*) meant a change in the conduct of one's life. It presupposed a sort of conversion (*conversio*)—not that fundamental conversion through repentance and the reversal of the will which a man achieves when he turns away from serving false gods to serving "the true God." In this case, Augustine was much more concerned with a new and special meaning of the word. Its content is a decision to live a celibate life, the renunciation of "hope in this world," and a promising of oneself "in a freely chosen servitude to God" in a monastic life of poverty and asceticism.[240]

Like Harrison and Lawless, Zumkeller emphasizes the role of early Christian monastic movements in the process of Augustine's life change. For example, Ponticianus' anecdote about the ascetic life of the hermit Antony had profoundly moved Augustine's transformation in the Milanese garden. For Zumkeller, Augustine's encounter with the anchoritic monasticism of Antony enabled Augustine to enter into the celibate and acetic life in community at Cassiciacum and then in Rome.[241]

Zumkeller insists that at Cassiciacum, Augustine and his friends were involved in Christian life in the community as well as in religious and philosophical discussions. Although the Cassiciacum community was not an explicitly monastic community, here Augustine had more determined to engage in the life of celibacy and asceticism and to

---

239. Zumkeller, *Augustine's Ideal*, ix. See Van Bavel, "Introduction to the Rule," 3.
240. Zumkeller, *Augustine's Ideal*, 210.
241. Ibid., 5–7.

participate in the Christian monastic movement of "serving God."[242] In 387, Augustine had unexpectedly spent nine months with his friends in Rome. Now Augustine had the opportunity not only to study the basic theory of Christian monastic asceticism, but also to observe its practical application (e.g., the pattern of prayer, the reading of Scripture, manual labor, and pious conversation).[243] In consideration of Augustine's encounter with Christian monasticism in Rome, Zumkeller pays attention to the impact of Pachomius (who was viewed as a founder of cenobitic monasticism) and Jerome (who was called the hermit of Bethlehem) on the learning process of Augustine of the eastern monastic ideal and the way of life.[244] He notes,

> St. Anthony of Egypt (d. 356) ranks as the true Father of Christian monasticism. In the second half of the third century he withdrew into the Libyan desert as a hermit, as many before him had also done. A larger settlement of hermits grew up around him, and he emerged as their spiritual leader. Monasticism entered a new phase when St. Pachomius, beginning about A.D. 320, united many hermit-monks in a single large monastery at Tabennisi in the Theban desert. Soon other foundations were made, so that at the time of Pachomius' death, in 347, this association of monasteries, which he himself had governed, comprised nine houses of men and two of women. The monks were said to number several thousand. Pachomius' Rule, the

---

242. Ibid., 7–13.

243. Ibid., 13–16. According to Elizabeth A. Clark, after his conversion to Christianity, Augustine learned more about Christian ascetic and monastic practices, at which point he rejected the view on the asceticism of the Manicheans. Clark remarks that, for Augustine, the Manicheans' motivation of asceticism was not appropriate because it was decided more by a rejection of material creation than by the love of God; as such, the Manichees mocked the stories of creation and production in Genesis 1–2, claiming that the highest principle, Light, or the Good, could never have enjoined such practices ("Asceticism," 69).

244. Zumkeller elucidates the influence of Jerome on the formation of Augustine's monastic ideal as follows: "In the midst of a pleasure-seeking world, a strongly ascetic movement was developing, as the spirit of Christian asceticism was asserting itself in [Rome], especially among its women, and penetrating the ranks of the nobility. . . . [I]t is certain at least that Jerome's ascetic ideals, and those of the Roman monasteries under his influence, were not without effect on Augustine. It must have been chiefly from Jerome's writings that Augustine learned more about Eastern monasticism at this time" (*Augustine's Ideal*, 15; see Schaff, "Monasticism," 205–14).

complete text of which is preserved only in a Latin translation by St. Jerome, influenced many later monastic rules.[245]

For Zumkeller, after studying the cenobites' lives in Rome, Augustine returned to North Africa. Influenced by the early Christian monastic movements, including the acetic ("anchoritic") life of Antony and the communal ("cenobitic") life of Pachomius, Augustine established a lay Christian community at Thagaste.[246] Further, as a monk and a priest, at the garden of the cathedral of Hippo, he founded the lay monastery within Valerius' agreement of monastery; as a monk and a bishop, he also founded the "clerics' monastery" (*monasterium clericorum*) at the "house of the bishop" (*domus episcopi*) as well as monasteries for women.[247] According to Zumkeller, Augustine's *Rule* had been employed by the members of the lay and clerical monasteries in order to foster Christian living in community. However, there was an essential difference between lay monks and clerics, that is, the "pastoral activity" of the cleric replaced the traditional "manual labor" of the lay monk. As such, the clerics' monastery ("the bishop's monastery") had combined the contemplative and active life.[248]

---

245. Zumkeller, *Augustine's Ideal*, 1; see 429–30. Harmless contends that the term "monk" (*monachos*) literally means "one who lives alone" (*Desert Christians*, 115; see Knowles, *Christian Monasticism*, 9). The word "monastery" (*monasterium*) refers to where those who live alone live together (ibid., 115). Harmless raises important questions: "How did monasteries arise? How did monks—those who choose to live alone—choose to live together?" (ibid.). Strictly speaking, the word monastery contains a separated but mutually informing dimension in light of a contradiction and symbiosis of the life of aloneness and the life of togetherness. Whereas Harmless views Antony as the founder of anchoritic monasticism, he understands Pachomius as the founder of cenobitic monasticism (from *coenobium*, 'community') (ibid.). Antony as a hermit tended to emphasize more Christian life in solitude, at which point he has been portrayed as a perfect model of the anchoritic life. On the other hand, Pachomius tended to focus more Christian life in community, at which point he has been depicted as the model of the communal ("cenobitic") life (which was called "the Pachomian *Koinonia*"). Harmless writes, "Pachomius . . . was certainly a pioneer [of the monastery]. He was also an organizational genius. By the time of his death, he headed a confederation of nine monasteries for men and two for women. These housed hundreds, perhaps thousands, of monks. His achievement earned him an international reputation, and the rules he composed provided a model for later monastic legislators, notably Basil of Caesarea in the Greek East, [Augustine of Hippo], and Benedict of Nursia in the Latin West" (ibid.; see 116–47).

246. Zumkeller, *Augustine's Ideal*, 24–32.

247. Ibid., 32–51.

248. Ibid., 41–42. For Zumkeller, Augustine's *Rule* gives us detailed information

Like Lawless, Zumkeller claims that Augustine's monastic life was deeply relevant to the service of Christ and of His members. Augustine had evenly devoted himself to his contemplation of God and his action for others. Zumkeller states, "Augustine shifted the notion of community to the center of monastic life. The chief thought behind his ideal of life was to form a community of Christian love and in that community to do everything possible to represent in its perfection the Christian ethic of living. This, above all, is the uniqueness of his monasticism."[249]

Zumkeller characterizes Augustine's concept of the monastic ideal and life as "Christian love" (*caritas*) in which all members of the community had attempted to engage in "the service of love" of God and neighbor: "Charity (love), the very heart of Christianity, is the center of Augustine's thought, especially of his monastic ideal."[250] In emphasizing the loving service of God and God's people within Augustine's monasteries at Hippo, Zumkeller writes, "Not continence or severe penances, not poverty or obedience, but love is the soul of the common life, the law of monastic perfection; love ought to form a monk's whole life. For [Augustine], love is the one fruit that life in his monasteries ought to bring to ripeness, his monks' dearest treasure, which they should cherish more than all the wealth of the world."[251]

---

about the mode of life that Augustine and his monks followed in the monastery of Hippo. Zumkeller writes, "The order of the day for the community was governed by strict rules. Time was divided into hours of prayer, Scripture reading, and physical labor. They came together in the oratory and the dining room. They all went outdoors together; they were together when they went into church, and, when reasons of health required it, to the public baths. And all their work was done for the benefit of the community.... The care of the sick was entrusted to one of the monks, the administration of the kitchen to another, and still others looked after books, clothing, and shoes" (ibid., 38; see 36, 172–99).

249. Ibid., 430; see 35–37, 41–42, 260–61, 431.

250. Ibid., ix. Bourke states, "The monasteries sponsored by Augustine cherished poverty for their residents, including Bishop Augustine, and offered hospitality to visitors and strangers, irrespective of their economic status.... His monasticism was no negative withdrawal from human interests and obligations.... Augustine's attempts at withdrawal were more efforts to avoid the wealthy than to evade his duties to the poor. Possidius wrote that it was a much greater privilege to live and converse with Augustine in his monastery at Hippo than to read all his great theological works. The monastery, for Augustine, provided a positive and enriched form of human living" ("Socio-Religious Issues," 211; see Collinge, "Augustine's Theology," 55–60; E. A. Clark, "Asceticism," 68–69).

251. Zumkeller, *Augustine's Ideal*, 260.

Getting Insights

Consequently, Zumkeller asserts that Augustine's transformation in the Milanese garden was inherently related to the early Christian monastic movements. This means that the early Christian monastic movements (including the anchoritic life of Antony and the cenobitic life of Pachomius) played a preeminent role in Augustine's conversion to Christianity, his resolution to enter into the life of celibacy and asceticism, his dedication to God as a servant of God, his establishments of the Christian and philosophical community at Cassiciacum, his formation of the monastic ideal of religious life, his foundations of the lay Christian community at Thagaste as well as the lay, clerical, and women monasteries at Hippo, and his loving service of God and God's people within the monastery and the church of Hippo.

In sum, from the perspective of anthropology of religion, Augustine's conversion has been regarded as a result of the influence of the Neoplatonic heritage (of Late Antiquity) on his thought, and a change through the Christian monastic movement in the context of the late fourth and early fifth centuries. On the whole, anthropological studies have explored Augustine's conversion process in specific cultural settings of his time. Thus, they have paid attention to the contextual matrix of Augustine's conversion that had occurred through long-term relationships with other persons or Christian communities.

Importantly, the anthropological studies of Augustine's conversion have contributed by elucidating the impact of cultural and philosophical forces on the complex process of his transformation. This means that in the consideration of the process of acculturation or cultural revitalization of Augustine, they have effectively elaborated the interplay of two levels of Augustine's conversion—personal and communal. As such, when we attempt to reinterpret Augustine's conversion in chapter 5, these anthropological studies guide us to recognize how the young Augustine had gradually undergone cultural and philosophical changes that resulted in the reconstruction of his religious identity, worldview, and belief in specific cultural values of the late fourth century. In doing so, they lead us to realize how Christian Neoplatonism helped the former Manichee Augustine 1) to reformulate his view on the divine nature from the material and divisible being to the immaterial and indivisible being, 2) to engage in his intellectual and spiritual journey toward union with the Truth (in light of knowing the divine and the soul), and 3) to acknowledge the Christian concept of the Incarnate

Christ (who is a mediator between temporal creation and the eternal God and who is a perfect example of humility).

Furthermore, these anthropological studies encourage us to look at 1) how the early Christian monastic movements (especially Antonian anchoritism and Pachomian cenobitism) had compelled Augustine to enter into the life of celibacy within the Christian philosophical community at Cassiciacum (386) and then at Rome (387), as well as 2) how these monastic movements had stirred Augustine to become a servant of God ("a monk") and to establish a monastery/lay Christian community at Thagaste (388) in North Africa, and then the lay and clerical monasteries at Hippo Regius (391, 395/6). However, these anthropological interpretations of Augustine's conversion are inadequate to investigate how the young Augustine's psychological crises were related to his personal and familial environments of his childhood because they have exclusively explored the influence of philosophical and cultural components on the process of his transformation. As such, they are not sufficient to elucidate the role of the divine, the sacred, or God in the process of Augustine's conversion in light of the correlation between divine intervention/grace and human transformation.

THEOLOGICAL STUDIES OF AUGUSTINE'S CONVERSION

Scholars in the field of Christian theology have examined the impact of religious factors on Augustine's conversion experience. In doing so, they have primarily paid attention to the dominant role of God in the process of Augustine's transformation. With respect to the complexity of the theological studies of Augustine's conversion, this section of the literature pays attention to four main themes because they are valuable for appreciating the religious dimension of conversion experience and because they are crucial for accomplishing a more coherent and integrated picture of Augustine's conversion process. These main themes are 1) Augustine's conversion and the transforming power of God's grace, 2) Augustine's conversion and the Christian Scriptures, 3) Augustine's conversion and Christian baptism, and 4) Augustine's conversion and the reciprocity of the love of God and neighbor.

Augustine's Conversion and the Transforming Power of God's Grace

Theologians have explored the interrelatedness between Augustine's encounter with God and his spiritual change. For example, David Burrell delves into the primacy and sufficiency of God's grace in the process of Augustine's transformation. Acknowledging psychological explanations of Augustine's personality and his life, Burrell emphasizes a theological reading of the *Confessions*, which involves an attempt to *understand* Augustine's conversion and his life story.[252] In this way, he regards Augustine's *Confessions* as an exercise in theological understanding, and as a "hymn of thanksgiving and praise to the Creator who revealed himself in Jesus."[253]

Burrell demonstrates how Augustine could continue in his attitude of self-reproach in the face of God's affirming mercy toward him: "One feels that the grace of God which Augustine celebrates so generously should in ten years have worked a greater self-acceptance than the continued tone of self-accusation betrayed in the *Confessions*."[254] According to Burrell, Augustine's self-reproach was rooted in an inability to acknowledge his sinfulness and to present himself available for forgiveness. In other words, his self-reproach actually reflected "a lingering unwillingness to surrender" himself to God. Whereas Freudian psychologists—Kligerman, Bakan, and Dittes—negatively describe Monica's role in the formation of Augustine's personality, worldview, and religiosity, Burrell positively depicts the influence of Monica on Augustine's life, his understanding of God, and his formation of theology (although he does not deny that Augustine's relationship to his mother was, at least to some degree, conflictual and ambiguous).[255] In

---

252. For Burrell, *understanding* engages in gaining insight into the working of a particular mind, whereas *explanation* involves accounting for a phenomenon by means of some universal law. In Burrell's view, Freudian studies (e.g., Kligerman, Bakan, and Dittes) attempts to *explain* Augustine's personality and his life, whereas the *Confessions* itself is an effort to *understand* them. The Freudian explanatory method has sought to fit Augustine within a psychoanalytic interpretive framework or model that has been developed and tested in other settings, with other subjects. In contrast, Burrell presents an alternate approach to understanding Augustine, largely by tracking Augustine's own self-understanding as revealed through the *Confessions* ("Reading the *Confessions*," 340–44).

253. Ibid., 350.

254. Ibid., 348.

255. Ibid., 341–42; see 348–49.

this sense, Burrell asserts that Augustine's relationship to his mother could be exemplary of his theology of grace.

Importantly, Burrell challenges the psychologist's assumption that autonomy and dependency must be polar opposites. More specifically, rejecting James E. Dittes' view that Augustine's surrender to his mother involves the relinquishment of his autonomy from his mother, Burrell raises a question: Are autonomy and dependency really opposed to one another? "Can it not be argued that the genuinely autonomous person is precisely the one who has come to accept the basic parameters of his life? Does not the person who acknowledges his dependency stand more of a chance for genuine autonomy and creativity?"[256] For Burrell, Augustine's autonomy resulted from the conversion itself; namely, his truly genuine autonomy came from an acceptance of his dependency on God, the ultimate source and ground of genuine human freedom. Augustine's reciprocal theme of his truly genuine autonomy with his dependency on God was deeply related to his theological views on God's grace; this theme was later based on Augustine's rejection of Pelagian views on human freedom.[257]

For Burrell, Augustine's heart was ever restless, ever in motion, until he found his ultimate rest in the relationship with God and himself. In becoming a Christian through God's grace, Augustine found a new way of confessing ("speaking") of God, and of the self in relation to God: "to be is to be related to God the Creator."[258] This new way of speaking of God and of himself enabled him to create a whole new way of life. As a result, theologically, Burrell understands Augustine's conversion as "the gracious gift of God" in which Augustine affirmed the primacy and sufficiency of God's grace for entering obviously into the creativity of his subsequent life. He concludes, "Linguistically, the *Confessions* is a carefully and a highly constructed work.... The double sense of 'confession' is well served by this hermeneutic hypothesis—praising God for all that He has made him and confessing how much he yet remains in need of purification."[259]

Similar to Burrell, Eugene TeSelle examines the efficacy of God's love in Augustine's conversion experience. Acknowledging psychological

256. Ibid., 346. See Dittes, "Continuities," 136–38.
257. Burrell, "Reading the *Confessions*," 344–46, 349.
258. Ibid., 332.
259. Ibid., 330–32.

(i.e., oedipal and narcissistic) readings of the *Confessions*,[260] TeSelle pays a great deal of attention to the theological reading of the *Confessions*, which primarily attempts to explore Augustine's relationships with God in his transforming process. For TeSelle, Augustine's concept of love involved the "appreciation of the other"; as such, theologically, Augustine viewed God as the object of his affections. TeSelle notes, "In Augustine's theory love at its best is an appreciation of the object and a finding of happiness through relationship with the object—in Augustine's view, first God, then all others 'in' God."[261] According to TeSelle, Augustine at least partially understood the Trinity to be this God's self-relatedness, whereas Plotinus finally understood the One to be the Alone.[262]

While describing the factors of Augustine's conversion, TeSelle stresses the internal dimension—"an inward presence of God"—rather than the external media of communication—"words, events, [or] rituals."[263] For TeSelle, "divine aid" through God's love (*caritas*) is a decisive factor for fostering Augustine's conversion in terms of God's calling, response, and conversion: "For many years Augustine assumed . . . that conversion is effected by the presenting of appropriate suasions through the channel of the understanding; the first assistance that is given to the will from within comes with the infusion of *caritas*, and this is given only to those who, responding to the call, have desired to do the good and have sought divine aid."[264] TeSelle asserts that as founded in the *Confessions*, God alone provides Augustine a sense of the coherence of his life in the past, present, and future. Consequently, he states,

> [Augustine] cannot bring himself to make a wholehearted commitment to the good because he is attached to many things, past

---

260. For TeSelle, the *Confessions* is psychologically revealing in light of development in such form as self-examination and autobiography ("Augustine as Client," 92). However, TeSelle finds oedipal and narcissistic readings of the *Confessions* inadequate. He contends that a historically sensitive and theologically informed interpretation of Augustine's relationships is far more illuminating (ibid., 92–93, 98–99).

261. Ibid., 99. According to TeSelle, the *Confessions* includes the following three significant sets of relationships: "with other people, either immediately or through institutions; with himself in his full concreteness; and with God as in his view the only adequate object of his affections" (ibid., 93).

262. Ibid., 100.

263. TeSelle, *Augustine the Theologian*, 332–35.

264. Ibid., 332.

and present, by the bonds of affection and is deeply involved with them because of his concerns and anxieties. The balance is tipped by a factor coming from beyond [him]. It is not something hidden and mysterious which overpowers the will or gives it some special impulse. The crucial factor is fully apparent, for it is simply the "call" which comes to [him]. It is something creaturely, and it enters [his] inner life through the channel of his understanding; then, by appealing irresistibly to his affections, it liberates them to act wholeheartedly in a single direction.[265]

As recent scholars, Colin Starnes and Carl G. Vaught agree with the idea that the transforming power of God's grace is a decisive factor in Augustine's conversion. In *Augustine's Conversion: A Guide to the Argument of Confessions I–IX*, Starnes explores how divine grace affected Augustine's conversion to Christianity. He provides an excellent "explanation of the move [Augustine] made from his birth in nature to his rebirth in grace."[266] More specifically, Starnes writes, "The argument of the *Confessions* has moved from Augustine's birth in nature which he called 'a dying life or a living death' (I,vi,7), to the point where he was about to be reborn in grace, 'to die to death and come alive to life' (VIII,xi,25)."[267] For Starnes, Augustine seriously underwent an inner division between his own habitual nature and his rational will; as such, his sexual desires were ceaseless and his old habits never consented to his going over Christ: "His habits were in conflict with his rational will. Neither could ever be fully satisfied nor could their conflict be truly resolved as long as he acted according to his nature, in which this division was now explicit and self-consciously manifest."[268] In this situation of his inability to help himself to get rid of the bondage of his will, Augustine heard from a neighboring house the voice of a child repeating a singsong refrain: "Pick it up and read it, pick it up and read it." Moved

---

265. Ibid., 42; see 191.

266. Starnes, *Augustine's Conversion*, xi. By using a trinitarian structure, Starnes formulates the Book I–IX of the *Confessions*: the first part (Books I–VII)—God as creator (the Father); the second part (Book VIII)—Christ, the Incarnate Son of God; and the third part (Book IX)—the Holy Spirit as the third person of the Trinity (ibid., 236). For Starnes, Augustine's conversion to Christianity, as found in Book VIII, was deeply related to his dedication to put himself on the Lord Jesus Christ.

267. Ibid., 234.

268. Ibid.

by this voice, he read one of Paul's letters and was transformed. Starnes writes,

> This is the sense of the *tolle lege* incident. Because he had acknowledged the impossibility of healing the division in his soul by himself he was at last open to a restoration and cure that would be effected by divine agency—by grace. . . . Presented as a divine command . . . he could now at last choose definitively between his habits and his rational will. . . . It was a command he obeyed voluntarily. In doing so his will was wholly and perfectly free since it was at last moved by end in which the division of reason and nature was not presupposed and from which their confusion, which had characterized his entire life to this moment, was totally excluded.[269]

Starnes emphasizes the impact of the transforming power of God's grace on the healing of Augustine's divided will in light of the process of becoming a Christian ("to walk on the way of God"). According to Starnes, in obeying the divine command, Augustine had freely committed to God. Divine grace alone cured his wounded soul and his division in the inner most nature: "God did not let him fall . . . The actual restoration, the healing of his divided soul, if it was to come at all, would have to come from God."[270]

Importantly, Starnes contends that during the healing of Augustine's divided soul through divine grace, Augustine was perfectly united with Christ. Augustine followed Christ with his whole will; he dedicated himself to Christ throughout the rest of his life. While agreeing with O'Connell's idea about Augustine's life of celibacy, Starnes states, "It was true that Augustine would not become a Christian unless he became celibate, yet his primary choice was about whether he would remain with his old habits in the confusion of reason and nature or else come to a position in which they were reconciled and united. He had found such a union objectively present in Christ."[271] For Starnes, Augustine's life of continence was a gift that expressed the grace of God rather than an achievement by his own effort and power: "The continence which

---

269. Ibid., 235; see 232.

270. Ibid., 235. See Fredriksen, "Paul and Augustine," 20–23, 26–27; Haight, *Experience and Language*, 50–51; Holtzen, "Therapeutic Nature," 110–15; Russell, "Augustine," 15; Stark, "Dynamics," 58; Van Fleteren, "Augustine's Theory," 67–68, 73.

271. Starnes, *Augustine's Conversion*, 233. See 213–14; O'Connell, *Augustine's Confessions*, 93–94.

Understanding Religious Conversion

had been impossible so long as he tried to achieve it by his own power had become actual in the moment that he placed his whole confidence in Christ."[272]

Like Starnes, Vaught in *Encounters with God in Augustine's Confessions* articulates the crucial role of divine interjection through God's grace in the process of Augustine's conversion in light of creation, fall, conversion, and fulfillment. According to Vaught, Augustine's *Confessions* unfolds on three important levels: "the author praises the greatness of God, confesses his sins by writing an autobiography, and defends his faith by describing the conditions that make memory, temporal experience, and existential transformation possible."[273] Acknowledging both the intellectual/philosophical dimension of Augustine's conversion in book seven ("the soul's ascent to God") and the communal dimension of his conversion in book nine ("shared mystical experience" with Monica), Vaught emphasizes the existential/volitional transformation of Augustine in book eight ("Augustine's conversion to Christianity") in terms of the transformation of the will.[274] For Vaught, Augustine's fundamental problem was "the distortion of [his] will" that led away himself from God at the deepest level. Although Augustine turned away from those among the Neoplatonists who knew God without glorifying him, preferred wisdom to piety, and embraced profession rather than confession, he remained separated from God because of his incapacity to orient his will toward God who created the world and who died to set him free.[275] In that sense, Vaught raises the following pivotal questions: "What does Augustine reject, and what does he accept during his conversion to Christianity?"; "What does he embrace, and what does he repudiate as he moves beyond the Neoplatonic vision to the Christian faith?" He writes,

> The most familiar answer is that for Augustine, becoming a Christian involves the abandonment of sexuality, the repudiation of worldly ambition, and the acceptance of the ascetic life of a monastery, first as a layman and then as a priest. However, this answer is inadequate because it focuses on the surface rather than the center of Augustine's existential transformation. . . . His

---

272. Starnes, *Augustine's Conversion*, 236. See Vaught, *Encounters*, 89.
273. Vaught, *Encounters*, ix; see x, 1–2; *Journey*, ix, 2.
274. Vaught, *Encounters*, 67. See Babcock, "Augustine," 180–82, 187.
275. Vaught, *Encounters*, 70, 82.

conversion to Christianity points beyond these relatively superficial phenomena to the transformation of his will. Augustine's attitudes toward sexuality and toward the advancement of his career are symptoms of an addiction that expresses a radical distortion of the will. Thus, when he responds to the voice of God in the garden, he not only relinquishes sexuality and renounces ambition at the surface of life, but also abandons the willfulness at the center of his being.[276]

Vaught asserts that Augustine himself understood his decisive moment in a garden of Milan (*conf.* 8.12.28–29) in light of a divine interjection that transforms his fragmented heart into a center of certainty and serenity.[277] Augustine's journey of dependence on the grace of God enabled him to move into the positive relation between God and his soul. During his conversion to Christianity, Augustine was willing to stand before God. Finally, he placed himself before "Jesus, the Christ" (8.7.16–8.12.30).

According to Vaught, in book eight, Augustine moved beyond his conversion to Neoplatonism to the transformation of his will. In other words, Augustine's shift from knowledge *about* God to a desire for more steadfastness *in* God led him beyond the Neoplatonic vision of *He Who Is* to a volitional transformation.[278] Vaught insists that at his decisive moment in the garden of Milan, Augustine needed existential transformation rather than philosophical reflection about his fragmented situation. Until hearing a divine voice (8.12.29), Augustine's search for wisdom was primarily intellectual. But now it began to shift in a voluntaristic direction; that is, he turned away from theoretical abstractions to the transformation of his will. Vaught notes,

---

276. Ibid., 68.

277. Ibid., ix; see 15. Vaught demands us to remember *four gardens* in order to understand Augustine's narrative about his conversion to Christianity: "The first is the garden where Adam and Eve eat the forbidden fruit and attempt to become gods. The second is the orchard where Augustine and his friends steal the pears and imitate omnipotence (2.6.14). The third is the place where Jesus prays before the crucifixion. And the fourth is the garden where Augustine leaves his friend behind to listen to a voice that speaks to him alone (8.12.28–29)" (ibid., 93). For Vaught, in the description of his conversion to Christianity, Augustine attempted to bind the Garden of Eden, the garden of his neighbor, and the garden where Jesus prayed together in the garden in Milan (ibid., 93).

278. Ibid., 69, 72, 95.

> The voice chants, "*Tolle, lege. Tolle, lege.*" . . . It is important to notice that these words come from a place beyond Augustine's reach and not simply from the "house of his soul." The self-enclosed garden in which Augustine weeps, the inner life to which it calls our attention, and the self-reflexivity of the soul to which it points cannot generate the transformation he needs. Rather, an encounter with a transforming source of power from beyond the circle of self-consciousness is necessary if Augustine is finally to come to himself. Yet since God not only transcends him infinitely, but is closer to him than he is to himself, God's voice can reach beyond the garden wall to address Augustine directly.[279]

Significantly, acknowledging that two Latin imperatives—*tolle lege*—mean "Take up and read," Vaught attempts to translate this passage, at least to some degree, "Destroy and read." More specifically, Vaught writes, "*Tollo* is irregular and its principle parts are *tollo, tollere, sustuli,* and *sublatum*. As Hegel points out in the *Phenomenology*, sublation has four stages: it means to take up, to destroy, to move beyond, and to embrace in a higher unity. The Latin *tollo* carries this significance as well. God not only asks Augustine to take up a book, but also to put off his old nature and to accept transformation by something new."[280]

Vaught argues that Augustine's "faith in Christ" was essential for his conversion to Christianity in light of embracing the Christ and creating a new way of living. After hearing a divine voice in the Milanese garden, Augustine read a passage from the book of Romans, which demanded him both to put off the lusts of the flesh and to put himself on Jesus, the Christ. Vaught states,

> In the phrase, "Put on Christ," the words "put on" translate *induo*. *Induo* sometimes means to put on a costume, but it also describes the moment when a Roman boy becomes a man by receiving a toga from his father. Augustine assumes many guises, not only in childhood, but also throughout his intellectual development. Now he must put these earlier stages behind him if the old costumes are to become a new creation. The need for a new creation leads us to the center of Augustine's transformation.[281]

---

279. Ibid., 91; see 79–80, 90.
280. Ibid., 94.
281. Ibid., 96; see 96–99, 102; *Access*, 16; *Journey*, 14.

Clearly, Vaught contends that during his conversion to Christianity, Augustine's embrace with the incarnation, the death, and the resurrection of Christ brought peace to his fragmented heart.[282] For Vaught, the Christ mediated the chasm between God and Augustine himself. *This* Christ enabled Augustine to turn away from his infinite self-accentuation, to accept his finitude and his fallenness, to set free from the bondage of the will that had enslaved him so long, and to become a newly created being.[283] As such, Augustine not only forsook "the chain of sexual desire" and "the slavery of worldly business," but also took his stand on the rule of faith that Monica had dreamed about.[284] As a result, Vaught concludes that through an encounter with a transforming power of God's grace, Augustine overcame his sense of willfulness, placed himself in Christ, and reestablished a peaceful relationship with God.

Augustine's Conversion and the Christian Scriptures

Scholars have examined the interconnection between the Christian Scriptures and the conversion experience of Augustine. For example, Karlfried Froehlich in "'Take Up and Read': Basics of Augustine's Biblical Interpretation" pays attention to the impact of the word of God on the process of Augustine's spiritual change. According to Froehlich, during years of his membership in the Manichean group, Augustine developed a rational criticism of the Bible, especially the Old Testament, for its crude anthropomorphisms and seemingly immoral teachings were unacceptable to the youth and young Augustine in his search of the truth. However, influenced by Bishop Ambrose, Augustine's view of the Bible had changed radically. Froehlich writes, "[The mature Augustine] now praised it as the book of books and celebrated the biblical God . . . whose eloquent word had the power to persuade, instruct, delight, and move beyond the power of anyone using the instrument of language."[285]

---

282. Vaught, *Encounters*, 98. According to Vaught, "the incarnation is a way of embracing finitude; accepting an unjust death is a way of taking sin on oneself; and the resurrection is a way of indicating that the one who dies on our behalf makes conversion and fulfillment possible" (ibid., 97).

283. Ibid., 94, 97–98; see *Access*, 96–99, 194; *Journey*, 102–3, 117.

284. Vaught, *Encounters*, 102.

285. Froehlich, "Take Up," 5.

Augustine understood the function of the Bible as a privileged means of God's interaction with humanity in the context of God-in-relation. For Froehlich, in book eight, Augustine portrayed his personal "discovery" which was deeply related to his experience of divine intervention through the word of God—"He had experienced God as the master rhetorician in the garden scene where the divine Word had moved him through the chant of a child and the words of the Apostle Paul."[286] More specifically, Froehlich writes,

> [Augustine's personal discovery/experience of the divine inspiration by the Christian Scriptures] becomes quite clear in the story of his last and decisive conversion, the scene in the garden with the unexplained sing-song of a child—*Tolle, lege!* ("take, read!"). In answer to this divine oracle, he takes the copy of Paul's letters form the table and reads Romans 13:13–14. The words hit home. Rather than the teacher of rhetoric interpreting the Bible, the Bible interpreted him through the providential action of God's Spirit. He had no other choice but to see it this way.[287]

Froehlich asserts that God communicated with Augustine in the Milanese garden by means of the word of God. That is, through the authoritative word of the Christian Scriptures, God the master rhetorician taught and moved Augustine who took up *this* word of God and read it. For Froehlich, in light of the christocentric understanding of the Bible, Augustine emphasized the link of Christian Scriptures with Incarnation, which essentially related to the theme of God's revelation to humanity and theme of paradoxical presence of God's perfect Word within imperfect human language. In that sense, Froehlich insists that the Incarnated God was revealed to Augustine through the Bible, and then enabled Augustine to enter into a new spiritual journey for fostering his faith, hope, and charity in light of the human soul to the love of God on the road to the blessed life.[288] As a result, Froehlich concludes that God's interaction with Augustine through Christian Scripture played an eminent role in Augustine's transformation.

Like Froehlich, Eugene TeSelle explores the link between the Bible and Augustine's conversion in terms of divine voice, Scripture, and

---

286. Ibid., 9; see 7, 10.
287. Ibid., 7.
288. Ibid., 5, 10–13. See *civ. Dei* 20.4.

Getting Insights

conversion. TeSelle reminds us to look at a crucial relation between hearing the voice of God and reading a biblical text when we account for Augustine's conversion. While Augustine's will was immobilized by inner conflict in the garden of Milan, Augustine heard a divine voice ("call")—*Tolle, lege*—beyond his own power, and acknowledged this voice as a divine command: "Do you still claim to be uncertain? The solution to your problem is right before your eyes. Pick it up and read."[289] At this decisive moment, Augustine did take up the Bible, opened, at random, the codex of Paul's letters, and read the words of Romans 13:13–14. This reading of a biblical text led Augustine to throw himself upon God.[290]

TeSelle pays attention to the transfiguring power of the word of God in the case of Augustine as well as the cases of Antony (who was an Egyptian monk) and Alypius (who was one of best friends of Augustine and was together with Augustine in the Milanese garden). He states,

> [Augustine] says first of Anthony that he was converted when he read a passage from the gospels—*Jesus said to him, "If you wish to be perfect, go, sell your possessions, and give the money to the poor, and you will have treasure in heaven; then come, follow me" (Matt 19:21)*—and felt that it was addressed directly to him (*Conf.*, VIII, 12, 29); then that his friend Alypius was given firm resolve and bound to a worthy purpose suited to his own character by reading another passage—*Welcome those who are weak in faith, but not for the purpose of quarreling over opinions (Rom 14:1)*; and then that he himself was turned toward God by still another passage—*Let us live honorably as in the day, not in reveling and drunkenness, not in debauchery and licentiousness, not in quarreling and jealousy. Instead, put on the Lord Jesus Christ, and make no provision for the flesh, to gratify its desires (Rom 13:13–14)*—in such a way that he would no longer vacillate, still entertaining hopes for marriage and [worldly] honor (*Conf.*, VIII, 12, 30). The words of Scripture, then, are the means by which God turns men toward himself, in each case by issuing

---

289. TeSelle, *Augustine the Theologian*, 41. TeSelle portrays the divine call that entered into the depths of the heart of Augustine: "The crucial factor is fully apparent, for it is simply the 'call' which comes to [Augustine]. It is something creaturely, and it enters [Augustine's] inner life through the channel of his understanding; then, by appealing irresistibly to his affections, it liberates them to act wholeheartedly in a single direction" (ibid., 42; see O'Brien, "Approach," 52).

290. TeSelle, *Augustine the Theologian*, 41–42. See Harrison, *Augustine*, 48–53, 88–93; Starnes, *Augustine's Conversion*, 235; Vaught, *Encounters*, 82.

an exhortation or presenting a possibility that is "congruous" with a man's condition.[291]

Similar to TeSelle, John M. Quinn in *A Companion to the Confessions of St. Augustine* probes how the word of God affected Augustine's conversion to Christianity. Quinn contends that "in brief, the *Confessions* praises God for the healing of sins confessed."[292] For Quinn, the story of Augustine's conversion was a tale of divine providence highlighting three major themes: "First, the Lord is a God of mercy, responding to Augustine's radical misery that is sin. Second, it is mercy constantly operative his whole life long, in every incident. . . . Third, this divine action works 'in wonderful and hidden ways' (4.4.7; 5.6.10; 7.21.27) . . . by employing the very depths of desolation of the prodigal son to vault him to the embrace of the Father."[293]

Quinn asserts that after studying Neoplatonic thought, Augustine's state of mind attested to the large-scale temptation to pride latent in an understanding of religious and metaphysical truths in the absence of saving grace. According to Quinn, as Augustine reached the summit of intellectual striving, he became subtly corrupted with egoism which rooted in his exclusive self-reliance: "the more apparently wise he became, the more actually unwise he grew, consumed by overweening pride"; "ironically, the more their philosophic vision was liberated, the more they were imprisoned by pride" which related to the enormity of his self-exaltation.[294] Quinn notes, "Even as [Augustine] capitulated to intellectual triumphalism, the wounds of his spirit throbbed with pain. General and abstract knowledge of the shape of things left him morally hollow; a feeling of stultification of spirit mitigated only when he began to feed on the Scriptures, whose nourishment soothed soul and self. The divine physician's fingers lovingly applied ointment to sores of his spirit so that his eyes were opened to the fine, sometimes undiscerned, line between presumption that is pseudo-salvation and confession indispensable in genuine salvation."[295]

For Quinn, Augustine's longing for conversion was hindered by his vacillating will; as such, in his mind, he might have just murmured "one

291. TeSelle, *Augustine the Theologian*, 42. Italics added.
292. Quinn, *Companion*, 1.
293. Ibid., 4.
294. Ibid., 397–98.
295. Ibid., 396–97; see 399.

word of true confession pleading for mercy."²⁹⁶ In other words, because of his exclusive self-reliance/exaltation, Augustine knew nothing of the cry of mercy to an offended God for forgiveness of inner misery. Quinn describes, in detail, Augustine's divided ("diseased") will as follows:

> So enchained, Augustine's spirit was condemned to a cruel slavery domineered by necessity, poles apart from the free servitude under the reign of charity got by grace [*en. Ps.* 99.8]. His fledgling new will was aiming to serve God unencumbered by self-interest that awards primacy to sexual pleasure or worldly honors; and through that loving service he was aiming at joy; God was to be his absolute source of delight, absolute, because the divine is immutable. Lamentably, his new desire could not eradicate his old will, affixed unshakably, apparently, in moral perversity. Conflict raged between the old or carnal will and the new or spiritual will, with the discord rivening his soul; civil war divided the one self into two warring camps.²⁹⁷

Quinn insists that in the culmination of his inner turmoil, God intervened to transfigure Augustine through the word of God. For Quinn, when Augustine experienced the peak of his divided will, he flung himself under a fig tree in the Milanese garden. He released lots of penitential tears. He heard the voice of a child chanting "Take and read" at which point he read Christian Scriptures (Rom 13:13–14). This reading of the Bible suddenly triggered his conversion to cast himself on the Lord.²⁹⁸

Like TeSelle, Quinn claims that as a specific scriptural text (i.e., Matt 19:21) affected deeply Antony's transformation and his monastic life in the desert, a specific verse of the Bible (i.e., Rom 13:13–14) influenced Augustine's conversion to Christianity in an "obscure" garden of Milan in 386; further like the cases of Antony and Augustine, another verse of the Christian Scriptures (i.e., Rom 14:1) played an important role in Alypius' transformation and his life.²⁹⁹ More specifically, Quinn depicts this garden scene of Milan as follows:

296. Ibid., 397; see 447, 449; *conf.* 8.8.19.
297. Quinn, *Companion*, 436.
298. Ibid., 457–59; see 399–400. See also Georgiou, *Last Transfiguration*, 70–71; Van Fleteren, "Augustine's Theory," 67.
299. Quinn, *Companion*, 458–59; see 471–72. See also *conf.* 8.12.29–30; Byasse, *Reading Augustine*, 50–51; Matter, "Conversion(s)," 24–25; TeSelle, *Augustine the Theologian*, 42.

> As the tears dried up completely, [Augustine's] mind was illumined with the insight that God was leading him to discover a clue to conversion in Scripture, after the pattern of St. Antony, whose life was wholly turned around by an apparently coincidental hearing of Matt 19:21. Snatching up the Epistle to the Romans near Alypius, he opened at random to Rom 13:13-14, which commanded him, in effect, to stop chasing women and the world, to stifle the clamor of the lower self and robe himself in the light of Christ. At the moment he finished reading the lines, his soul was flooded with light, banishing all anxiety and bathing him in profound peace. . . . When he related his inner transformation to Alypius, remarkably, he learned, Alypius had been graced with a like interior transmutation, applying to himself the following line, "But receive the man who is weak in faith" (Rom 14:1).[300]

Clearly, Quinn elucidates that before his conversion in the garden, the young Augustine had rated the style of Scriptures barbarous in contrast to the eloquence of Cicero, that is, he might have put down the Scriptures as unworthy and unscientific in comparison with the analytical yet stylish superiority of Neoplatonic writings.[301] However, after his conversion, Augustine regarded the Scriptures as a treasure trove of wisdom. For Quinn, Augustine employed two keys in order to unlock Scriptural treasures: "*faith*, for which humility disposes the mind, and *understanding*, which explicates the data of faith. *Faith* is the introductory acceptance, *understanding*, the developed grasp of Scriptures."[302]

As a result, emphasizing the historicity of Augustine's conversion scene in an "obscure" garden of Milan in 386,[303] Quinn pays attention

---

300. Quinn, *Companion*, 458–59.

301. Ibid., 398. See *conf.* 3.4.8–3.5.9.

302. Quinn, *Companion*, 134. Italics added. See 135, 399; *s.* 60 A.1.

303. According to Quinn, Pierre Courcelle casts a doubt on the historicity of Augustine's conversion scene in the garden of Milan. Courcelle claims that while Augustine's interior conversion was unquestionable, the exterior details of his conversion scene were intentionally constructed in his literary imagination (ibid., 460). However, rejecting Courcelle's fictional interpretation of Augustine's conversion, Quinn emphasizes the factual character of Augustine's narration. Quinn writes, "In Book 8 Augustine simply records the fact that he threw himself under a [real] fig tree" (ibid., 461). As such, for Quinn, the child's (i.e., a real boy or girl's) chanting of *Tolle, lege* truly appeared to be coincidental (ibid., 460–63; see Starnes, *Augustine's Conversion*, 241–42; Wills, *Augustine's Conversion*, 31–34).

On the other hand, influenced by Courcelle, Leo C. Ferrari suggests that Augustine's

to the inner workings of the divine word in Augustine's transformation. Through reading of the Bible, Augustine overcame his sense of exclusive self-reliance, that is, his divided will became one; he opened his mind to hear the inward divine locution—"It is I who am with you now as always."[304] Further, Augustine actually committed himself to God in terms of right relationship with God.

Augustine's Conversion and Christian Baptism

Scholars have speculated about the link between Christian baptism and Augustine's spiritual change. For example, Richard Fenn probes the ritual dimension of Augustine's transformation in terms of "the magical power of ritual."[305] Fenn articulates how the holy waters of baptism enabled Augustine to be recreated and to be anew. According to Fenn, in spite of his garden experience in the summer of 386, Augustine as a (former) professor of rhetoric had still suffered from a serious disease of his lungs.[306] Specifically, Fenn describes,

> [Augustine's] conversion [in the Milanese garden] was not enough . . . to undo the damage that he had done by teaching

---

conversion did replicate that of St. Paul in light of the intentional literary reconstruction. Ferrari views Augustine's *Confessions* as "not strictly a historical document, but was rather written basically as a romantic story to be read aloud before a live audience" ("Book Eight," 136). For Ferrari, Augustine's conversion scene in book 8 of the *Confessions* is dependent upon St. Paul's conversion on the road to Damascus as found in Acts 9:1–9; 22:6–16; 26:12–18. As such, the *tolle lege* scene is a fictional composite based in part upon an earlier experience of Pauline discovery ("Book Eight," 132–36; *Conversion*, 50–70; "Paul," 8–20).

However, repudiating Ferrari's idea that Augustine's conversion scene is fictional, Quinn argues that Augustine's conversion was not a Damascan experience; he prepared himself for the breakthrough step by step, through prayer, reading, and dialogue with friends (*Companion*, 471–72). For Quinn, Augustine's conversion scene is more paralleled with the conversion story of Antony rather than that of Paul: "The chanting of the child's voice reminded Augustine not of Paul but of Antony. *Like him, [Augustine] felt admonished to consult the Scriptures*, and in line with a similar oracle or sign from heaven he was at once converted" (ibid., 465; italics added; see Matter, "Conversion(s)," 24–25; cf. Fredriksen, "Paul and Augustine," 20–26; Kreidler, "Conversion," 511).

304. Quinn, *Companion*, 458.

305. Fenn focuses on the link of transfiguring ("magical") power of ritual with language ("Magic," 78–81; see Elledge, "Augustine," 82).

306. Fenn, "Magic," 84.

people to harm others through the techniques of speech; he developed a symptom that left him too breathless to teach anyone further as his lungs "began to decay," and he therefore became unable to speak "too loud or too long" (Book 9, 2). This is a fitting punishment for [Augustine] who prided himself on being able to take others' breath away by the powers of his own rhetoric. . . . [Augustine's] conversion was therefore not enough to stop this cycle of cruelty and self-destruction; only the "holy waters of baptism" could provide pardon for his "most horrible and deadly sins" (Book 9, 4).[307]

Looking at the context of Augustine's illness and his sense of pride, Fenn emphasizes the healing ("cure") power of the baptismal waters for Augustine.[308] For Fenn, through immersion into the holy waters, Augustine has been soothed and transfigured; namely, his sin was forgiven by God and he became a humble person. As a result, Fenn concludes that the rite of Christian baptism at Milan played a preeminent role in the process of Augustine's healing and regeneration.

Similar to Fenn, David F. Wright in "Augustine and the Transformation of Baptism" articulates the link of Christian baptism with Augustine's change in light of the power of ritual process. According to Wright, by the time of his writing of the *Confessions*, Augustine portrayed his baptismal experience as a dramatic turning-point of his life. Wright insists that the sacrament of Christian baptism enabled Augustine to enter into "the decisive transition from an old life to a new that marked early Christian baptism."[309] Clearly, Wright depicts Augustine's transformation of his life through the Milanese baptismal rite as follows:

> The abandonment of his profession of rhetoric, and of all expectation of a successful career in the public eye; a final turning away from the pleasures of the flesh, within or without marriage; the divine remission of all his "horrendous and mortal sins"; the ultimate reconciliation with his devoted mother, sealed in the climactic vision of Ostia; the new delights of the Psalms, of the

307. Ibid., 84.

308. Elledge asserts that there is an analogy between Monica's tears and the baptismal waters for Augustine ("Augustine," 78–79; see Fenn, "Magic," 81). For Elledge, as baptismal waters functioned as "a means to and guarantor of salvation" for Augustine, Monica's tears became "spiritually engendering, ontologically regenerative, and . . . amniotically protective of" his son ("Augustine," 78).

309. Wright, "Augustine," 291.

hymns and chants of worship in Milan, and fresh plans for a shared life in the service of God back in Africa.[310]

In the same way, William Harmless in *Augustine and the Catechumenate* examines how the ritual of Christian baptism was interwoven with Augustine's transformation in light of a movement of Augustine the catechumen, Augustine the petitioner, and Augustine the neophyte. Harmless views Christian baptism as "a sharing in the death and resurrection of Christ."[311] According to Harmless, Augustine became a catechumen while he was still a child; that is, he was regularly sanctified from birth by the sign of the cross on his forehead and was seasoned with God's blessed salt on his tongue as an act of exorcism ("a sort of inoculation").[312] However, Augustine's baptism was delayed by his mother; as such there was a conventional wisdom for him: "Leave him alone and let him do it; he is not yet baptized";[313] he was not eventually baptized until age thirty-three. Only after his dramatic garden experience, Augustine publicly became a candidate for Christian baptism in Milan. He participated in the baptismal liturgy on March 10, 387; he had undergone the demand regimen of Lent, including asceticism, exorcism, and catechesis. Finally, at the Easter vigil service April 24–25, 387, Augustine was baptized by Bishop Ambrose with his son, Adeodatus, and his closest friend, Alypius.[314]

While agreeing with Peter Brown's view on Augustine's baptism and his transformation,[315] Harmless asserts that through the sacrament of Christian baptism, Augustine was transfigured; that is, his baptism was effective for the remission of his sin and for the rebirth of his life. In other words, Augustine was delivered from evil, reconciled with God, enlightened by the Spirit, and incorporated into the body of Christ, the church. For Harmless, after his baptism, Augustine had retired from his professorship of rhetoric; he had set aside any prospect for a com-

---

310. Ibid., 291–92.

311. Harmless, *Augustine*, 16.

312. Ibid., 80. See *conf.* 1.11.17.

313. Harmless, *Augustine*, 81. See *conf.* 1.11.18. According to Harmless, in the context of the North African church of the fourth century, parents had usually stopped short of having their children baptized (80).

314. Harmless, *Augustine*, 79–81, 93–104. See *conf.* 9.5.13; Quinn, *Companion*, 494–96; Smith, *Transforming Conversion*, 50–57; Starnes, *Augustine's Conversion*, 254.

315. See Brown, *Augustine*, 118.

fortable marriage and had committed himself to a celibate life.[316] As a result, Harmless concludes that the ritual of Christian baptism in Milan played a pivotal role in Augustine's rebirth and change.

Influenced by Harmless, Thomas M. Finn in *From Death to Rebirth: Ritual and Conversion in Antiquity* deals with Augustine's change through ritual act of baptism within the Christian community. For Finn, the early Christians had a strong conviction "(1) that Jesus had risen from the dead, (2) that his resurrection established an entirely new relationship between God and humankind, and (3) that baptism symbolized that relationship."[317] In this sense, Finn states,

> Baptism as the passage from death to life gave rise to the image of the baptismal font as tomb and womb. . . . The baptizands are . . . immersed in the baptismal waters, which Ambrose's contemporary, John Chrysostom (c. 345–407 C.E.), regularly calls a tomb (*taphos*), insisting that the "old self has been crucified with him, in order that the body of sin may be destroyed." The font as womb emphasizes the passage to life, with rebirth and resurrection used almost interchangeably. The same Chrysostom remarks, "Conception without womb, begetting without bosom, birth without flesh!" Yet he insists that in baptism there are both burial (*taphe*) and resurrection (*anastasis*) at the same time.[318]

While employing a dominant metaphor of death and rebirth, Finn explores how Milanese baptismal liturgy affected Augustine's transformation. He argues that Augustine's conversion "was embedded in complex and richly articulated ritual processes."[319] According to Finn, after recovering from a serious infection in his lungs at Cassiciacum, Augustine as a catechuman returned to Milan to be baptized within the approval of Bishop Ambrose. After enrollment in the Milan cathedral, Augustine as a "competent" began his Lenten catechumenate with others, including Adeodatus and Alypius. This Milanese Lenten catechumenate was composed of 1) enrollment and the fast, 2) instruction, 3) scrutinies, 4) the creed, 5) holy week, and 6) the vigil.[320] For Finn, after completing successfully the Lenten catechumenate, Augus-

---

316. Harmless, *Augustine*, 104.
317. Finn, *Death to Rebirth*, 141. See Georgiou, *Last Transfiguration*, 106–7.
318. Finn, *Death to Rebirth*, 255–56.
319. Ibid., 34; see 254.
320. Ibid., 221–26; see "It Happened," 590–94.

tine participated in the Milanese baptismal liturgy which consisted of 1) the opening ceremony (*ephphatha*), 2) the anointing, 3) renunciation and profession, 4) consecration of the waters, 5) immersion, 6) anointing and foot washing, and 7) the white garment and the sealing. More specifically, Finn describes this process of Augustine's baptismal liturgy as follows:

> At the end of the [Easter] vigil, the competents assemble at the door to Ambrose's new baptistery for the first rite, *ephphatha* [which refers literally to] "be opened." . . . Ambrose touches Augustine's ears and nostrils to open his mind to understand the rites and his experience of them. . . . Next Augustine enters the baptistery proper . . . where he ritually removes his clothes. A priest anoints him from head to toe with olive oil to strengthen him. . . . Thus prepared, a naked and glistening Augustine stands upright, facing west, and hears two questions. "Do you renounce the devil and his works?" "Do you renounce the world and its pleasures?" To both he answers, "I do renounce them." . . . Ambrose now consecrates its waters in the name of the Father and of the Son and of the Holy Spirit. . . . Augustine then enters and stands waist-deep in the font. Baptism is by triple immersion, and the form is interrogatory. Three questions are put to him: "Do you believe in God the Father?" "Do you believe in our Lord Jesus Christ and in his cross?" "Do you believe also in the Holy Spirit?" Each time he answers, "I believe," he is immersed. . . . When Augustine emerges from the font, a priest awaits to anoint him with chrism on the forehead with the words, "God the Father All Powerful, who has given you new birth through water and the Holy Spirit and has forgiven your sins, he is the one who anoints you for eternal life." After [Augustine and his fellows] are anointed . . . a deacon reads from the Last Supper account the words about Jesus tying a towel around his waist, washing, and then drying the feet of the disciples (John 13:1–11). Ambrose does the same for the newly anointed, with help from the priests. . . . Augustine dries, puts on a new linen garment, and takes his place in the white-robed line before Ambrose. Ambrose anoints him on the forehead with the sign of the cross in the name of the Trinity, thereby stamping him as their possession and strengthening him with the fullness of the Holy Spirit.[321]

---

321. Finn, *Death to Rebirth*, 226–29; see "It Happened," 594.

For Finn, after baptism, Augustine was welcomed as a newborn member of the Christian community. He celebrated his first Eucharist with other newly baptized. Finally, Augustine became fully Christian, namely, he was reborn and was now risen.[322]

Importantly, Finn views Augustine's experience of Christian baptismal rite on Easter (387) as a climax of Augustine's life history. According to Finn, Augustine clearly understood that baptism in the Milan cathedral, not his experience in the garden in Milan, established his conversion and regeneration, although he said nothing about the baptismal rites themselves in the *Confessions*. In emphasizing Augustine's baptismal experience in Milan, Finn summarizes the movements of Augustine's life as follows: "[Augustine's journey of conversion] began with his inscription in the catechumenate in 354 and culminated in the mysteries of baptismal initiation on Easter 387. His home and family, his education, his mistress, Adeodatus, the Platonic books, the Manichees, Ambrose's homilies, the garden in Milan, Monica's incessant pressure—they were part of the process, currents in a sea change about which Augustine might say, 'It is not a lie but a mystery' (*non est mendacium sed mysterium*)."[323] As a result, Finn asserts that Augustine's conversion happened within the ancient ritual process known as the catechumenate. He concludes that through the baptismal liturgy of Milan, the old Augustine died and was buried; now the new one was reborn and was risen; publicly, the newly baptized Augustine became a member of the Christian church.

Augustine's Conversion and the Reciprocity of the Love of God and Neighbor

Scholars have probed the symbiotic relation between love of God and love of neighbor in Augustine's conversion process. For example, Bernard McGinn and Patricia F. McGinn understand Augustine's conversion experience as an ongoing transformative process in which he moved into the connection with God as well as the connection with God's people. According to McGinn and McGinn, after making a decisive commitment to "the Incarnate Christ" in the Milanese garden,

---

322. Finn, *Death to Rebirth*, 229–30.
323. Ibid., 230–31.

Getting Insights

Augustine involved "not only baptism but also the choice of a celibate life typical of emerging Christian ideals of perfection."[324] Clearly, McGinn and McGinn depict the rest of life of Augustine after his conversion to Christianity as follows: "Augustine returned to Africa . . . where he founded a monastic community and was ordained priest. . . . [He] was made bishop of Hippo, a small coastal town, where he spent the remaining thirty-five years of his life caring for his flock and engaged in a series of doctrinal disputes that shaped later Western theology."[325]

McGinn and McGinn elucidate how Augustine intended to establish a more refined ideal of Christian charity that fully integrated the love of God and neighbor (the "precepts of the Great Commandment").[326] They claim that for Augustine, the authenticity of the love of God is only proved by the love of neighbor. For McGinn and McGinn, Augustine had experienced a deep and transforming awareness of God's immediate presence in his participation in the corporate life of the church ("Christ's body"). They insist that Augustine viewed the love of charity as "a higher glue that binds [God's people] to God"; that is, he spoke of union with God in terms of the loving bond that knits all believers into the one Body of Christ.[327] McGinn and McGinn write, "Augustine's insistence that true progress toward God must be thought of as social, that our pursuit of God is not a solitary effort, but one that takes place in the bosom of the church and by means of the exercise of loving charity toward all, is the core of his message."[328]

As a result, McGinn and McGinn assert that Augustine sought to harmonize the mutually enriching dimensions of Christian living—contemplation and action. They conclude that there was a reciprocal relation between Augustine's movement toward God and his movement toward neighbors: "No one should be so contemplative that in his contemplation he does not think of his neighbor's needs; no one so active that he does not seek the contemplation of God."[329]

Like McGinn and McGinn, Thomas F. Martin explores the link of Augustine's turning toward God with his turning toward others in his

---

324. McGinn and McGinn, *Christian Mystics*, 153.
325. Ibid.
326. Ibid., 161–69. See *Trin.* 8.8.12.
327. McGinn and McGinn, *Christian Mystics*, 163; see 154.
328. Ibid., 167.
329. Ibid., 168. See *civ. Dei* 19.19.

conversion experience. Viewing Augustine's conversion not as a single event but an ongoing "progress" (*proficere, proficiens*), Martin emphasizes that Augustine's conversion did bring him into a new relationship with God ("solitude") and with other human beings ("community"): "The emphasis on interiority is matched by a just as insistent emphasis on the shared nature of Christian existence."[330] Along with his putting on the Lord Jesus Christ, Augustine embraced the ascetical life, foregoing marriage and family, wealth and career. After he returned to Africa, his unexpected call to serve the church of Hippo Regius led him both to establish a Christian monastery there and to confront the historical and social milieu of the North African Church.[331] While repudiating Gerhard Lohfink's idea that Augustine had diverted "ancient Christianity from community to individualism," Martin pays attention to Augustine's living of "ongoing conversion," which was deeply rooted in the interplay of his sense of solitude and community.[332] Martin argues, "Does Augustinian spirituality lead to a privatized spirituality? While it is clear that Augustine privileges the heart and the journey within, he would be the first to decry any reading of him that would turn the Christian life into a solitary journey. It is always a shared pilgrimage, a community of fellow believers on a journey of faith to God."[333]

Clearly, Martin states that Augustine's "emphasis on interiority, its intention is never meant to lead to an introverted spirituality"; that is, Augustine's concept of solitude never means individualism.[334] For Martin, Augustine was never journeying alone but journeying with others, especially his friends (e.g., Alypius) as found in the *Confessions*. Based on the dynamic interaction of God, self, and community, Augustine's spiritual life was "imbued with a personalism that defuses its rigour and a sense of community that challenges all individualism."[335] Martin contends that Augustine had struggled to follow God's commandments of love of God and neighbor in his life, while serving his church and taking care of his flock. More specifically, Martin writes,

---

330. Martin, "Augustinian Spirituality," 137; see 138.
331. Ibid., 138; *Restless Heart*, 21–50.
332. Martin, *Restless Heart*, 47. See Lohfink, *Jesus and Community*, 181–85.
333. Martin, *Restless Heart*, 47.
334. Ibid., 43, 48.
335. Ibid., 159; see 46–47, 61–62, 88–89.

[Augustine] explored in depth the relationship between love of God and love of neighbour, one result being his classic *frui/uti* distinction: God alone is to be loved as an end—effectively subordinating all other loves to this end. Both enthralled and terrified with the scriptural affirmations that "God is love" (1 John 4:6) and Christ's own description of the final judgement in terms of neighbourly love of the poor Christ (Matt 25:31–46; see s. 389.5), Augustine consistently placed Jesus' love command as the summation of the whole Christian life.[336]

According to Martin, Augustine's life was "a pilgrimage, demanding ongoing conversion, the taking up of new challenges, requiring an ever-fresh response to God's call" and engaging in the historical and social context of the Christian community.[337] Martin echoes Augustine's sensitive and insistent awareness that "there is a mysterious interpenetrating dynamism between self, God, community and grace."[338] In emphasizing Augustine's new spiritual "journey" (*peregrinatio*) for union with God and his new participation in the Christian community, Martin concludes that Augustine's conversion was not only turning toward God, but also turning toward neighbors.

In the same way, Raymond Canning probes the link of Augustine's spiritual life with his encounter with Jesus' two great commands—the love of God and neighbor. Canning contends that Augustine viewed love for neighbor as "a step (*gradus*) to love for God" and as a "virtuous action cleansing the eye and the heart for contemplation."[339] According to Canning, Augustine stressed a deeper unity of love for God and the neighbor: "Love of God can be tested in everyday practice of love of neighbour."[340] That means that for Augustine, Christ is present in the poor generally—in any needy neighbor. Indeed, to love this neighbor is to love God: "God and the neighbour are loved with one and the

---

336. Martin, "Augustinian Spirituality," 137.

337. Ibid., 138.

338. Martin, *Restless Heart*, 89. Martin states, "Augustine's emphasis on 'a spirituality of the self' fits into a particular historical context that seemed all too prone to eliminate the necessary tension between self and community. [Augustine] decried a dualistic and Gnostic Manichaeism that postured as true Christianity and dismantled human autonomy.... God, self, and community are inextricably bound together in the spirituality of Augustine" (ibid., 49).

339. Canning, "Love of Neighbour in St. Augustine," 12, 31.

340. Canning, "Unity of Love," 72.

same love: the more we love God, the more we love ourselves, and consequently the more we are able to 'consider all that is mortal of no value in comparison to love for people by which we desire that they live righteously.'"[341]

Importantly, Canning claims that the love of God and the love of neighbor stand in an analogous relation within the process of Augustine's transformation. According to Canning, while emphasizing the identification of the love of God with the love of the neighbor, Augustine pointed out that "love itself makes God present" and that "to love the neighbour is to follow Christ's path to the Father which goes by way of the cross."[342] As a result, Canning asserts that "[Augustine's] turning to the neighbour form[ed] such an integral part of [his] turning to God";[343] that is, during the process of his spiritual change, Augustine's sense of love of neighbor played a vital role within his movement of love toward God.

Like Canning, Mary T. Clark examines an interaction between Augustine's new relationship with God and his new commitment to the Christian community. Clark pays attention to Augustine's "continued conversion" in which he entered into "union with God, communion with his neighbors, and ministry to those in need of spiritual and material assistance."[344] For Clark, Augustine understood the love of God and neighbor as an essential Christian value in which God's call to the inward life of love for God expands into a community life of love for one another; as such, the whole members of the Christian community could be "united in love of God, one heart, one soul."[345] Clark contends that after his encounter with the Incarnate Christ in the garden of Milan, Augustine did not escape from the material or external world. Rather, he had continuously applied the meaning of "the Word made flesh" in the historical and social context of the Christian community.[346]

---

341. Ibid., 120; see "Love Your Neighbour," 146, 183, 197. See also *Trin.* 8.8.12; Corrigan, "Love of God," 103, 106; DeSimone, "Augustine," 20; Froehlich, "Take Up," 5, 11; Harrison, *Augustine*, 65–67, 96–100; Kreidler, "Conversion," 516–20; Van Bavel, "Double Face," 169, 177, 181.

342. Canning, "Love of Neighbour in St. Augustine," 48, 50; see 5; "Augustine on the Identity of the Neighbour," 232; "Unity of Love," 119–20.

343. Canning, *Unity of Love for God and Neighbour*, 420.

344. Clark, "Spirituality," 814–15.

345. Ibid., 815; see *Augustine*, 87–90.

346. Clark, "Spirituality," 814–15; see *Augustine*, 30, 44; "Eye of the Heart," 30.

Getting Insights

Significantly, Clark shows how the personal and communal aspects of Augustine's conversion belong together in the process of his transformation. According to Clark, Augustine's spiritual life was involved in "a longing for mystical union with God [and] it is firmly rooted in the biblical command to love one's neighbor."[347] While Augustine as a layman, a priest, and a bishop lived in Christian communities, including his monastery and his church of Hippo of Regius, he realized that "an 'interior life' of love for God . . . externalized itself in [and expanded into] a community life of respect and love for one another."[348]

As a result, Clark insists that during his process of spiritual transformation, Augustine actively responded to God's calling. This calling through God's intervention in the Milanese garden enabled Augustine to establish a new relationship with God; this relationship with the divine also enabled him to enter into a new living with other people.

In conclusion, there are various understandings of Augustine's conversion experience in the field of theology of conversion. Augustine's conversion has been regarded as a result of the transforming power of God's grace, a turning from godlessness to God portrayed in the Bible, a change through ritual act of baptism within the Christian community, and a consequence through the mutual interplay between love of God and love of neighbor. On the whole, theological studies of conversion have primarily emphasized the efficacy of encounter with God through divine grace in process of Augustine's spiritual change.

Indeed, the theological studies of Augustine's conversion have contributed by articulating the impact of religious factors (especially the encounter with the divine) on the process of religious change. While emphasizing the impact of the religious forces on Augustine's transformation, they have primarily depicted the correlation between the experience of the self and the experience of the divine in the complex process of his spiritual change. In that sense, they have profoundly elucidated how the divine intervention or grace—a primary factor—has

---

347. Clark, "Spirituality," 815. Similarly, T. J. Van Bavel states, "Modern individualism contrasts with Augustine's thought, which is basically corporative. He envisions the whole present in the parts, and, conversely, the parts present in the whole. Consequently, Christ is for him not only an 'I,' but also a 'We.' Christ incorporates us into Himself. Through love, Christ is present in mankind, and mankind in Him" ("Double Face," 175); "'The absolute Other is the source of all other relations.' Love has a double face" (ibid., 181).

348. Clark, *Augustine*, 92; see 87.

affected the transformation of Augustine. As such, they have contributed by speculating a crucial relation between hearing the voice of God and reading a biblical text in Augustine's conversion process as well as an inherent link between the ritual performance of Christian baptism (i.e., the Milanese baptismal liturgy) and Augustine's spiritual change. Moreover, while emphasizing the interaction of Augustine's turning to God and his turning to others, these theological studies have contributed by demonstrating how the convert Augustine has moved into loving relationships with himself, others, and God; that is, how he has committed himself into both the service of God (i.e., Christian living in solitude) and the service of neighbors (i.e., Christian living in community).

As such, when we attempt to understand Augustine's conversion, these theological interpretations strongly encourage us to recognize the impact of the transforming power of God's grace on the healing of Augustine's divided soul/will in light of the process of becoming a Christian. In doing so, these interpretations lead us to look at how God intervened to transfigure Augustine through the word of God in the context of the culmination of his inner turmoil as well as how the Milanese baptismal liturgy was interwoven with Augustine's transformation in terms of a movement of Augustine the catechumen, Augustine the petitioner, and Augustine the neophyte. Furthermore, they help us to pay attention to the ongoing transformative process of the convert Augustine in which he had continuously engaged in the connection with God as well as in the connection with God's people in light of the reciprocity of his monastic life and his pastoral ministry. However, on the whole, these theological studies of Augustine's conversion have tended to consider the personal, social, and cultural factors as subordinate to the theological factor (e.g., sin and God's grace) in the process of Augustine's transformation. As such, in order to foster a better understanding of Augustine's conversion, the theological studies need to respect more human science approaches to Augustine's transformation, while acknowledging the influence of the transforming power of the divine on the process of his spiritual change.

INTERDISCIPLINARY QUESTIONS FOR EXTENDING THE CONTRIBUTIONS OF THE LITERATURE

This section of the chapter attempts to formulate interdisciplinary questions for critically extending the contributions of the literature of Augustine's conversion. By applying Rambo's interdisciplinary framework, this section claims that the study of Augustine's conversion is profoundly enriched by an interdisciplinary approach, which pays attention to the personal, socio-cultural, and religious contexts of his transformation. In order to understand the complexity and richness of the phenomenon of Augustine's conversion, it proposes a main interdisciplinary question as follows: *How might we investigate the interrelated influence of personal, social, cultural, and religious factors on the lifelong process of Augustine's conversion?*

There is no common theoretical definition of Augustine's conversion. Previous studies have tended to explore Augustine's conversion process from the perspective of a specific theoretical discipline. This implies that there is a great demand for enhancing a mutually-informing conversation among theological and social scientific studies of Augustine's conversion. As such, the above interdisciplinary question leads us to respect the religious/theological approach to Augustine's transformation while also incorporating the importance of personal, social, and cultural issues. This question helps us to establish a more integrated understanding of Augustine's conversion narrative in his *Confessions*.

Based on the main interdisciplinary question, this section of the chapter suggests the following six substantive and mutually-informing questions in order to facilitate a more accurate and effective investigation of Augustine's conversion. These questions provide us an insight into portraying a coherent picture of how multiple factors work together, simultaneously and cumulatively, in the process of Augustine's lived experience of change.

1. How had Augustine's psychological crises affected his earnest quests for knowing himself and the divine?

This question provides an insight into a connection between Augustine's experience of psychological distress and his yearning for knowing himself and the divine. It attempts to demonstrate that

Augustine's conversion process might begin within the context of his restlessness of the heart—his "soul's sickness"—which could not find a resting place on earth (e.g., *conf.* 7.7.11, 8.5.10). As such, this question helps us to explore the process of Augustine's interior transformation from the divided self to the integration of the self in relation to his profound experience with the divine (e.g., 8.12.28–29).

2. How were Augustine's interior journey for union with God and his search for community with others knit together in the process of his conversion?

This question intends to demonstrate how turning to God is related to turning to neighbor in Augustine's conversion experience. It leads us to investigate a symbiotic relation between Augustine's search for union with God and his search for others in terms of solitude and community (*civ. Dei* 19.19; *f. et op.* 16.17; *s.* 261.8). This implies that Augustine's conversion was deeply rooted in the reciprocal process of his love of God and his love of neighbor in light of his contemplation of God and his action for others.

3. How had significant other people in the Christian community provided love, support, and belonging to fulfill Augustine's psychological needs and to make up for his frustration with his deprivations in the social and cultural conditions of his time?

This question emphasizes intimate interactions between Augustine and other persons within Christian communities. During the period of the depths of his agony and spiritual darkness, Augustine experienced loving care and support from other persons (e.g., Ponticianus [*conf.* 8.6.14–15] or Alypius [8.11.27]). As such, this question provides us with an insight into examining how significant other persons (e.g., Ambrose [5.13.23–5.14.25] or Simplicianus [8.2.3–5]) had affected Augustine to overcome his dualistic materialism (i.e., the Manichean belief [3.7.12]) and his skeptic thinking in the Academy (5.14.25) as well as how they supported Augustine to fill his (psychological) needs (e.g., a sense of belongingness) and to find a new way of life in the Christian community. Further, this question helps us to elucidate the influence of significant others' conversion stories (e.g., conversions of Victorinus

Getting Insights

[8.2.3–5], Antony [8.6.14–15], and Ponticianus' two friends [8.6.15]) on Augustine's own conversion.

4. How had Augustine reshaped his (personal and religious) identity, worldview, and belief through his ongoing interactions with others, through his participation in Christian communities, and through his experiences of cultural change?

This question pays attention to the impact of institutional and cultural-philosophical factors on the complex process of Augustine's transformation. It enables us to elaborate the influence of the Neoplatonic heritage (e.g., Plotinus' concept of the soul's ascent to the One [see *conf.* 7.10.16, 9.10.23–25; *sol.* 1.2.7, 2.1.1; Plotinus, *enn.* 1.6.9]), Christian monastic movement (e.g., a type of the solitary hermitage of the desert anchorites—Egyptian monk Antony's life [*conf.* 8.6.14–15]—or a type of the community life of the cenobites [Possidius, *v. Aug.* 3, 5]), and the North African context on Augustine's thought and his conversion process.

5. How were Augustine's interpersonal relationships, his God representations, and his encounters with God bound together in his conversion process?

This question leads us to delve into the interplay of human relationships, the God representations, and the experiences of the divine in the process of Augustine's transformation. More specifically, it helps us to examine how Augustine's (interpersonal) relationships might have affected and have been affected by his God representations, and how his God representations might have affected and have been affected by his experiences of the divine in the process of his conversion.

In this study, *the God representation* refers to an internal structure through which one's experience of and relationship with God is mediated. It is comprised of images, ideas, feelings, sensations, and memories that are unconscious as well as conscious. The God representation evolves throughout the human life span, influenced by the complex and rich interplay of the person with personal, social, cultural, and religious forces. There are three concurrent types of the God representation in the literature. From a psychoanalytic object relational perspective,[349]

---

349. Winnicottian object relational psychologists have implored how past

Understanding Religious Conversion

Ana-Maria Rizzuto in *The Birth of the Living God* focuses on the impact of human interpersonal relationships on the formation of God representations during childhood, in addition to its transformations and utility throughout life.[350] Rizzuto's psychoanalytic research tends to emphasize almost exclusively on internally constructed and experienced representations of God. Because Rizzuto limits herself to a discussion of the formation of the individual's private representations of God,[351] she does not pay attention to the workings of an institution consisting of culturally patterned interactions with cultural representations of God, and she does not explore the relationship that many people develop with God as an external being in which they experience God as a real presence which transcends their representations.[352] From psychological

---

interpersonal relationships shape relationships in the present, including the relationship with the sacred (e.g., A. B. Ulanov; C. R. Schlauch; D. W. Winnicott; J. W. Jones; J. McDargh; M. Clair; W. W. Meissner). Object relations theory emphasizes the significance of the earliest relational experiences in the formation of one's personality as well as in the development of the God representation. The studies of the interaction of human relationships, God representations, and the experiences of the divine are closely related to the following issues in the literature: the impact of human interpersonal relationships on formation and reformation of the God representation (Clair, *Human Relationships*; McDargh, *Psychoanalytic Object Relations Theory*; Rizzuto, *Birth*); the interplay of human psychological development with religious experience (Meissner, *Psychoanalysis*); the interaction of a new sense of the self, the transformation of the God representation, and the experience of the sacred (Jones, *Psychoanalysis & Religion, Religion and Psychology*); the link between creative playing, imagination, and religiosity in transitional ("illlusionistic") world (Pruyser, *Play of the Imagination*); the interaction of the self with the lived experience in transitional process/space (Schlauch, *Faithful Companioning*). In this dissertation, object relations theory helps us know how Augustine's interpersonal life experiences might have influenced his personality and religiosity in his life span. In doing so, it leads us to explore how Augustine's conversion experience may enhance his play, imagination, creativity, and symbolization in the terms of the relational self and transitional space. More specifically, it provides us an insight into exploring the correlation between Augustine's divided self and his fragmentation anxiety, between Augustine's abuse experience in childhood and his negative representation of God, between Augustine's experiences of loving care by others, his experience of the divine, and his positive representation of God, and between Augustine's creative playing and his conversion experience in light of the relational self, creative playing of imagination, and the transformation of the God representation in transitional space.

   350. Rizzuto, *Birth*, 3, 177–201.

   351. Ibid., 3.

   352. John McDargh argues that God representations are not to be reduced to the collections of human object relationships "without leaving room for the possibility that the reality of God him/her/itself may be an essential contributor to the

Getting Insights

and anthropological perspectives, Melford E. Spiro in "Collective Representations and Mental Representations in Religious Symbol Systems" suggests a developed explanation of the representations of God, which includes both the cultural/anthropological ("collective") element and the psychological ("mental") element.[353] Spiro claims that beginning at birth children develop *socially-constituted* conceptions of the world as a consequence of transactions with parents or other primary caretakers.[354] For Spiro, God representations are not only mentally and individually derived, but also collectively and culturally derived from one's relationships within social groups. From psychological and theological perspectives, Moshe H. Spero in *Religious Objects as Psychological Structures* proposes that there are two sources of God representations: 1) interpersonal relationships (an "anthropocentric" source) from an object relational perspective and 2) direct or indirect relationships with an objective God (a "deocentric" source) from Judaism's view of religious experience. For Spero, God representations are not only internally derived, but also externally derived from one's relationship with God.[355] Spero's model includes a real Deity object in the external environment, which is internalized. From an interdisciplinary and integrative approach, Rizzuto's, Spiro's, and Spero's models give us insight into how we can explore together the individual, social/cultural, and deocentric representations of God for a more integrated understanding of religious conversion.

Augustine described his own God representations in his works, especially his spiritual autobiography—*Confessions*—when he (now a mature middle-aged adult) recollected his life history before God and his community members. Augustine portrayed his traumatic injuries in childhood, his negative image of the self, and his negative God representations (e.g., his experiences of beatings at school and parents' laughing at his stripes/God's silence about it [*conf.* 1.9.14–15]).[356] While

representational process" ("Research Paradigm, 192).

353. Spiro, "Collective Representations," 45.

354. Spiro emphasizes the human psyche at the center of anthropological inquiry, seeking to understand the psychological existence of human beings as an integral and dynamic part of social and cultural life.

355. Spero, *Religious Objects*, xvi. Spero's model goes beyond Rizzuto's model of the God representation which describes how internal God representations are formed from internalized human object representations.

356. See Capps, "Scourge of Shame," "Vicious Cycle"; Ferrari, "Boyhood Beatings."

expressing his low self-esteem (e.g., 1.19.30), Augustine negatively characterized his representations of God as follows: 1) God as punishing—"And my reluctance to learn you used for a punishment which I well deserved: so tiny a child, so great a sinner" (1.12.19); 2) God as whipping—"I will not pass over in silence the acute pain of your chastisement" (9.4.12; 3) God as laughing—"So let the mighty and powerful laugh at our expense" (4.1.1).

However, during the depths of his agony, Augustine experienced loving care and support from other persons (e.g., Ponticianus [8.6.14-15] or Alypius [8.11.27]). During the depths of intellectual disruption in the Manichean dualistic materialism, he found a new way of life through his cultural change resulting in the reconstruction of his (personal and) religious identity, worldview, and belief (e.g., 7.12.18). During the depths of spiritual darkness, he felt the initiating activity of God's loving grace (e.g., 8.12.28-29). This means that Augustine re-created his relationships with himself, others, and the divine. Through these relationships, he underwent progressive restoration and healing. Accordingly, his negative God representations were changed into the positive God representations as a loving, accepting, and encouraging Being. As such, Augustine depicted 1) God as merciful—"then little by little, Lord, with a most gentle and merciful hand you touched and calmed my heart" (6.5.7); 2) God as caring—"I tasted you, and I feel but hunger and thirst for you. You touched me, and I am set on fire to attain the peace which is yours" (10.27.38); and 3) God as healing—"By inward goads you stirred me to make me find it unendurable until, through my inward perception, you were a certainty to me. My swelling was reduced by your hidden healing hand, and my mind's troubled and darkened eye, under the hot dressing of salutary sorrows, was from 'day to day' (Ps 60:9) brought back to health" (7.8.12).

6. How were Augustine's relationships with himself, others, and the divine related to human development and spiritual maturity?

This question provides us with an insight into realizing that to be converted means to be (properly) related with oneself, others, and the divine in terms of human development and spiritual maturity. This implies that the conversion experience involves an ongoing process of one's transformation to search for connection and negotiating disconnection and reconnection with oneself, others, and the divine in terms

Getting Insights

of the interaction of self-self, self-other, and self-divine relationships. In this sense, this question demonstrates that Augustine's conversion was a process of transformation ("turning"), which engaged in the new connection with himself, others, and God. As noted earlier, the garden experience at Milan (*conf.* 8.8.19, 8.11.27, 8.12.28–30) enabled Augustine to make a new decision for reorganizing the rest of his lifetime. During the process of his transformation, Augustine became reconciled to himself through his encounter with the divine (8.12.29) and he committed himself to the monastic life (9.2.2–3). Further, he actively responded to God's calling and he participated with other community members in God's mission to the world (i.e., his church ministry as a priest or bishop). As such, this question clarifies how the personal, communal, and spiritual aspects of Augustine's conversion belonged together in his transforming process in the light of a mutual interaction of human development and spiritual maturity.

SUMMARY

Due to the complexity and diversity of the phenomenon of Augustine's conversion, scholars have offered diverse interpretations of his narrative of transformation. From psychological perspectives, scholars have viewed Augustine's conversion as an effort to resolve his oedipal conflicts, the process of unifying his divided self, or the process of self-becoming through his mental development and progressive maturity. From social/communal perspectives, scholars have regarded Augustine's conversion as a consequence of the impact of the conversion narratives of other people on his transformation ("a story within a story"), and a change through his interpersonal bonds and Christian friendships within the Christian community. From cultural and philosophical perspectives, scholars have considered Augustine's conversion as a result of the influence of Neoplatonism of Late Antiquity on his intellectual change, and a change through Christian monastic movements of the late fourth and early fifth centuries. From theological perspectives, scholars have understood Augustine's conversion as a result of the transforming power of God's grace, a turning through hearing the voice of God and reading a biblical text, an experience of rebirth or regeneration through the baptismal liturgy of Milan, and a lifelong transformation by way of his engagement in Christian life in love of God and neighbor. Indeed, the contributions of the previous conversion studies have tended to remain isolated from one another (like tracks of a metropolitan train yard running parallel to each other), because the perspectives are established independently. They have not critically integrated religious and social science perspectives for understanding his conversion.

In order to extend critically the contributions of the literature by bringing together various disciplines, this chapter offers the main interdisciplinary question how personal, social, cultural, and religious factors might have affected the unfolding process of Augustine's conversion. Following this main question, six substantive and mutually-informing questions guide us to explore the complexity and richness of Augustine's religious change, and thus demonstrate the benefits of constructing an interdisciplinary approach to the process of his transformation.

5

Playing Together
An Integrated Understanding of Augustine's Conversion

> What is most essential in facing the abundant new readings of Augustine is to keep these readings in conversation with one another as well as with Augustine's own rich complex: Augustine the God-seeker, Augustine who "put on Christ," Augustine the monk and pastor, Augustine the thinker, Augustine whose life was nourished by prayer and evangelical love, Augustine the historical figure, living in a real world with all of its blindness and all of its insight. Any spirituality that claims the name "Augustinian" faces the challenge and responsibility to take into account the "whole" Augustine, joining him on that same journey that was closest to his own heart.
>
> —Thomas F. Martin[1]

THIS CHAPTER PRESENTS AN integrated understanding of Augustine's conversion process through the critical and mutually-informing conversation of personal, social, cultural, and religious dimensions within Rambo's interdisciplinary framework. In other words, it shows

1. Martin, *Restless Heart*, 156–57.

a coherent picture of how the complicated and multi-layered components of Augustine's conversion process interact with and reinforce one another. Following this reinterpretation, it proposes a holistic pattern of the conversion process from the *Confessions*.

In consideration of the complexity and richness of the re-readings of Augustine and his life history, this study argues that the case of Augustine's conversion experience illustrates well the complex and multidimensional process of religious change. As noted earlier, Augustine's conversion was not simply "a [crucial] single event" in his life, but "an ongoing process" in which multiple factors worked together simultaneously and cumulatively, requiring the continuing transformation and dedication of his whole life. In this chapter, the main interdisciplinary question and six substantive and mutually-informing questions help us to investigate the impact of complicated and multiple components on Augustine's conversion process as well as to demonstrate the benefits of formulating an interdisciplinary approach to the process of his whole change of life.

PRESENTING A COHERENT PICTURE OF AUGUSTINE'S CONVERSION PROCESS

This section of the chapter accomplishes an integrated account of Augustine's narrative of transformation. More specifically, it presents a reinterpretation of Augustine's conversion through the critical and collaborative dialogue of the personal, social, cultural, and religious dimensions. This means that by critically extending the contributions of the literature, it depicts a more coherent and integrated picture of how the complex and multiple factors involved in Augustine's conversion are knit together.

Indeed, Augustine's lived experience of conversion depicts well the lifelong process of human transformation. In "The Dynamics of the Will in Augustine's Conversion" (1990), Judith C. Stark characterizes Augustine's conversion as a progression and summarizes it as follows:

> Many years of searching, growing, and struggling preceded Augustine's conversion in the garden in Milan in 386. Augustine himself considers his first reading of Cicero's *Hortensius* when he was nineteen years old to have been a decisive moment in his years of struggle. Many other important elements contributed

to Augustine's intellectual, moral, spiritual and psychological growth and development from age nineteen until his conversion to Christianity when he was thirty-one years old. Among these important elements, the following certainly merit consideration: Manicheanism, skepticism, Stoicism, Neoplatonism, as well as the influence of important persons in his life, for example, Ambrose and Simplicianus. The full story of both the persons and ideas that influenced Augustine is best revealed by Augustine himself in his *Confessiones*.[2]

While emphasizing the diversity and richness of Augustine's conversion, this study articulates how and why the young Augustine converted to Christianity in the summer of 386 and what specific experiences led him to conversion. In doing so, it sheds light on the symbiotic relation between Augustine's inner journey toward encounter with God and his sense of solidarity with others within Christian communities in terms of knowing oneself, others, and the divine. Moreover, it elaborates how Augustine had gradually reestablished his identity, worldview, and belief by way of his affective interpersonal bonds and his intensified affiliations with religious/philosophical groups, impacted by Neoplatonism and Christian monasticism of the late fourth and early fifth centuries.

The portrayal of an integrated reinterpretation of Augustine's conversion is based on Rambo's systemic stage model of religious conversion which includes context, crisis, quest, encounter, interaction, commitment, and consequences. It consists of the following main themes: 1) the macro and micro context of Augustine's time; 2) the experience of psychological distress and crisis; 3) the quest for knowing himself and the divine; 4) encounters with significant others and participation in Christian communities; 5) the experience of cultural change related to the Neoplatonic heritage and the Christian monastic movement; 6) the experience of divine intervention and grace; 7) the acceptance of Christian baptism and the experience of the vision of Ostia; and 8) engagement in the service of God and God's people.[3]

2. Stark, "Dynamics," 45.

3. The interdisciplinary questions play a crucial role of the connection—a "bridge" or "glue"—between the main factors of Augustine's conversion in order to overcome isolation from one another; that is, they are helpful and beneficial for coordinating a range of main factors which work together in the unfolding process of Augustine's religious change.

Understanding Religious Conversion

These themes are inherently interwoven in Augustine's evolving process of transformation. They demonstrate that Augustine's conversion occurred in the relational contexts of himself, others, and the divine; as such, it took place within the personal/familial, social, cultural, and religious contexts of his time. This implies that Augustine was involved in a web of relationships; in this meaningful web, he had experienced persons in the moment, persons from the past, persons about whom he'd been told or had read, and a divine agent all acting (and responding) in an unfolding process.

While reinterpreting Augustine's narrative of transformation, we need to imagine that we are chanters participating in a choral performance. In order to demonstrate effectively the talents of personal voices as well as to show successfully the richness and meaning of the hymn itself, each person has to respect other people's voices while listening to one's own voice within the spirit of harmony and balance. Like the cooperative performance of the members of the choir, we need to respect another person's unique account of Augustine's lived experience, and thus integrate a range of various voices ("interpretations") of Augustine's conversion.

Macro and Micro Context of Augustine's Time

For the first stage of Augustine's conversion process, this section of the chapter focuses on the specific *context* of his time in order to help us accomplish a comprehensive account of his religious change. More specifically, the exploration of the initial stage of the process of Augustine's conversion helps us to understand the basic background and motif of his transformation as well as to establish a more coherent and integrated picture of his religious change. It is consonant with stage 1—*context*—of Rambo's model of religious conversion. As Rambo emphasizes context in the formulation of his model of religious conversion to depict the ecology of the conversion process, this study begins with the description of *macro and micro context* of Augustine's conversion. Augustine was born in the province of Numidia, North Africa. Although he had greatly influenced the construction of Western culture, Augustine had remained a North African. This means that he had lived in the Roman world of North Africa during all of his seventy-six years of life, except five years in Italy.

There is the *macro context* of Augustine's conversion which includes the social, cultural, religious milieu of North Africa. In Augustine's day, North Africa was an important place within the Roman Empire. At that time, by cultivating the fertile plains in the Northern coastal region, North Africans had played a crucial role in supplying a tremendous amount of grain and olive oil to Romans. In that sense, Brown describes the plains of grain and olive in North Africa: "By the third century A.D., the high plains and valleys of the plateau—the old Numidia—where Augustine was born, had been planted with grain, criss-crossed with roads, settled with towns. Even farther south, beyond the Aures mountains, a chain of forts guarded the boundary between intensive cultivation and its absence, on the very edge of the Sahara."[4] More specifically, Harrison points out the link between the rich plains of North Africa and the life of Romans as follows: "Augustine's Africa lay at the heart of the Roman Empire. Its northern coast bordered the Mediterranean and its roads led to seaports whose busy traffic ensured that the roads ultimately led to Rome. The traffic was largely one-way however, for Rome depended upon the fertile plains of the coastal strip for its bread—at least two-thirds of its wheat supply came from Africa—which it exacted as part of the land tax, or *annona*. Huge granaries dominated the ports, their importance evidenced by neighbouring Roman garrisons."[5]

According to Harrison, Rome controlled about 140,000 square miles of North West Africa which was divided originally into four, and later, under Diocletian's reforms, eight provinces that consisted of about 650 towns. Carthage, its capital city, was one of the biggest and busiest places in the Empire in which a lot of ships had continuously carried wheat and olive to the port of Italy (e.g., Ostia or Naples) for Rome.[6]

In the context of the movement of the Romanization of the Empire (especially the era of Caracalla's edict [212 A.D.]), North African society was influenced by Rome's distinctive culture and civilization at which point North Africans, especially those of the coastal region near Mediterranean Sea, were gradually civilized and Latinized/Romanized. However, inland areas (which were away from the fertile olive and wheat plains of the coast) were still predominated by the traditional village culture; that is, they were proportionately less Romanized than

---

4. Brown, *Augustine*, 7.
5. Harrison, *Augustine*, 117.
6. Ibid.

coastal areas. In these inland areas, Punic was still spoken, as opposed to Latin, and rural traditions and beliefs were more persistent.[7]

As such, the exploration of the African social and cultural background is essential for understanding Augustine, his conversion, and his thought, as Lancel points out: "A large part of what motivated Augustine as an adolescent and young man cannot be understood unless we are sufficiently aware of both the cultural formation of his deep-rootedness in Africa and the social milieu into which he was born."[8] As a North African, Augustine was deeply influenced by the African life-style and culture. In this sense, John H. McClanahan looks at how the traditional Roman-African temperament had affected the formation of Augustine's personality and his thought:

> The African temperament manifested itself in various ways in the experience of Augustine. A strong licentiousness was nourished in the culture. Among some Roman remains in a North African city this inscription has been discovered: "To hunt, to bathe, to play, to laugh—this is to live." In his early life Augustine apparently acted in the spirit of this motto. Vigor and intensity were a part of the North African environment. These characteristics are reflected in Augustine's style of writing, in his vivid memory, in his strong and energetic will. The climatic influence in the African provinces seemed to nurture a hardness and coarseness of fibre in the people. It was evident in ecclesiastical controversy. T. A. Lacey attributes the brutality displayed by [the young] Augustine in his treatment of women to this influence.[9]

According to McClanahan, in the North Africa of Augustine's time, many people had sought relief from the lethargy and decay of the age by becoming sensual materialists. These people were popularly impacted by the distortion of the Epicurean philosophy that was heavily rooted in a motto—"Live and let live; tomorrow we die."[10] This means that such cultural and philosophical movement (which was deeply related to the

7. Ibid. See Lancel, *Saint Augustine*, 5–6.

8. Lancel, *Saint Augustine*, 5.

9. McClanahan, "Psychology of the Self," 25–26. See Brown, *Augustine*, 7.

10. McClanahan, "Psychology of the Self," 28. At that time, many adolescent and young people were deeply affected by the movement of sensual pleasure and materialism in African society. For example, Alypius (who was a student of Augustine) was seriously involved in the entertainment of worldly games rather than studying: "The whirlpool of Carthaginian morals, with their passion for empty public shows, sucked [Alypius] into the folly of the circus games" (*conf.* 6.7.11).

rigidity of North African society [e.g., the issue of social class]) had compelled many African people to be satisfied with a sensual pleasure based on the materialistic attitude or life-style.

In contrast to the movement of the sensual materialists, there was a different movement in North African society and culture which was profoundly related to (Christian) monasticism. This means that for McClanahan, while repudiating the voluptuous approach to life, Christian monasticism had represented a deep quest for moral earnestness and purity. The movement of monasticism had challenged the sensual materialists to escape from the drag of carnal life, to reformulate their self-image and the goal of life in the newly monastic ideal, and to enter into the spiritual and monastic life in solitude and/or community.[11] Indeed, the Christian monasticism of Augustine's time was rooted in the Egyptian monasticism of the desert. In this sense, Harmless states, "Christian Egypt has long been regarded as the birthplace of monasticism. That view . . . is only partially true. Still, its desert monasteries and its sage monks would imbue Egyptian Christianity with a distinctive flavor, and by the mid-fourth century would earn it international fame. The writings and example of these desert Christians would influence monastic life for centuries, both in the Greek East and in the Latin West."[12] In particular, both the anachoritic monasticism of Antony—Christian living in solitude—and the cenobitic monasticism of Pachomius—Christian living in community—were crucial for fostering Christian monastic movements of Augustine's time in the Greek East as well as in the Latin West.[13]

Indeed, the exploration of the religious context of North Africa in Augustine's time is also essential for understanding Augustine, his conversion, and his religious identity. Harrison portrays the condition of early Christianity in North Africa:

> We know, in fact, very little about early Christianity in Africa. Our first real evidence is the account of the seven men and five women from Scilli, somewhere in Numidia, who were brought before the Proconsul Saturninus in Carthage, in AD 180, for "refusing to swear by the genius of the Emperor" and who were

---

11. McClanahan, "Psychology of the Self," 29–31.

12. Harmless, *Desert Christians*, 17.

13. Ibid., 57–100, 115–41; Harrison, *Augustine*, 177–93; Knowles, *Christian Monasticism*, 9–36; Markus, *Ancient Christianity*, 157–77; Walker, *History*, 125–26.

subsequently martyred. Towards the end of the second century Victor I (189–99) became the first African Bishop of Rome. Of course, we also have the work and witness of Tertullian (c. 160–c. 225) during the early, unsystematic period of persecution, and later, that of Cyprian (d. 258) who, after ten eventful years as Bishop of Carthage, including the periods of systematic persecution by Imperial edict, was martyred under Valerian. That Cyprian was able to assemble 85 bishops to meet in council at Carthage is some indication of the contemporary extent in Numidia and the Proconsular Province.[14]

As such, the conversion of the Emperor Constantine in 312 A.D. was crucial for facilitating a great change of early Christianity which was deeply related to a shift from a persecuted religion to an officially approved religion within the Roman world. More specifically, after his conversion to Christianity, the Emperor Constantine (who was "a friend of the church") had declared freedom of religious belief and worship and had tolerated Christianity. This means that he had prohibited public persecution by imperial legislation, at which point he had eventually attempted to establish Christianity as an acceptable official religion for Roman society. In line with Constantine's new religious allegiance, throughout the course of the fourth and fifth centuries, the post-Constantinian emperors had kept their official attitude for protecting and supporting the Christianization of the Roman world, except the reign of Constantine's pagan nephew Julian (361–363) (although after the reign of Constantine, the Roman Empire was politically split into the West and East).[15] In particular, the Emperor Theodosius I had systematically attempted to establish Christianity as an imperial Roman religion, and to wipe out paganism by imperial law in 391.[16]

14. Harrison, *Augustine*, 119. Gillian Clark explores the persecution of early Christians within the Roman Empire. Clark writes, "Jesus died on a cross: a public, agonizing death, legally inflicted by a Roman provincial governor as the standard punishment for rebels. For almost three hundred years, his followers were also at risk of legally inflicted death, sometimes as a public spectacle. Roman law allowed Christians to be burned alive or thrown to wild animals or inventively tortured" (*Christianity*, 38); "Christians were executed because their refusal to worship the Roman gods entailed refusal to obey the Roman authorities, and because they aroused suspicions of anti-social behaviour" (ibid., 39; see 40–59).

15. Peter Brown views Christianization as "knowledge of yet another world-wide category of persons whose deeds were open to the eye of an effective goddess of the post-Constantinian age" (*Authority*, 3).

16. David Knowles examines the correlation between the conversion of

Playing Together

In the context of Constantine's conversion to Christianity and subsequent emperors' toleration of Christianity, the movement of Christianization was widespread and far-reaching in Roman society. In this sense, Robert A. Markus in *The End of Ancient Christianity* (1990) pays attention to the process of the Christianization of the Roman world in the fourth and fifth centuries (especially the half century from about 380 to about 430) in which Roman society had reached a climax of dramatic socio-cultural and religious changes. Markus notes, "These two centuries correspond roughly to the timespan of the Christian Roman Empire in the West. The starting point . . . is the age of the large-scale christianisation of Roman society at the end of the fourth century and the beginning of the fifth: the age of Theodosius I, of Augustine of Hippo and their contemporaries. The end-point is the time, more or less, of the 'end of the Western Empire,' its fragmentation into the barbarian kingdoms of Europe."[17]

Following the widespread process of the Christianization of Roman society, the North African church had moved from the age of systemic persecution by Imperial edict to the new era of the publicly accepted Christianization in the Roman world. This means that North Africans had entered into the preeminent transition from paganism to Christianity. In a related vein, Harrison states,

---

Constantine and the end of the persecution of Christians. Knowles states, "For more than a century after Pentecost Christians formed small and fairly compact groups in cities and towns, regarded by others with distaste and suspicion, and when their numbers increased they were liable to persecution and spoliation, but these were far less universal and continuous than was later generally supposed. They were nevertheless sufficiently exacting to restrict membership of the church to serious believers, and to make of martyrdom, the supreme sacrifice of life, the height of a Christian's glory and his ideal of perfection. Towards the middle of the third century, however, the threat of persecution had receded and the numbers of Christians had increased. Through persecution was to recur under Decius (249–52) and Diocletian (284–305) in a form fiercer than ever before, this was in a sense a desperate measure, and was immediately followed by the conversion of Constantine and the swift transformation of the Christian church from a persecuted and fervent sect into a ruling and rapidly increasing body, favoured and directed by the emperor, membership of which was a material advantage" (*Christian Monasticism*, 11–12; see Brown, *Authority*, 3–5; *Augustine*, 207–39; G. Clark, *Christianity*, 93–100; Fredriksen, "Christians," 587–89; MacMullen, *Christianizing*, 43–51, 86–101; Markus, *Ancient Christianity*, 125–35; Walker, *History*, 99–102).

17. Markus, *Ancient Christianity*, xiii.

> The question of just how far the Roman Empire was 'christianized' in Augustine's time is . . . not an easy or straightforward one to answer. We have seen just how limited Christianity's influence was in some instances, especially in respect of its place in the traditional Roman town. In its organization, jurisdiction, municipal offices and even its sense of identity, coherence, and public events, the Church seems to have played but a marginal role. Legislation against paganism seems to have done little but secularize what was once understood on the basis of ancient religious traditions, but not to have Christianized them. . . . . [As such] the Church . . . came to affirm its identity and self-understanding, its sense of the sacred and its place in relation to the world.[18]

Indeed, the process of Christianization was complex and difficult in the Roman world, including North Africa. It was continuously challenged by serious religious conflicts between Christianity and paganism (although Christianity was in the condition of toleration and became a state religion of the Roman Empire). As Harrison points out, "Even in Augustine's day . . . it is difficult to know exactly why people became Christian or to estimate just how widespread it was, especially where, for reasons of class, language, culture or geography paganism, or the old cults of Saturn and Ceres still held sway in people's minds (and were, indeed, sometimes syncretistically mixed up with Christianity)."[19] During the late fourth and early fifth centuries, political unrest, social upheaval, and religious conflicts had continuously challenged "the Christianity of Church communities and those who ministered to them."[20]

Along with the exploration of the macro context of Augustine's time, let us look at the *micro context* which includes the personal and familial milieu of the early and adolescent Augustine. Augustine (Aurelius Augustinus) was born at Thagaste, which was a Roman provincial town in North Africa (*b. vita.* 1.6; *ep.* 126.7; Possidius, *v. Aug.* 1).[21] Like other Roman towns, Thagaste had officially protected and supported the movement of Christianization (that sometimes had used "religious

---

18. Harrison, *Augustine*, 140.

19. Ibid., 119. See Brown, *Authority*, 4.

20. Kreidler, "Conversion," 509. See Harrison, *Augustine*, 132–57.

21. Michael M. Gorman contends that St. Augustine's name was Aurelius Augustinus and that Aurelius is the gentilitial/clan name ("Aurelius Augustinus," 475–80; see Lancel, *Saint Augustine*, 5, 480).

coercion" in order to proselytize people to Christianity), in which there were serious religious conflicts between Christianity and paganism in North Africa. Harrison depicts the town of Thagaste as follows: "Augustine's birthplace, the small, rather insignificant, and traditionally Berber town of Thagaste (modern Souk Ahras), in the [south-]eastern part of Numidia, had, like many provincial towns from the second century onwards, undergone a slow but sure *process of Romanization* in its legal, administrative, and social life."[22] The region of Thagaste consisted of fertile plains in which people had widely cultivated lots of grain and olive. This rural environment of Augustine's hometown had deeply affected the early and adolescent Augustine's development, at which point the young Augustine was familiar with the landscape of the plains of olive and wheat. As Brown points out, "Forests of olive-trees had come to cover the hillsides of south[-eastern] Numidia. [The adolescent and young] Augustine could work all night in Africa, his lamp stocked with plentiful supplies of the coarse African oil: it was a comfort he would miss during his stay in Italy."[23] (At this point, we should note that Augustine's conversion to Christianity in the summer of 386 occurred in the Milanese garden which consisted of olive and fig trees.)

In the context of Romanization, Augustine's forebears had lived in the south-eastern part of Numidia of North Africa (although we are unable to know exactly when and why his Roman ancestors came from Italy to North Africa).[24] His father, Patricius, was a Roman-African pagan. He was only baptized on his deathbed (*conf.* 2.3.6, 3.4.7, 9.9.22); he was an affective man, but authoritarian and hot-tempered (9.9.19) (because he might have been deeply impacted by the African temperament of sensual pleasure and materialism—"The hunt, the baths, play and laughter: that's the life for me!"[25]). His mother, Monica, was a sincere and earnest Christian who was born in a Christian family (9.8.17). She was friendly, but strong-willed (9.9.19–21). Augustine had siblings, including at least a brother, Navigius (*conf.* 9.11.27; *b. vita* 12) and a sister, Perpetua (*ep.* 211.4; Possidius, *v. Aug.* 26).[26] Indeed, Monica had dedicated herself to bring up her son, the child Augustine, in the Christian

22. Harrison, *Augustine*, 118.
23. Brown, *Augustine*, 8.
24. Ibid.; Lancel, *Saint Augustine*, 5.
25. Brown, *Augustine*, 7.
26. See Bonner, *St. Augustine*; Bourke, *Augustine's Quest*.

living of faith; that is, Augustine drank in the name of Christ with his mother's milk, at which point her devotion to Augustine had played a crucial role in his later spiritual life (*conf.* 1.6.7, 1.11.17).

Augustine had superior academic talents through elementary training at Thagaste. He went to advanced school at a neighboring town, Madauros, in order to learn oratory. However, at the age of sixteen, Augustine was unable to study more and returned home due to the lack of his family funds (*conf.* 2.3.5). In a related vein, while paying attention to Patricius and Monica's strong ambition for their son's worldly successful career or life, Brown states,

> To be a full member of a Roman town, Augustine had to be free and civilized: he did not have to be rich. His father, Patricius, was a poor man, a *tenuis municeps*, a burgess of slender means. Augustine will grow up in a hard, competitive world, among proud and impoverished gentlefolk. A classical education was one of the only passports to success for such men; and he narrowly avoided losing even this. His early life will be overshadowed by the sacrifices his father made to give him this vital education: Patricius and his family had to go poorly-dressed; he had to scrape; for one disastrous year Augustine found himself condemned to give up his studies at a pleasant "university-town" at Madaura (or Madauros: modern Mdaourouch) to run wild in primitive Thagaste.[27]

During his adolescence (especially at the time of his return from Madauros to Thagaste), Augustine (who was influenced by the African temperament of sensual materialists) entered into the turbulent life in which he amused himself by seeking for the life of sensual pleasures (e.g., his pear-stealing with his friends [2.4.9–2.6.12]). At the age of seventeen, Augustine came to Carthage in order to study continuously under the financial support of his relatives. In his stay in Carthage, Augustine met and fell in love with a young lower-class (and Christian) woman. He had lived with this woman, whose name is unknown, for fifteen years, although Garry Wills suggests her name as "Una" based on the words—*unam habebam*—"I lived with a woman" (*conf.* 4.2.2).[28] As such, his son, Adeodatus was born in 371 (4.2.2). During the study of

---

27. Brown, *Augustine*, 9. During his schooling, Augustine was seriously burdened with his parents' expectations for him to acquire worldly honor (*conf.* 1.9.14, 1.19.30, 2.3.8; see Ferrari, "Boyhood Beatings," 5).

28. Wills, *Saint Augustine*, 16.

rhetoric, Augustine read Cicero's *Hortensius* which compelled him into an earnest inquiry for truth and philosophy (3.4.7–8; *sol.* 1.10.17). In the context of seeking for intellectual and spiritual comfort, he was also involved in Manichaeism. During nine years, the Manichee Augustine had taken refuge within the Manichean sect in order to articulate conveniently the existence of evil by positing a conflict between God (the cause of all good) and matter (the source of the evil) (3.6.10–3.7.14, 7.5.7).

After his study in Carthage, Augustine (who became a Manichee and a rhetorician) returned to Thagaste in 375. At that time, Monica felt a deep discontent with her son because Augustine had an unlawful marriage and accepted Manichean dualism against Christian belief. Here Augustine attempted to convert his Christian friends to Manichaeism (3.11.19). Especially, the Manichee Augustine mocked an unnamed friend, who was baptized before death because he gravely fell ill (4.4.7–9). After hearing the death of his unnamed friend, Augustine was very ashamed and decided to depart his home town (4.7.12). While reflecting on the death of his unnamed friend, Augustine later regretted mocking the baptism of his friend and emphasized the correlation of Christian baptism with the remission of sins and the rebirth for the newness of life in Christ (*bapt.* 3.14.19, 6.25.46; *epp.* 23.4, 55.2.3; *s.* 213.9).

Augustine came again to Carthage in 376. As a great scholar, he acquired striking success of teaching and became a winner in the oratorical contest of Carthage (*conf.* 4.2.3, 4.3.5). During this time, Augustine began to doubt the intellectual and moral adequacy of Manichaeism. In particular, after meeting with Faustus, the Manichaean bishop, Augustine lost respect for Manichean cosmology because he was not able to satisfy his intellect and the religious issues which were disturbing him (5.3.3–5.7.13). In the context of his intellectual and religious frustration within the Manichean sect (as well as his feeling of disenchantment which resulted in the rudeness of his students), Augustine decided to move to Rome, although Monica stood against her son's going away to a distant place (5.8.14–15).

Augustine arrived in Rome in the fall of 383 (5.9.16). He suffered from a serious illness, but did not attempt to receive any Christian ritual of baptism—"I still remained sick in my sacrilegious heart, for though in such great danger, I had no desire for [Christian] baptism" (5.9.16).

This means that the young Augustine was in a serious condition of completely turning away from God as well as the traditional Christian belief. After recovering his health, Augustine became a professor of rhetoric in Rome. In the context of the strong support of the Manichee Symmachus as well as the problematic economic condition related to the non-payment of tuition by students in Rome, Augustine decided to move to Milan, the Western capital of the Roman Empire, in order to acquire a new professorship (5.12.22).

Apparently, the depiction of the macro and micro contexts of Augustine's time is preeminent for making a better understanding of the background and initial stage of his ongoing journey of change. Under the far-reaching movement of Christianization in the Roman world relevant to Constantine's conversion to Christianity, Augustine had lived at a time of transition from a classical pagan past to a new Christian empire. Augustine's conversion occurred within specific contexts; that is, the personal/familial, social, cultural, and religious contexts of his time had profoundly affected the whole process of his transformation.

The Experience of Psychological Distress and Crisis

Consistent with the exploration of the macro and micro contexts of Augustine's conversion, this section of the chapter describes *the young Augustine's psychological distress and crisis* in the ongoing process of his transformation. In doing so, it demonstrates how Augustine's psychological distress and crisis were relevant to his inner division of the mind and his relational problems with others and the divine. This section is resonant with stage 2—*crisis*—of Rambo's model of religious conversion. As Rambo views the crisis stage as catalyst for human change, this study regards Augustine's experience of psychological distress and crisis as the initial and crucial trigger of his transformation.

The portrayal of Augustine's psychological distress and crisis helps us to construct a more integrated account of the unfolding process of his change. By way of Rome, Augustine, as a Manichee and a skeptic, came to Milan in the autumn of 384. Here Augustine had a strong desire for a worldly successful career or life and eventually became a municipal chair of rhetoric (*conf.* 5.13.23). As Capps portrays, "His father's soul [of sensual pleasure and materialism] was now dominant in him."[29] However, the young rhetorician Augustine had experienced a sense of the inner division in his mind which was deeply related to the sickness of the soul, as James points out: "[He was] distracted by the struggle between the two souls in his breast, and ashamed of his own weakness of will . . . [in the condition of] the shackles of sensuality. . . . Augustine's psychological [distress and crisis] has given an account of the trouble of having a divided self."[30] Augustine himself confessed, "The new will, which was beginning to be within me a will to serve you freely and to enjoy you, God, the only sure source of pleasure, was not yet strong enough to conquer my older will, which had the strength of old habit. So my two wills, one old, the other new, one carnal, the other spiritual, were in conflict with one another, and their discord robbed my soul of all concentration" (*conf.* 8.5.10; see 8.10.22-24). Augustine's interior world was a battle-ground in which two deadly hostile selves—one actual and the other ideal—were at war (8.8.19).[31] This means that the restless Augustine had vigorously struggled "between the two souls" in his mind. He did not do the good he wanted, but did the evil he did not want, as the Apostle Paul says: "I do not understand my own actions. For I do not do what I want, but I do the very thing I hate" (Rom 7:15; see 7:19). The more Augustine had sought for sensual pleasures and worldly honors, the deeper he (who was an "injured narcissist") had undergone a sense of disconnection—*shame* experience—and a feeling of restlessness in his heart.[32]

Importantly, there is an inherent link between the young Augustine's psychological distress/crisis and his early traumatic injuries within the specific personal and familial contexts of his childhood. In that sense, this study attempts to investigate the following two crucially life-effective events of Augustine in his early life (which were profoundly related to the formation of his personal and religious identity as well as his inner division of the mind): 1) Augustine's experience of beatings

29. Capps, "Divided Self," 562.

30. James, *Religious Experience*, 171-72. See O'Connell, *Augustine's Confessions*, 97.

31. Capps, "Divided Self," 560-62; O'Connell, *Augustine's Confessions*, 96-98; Quinn, *Companion*, 448-53.

32. See Capps, "Augustine as Narcissist," *Depleted Self*, "Divided Self," "Parabolic Events," "Self-Reproach," "Scourge of Shame," "Vicious Cycle"; Dixon, *Augustine*; Gay, "Augustine"; Niño, "Restoration"; Paffenroth, "Book Nine"; Parsons, "St. Augustine."

at school and his parents' mocking at his stripes/God's silence about it; and 2) Augustine's familial conflict related to the religious difference between his father (who was a pagan) and his mother (who was a Christian).

In the school life of his childhood, the boy Augustine was frequently beaten by teachers, although he was an able and competitive student at school (*conf.* 1.9.14–15). In this time of Augustine, corporal punishment was widespread in schools, as Augustine himself stated: "This method [of corporal punishment] was approved by adults [in the Roman world], and many people living long before me had constructed the laborious courses which we were compelled to follow by an increase of the toil and sorrow" (1.9.14). In the milieu of corporal punishment in schools, Augustine's early experiences of beating were painful and unbearable for him. Like other adults, Augustine's parents had not paid attention to his difficult schooling which was rooted in his beating experiences. Rather, they had critically mocked at his physical stripes— "My parents, who wished no evil to come upon me, used to laugh at my stripes, which were at that time a great and painful evil to me" (1.9.14). In the context of his fear of being beaten as well as his feeling of being ignored, the boy Augustine had attempted to pray to God in order to receive God's help. This means that through God's help, Augustine wanted to escape from his intolerable condition of beatings. However, here the early Augustine had experienced God's deep silence about his prayer because he was still beaten at school and because he was laughed by his parents at home: "O God, my God, 'what miseries I experienced' at this stage of my life. . . . I was beaten. . . . As a boy I began to pray to you. . . . Though I was only a small child, there was great feeling when I pleaded with you that I might not be caned at school. [However] you did not hear me" (1.9.14). Later the aged Augustine described his painful memory related to his traumatic experiences of his schooling as follows:

> Children are compelled, by dint of painful punishments, either to learn a craft or to acquire a literary education. And the process of learning with its attendant punishment is so painful that children not infrequently prefer to endure the punishments designed to compel them to learn, rather than to submit to the process of learning. In fact is there anyone who, faced with the choice between death and a second childhood, would not

shrink in dread from the latter prospect and elect to die? (*civ. Dei* 21.14)

Significantly, there is a correlation of Augustine's beating experiences in his childhood with the formation of his personality and his God representations. Augustine's traumatic injuries ("emphatic failures" or "internalized bad objects") had negatively impacted the formation of his self-image as well as the formation of his representations of God in light of the interaction of a deep sense of self-reproach, inability to relate to others/Other, and suffering.[33] More specifically, Augustine's early traumatic experiences had compelled him to establish his low self-esteem as well as his deep sense of disconnection or isolation. In that sense, while paying attention to the interrelatedness between Augustine's early experiences of floggings and his enduring sense of shame in his life, Donald Capps states,

> The traumatic aspect of [Augustine's childhood experiences of being beaten] was more related to shame than to guilt. . . . The most painful feature of the beatings was not the physical pain inflicted by his teachers, but the mocking laughter of his parents when he reported the floggings to them. The physical pain soon subsided, but he was never quite able to come to terms with his parents' mockery, as he remained sensitive to ridicule throughout his life. It was the ridicule he endured, more than the flogging itself, that sowed his "first seeds of disenchantment with the adult world." In other words, the trauma he experienced at the time was the trauma of shame.[34]

As such, the early and adolescent Augustine had negatively depicted himself as "a wretched boy" (1.19.30), "the lowest of the low" (1.19.30), "the most wicked slave of evil lusts" (4.16.30; see 2.2.4, 4.6.11), or "so great a sinner" (1.12.19). At that time of his feeling of low self-esteem and his sense of negative self-image, Augustine's early traumatic experiences had also compelled him to formulate the negative representations of God. In that sense, Leo C. Ferrari in "The Boyhood Beatings of Augustine" (1974) writes,

---

33. Capps, "Augustine as Narcissist," 127; "Scourge of Shame," 72–74; "Vicious Cycle," 136; Dixon, *Augustine*, 54–57, 131–32; Dodds, "Augustine's *Confessions*," 45; Ferrari, "Boyhood Beatings," 2–8.

34. Capps, "Scourge of Shame," 72.

> The irate schoolmaster of Augustine's infancy . . . becomes the scourging God who purifies his soul through the many punishments of life. In this regard it is to be noted that a favoured theme of the *Confessions* is that of the scourging God. . . . Again, there are grounds for arguing that the traumatic terror of his first floggings as a very young schoolboy contributed to an enduring sense of culpability and the formation of a temperament disposed to self-reproach and suffering. It would seem that these characteristics can be found in his writings, as well as in his frequent use of the image of the scourging God.[35]

Indeed, Augustine's negative representations of God were inherently rooted in his experiences of God's silence or indifference to his prayer in the context of his unendurable experiences of beatings.[36] Now the adolescent and young Augustine had portrayed 1) God as scourging—"You, Lord, put pressure on me in my hidden depths with a severe mercy wielding the double whip of fear and shame" (8.11.25; see 1.12.19, 2.2.4, 5.9.16, 6.6.9, 9.4.12); 2) God as mocking—"I aspired to honours, money, marriage, and you laughed at me" (6.6.9; see 4.1.1); 3) God as indifferent—"As a boy I began to pray to you . . . [but] you did not hear me . . . [when] adult people, including my parents . . . used to laugh at my stripes" (1.9.14; see 5.9.16); and 4) God as wrathful—"You beat me with heavy punishments. . . . My stiff neck took me further and further away from you. I loved my own ways, not yours" (3.3.5); "You had not yet forgiven me in Christ for any of them, nor had he by his cross delivered me from the hostile disposition towards you which I had contracted by my sins" (5.9.16; see 1.12.19, 2.2.4, 4.6.11, 8.7.18, 9.4.12).

Along with the exploration of the impact of the early Augustine's traumatic experiences of beatings on the formation of his self-image and his representations of God, this study articulates how Augustine's familial conflict (which was rooted in the religious difference between his pagan father and his Christian mother) had affected the formation of his personal and religious identity as well as his psychological distress

---

35. Ferrari, "Boyhood Beatings," 7, 14

36. Capps notes, "When the [boy] Augustine first experienced flogging as an experience of shame . . . he felt, at best, God had abandoned him, and, at worst, was joining with his parents in mocking laughter. . . . He had noted that God must be 'laughing' at him for asking questions for which there are presumably no answers" ("Scourge of Shame," 73).

Playing Together

and crisis. Indeed, there was no serious hostility between Augustine's father (Patricius) and his mother (Monica) because she (who was mild and patient) had wisely acted to foster a good relationship with her husband as well as to reduce problems within the familial context (9.9.19–20, 9.13.37).[37] Later Augustine recalled and described the tolerant attitude or suitable relation of his mother with his father as follows:

> [Monica] tried to win [Patricius] for you, speaking to him of you by her virtues through which you made her beautiful, so that her husband loved, respected and admired her. She bore with his infidelities and never had any quarrel with her husband on this account. . . . She knew that an angry husband should not be opposed, not merely by anything she did, but even by a word. Once she saw that he had become calm and quiet, and that the occasion as opportune, she would explain the reason for her action, in case perhaps he had reacted without sufficient consideration. (9.9.19)

However, basically agreeing with Dodds' and Capps' views on the correlation of the origins of Augustine's divided self with his family history,[38] this study contends that to some extent, there was an inevitable familial conflict which was inherently related to the religious difference between the pagan Patricius and the Christian Monica, although Patricius had respected Monica's faith and left the raising of the children to her (1.11.17). As such, Monica had undergone an uncomfortable religious conflict between her husband and herself, although it was not explicitly and vigorously manifest within the context of the whole fam-

---

37. While paying attention to Daly's emphasis on no fundamental hostility between Patricius and Monica (see Daly, "Psychohistory"; Fredriksen, "Augustine"; O'Meara, *Young Augustine*), we need to recognize that there were commonly "mixed marriages" in the Roman world of Augustine's time like that of Patricius and Monica (Starnes, *Augustine's Conversion*, 166) and that there still existed the African temperament of sensual pleasures in North African society based on the materialistic life-style (*conf.* 6.16.26; McClanahan, "Psychology," 25–28), although the far-reaching movement of Christian monasticism took place in the Roman world (Harmless, *Desert Christians*; Harrison, *Augustine*; Knowles, *Christian Monasticism*; Markus, *Ancient Christianity*; Walker, *History*). This means that the parental conflict of the child Augustine was deeply related to religious difference which was involved in their different personalities and worldviews within the socio-cultural and philosophical context of the fourth and fifth centuries.

38. For Capps, the division of Augustine's self "was due to the fact that he was raised by parents of very different personalities and conflicting worldviews" ("Divided Self," 559; see Dodds, "Augustine's *Confessions*," 44).

Understanding Religious Conversion

ily. Later Augustine recalled and described this religious conflict of his parents as follows: "At the end when her husband had reached the end of his life in time, she succeeded in gaining him for you. *After he was a baptized believer, she had no cause to complain of behaviour* which she had tolerated in one not yet a believer" (9.9.22, italics added). As earlier noted, in the childhood of Augustine, Patricius (whose name was common in the Roman world) was a pagan; he was hot-tempered and licentious because he might have been more influenced by the African temperament of sensual pleasure and materialism than the movement of Christian monasticism. Unlike Patricius, Monica (whose name was deeply related to a religious deity) was a devout Christian who might have been more affected by Christian monasticism than the licentious and material movement of North African society. As Lancel points out, "Although his father's name, Patricius, is one of the common-or-garden [variety] Latin names of the Late Empire, his mother's, Monnica (Monica), which occurs particularly often in the region, is the diminutive of Monna, a well attested indigenous name which also belongs to a local deity whose cult is mentioned on an inscription at Thignica."[39] His mother, Monica, attempted to raise the child Augustine as a faithful Christian (*conf.* 1.6.7). In the context of his Christian mother's rearing of the child Augustine (as well as in the process of Christianization of the Roman world), Augustine began his life as a catechumen—"I was already signed with the sign of the cross and seasoned with salt from the time I came from my mother's womb" (1.11.17).

As such, the religious difference or conflict of Patricius and Monica (which was involved their different personalities and worldviews) had affected the formation of the early Augustine's personality, his religious identify, and his mental development. At this point, Capps states,

> Augustine's father, Patricius, a civil servant of the Roman state, was a sort of magistrate or tax collector-and a pagan. The mother, Monica, later St. Monica, was a devout Christian from a Christian family. This religious difference led to intense parental conflict which was decisive for Augustine's entire development.... Augustine had the misfortune to be the fruit of this ill-assorted union.... It was his tragic destiny to combine in a

---

39. Lancel, *Saint Augustine*, 5.

small and sickly body the warring souls of both his parents and a fastidious intellect which served each soul in turn.[40]

The child Augustine might be deeply influenced by his father's temperament of North African society which preferred to seek sensual pleasure within the materialistic life-style, at which point the adolescent and young Augustine had continuously tried to establish an external and worldly success as well as to achieve his gratification within his voluptuous life-style ("Epicurean pleasure" [*conf.* 6.16.26]). As O'Meara says, "For the important first sixteen years of his life [Augustine] cannot have escaped altogether from the influence of his father."[41] (At this point, we are able to realize that the *concubinage* of the young Manichee and skeptic Augustine might be inherently connected to his North African temperament of sensual pleasure or materialism [4.2.2, 6.15.25].) Meanwhile, the child Augustine might also be impacted by his mother's raising or life-style of Christian faith which was centered in the quest for moral earnestness and purity, as Quinn points out: "The seeds [of Christian faith] may have been implanted as part of the Christian teaching gathered from Monica's informal instructions."[42] In this way, we are able to recognize that Monica's child-rearing and her expectation for his son within the Christian faith had later deeply affected both the young Augustine's spiritual change in the Milanese garden in 386 and the new convert Augustine's living in Christian faith for the rest of his life.

Influenced by his father's temperament of sensual pleasure and materialistic life-style as well as his mother's life-style of moral earnestness and purity, the adolescent and young Augustine had continuously involved his inner struggles between the licentious life and the moral/ascetic life. This means that Augustine was conflicted between the dissonant and fragmented life-styles of carnal pleasure and moral purity. More specifically, Augustine (who was "a slave of lust" [6.15.25]) had vigorously attempted to satisfy his desires of sensual pleasure (by using concubinage—his first concubine [4.2.2]; his second concubine [6.15.25]) and worldly ambitions (e.g., a victory of a poetry competition at the theatre [4.2.3]; a desire of higher position of the Empire

---

40. Capps, "Divided Self," 559, 561. See Dodds, "Augustine's *Confessions*," 44–45.
41. O'Meara, *Young Augustine*, 213.
42. Quinn, *Companion*, 327.

[6.15.25]). At the same time, he had earnestly attempted to seek for the philosophical and religious truth or the Truth (e.g., the reading of Cicero's *Hortensius* in Carthage [3.4.7–8]; the learning of Neoplatonism in Milan [7.10.16]). In the summer of 386, here Augustine had seriously experienced his division of the will; that is, he was involved in the worst fragmentation or split of the self, at which point he had felt a sense of deep estrangement or restlessness of the heart.

In the context of his psychological distress and crisis, Augustine had also undergone relationship problems with others; namely, he had felt a lack of ability to relate with others, as later he recalled and described: "I was on the way to the underworld, bearing all the evils I had committed against you, against myself, and against others" (5.9.16); "all positions are uncomfortable" (6.16.26). Indeed, at the time of his relationship problems with himself and the divine, the adolescent and young Augustine had experienced disruptions of relationships with other people, including his critical mocking at the Christian baptism of his unnamed friend (4.4.7–9), his trouble with Monica due to his Manichean belief and his concubinage (3.11.19), his dissatisfaction of the academic meeting with Faustus (5.3.3–5.7.13), the separations from his students in Carthage (5.8.14) and Rome (5.12.22), and no delight or interest of dialogues with his friends—"In my somber state I did not consider from what fountain came the flow of delightful conversation with friends" (6.16.26).

Consistent with his above relational problems with others, now Augustine had undergone another serious disruption of the relationship with his "unlawful" wife. More specifically, at the time of his inner division of the will, Augustine had struggled with the issue of the dismissal of his unmarried wife ("a long-term partner") because she was a hindrance to his legitimate marriage with a woman of a higher class as well as to his ambitions for worldly fame and money. After arriving in Milan, his mother, Monica (who had supported her son, Augustine, to be a worldly successful man within both the condition of the poor economy and the condition of the absence of her husband [*conf.* 3.4.7]) had persuaded Augustine to discharge his unlawful wife. As Elizabeth A. Clark points out: "Monica was eager for her son to undertake a [legitimate] marriage suitable to his career ambitions."[43] In the condition of his mother's demand of discharge, the young rhetorician Augustine

---

43. E. A. Clark, "Asceticism," 68.

had finally dismissed his son's mother (who had lived for fifteen years [371–86]) in order to undertake a marriage with a young noble woman for achieving a higher status in the Empire (e.g., a governor of the province). As such, Augustine's unlawful wife (whose name was unknown) returned to North Africa, vowing never to live with another man again—*continence*—and leaving their son with Augustine (6.15.25), as Brown states: "This nameless woman [came back] to Africa. . . . In all probability she had been a good Catholic throughout her life with Augustine; and, by this vow, she intended either to become eligible for baptism, or to be re-admitted to the Eucharist."[44] Apparently, the departure of his beloved woman had compelled Augustine to enter into the depths of agony and misery, as F. B. A. Asiedu points out: "When his concubine departs [Augustine] tries to soften the blow by seeking the embrace of another woman. Instead what he discovers is a misery much deeper and more intolerable."[45] Later the mature adult Augustine recalled that he had dearly loved his unmarried wife, and that he underwent psychological distress and existential abyss due to his separation with his woman, although he (who was "not a lover of [lawful] marriage") began to live with her in the condition of "a slave of lust." More specifically, Augustine stated, "In those years I had a woman [in Carthage]. She was not my partner in what is called lawful marriage. I had found her in my state of wandering desire and lack of prudence. Nevertheless, she was the only girl for me, and I was faithful to her (4.2.2). . . . [Now] my heart which was deeply attached was cut and wounded, and left a trail of blood. . . . She left with me the natural son I had by her. . . . I was unhappy, incapable of following a woman's example [of continence]" (6.15.25).

Basically agreeing with Garry Wills' argument that Augustine did love his woman to whom he had been faithful for so long,[46] this study

---

44. Brown, *Augustine*, 80; see 52. See Chadwick, *Augustine*, 15–16; O'Donnell, *Augustine: Confessions*, vol. 2, 383–85.

45. Asiedu, "Example of a Woman," 304.

46. Margaret R. Miles contends that Augustine did not love his long-term companion. In that sense, Miles portrays Augustine's woman as a concubine who had lived with him for satisfying his sexual desires (*Desire*, 27–29). Miles has diagnosed Augustine's continuous sexual desires as addiction in which he was enslaved ("Infancy," 358). Unlike Miles, Wills suggests that Augustine was faithful for his beloved woman; namely, he had loved her. Wills depicts this woman as not simply a concubine for Augustine's sexual gratification, but as a partner of Augustine himself (who had

contends that Augustine's disruption of relationship with his unlawful wife was crucial and fatal because his inner division or restlessness of the heart grew worse. As Asiedu states, "The concubine makes a vow to God to live a life of continence. . . . [At least] Augustine does not get reconciled to . . . his concubine until the day of his conversion in 386 when . . . he embraces continence."[47] Augustine himself was entirely silent about the name of his unlawful wife in his whole life, including the period of his writing of the *Confessions*. Augustine's deep *silence* about her name or her being itself was inherently related to his sense of disconnection and estrangement—the peak of shame experience—namely, his deep silence was involved in his deep agony and pain for a long time. This means that Augustine's inner conflict of the mind as well as his relational problem with others were culminated at the time of his dismissal of the unlawful wife in order to marry an aristocratic heiress for gaining his worldly honor. As Eric Plumer points out, "[Augustine's] pain over her dismissal was very great and did not heal over time, but instead turned into 'a cold despair.'"[48]

Significantly, the young Augustine's experience of separation from his beloved woman had compelled him to look at the inner division in his mind or his existential predicament in his life. At the same time, it had led him to realize his lack of ability to love others as well as his ceaseless desires for achieving worldly fame in the Roman world. Moreover, it had stirred Augustine to pay attention to his lack of power to be continent as well as his unnamed woman's ability to enter into the life of celibacy (6.11.20–6.15.25).[49] In this way, Asiedu in "Following the Example of a Woman: Augustine's Conversion to Christianity in 386" shows well the impact of Augustine's unnamed woman's vow of continence to "the Christian God" on the process of his religious change as follows:

> [Augustine's unnamed woman's] desire for continence may have been an attempt to give divinity to her hopelessness: converting

---

continuously influenced his life time) (*Saint Augustine*, 16–18, 41–42; see Plumer, "Book Six," 104–5; Vaught, *Journey*, 152).

47. Asiedu, "Example of a Woman," 304.

48. Plumer, "Book Six," 105. See Vaught, *Journey*, 152.

49. See Asiedu, "Example of a Woman," 304–6; Plumer, "Book Six," 104–5; Quinn, *Companion*, 326–27; Starnes, *Augustine's Conversion*, 158–59; Vaught, *Journey*, 152–53.

her shame in a declared act of renunciation that would lend to her life a "divine" or religious purpose. . . . Since Augustine recognized his concubine's vow to continence as an example he was too weak and unhappy to follow at the time, his later acceptance of that way of life should be acknowledged as a witness to the influence of his concubine on the choice he came to make, The *Confessions*, after all, makes an implicit claim as a meta-narrative of conversion. . . . By recounting this episode, Augustine offers a veiled tribute to a woman whose decision to commit herself to a life of continence prompted Augustine's journey down that road. By recognizing the mother of Adeodatus, the woman with whom he was in the habit of sleeping, as "flesh of his flesh" Augustine the catechumen came to see in sexual renunciation the only credible embodiment of his possible conversion to Christianity.[50]

At the time of his psychological distress and crisis as well as his relational problems with others (especially with his unlawful wife), the young rhetorician Augustine was unable to discover a resting place on earth. He noted, "That was inward, while I was still externals. It was not in a place; but I was fixing my attention on things contained in space, and [yet] I found no place to rest in, nor did those external things receive me so that I could say 'It is enough and it is well'" (*conf.* 7.7.11; see 8.12.28); "The only thing left to it was a mute trembling, and as if it were facing death it was terrified of being restrained from the treadmill of habit by which it suffered 'sickness unto death' (John 11:4)" (8.7.18); "*Alas, alas, how long-drawn-out is my exile!* I have gone so far away from you. My pilgrimage is so wearisome! I have not yet arrived in that homeland where I shall live untroubled by any evil. . . . Why am I not yet there?" (*en. Ps.* 119.6).

The Quest for Knowing Himself and the Divine

Consistent with the depiction of Augustine's psychological distress and crisis, this section examines *his quest for knowing himself and knowing the divine* in the ongoing process of his conversion. It is relevant to stage 3—*quest*—of Rambo's model of religious conversion. Rambo pays attention to the quest stage in order to articulate the active search of

---

50. Asiedu, "Example of a Woman," 304–5. See the Appendix on the implications of the role of Augustine's unnamed woman in his conversion.

the potential convert who seeks resolutions to his or her problems and strives to discover meaning, purpose, and transcendence in life. In line with Rambo, this study attempts to elucidate how Augustine had deeply responded to his experiences of the inner division of the mind and his relational problems with others/the divine in order to establish a more valid and meaningful life. As such, question 1 asks how Augustine's psychological crises had affected his earnest quests for knowing himself and the divine.[51] This question is helpful for exploring Augustine's inquiry to know himself and the divine resonant with his psychological distress and existential restlessness in light of the interaction of the experience of the self and the experience of the divine. More specifically, while establishing a coherent and integrated picture of Augustine's conversion process, it guides us to look at the correlation of the adolescent and young Augustine's psychological distress and crisis with his early traumatic injuries within the specific personal and familial contexts of his childhood as well as the correlation of Augustine's inner division of the mind ("the sick soul") with his struggles to find or experience himself in relation to the divine.

During the peak of his sense of inner division and his relational problems with others (especially his disruption with the unnamed woman), the restless Augustine had seriously attempted to rethink the goal and meaning of his life (6.16.26).[52] More specifically, after realizing that he could not find the resting place on earth (7.7.11), Augustine had moved into his inner world to know himself and to know the divine. This means that Augustine's psychological crisis and existential abyss had affected himself to recollect and reflect upon his life history. That is, he had attempted to think about what the real problem is in his life as well as to recognize the roots of his inner conflict, at which point he was able to open his mind to feel the inward divine location. Here Augustine had entered into a movement for remedying his inner incompleteness and for reducing his inner discord, as James points out: "Augustine [began to flow into] inner unity and peace. . . . The process of unification [of his divided self might] come gradually, or it [might]

---

51. Question 1 is deeply rooted in the collaborative dialogue between the factor of the experience of psychological distress and crisis (e.g., *conf.* 7.7.11, 8.5.10, 8.12.28; *en. Ps.* 119.6) and the factor of the quest for knowing himself and the divine (e.g., *conf.* 7.10.16, 9.1.1; *sol.* 1.2.7, 2.1.1; *ord.* 2.18.47).

52. See Quinn, *Companion*, 327–30.

occur abruptly; it [might] come through altered feelings, or through altered powers of action; or it [might] come through new intellectual insights, or through experiences which we shall later have to designate as 'mystical.'"[53]

Indeed, Augustine's active search for the meaning in life and his yearning for knowing himself and the divine stirred him to open himself to the divine, namely, to disclose/confess his sense of hopelessness and powerlessness (i.e., his painful condition of "tragic estrangement") to God. As Capps states, "His mother's soul [for seeking the life of moral earnestness and spiritual purity] began its works in him."[54] Now Augustine had no reason to hide himself from God, as he recalled and described: "Before you I lay my heart and my memory. At that time you were dealing with me in your hidden secret providence, and you were putting my shameful errors before your face" (*conf.* 5.6.11). As such, the young Augustine had gradually perceived God, not outside of himself, but within himself: "I was walking through darkness and 'a slippery place' (Ps 34:6). I was seeking for you outside myself, and I failed to find 'the God of my heart' (Ps 72:26)" (6.1.1); "You were more inward than my most inward part and higher than the highest element within me" (3.6.11).

Moreover, Augustine's interior journey toward union with God has led him to recognize his crucial and fundamental problem in his life which was profoundly rooted in his turning away from God (5.9.16, 7.10.16). More specifically, during his inner struggles to himself and the divine, Augustine found himself far from God—"the ground of being"—at which point he realized that the primary cause of both his inner division (and his relational problems with others) was deeply derived from his disconnection with the ground of Being. As Vaught points out, "Augustine's basic problem [was] the distortion of the will that [led] away from God."[55] Augustine himself noted, "For wherever the human soul turns itself, other than to you, it is fixed in sorrows, even if it is fixed upon beautiful things external to you and external to itself, which would nevertheless be nothing if they did not have their being from you" (4.10.15); "How fearful a fate for 'the rash soul' (Isa 3:9) which nursed the hope that after it had departed from you, it would

---

53. James, *Religious Experience*, 175.
54. Capps, "Divided Self," 563.
55. Vaught, *Encounters*, 82.

find something better!" (6.16.26). As such, here Augustine needed to turn from his worldly ambitions/honors to God—the ground of Being; that is, he needed to shift from the life of sensual materialism ("Epicurean pleasure" [6.16.26]) to the life of asceticism and celibacy (e.g., 9.1.1–9.2.4). This means that the young Augustine needed to accept God's presence in the depth of his soul and his life as well as to create a new way of living in light of the interplay between the soul and the ground of its existence. In this way, Plumer writes, "Augustine's despair was so unbearable that he would gladly have allowed himself to be 'sucked still deeper into the whirlpool of carnal lusts' in order to escape it, but he could not. . . . His growing sense of powerlessness and hopelessness was being used by God to prepare his heart to receive grace. Augustine was slowly coming to the realization that he faced utter loss unless he surrendered his life to God unconditionally."[56]

At the time of his earnest quest for meaning in life and for knowing himself and the divine, Augustine began to enter into the transformative process of unifying his divided self ("twice born"). That is, he began to shift from the state of storm, stress, and inconsistency to the state of firmness, stability, and equilibrium.[57] As such, Augustine was involved in a movement for overcoming his sense of shame as well as for healing his narcissistic injuries in the process of self-disclosure or self-becoming; he had gradually re-established empathic relationships with others and the divine which indicated a sign of developmental and progressive maturity.[58] Indeed, the young Augustine had greatly moved into the painful yet meaningful process of his interior transformation from the divided self to the integration of the self which was deeply related to his profound experience with the divine/God ("a More"), as Elledge states: "The process of conversion takes Augustine from restraint through renunciation and release into a repossession which includes an escape hatch, i.e., from the closed embrace of mundane attachments into God's open one that neither empties itself nor ceases by its openness to embrace."[59]

56. Plumer, "Book Six," 105.
57. See Capps, "Divided Self"; Elledge, "Augustine"; James, *Religious Experience*.
58. See Capps, "Augustine as Narcissist," *Depleted Self*, "Divided Self," "Parabolic Events," "Self-Reproach," "Scourge of Shame," "Vicious Cycle"; Dixon, *Augustine*; Gay, "Augustine"; Niño, "Restoration"; Paffenroth, "Book Nine"; Parsons, "St. Augustine."
59. Elledge, "Augustine," 81–82. See *conf.* 8.12.28–29.

Apparently, as discussed in question 1, there is an intimate connection between Augustine's experiences of psychological distress and his yearning for knowing himself and the divine. That is, the restless Augustine (who had felt a sense of dividedness and who had suffered from "sickness unto death") was unable to discover a safe resting place on earth, and thus he had begun to recollect his own life as well as to enter into his inner world to know (or experience) himself and the divine. In this way, the depiction of Augustine's search for the knowledge of the self and the knowledge of the divine is crucial for understanding how Augustine had moved toward to resolve his psychological crisis and existential predicament, to overcome his isolated and selfish lifestyle, and to establish newly the purpose and meaning of his life.

Encounters with Significant Others and Participation in Christian Communities

In consideration of Augustine's quest for knowing himself and the divine as well as his search for meaning in life, this section of the chapter explores *his encounters with significant others and his participation in Christian communities* in the process of his transformation. It is consonant with stage 4—*encounter*—of Rambo's model of religious conversion, while it gradually involves stage 5—*interaction*. While describing the encounter stage as the initial contact between the advocate and the potential convert (who relate mutually and dialectically to one another), Rambo pays attention to the interaction stage—the matrix of change—in which they engage in a more intensive and extended exchange/interchange within the religious community. In line with Rambo, while acknowledging the correlation of Augustine's quest for the divine with his quest for others, this section focuses on the influence of others' conversion stories on Augustine's own conversion narrative in light of the metaphor of the ongoing-containing Korean/Chinese box of stories of conversion ("a story within a story"); it also pays attention to the impact of his affective bonds and intensive interactions with other people as well as his engagement in the newly alternative community (i.e., the Milanese cathedral) on the process of his transformation.

In this way, question 2 asks how Augustine's interior journey for union with God and his search for community with others were knit together in the process of his conversion.[60] This question is valid for recognizing that Augustine's turning toward the divine is deeply interwoven with his turning toward others. More specifically, while achieving a coherent and integrated picture of Augustine's narrative of transformation, this question guides us to pay attention to the correlation of the experience of the self with the experience of the divine as well as the correlation of Augustine's quest for the divine and his quest for others in the Christian community. Importantly, the young Augustine began to establish good and suitable relationships with himself and with God. At the same time, now Augustine also began to rebuild his relationships with other persons (e.g., his fellow-African Ponticianus [8.6.14–15] or his spiritual mentor Simplicianus [8.2.3–5]) in the Christian community. Along with question 2, question 3 asks how other people in the Christian community had provided love, support, and belonging to fulfill Augustine's psychological needs and to make up for his frustration with his deprivations in the social and cultural conditions of his time.[61] As an active seeker for knowing himself and the divine, the young Augustine had intensively participated in Christian communities, while he was intimately related to significant other people. As such, this question 3 encourages us to look at the interaction between the experience of the self and the experience of others in the complex process of Augustine's "resocialization" or institutionalization. Particularly, it provides an insight into investigating how significant other persons had affected Augustine to overcome his dualistic materialism (i.e., the Manichean belief [3.7.2, 3.7.12]) and his skeptic thinking in the Academy (5.14.25), at which point they supported Augustine to

---

60. Question 2 is related to the collaborative dialogue between the factor of the quest for knowing himself and the divine and the factor of encounters with significant others (e.g., Ambrose [*conf.* 5.13.23–5.14.25, 6.3.3–4, 9.6.14]; Simplicianus [8.2.3–5, 8.5.10]; Ponticianus [8.6.14–15, 8.7.16–18]; Alypius [8.6.14–15, 8.8.19, 8.11.27, 8.12.30]; Monica [6.2.2, 9.7.15, 9.10.23–26]).

61. Question 3 is primarily relevant to the collaborative conversation between the factor of intimate interactions with other people and the factor of participation in Christian communities (e.g., 5.13.23–5.14.25, 9.6.14).

feel a sense of belongingness or solidarity and to find a new way of life in the Christian community.

During the depths of his existential struggles to know himself and the divine as well as to reconstruct purpose and meaning in life, Augustine was related to and was influenced by significant others. Augustine's interior journey for union with God was not simply an alienated experience of a person; it did not occur "in a vacuum." Rather, his ontological and spiritual journey for the Truth was interwoven with the specific philosophical and socio-cultural conditions of his time, at which point his intellectual and spiritual odyssey was deeply connected to his intensive interactions with other persons and his participation in Christian communities. At this point, Kreidler states, "Augustine's conversion [did] not remain the isolated experience of an individual. It took place within an ecclesial community and was subsequently lived out in a religious community which Augustine understood to model the larger Church. [Augustine's] experiences of friendship and even various forms of community predate his conversion to Christianity."[62]

Paradoxically and gracefully, here Augustine (who was a young rhetorician and an active seeker) had experienced loving ("good-enough") care and support from significant persons (especially Ambrose, Simplicianus, Ponticianus, Alypius, and Monica) within the Christian community (as well as he had undergone the divine grace and intervention into his life), when he was in the unbearable and intractable conditions of his sickness of the soul and his relational problem with others (e.g., his unlawful wife [6.15.25]). While engaging in the Milanese circle of the Neoplatonists, the young Augustine had met Bishop Ambrose of Milan who was a former governor of a Roman province with a powerful personality and great integrity as well as a Christian Neoplatonist. Here Ambrose had welcomed the rhetorician Augustine's visit to his church, although he might have known that Augustine was still a Manichee and a skeptic and that he just began to study Neoplatonism within the Milanese intellectual circle. Later Augustine recalled their meeting and confessed, "I came to Milan to Ambrose the bishop, known throughout the world as among the best of men, devout in your worship. . . . I was led to him by you, unaware that through him, in full awareness, I might be led to you. That 'man of God' (2 Kgs 1:9) received

---

62. Kreidler, "Conversion," 515.

me like a father and expressed pleasure at my coming with a kindness most fitting in a bishop" (5.13.23).

In the context of Ambrose's hospitality, Augustine had regularly participated in the worship service in the Milanese cathedral and had heard the sermons of Ambrose. Augustine had discovered himself becoming interested in the content as well as the rhetoric technique of his sermons. This means that through Ambrose's gifted interpretations of the Christian Scriptures, Augustine had learned a new way of reading the Bible; that is, he began to realize the great depth of Christian faith and living (*conf.* 5.13.23–5.14.25; see 6.3.3–4).[63] As noted earlier, the adolescent Augustine previously thought that the literary quality of the early Latin version of the Bible was unsophisticated and "unworthy" compared to the Latin classics (especially Cicero's *Hortensius*) (3.5.9). However, here the young Augustine came to believe that Christianity, with its doctrines of creation, fall, and redemption, possessed a much more compelling explanation of evil and good than anything he had found among the Manichees or elsewhere, as later he stated: "My pleasure was in the charm of [Bishop Ambrose's] language [of sermons]. It was more learned than that of Faustus [the Manichean bishop], but less witty and entertaining, as far as the manner of his speaking went. But in content there could be no comparison. Through Manichee deceits Faustus wandered astray. Ambrose taught the sound doctrine of salvation. From sinners such as I was at that time, salvation is far distant. Nevertheless, gradually, though I did not realize it, I was drawing closer" (5.13.23).

Indeed, Bishop Ambrose had affected Augustine to resolve his intellectual problem of conceiving of the divine as a corporeal being, at which point he had stirred Augustine to become a Christian. Especially, Ambrose's sermons (which reflected Christianized Neoplatonism) had inspired the rhetorician Augustine to have a positive attitude towards the Bible; his sermons had challenged Augustine to make interior journey for union with the Truth in light of the relation between God and the soul. As Cary points out, "That is why Bishop Ambrose understands Scripture so much better than young Augustine: Ambrose teaches the spirit rather than the letter of Scripture, because he knows

---

63. See Bourke, *Augustine's Quest*, 50–51; Brown, *Augustine*, 74–77; O'Donnell, *Augustine*, 54–55; O'Meara, *Young Augustine*, 109–24.

Playing Together

the incorporeal realities."[64] As such, the young Augustine had a strong resolution to give up his membership of the Manichean sect—"in the fluctuating state of total suspense of judgement I decided I must leave the Manichees" (5.14.25), at which point he had newly engaged in the Milanese cathedral—"the resocialization into an alternative community"—for fostering his new quest for the Truth. Now Augustine decided to become again a catechumen in the Milanese cathedral, although he remained skeptical about the possibility of finding any truth and although he had still hesitated to become a faithful Christian—"At that period of my skepticism . . . I . . . refused to entrust the healing of my soul's sickness. I therefore decided for the time being to be a catechumen in the Catholic Church" (5.14.25).

During the period of Augustine's interactions with Ambrose as well as his participation in or his affiliation with the Milanese cathedral, Bishop Ambrose had strongly attempted to keep the Nicene faith based on the Creed of the Council of Nicaea in 325.[65] This means that Ambrose had struggled to defend the church against the Roman army during the time of religious controversy against the Arians. At that time, the Arian Justina (who was the wife of Valentinian I) came to Milan with her son Valentinian II in 371; she had participated in a vehement and lengthy struggle against Ambrose in January 386. In the condition of the aid of the Empress Justina and the Roman army, the Arians demanded the surrender of Ambrose for permitting Arian worship service within basilicas. However, Bishop Ambrose made no compromise with the Arians. Ambrose and his flock (including Augustine's mother) had tried to prevent military force from confiscating any churches for the Arian Goths to use at Easter 386, as later Augustine stated: "Only a year or a little more had passed since Justina, mother of the young king Valentinian, was persecuting your servant Ambrose in the interest of her heresy. She had been led into error by the Arians. The devout congregation kept continual guard in the Church, ready to die with their bishop, your servant. There my mother, your handmaid, was

---

64. Cary, "Book Seven," 122. See Lancel, *Saint Augustine*, 82, 85; O'Connell, *Augustine's Confessions*, 64–65; Vaught, *Encounters*, 57, 139, 146.

65. The Council of Nicaea emphasized the unity of substance between Christ and the Father. This Council of Nicaea confirmed that the Son was eternal, "begotten, not made," and "of one essence (*homoousion*) with the Father" (Walker, *History*, 76, 107–11).

a leader in keeping anxious watch and lived in prayer" (9.7.15).[66] In that sense, it is fair to assume that Bishop Ambrose and Monica's struggles to defend the church against the Arians might have challenged the young Augustine who had deeply indulged his desires for sensual pleasures and worldly ambitions (although he was not engaged in the provocative movement to protect the Milanese churches). This means that Ambrose and Monica's desperate dedication to the church had enabled Augustine to reflect on his life history—"Who am I and what am I?" (9.1.1)—and to ponder the becoming of a Christian as well as the meaning of Christian friendships in the specific human conditions.[67]

At the time of the summer of 386, the catechumen Augustine still held back from seeking Christian baptism, although he had regularly participated in the worship services of the Milanese cathedral. This means that Augustine was still in the condition of his inner division of the mind, that is, he had struggled to achieve a safe resting place for his soul, although he was intellectually convinced of the truth of Christianity (based on his learning of the doctrines of Christian Neoplatonism). In doing so, as Ambrose once had done, Augustine put himself in the hands of Simplicianus in order to consult his spiritual mentor about his troubles—"So I visited Simplicianus, father to the then bishop Ambrose in the receiving grace. . . . I told him the story of my wanderings in error" (8.2.3).[68]

---

66. Justina, the Arian wife of Valentinian I, came to Milan with her son Valentinian II in 371, and engaged in a lengthy struggle against Ambrose in January 386. She demanded the surrender of Ambrose for permitting Arian worship service within basilicas. Ambrose arranged for his people to provide a permanent sit-in to prevent military force from confiscating any Churches for the Arian Goths to use at Easter 386 (Brown, *Augustine*, 71–72; Chadwick, "Introduction and Notes," 164).

67. In line with Bishop Ambrose, later Augustine had supported the Creed of the Council of Nicaea in 325. He had refuted Eastern remains of subordinationism that the Father is the sole source of all and that the Holy Spirit proceeds from the Father alone. Augustine had fully developed his understanding of God in terms of God's trinitarian nature—"God one in three and three in one" (*Una trinitas et trina unitas*) (*conf.* 12.7.7; 13.11.12). In other words, he had formulated his concept of the Trinity—the Father, the Son, and the Holy Spirit—through his debates with the Arians (e.g., Maximinus, the Arian bishop, in Hippo in 428) (see *Trin.* 4.21.30; 6.3.4–6.7.9; 7.6.12).

68. In emphasizing Augustine's visit to Simplicianus, Vaught writes, "What [the young Augustine] needs . . . is a spiritual adviser, who can respond to his existential predicament and can help him move beyond his conversion to Neoplatonism to the transformation of his will" (*Encounters*, 72).

Playing Together

Simplicianus was a convert from Paganism to Christianity. Now Simplicianus, as a senior priest and a Christian Platonist, had been a humble servant of Christ for many years. In doing so, Simplicianus baptized Ambrose (who was the provincial governor, but was suddenly nominated to be a bishop of the Milanese cathedral) and became a spiritual father for Ambrose—"Ambrose truly loved him as one loves a father" (8.2.3).[69] Throughout his meetings with Augustine, Simplicianus illustrated how he had shifted from paganism to Christianity; then he advised Augustine how to deal with his existential predicament and spiritual abyss as well as how to follow Christ's example of humility. In particular, Simplicianus had encouraged the intellect Augustine to read the letters of the Apostle Paul. Later Simplicianus' appropriate recommendation of reading the letters of Paul would prove essential for Augustine's spiritual change in the Milanese garden in 386.

In the context of Augustine's endless quest to know himself and to know the divine as well as his struggling to read the Bible and to learn about the basic themes of Christian faith, Simplicianus told Augustine about his old friend Victorinus' conversion story who became a role model of Christian humility through dedication to Jesus Christ (8.2.3–5, 8.5.10).[70] Marius Victorinus, as a pagan Neoplatonist, was a famous professor of rhetoric at Rome. Victorinus wrote books on grammar, rhetoric, and dialectic; he translated some books of the Platonists which had affected Augustine's intellectual transformation, as Augustine himself stated: "Victorinus was extremely learned and most expert in all the liberal disciplines. . . . I had read some books of the Platonists, which had been translated into Latin by Victorinus" (8.2.3). Before his conversion to Christianity, Victorinus was an ardent believer of the traditional Roman cults—"Until [Victorinus] was of advanced years, he was a worshipper of idols and took part in sacrilegious rites. At that time almost all the Roman nobility was enthusiastic for the cult of Osiris and Monstrous gods of every kind and Anubis the barking dog, Monsters who once bore arms against Neptune and Venus and against Minerva, gods that Rome once conquered but then implored for aid. The old Victorinus had defended these cults for many years with a voice terrifying to opponents" (8.2.3). Later, Victorinus, who

---

69. See Bourke, *Augustine's Quest*, 44, 83; Chadwick, "Introduction and Notes," 133–34; Vaught, *Encounters*, 72; Walker, *History*, 128–29.

70. See O'Brien, "Approach"; Vaught, *Encounters*.

was an aged man and learned in all the liberal sciences, had read the Holy Scriptures and Christian literature (which was profoundly related to Christian conversion). After his intensive readings, the old Victorinus made a decision to convert to Christian faith, at which point he received the sacrament of baptism within the Christian community in 355 (8.2.4).

At the time of his conversion to Christianity and his rebirth through Christian baptism, Victorinus wanted to confess, explicitly and publicly, his Christian faith before the former fellow pagans as well as before the church members, although it was not an easy task for him in the context of the reign of the emperor Julian. His public confession of Christian faith might have compelled his former fellow pagans to turn away from their traditional religious beliefs and cults, that is, to convert to Christianity. Now it might also have enabled his fellow Christians to share his transformative story of conversion and to join together in his joy in faith in Christ:

> [Victorinus] preferred to make profession of his salvation before the holy congregation. For there was no salvation in the rhetoric which he had taught; yet his profession of that had been public. How much less should he be afraid in proclaiming your word, when he used to feel no fear in using his own words before crowds of frenzied pagans. When he mounted the steps to affirm the confession of faith, there was a murmur of delighted talk as all the people who knew him spoke his name to one another. . . . A suppressed sound came from the lips of all as they rejoiced, "Victorinus, Victorinus!" As soon as they saw him, they suddenly murmured in exaltation and equally suddenly were silent in concentration to hear him. He proclaimed his unfeigned faith with ringing assurance. All of them wanted to clap him to their hearts, and the hands with which they embraced him were their love and their joy. (8.2.5)

After his public confession of Christian faith, Victorinus resigned his professorship in Rome because the edict of the emperor Julian was "promulgated forbidding Christians to teach literature and rhetoric" (8.5.10). Here Victorinus welcomed Julian's edict; namely, he preferred to give up "the school of loquacious chattering" (8.5.10). As O'Brien, Matter, and Van Fleteren point out, this story of Victorinus' conversion had enabled Augustine to pay attention to his state of bondage of the will, especially his inner division, which now he had struggled to resolve; further, it had stimulated in the rhetorician Augustine's heart a desire to imitate his example of humility—"As soon as your servant Simplicianus told me this story about Victorinus, I was ardent to follow his example" (*conf.* 8.5.10; see 8.5.11–12).

During the period of Augustine's intimate interactions with his spiritual mentor Simplicianus, Augustine (and Alypius) received a surprise visit at home from Ponticianus who was a baptized African Christian and a servant of the emperor. Ponticianus was amazed and glad because he realized that Augustine had read the Epistles of Paul—"By chance [Ponticianus] noticed *a book on top of a gaming table* which lay before us. He picked it up, opened it, and discovered, much to his astonishment, that it was the apostle Paul. . . . I had indicated to him that those scriptures were the subject of deep study for me" (8.6.14, italics added). Ponticianus had paid attention that the young Augustine had vehemently struggled to overcome his existential predicament and spiritual abyss. As such, he was moved to tell Augustine (and Alypius) about the existence of a monastery in Milan under the care and support of Bishop Ambrose (8.6.15). In particular, as Simplicianus told Augustine about his friend Victorinus' conversion story, here Ponticianus also told Augustine (and Alypius) about the life story of Antony the Egyptian monk, who was a pioneer of desert monasticism, as well as the conversion story of his own friends, who were members of the emperor's court that the rhetorician Augustine aspired to join (8.6.14–15). More specifically, Ponticianus told Augustine (and Alypius) how his two friends had been affected by the ascetic life of Antony. Ponticianus' two friends went to Trier with the royal court. One day, while wandering in the gardens adjacent to the city walls, they arrived at "a certain house where there lived some of [God's] servants, poor in spirit: 'of such is the kingdom of heaven' (Matt 5:3)" (8.6.15). They discovered a book, *The Life of Antony,* and read it. Ponticianus' two friends' reading of the life of Antony had compelled them to abandon their high positions of the imperial court as well as to move into the monastic community, as later Augustine stated:

> [Ponticianus' two friends] found there a book in which was written the Life of Antony. One of them began to read it. He was amazed and set on fire, and during his reading began to think of taking up this way of life and of leaving his secular post in the civil service to be your servant. . . . Suddenly he was

filled with holy love and sobering shame. Angry with himself, he turned his eyes on his friend and said to him: "Tell me, I beg of you, what do we hope to achieve with all our labours? What is our aim in life? . . . As for myself, I have broken away from our [worldly] ambition, and have decided to serve God, and I propose to start doing that from this hour in this place. If it costs you too much to follow my example, do not turn against me." His friend replied that he would join him and be associated with him for such great reward and for so great a service. (8.6.15)

Influenced by Ponticianus' two friends' example of humility and asceticism, their two affianced women had decided to commit to the life of celibacy—"Both had fiancées. When later their fiancées heard this, they also dedicated their virginity to you" (8.6.15). As such, there Ponticianus had also decided to become a Christian, at which point he was baptized in the Christian church, although he had not participated in the Christian monastic community ("'flocks' [*greges*] of monastic saints") in which his two friends (and their fiancées) were involved. After hearing the life story of Antony as well as the conversion story of Ponticianus' two friends (and their two fiancées), Augustine was surprised because (Alypius and) he had never heard of them (8.6.14–15). Now the young Augustine had reflected on his life history, as later he confessed: "While [Ponticianus] was speaking, Lord, you turned my attention back to myself" (8.7.16). Indeed, Augustine had realized that after reading Cicero's *Hortensius* at the age of nineteen, he had made little progress in resolving his intellectual and spiritual quest for wisdom or the Truth, although he had engaged in the sequence of the religious and philosophical groups of Manichaeism, astrology, skepticism, and Neoplatonism (8.7.17; see 3.4.7–8). As such, the rhetorician Augustine had felt a deep sense of shame—"I felt for myself in comparison with them" (8.7.17). He was angry with himself who did not completely abandon his desire for worldly ambition and who had still hesitated to become a Christian, as later he stated:

> The day had now come when I stood naked to myself, and my conscience complained against me: "Where is your tongue? You [as a skeptic] were saying that, because the truth is uncertain, you do not want to abandon the burden of futility. But look, it is certain now, and the burden still presses on you. Yet wings are won by the freer shoulders of men who have not been exhausted by their searching and have not taken ten years or more

to meditate on these matters." This is how I was gnawing at my inner self. I was violently overcome by *a fearful sense of shame* during the time that Ponticianus was telling his story. When he had ended his talk and settled the matter for which he came, he went home and I was left to myself. (8.7.18, italics added)

Like Ambrose and Simplicianus, Ponticianus had played a crucial role in the process of Augustine's spiritual transformation in terms of interactions with companions and a network of Christian friendships. That is, Ponticianus had guided the rhetorician Augustine to become a Christian; he had encouraged Augustine to engage in a turning toward God and to embrace the humility of the cross in the light of the radical reorientation of the will.[71] Like the conversion story of Victorinus, the ascetic life of Antony and the conversion story of Ponticianus' two friends (and their fiancées) had profoundly challenged the young Augustine to commit himself to serve God and to imitate their life-style of asceticism and celibacy.[72] In that sense, while paying to the accretive

---

71. See Matter, "Conversion(s)"; O'Brien, "Approach"; Vaught, *Encounters*; Wills, *Augustine's Conversion*.

72. I would like to suggest paying attention to the correlation between Augustine's description—"a book [of the Apostle Paul] on top of a gaming table" (8.6.14)—and his inner change of the mind. It is fair to assume that while employing the metaphor of the "gaming table" and the book of Paul in *Confessions* 8.6.14, here Augustine had tacitly expressed his inner state of division which was deeply related to his opposed two wills or desires in his mind. Symbolically, the term *the gaming table* indicates Augustine's endless desire—"a blind and rash enthusiasm for empty games" (6.7.12)—to achieve worldly honors and to satisfy sexual pleasures; in contrast, the term *the book of the Apostle Paul* points to his vehement desire to be continent and to become a Christian. As noted earlier, Augustine's desire of sensual pleasure and worldly ambition was deeply influenced by the personality and life-style of his father Patricius which was inherently related to the African temperament of sensual materialism of Augustine's time. Augustine's another desire of the life of asceticism and celibacy was profoundly affected by the personality and religiosity of his mother Monica which was inherently related to the movement of early Christian monasticism within African society. In this way, I raise important questions: "How can we effectively Augustine's own description—'a book [of the Apostle Paul] on top of a gaming table' (8.6.14)?" "What is the implication of Augustine's description?" In order to understand better Augustine's description of "a book [of Paul] on top of a gaming table," I suggest supposing that there was Augustine's another hidden description such as *a book of the Apostle Paul under the gaming table*. It is fair to assume that as a Manichee and a skeptic, Augustine had lived in the condition of the dominant impact of his father—*a book of the Apostle Paul under the gaming table*—at which point Augustine had more pursued the life of sensual pleasure and worldly success than the life of moral earnestness and purity (see Capps, "Divided Self," 562–63; O'Meara, *Young Augustine*, 213). However, during

Understanding Religious Conversion

and accelerative force of others' conversion stories toward the climax of Augustine's own conversion, Elledge writes,

> Conversion narratives prefigure this conversion [of Augustine] and mirror some features of Augustine's unreformed life. . . . Antony's, Victorinus,' which Augustine wishes "with fervour to imitate," and Ponticianus' story of his two friends' conversions. These dramatic, even melodramatic, emotionally charged accounts would naturally appeal to Augustine the rhetorician, skilled in the arts of persuasive composition. But they also amaze and instruct the indecisive, embattled man, and almost certainly function as motivating precedents, as authorized models to imitate, especially those that involve human as well as divine bondings.[73]

During Augustine's journey to know himself and to know the divine as well as his interactions with others and his participation in the Christian community, Alypius was *together* with Augustine. Especially, at the time of Ponticianus' visit to Augustine, Alypius was present with him (e.g., 8.6.14–15). As such, after hearing the life of Antony and the conversion story of Ponticianus' two friends and their fiancées, Augustine had shared with Alypius his feelings of inner division and restlessness. As one of Ponticianus' two friends had asked the other friend how to resolve his inner disturbance of becoming a servant of God at Trier— "What do we hope to achieve with all our labours [for the emperor]? What is our aim in life?" (8.6.15), Augustine had also asked Alypius how to handle with his turbulent hesitation of becoming a Christian:

> In the middle of that grand struggle in my inner house, which I had vehemently stirred up with my soul in the intimate chamber of my heart, distressed not only in mind but in appearance, I turned on Alypius and cried out: "What is wrong with us? What is this that you have heard? . . . . Do we feel no shame at making

---

and after his intimate interactions with significant others (i.e., Ambrose; Simplicianus; Ponticianus; Alypius) and his participation in the newly alternative community (i.e., the Milanese cathedral) as well as his hearing the conversion stories of other persons (i.e., the conversion stories of Victorinus, Antony, and Ponticianus' two friends) and his reading of the Bible, here the young Augustine was involved in the condition of the dominant influence of his mother—*a book of the Apostle Paul on top of the gaming table*—at which point Augustine had more pursued the life of moral earnestness and purity than the life of sensual pleasure and worldly success (see Capps, "Divided Self," 563–64; Quinn, *Companion*, 327).

73. Elledge, "Augustine," 82.

not even an attempt to follow" (8.8.19). . . . This debate in my heart was a struggle of myself against myself. Alypius stood quite still at my side, and waited in silence for the outcome of my unprecedented state of agitation. (8.11.27)

The presence of Alypius was crucial for Augustine and his spiritual change because Alypius was not only a witness of Augustine's conversion process, but also a faithful companion who had supported, implicitly and explicitly, his friend Augustine in overcoming his existential predicament and spiritual abyss (8.8.19, 8.11.27, 8.12.28–30). As Martin points out, "In the garden of Milan, at the precise moment of Augustine's deepest spiritual crisis, we . . . find close at hand his dearest friend Alypius."[74] Alypius was a pupil of Augustine in Carthage (6.7.11) and became a Manichee with Augustine (6.7.12). Alypius accompanied his professor, Augustine, to Rome and then to Milan—"I found Alypius at Rome. He attached himself to me with the strongest bond and was to accompany me to Milan" (6.10.16). Later Alypius became the closest friend of Augustine.[75] Indeed, Augustine's intimate interactions with Alypius had tremendously affected his spiritual change in 386 and his ongoing transformation for the rest of his life, as Wills states: "Augustine is setting up a network of friendships that will correspond to the network of friendship exemplified in Pontician's immediately following and crucial account of the four friends (and their two affianced women) in Trier."[76] As noted earlier, the adolescent Augustine was involved in pear-stealing with his peer group which he later regarded as a senseless and sinful act based on the "worldly friendship" (2.5.10–2.9.17). However, through his properly developed relationships with Alypius, here the young Augustine began to enter into the newly established community which was based on Christian friendship and faith in Christ.

---

74. Martin, *Restless Heart*, 46.

75. Surprisingly, Alypius was present in the crucially life-changing events of Augustine: for example, Augustine's meeting with Pontiscianus (8.6.14–15), his conversion to Christianity in the Milanese garden (8.12.28–30), his experience of Christian baptism in Milan (9.6.14), his Christian philosophical community at Cassiciacum (9.4.8) and in Rome, his lay Christian community at Thagaste, his Christian monastery at Hippo Regius, his pastoral ministry at Hippo, and his vehement and endless debates with the Manichees, Donatists, Arians, and Pelagians in North Africa (see Possidius, *v. Aug.* 11; Bonner, *St. Augustine*, 113–14; Bourke, *Augustine's Quest*, 126–28; Brown, *Augustine*, 136–37; Fitzgerald, "Alypius," 16–17).

76. Wills, *Augustine's Conversion*, 117.

In that sense, the intimate relationship between Augustine and Alypius could be a preeminent role model of Christian friendship.

As emphasized in question 2 and 3, in the process of Augustine's conversion, there is a close link between his interactions with others, his participations in the Christian community, and his spiritual change in the Milanese garden in summer of 386. In the context of Augustine's inner division of the mind ("the deeper predicament of the bondage of the will") as well as his endless quest for knowing himself and the divine, significant persons—Ambrose, Simplicianus, Ponticianus, Alypius, and Monica—had played a preeminent role of "drumbeat" leading up to Augustine's own conversion to Christianity in the Milanese garden as well as fostering his participation in the Christian community. More specifically, they had affected the rhetorician Augustine to overcome his desire of worldly honor and sensual materialism which was related to the dualistic Manichean belief (3.7.12) and the Epicurean philosophy of pleasure (6.16.26) as well as to fulfill his need for belongingness or Christian friendship. They had also stirred the intellect Augustine to move from the Manichean group or the (skeptic) Academy to the alternative Christian community (i.e., the Milanese cathedral) in light of resocialization and institutionalization within the Christian community. In this way, the interlocking stories of conversion of Victorinus, Antony, Ponticianus' two friends (and their fiancées) had challenged Augustine to rethink the goal of life, to become a Christian, and to follow their example of humility and celibacy, as Wills states: "All the stories of conversion in this book [*Confessions*] are either intended by their tellers, or by God in providentially putting them in Augustine's way, to shape a journey into and through the garden of 'conversion.'"[77]

The Experience of Cultural Change

Along with the description of Augustine's encounters with significant others and his affiliations with Christian communities, this section of the chapter delves into *his experience of philosophical and cultural changes* related to the Neoplatonic heritage and the Christian monastic movement in the late fourth century. It is relevant to stage 5—*interaction*—of Rambo's model of conversion, while it gradually involves

77. Ibid., 112.

stage 6—*commitment*. Rambo views the commitment stage as the consummation and consolidation of transformation in which the (potential) convert embarks on a series of actions that solidify a new spiritual orientation and incorporate its meaning into daily life. While acknowledging Augustine's continuous interactions with other people (especially Christian Neoplatonists) and participation in the religious/philosophical group, this section examines the correlation between Augustine's experience of cultural renewal/revitalization and his life change. In doing so, it articulates the influence of Neoplatonism and Christian monasticism on the ongoing process of his intellectual and spiritual transformation.

As such, question 4 asks how Augustine had gradually reshaped his (personal and religious) identity, worldview, and belief through his ongoing interactions with others, through his participation in Christian communities, and through his experiences of cultural change.[78] In the conditions of his experiences of loving care and support from others as well as his affiliations with the Milanese cathedral and the Milanese group of intellects, the young Augustine had undergone his philosophical and cultural changes which had been deeply affected by the Neoplatonic heritage and the Christian monastic movement of his time. In this way, this question is beneficial for discussing the interrelatedness between the experience of the self and the experience of others in the process of Augustine's transformation as well as the interrelatedness between Augustine's quest for the divine and his quest for community. More specifically, while paying attention to the dynamic process of his cultural renewal and revitalization, this question helps us to deal with how the young Augustine had experienced intellectual and cultural transformation which resulted in the reformation of his personal and religious identity, worldview, and belief within the specific philosophical and socio-cultural milieu of the late fourth and early fifth centuries.

Around the same time of his intimate interactions with other people and his participation in the Christian community (i.e., the Milanese cathedral), the rhetorician Augustine was engaged in the

---

78. Question 4 focuses on the factor of the experience of cultural change related to the impact of Neoplatonism and the Christian monastic movement, while acknowledging the factors of interactions with others and participation in Christian communities.

"Milanese circle" of the intellects in which some members were Christians (e.g., Ambrose or Simplicianus) and others were pagans. Within this intellectual circle of Milan, Augustine had read some books of the Neoplatonists (especially those of Plotinus and Porphyry).[79] Through his readings of Neoplatonic books, he had learned about Neoplatonic themes or doctrines (e.g., the sovereign good, the origin of evil, the ascent of the soul towards God to the point of ecstasy, the celestial fatherland, the liberation achieved by the death of the body, and the perpetual life of the Blessed).[80]

The young Augustine had searched for knowing who he was in relation to the divine as well as for knowing who God was for him in light of interplay between God and the soul. This means that he had sought for his cognitive satisfaction of Truth which was related to the Christian Neoplatonic concept of the ascent of the soul to the One or the return of the soul to the Origin ("Plotinian ecstasies" [Plotinus, *enn.* 1.6.8])—"Beauty seen not by the eye of the flesh, but only by inward discernment" (*conf.* 6.16.26). Augustine had depicted his intellectual and spiritual journey toward God as follows:

> I entered and with my soul's eye, such as it was, saw above that same eye of my soul the immutable light higher than my mind—not the light of every day, obvious to anyone, nor a larger version of the same kind which would, as it were, have given out a much brighter light and filled everything with its magnitude.... When I first came to know you, you raised me up to make me see that what I saw is Being, and that I who saw am not yet Being. And you gave a shock to the weakness of my sight by the strong radiance of your rays, and I trembled with love and awe. And I found myself far from you "in the region of dissimilarity," and heard ... your voice from on high. (*conf.* 7.10.16; see 9.1.1, 10.7.11; *sol.* 1.2.7; 1.12.20, 2.1.1, *ord.* 2.18.47)

Indeed, Augustine's readings of the books of Neoplatonists as well as his encounters with Christian Neoplatonists had deeply affected his

---

79. Van Fleteren contends that "Plotinus's treatise on Beauty, *Enneads* 1.6, and Porphyry's *De regressu animae* were among the books which Augustine read at that time. These books lit 'an incredible fire' within the young rhetor (*c. Acad.* 2.2.5)" ("Ascent," 64; see Chadwick, *Augustine*, 17–24; Harrison, *Augustine*, 13; *Augustine's Early Theology*, 27–28; O'Meara, *Young Augustine*, 127–28, 131, 152–53).

80. See Brown, *Augustine*; Harrison, *Augustine's Early Theology*; Lancel, *Saint Augustine*; O'Donnell, *Augustine*; O'Meara, *Young Augustine*.

intellectual and spiritual transformation in light of the submission of intellect.[81] This means that Christian Neoplatonism had stimulated the Manichee and skeptic Augustine to reconstruct his conceiving of the divine nature *from* the material and divisible being—"God [is] confined within a corporeal form" (3.7.12)—*to* the incorporeal and indivisible/spiritual being—"God is a Spirit (John 4:24), not a figure whose limbs have length and breadth and who has a mass" (3.7.12; see 7.20.26). In doing so, it had also stirred the intellect Augustine to be convinced that the divine is not stretched out or poured out part-by-part in space, but is present as a whole everywhere (7.1.2, 7.5.7; see *ep.* 118.23; Plotinus, *enn.* 6.4.1–6.5.12).[82] Furthermore, Christian Neoplatonism had enabled Augustine to reestablish his understanding of evil from a real existence to no substance or an absence of Good (*privatio boni*)—"Evil has no existence except as a privation of good" (*conf.* 3.7.12); "As you did not make all things equal, all things are good in the sense that taken individually they are good, and all things taken together are very good. For our God has made 'all things very good' (Gen 1:31)" (7.12.18; see 7.5.7; *civ. Dei* 14.11; *c. Jul. imp.* 3.206). Augustine's new concept of the divine and his new understanding of the nature of good and evil had greatly stimulated him to make his inner spiritual journey toward union with the Truth.

In the conditions of his struggles with his interior journey for the divine and his intimate interactions with others as well as his readings of the books of the Neoplatonists and his reformation of his view on the divine and the origin of evil, here the young Augustine (who became a catechumen) had been affected by the public sermons of Ambrose, at which point Augustine's attitude to the Bible was positively changed. At that time, Augustine had also received a strong recommendation from his spiritual mentor, Simplicianus, for reading the Christian Scriptures,

81. See Cary, "Interiority," *Augustine's Invention*, "Book Seven"; Lancel, *Saint Augustine*; O'Meara, *Young Augustine*.

82. The Manichee Augustine had undergone the intellectual and philosophical problem of conceiving of God as taking up space: "God is present everywhere, young Augustine knows, but how? His materialistic heart can only imagine God as spread out through all the places in the universe, like water filling a sponge. But that means one part of God must be in one place, and another part in another place, and more of him in an elephant than in a sparrow" (Cary, "Book Seven," 109). However, after understanding the nature of divine omnipresence, Augustine realized that his return to the divine is not a physical journey through space—"One does not go far away from you or return to you by walking or by any movement through space" (*conf.* 1.18.28).

especially the Epistles of the Apostle Paul. As such, the young Augustine had (re)-read the Bible. While reading the Bible, Augustine had gradually discovered the specific and crucial difference between the Holy Scriptures and the Neoplatonic books (although he was deeply influenced by the themes of Neoplatonism which had helped the intellect Augustine to reestablish his view on the nature of the divine as well as the nature of good and evil). In particular, Augustine had realized that the pagan Neoplatonists (e.g., Porphyry) had viewed Christ as an excellent man; that is, they had not accepted any virtue of the divine nature of Christ, but had emphasized the virtue of his human nature: "[For Porphyry] Christ is represented by an imaginary portrait of another person" (*civ. Dei* 10.27). At that time, influenced by pagan Neoplatonism, the intellect Augustine had also thought that Christ was simply a wise man, as later he stated, "[Before my reading of the Bible] I had a different notion, since I thought of Christ, my Lord only as a man of excellent wisdom which none could equal" (*conf.* 7.19.25). However, after his reading of the Bible, Augustine had recognized that unlike Paul's letters, the books of the Neoplatonists did not contain the Christian belief or message which is profoundly related to the Christian concept of the Incarnate Christ—"The Word made flesh (John 14:6)" (*conf.* 7.18.24)—who is a mediator between God and humanity and who is a perfect example of humility (*civ. Dei* 10.27–29).[83] As later he stated,

> These philosophers [e.g., Plotinus or Porphyry] . . . were without Christ's saving name (*conf.* 5.16.25). . . . Who will deliver him from this body of death except your grace through Jesus Christ our Lord (Rom 7:24), who is your coeternal Son, whom you "created in the beginning of your ways" (Prov 8:22). . . . None of this is in the Platonist books. Those pages do not contain the face of this devotion, tears of confession, your sacrifice, a troubled spirit, a contrite and humble spirit (Ps 50:19), the salvation of your people, the espoused city (Rev 21:5), the guarantee of your Holy Spirit (2 Cor 5:5), the cup of our redemption. In the Platonic books no one sings: "Surely my soul will be submissive to God? From him is my salvation; he is also my God and

---

83. See Bonner, "Starting with Oneself," 165; Cary, "Book Seven," 120; Harrison, *Augustine*, 30–38; *Augustine's Early Theology*, 32–33; O'Connell, *Augustine's Confessions*, 79–80; O'Meara, *Young Augustine*, 139–41.

Playing Together

my savior who upholds me; I shall not be moved any more" (Ps 61:2–3). (*conf.* 7.21.27; see 7.18.24, 7.20.26)[84]

At the time of his readings of the Bible and his realization of the key difference between the books of Neoplatonism and Christian Scriptures, the young Augustine had learned the early Christian monasticism. There is interrelatedness between the Christian monastic movement and the social and cultural milieu of the fourth century in the West. After the Emperor Constantine's conversion to Christianity in 312, persecution came to end in the Roman world; as such, Christian asceticism gradually held to replace martyrdom. In the widespread context of the growth of Christian monasticism, here the young Augustine had heard from his Christian fellow-African, Ponticianus, about the Milanese monastery which was under the guidance of Bishop Ambrose (8.6.15) as well as the early Christian monastic movement—the ascetic life of the Egyptian Antony who was the architect of the desert monasticism (which is called "anchoritic monasticism") (8.6.14–15, 8.12.29). In doing so, Augustine had also heard about the life of asceticism and celibacy of Ponticianus' two friends and their fiancées (who were influenced by the life of Antony the Egyptian monk) (8.6.15, 8.7.17).

Indeed, Christian monastic movements, especially the Antonian tradition of the life of asceticism, had played a crucial role in Augustine's spiritual transformation in the garden of Milan in 386, as Harrison states: "Ponticianus' words [of Christian monastic movements] . . . gave [the young Augustine] an appalling vision of his own vileness from which he could not escape except by heeding them and suffering their judgement upon his own situation. [They compelled] Augustine . . . to embrace the celibate, ascetic life."[85] Specifically, these monastic movements had encouraged Augustine to overcome his vacillation of becoming a Christian—"the turbulent hesitations of his heart"—and to stand humbly before God—"the humble Incarnate Christ"—in the Milanese garden. This means that they had stimulated Augustine to become a servant of God ("a monk") and to engage in the renunciation of the worldly ambition and the life of asceticism and celibacy in the Christian

---

84. See Cary, *Augustine's Invention*, 31; "Book Seven," 119–20; Harrison, *Augustine*, 88–93; Lancel, *Saint Augustine*, 87–88; O'Donnell, *Augustine: Confessions*, vol. 3, 3; O'Meara, 155–58, 191.

85. Harrison, *Augustine*, 179.

monastic community.[86] Later Augustine's encounter with the anchoritic monasticism of Antony had profoundly affected him to enter into the celibate and acetic life in community at Cassiciacum and then in Rome ("the revitalized commitment to a faith"), although Augustine himself had preferred to pursue the life of the community rather than the life of the hermit.

Apparently, Augustine's learning of Christian Neoplatonism and Christian monasticism had led him to move from the life of sensual pleasure and worldly ambition to the life of moral earnestness and purity. In doing so, Augustine's reading of the Bible and his learning of Christian faith and living in the Christian community had helped him to overcome the Epicurean philosophy of pleasure.[87] More specifically, although Augustine had been influenced by the predominant pleasure-motif in Epicurus, he had eventually rejected the Epicurean way of life because Epicurus had denied any divine intervention into or concern in human affairs and because Epicurus had refused to believe in the life of the soul after death and God's future judgment,[88] as later Augustine noted:

> Nothing kept me from an even deeper whirlpool of erotic indulgence [based on Epicurus' philosophy of pleasure] except fear of death and of your coming judgment. . . . To my mind Epicurus would have been awarded the palm of victory, had I not believed that after death the life of the soul remains with the consequences of our acts, a belief which Epicurus rejected; and I asked: If we were immortal and lived in unending bodily pleasure, with no fear of losing it, why should we not be happy? What else should we seeking for? . . . For I was so submerged and blinded that I

86. See E. A. Clark, "Asceticism"; Harrison, *Augustine*; Lawless, *Augustine*; Van Bavel, "Double Face"; Zumkeller, *Augustine's Ideal*.

87. While exploring the impact of Epicurus' philosophy of pleasure on the skeptic Augustine, Colin Starnes states, "Epicurus' doctrine was a determined worldliness. All things were composed of matter—of atoms and the void—including the human soul, which was simply annihilated in the dissolution of its material elements once they were no longer held together by the body. Sense-perception, produced by images streaming off the surface of things, passing through the senses and imprinting on the soul, was true and indubitable. . . . The truth or falsity of opinion was determined by experience. Good and evil were simply pleasure and pain—although by pleasure Epicurus meant the pleasures of the entire person and an entire life, both bodily and mental. He understood pleasure as the absence of pain since, on his view, it consists chiefly in the satisfaction of a need and thus the removal of pain" (*Augustine's Conversion*, 160).

88. See Quinn, *Companion*, 327–28; Starnes, *Augustine's Conversion*, 161.

could not think of the light of moral goodness and of a beauty to be embraced for its own sake—beauty seen not by the eye of the flesh, but only by inward discernment. (*conf.* 6.16.26)[89]

Consistent with his departure from the Epicurean life of sensual pleasure, the young Augustine began to enter into his spiritual journey toward union with the divine, at which point he was engaged in the process of becoming a Christian in light of shift from the eye of the body to the eye of the soul. At this point, Quinn notes, "Epicurus' goods are strictly accessible only to the eye of the body whereas these goods [of Christian Neoplatonism] are seen within, by the eye of the soul. . . . Loosing him from all ties of temptation to *the garden of Epicurus*, God would bear him up in *the garden of Milan* (8.12.28–9), then later bear him up to shoulder all the grinding labors of the priestly vocation mapped out for him."[90]

Indeed, as discussed in question 4, in the process of Augustine's conversion, there is a correlation between his interactions with others, his participation in the Christian community, and his cultural changes. In the contexts of his struggles to know himself and the divine and to reconstruct purpose and meaning in life as well as his affective bonds with significant others and his affiliations with the Milanese cathedral/ the Milanese intellectual group, Augustine's learning of both Christian Neoplatonism and early Christian monasticism had played an important role in facilitating his intellectual and spiritual change. In the dynamic process of his transformation and acculturation/cultural revitalization, the young Augustine had newly reconstructed his view of the divine nature and the origin of evil; through his reading of the Bible, he had recognized the Christian concept of "the humble Incarnate Christ" (who had later compelled the young philosopher Augustine to look at his own "intellectual pride" in which he had understood "himself as the

---

89. According to Starnes, in antiquity, Epicurus had earned "an undeserved reputation as a hedonist who sought only pleasure" and who emphasized exclusively worldly view (*Augustine's Conversion*, 160). Likewise, Quinn contends that the life of dedication for others ("self-giving in friendship") is meaningless in the Epicurean way of sensual pleasure. In that sense, Roman intellects had generally interpreted Epicurus as one who would prefer "to be a pig satisfied than Socrates dissatisfied," although Epicurus himself never proposed pursuit of pleasure in a brutish manner (*Companion*, 329; see *en. Ps.* 73.25).

90. Quinn, *Companion*, 329–30. See Plumer, "Book Six," 105; Starnes, *Augustine's Conversion*, 160–62; Vaught, *Journey*, 153–54.

source of his wisdom"). Further, Augustine had learned about the early Christian monastic movements which had greatly encouraged him to overcome his sensual pleasure and worldly ambition as well as to follow the example of humility and celibacy.

The Experience of Divine Intervention and Grace

Along with the depiction of Augustine's philosophical and cultural changes, this section of the chapter explores *his experience of the transforming power of God's grace* in the Milanese garden in the summer of 386. While corresponding to the commitment stage and interlocking with other stages of Rambo's model of religious change, it moves into stage 7 (*consequences*), which is regarded as the cumulative effects of the conversion process over time.[91] While acknowledging Augustine's intensified interactions with others within the Christian community and his reformation of (personal and religious) identity, worldview, and belief within social and cultural milieu of his time, this section pays attention to the inherent link between Augustine's experience of God and his spiritual change. Specifically, it elucidates the divine intervention and grace into Augustine's life through the word of God in the Milanese garden.

As such, question 5 asks how Augustine's interpersonal relationships, his God representations, and his encounters with God were bound together in his conversion process.[92] In the cumulative and consummated contexts of his interior journey for union with the divine, his newly established relationships with others, his commitment to the Christian community, and his philosophical and cultural changes through learning Christian Neoplatonism and Christian monasticism, the young Augustine had experienced divine intervention; that is, he felt the initiating activity of God's loving grace (by way of the word of God) in the garden of Milan (*conf.* 8.12.28–29). In this way, while

---

91. Rambo's term *consequence* refers to not simply a static phenomenon or result of conversion (event), but an ongoing engagement in the transformational life of the convert. In the stage of consequences, the convert is able to enter into the lifelong process of changing for the rest of one's life.

92. Question 5 focuses on the factor of the encounter with God, while acknowledging the factors of the experience of psychological distress and crisis, interactions with others, participation in Christian communities, and the experience of cultural change.

achieving a coherent and integrated picture of Augustine's narrative of transformation, this question is valid for investigating the interaction between the experience of the self and the experience of the divine in the process of Augustine's spiritual change as well as the interaction between Augustine's search for the divine and his search for others. More specifically, this question encourages us to recognize the correlation of human relationships, God representations, and the experiences of the divine in the dynamic process of Augustine's transformation. In doing so, it leads us to pay attention to the impact of the transforming power of God's grace on Augustine's spiritual change in terms of the encounter with God and the healing of the divided self/will. It also provides us an insight into how the word of God had affected Augustine's conversion to Christianity in terms of divine voice, Scripture, and conversion.

During the depths of his existential predicament and spiritual darkness, the young Augustine (who had hesitated to become a Christian [8.1.1–2, 8.8.19–8.11.27]) had confronted himself and God in the Milanese garden in the late summer of 386 (8.12.28–30). Although he had experienced his intellectual transformation of the divine nature and the origin of evil, Augustine had still struggled to find a resting place for his soul.[93] This means that he had still experienced inner turmoil which was rooted in the division of his soul/will—"I was deeply disturbed in spirit, angry with indignation and distress that I was not entering into my pact and covenant with you, my God, when all my bones (Ps 34:10) were crying out that I should enter into it and were exalting it to heaven with praises" (8.8.19).[94] In the condition of his restlessness of the heart and his inner struggle to experience God, Augustine rushed into the garden, as he stated: "Our lodging had a garden. . . . The tumult of my heart [due to my divided will] took me out into the garden where no one could interfere with the burning struggle with myself in which I was engaged, until the matter could be settled" (8.8.19). (Alypius also went to the garden, namely, he was present while Augustine was struggling to overcome his existential predicament and to seek for the union with God [8.7.28; 8.8.19; 8.11.27].)[95] Here Augustine had paid attention to his vacillation of becoming a Christian in his mind, although he had

---

93. See Vaught, *Encounters*, 70.
94. See Starnes, *Augustine's Conversion*, 159.
95. See Martin, *Restless Heart*, 46; Vaught, *Encounters*, 79.

Understanding Religious Conversion

felt a strong desire to devote himself wholly to the search for the Truth as well as to be continent, as later he recalled:

> In my temporal life everything was in a state of uncertainty, and my heart needed to be purified from the old leaven (1 Cor 5:7f.). I was attracted to the way, the Saviour himself, but was still reluctant to go along its narrow paths (*conf.* 8.1.1).... And now I had discovered *the good pearl* [which might refer to the humble Incarnate Christ who is mediator between the Creator and the created and who is a perfect example of humility]. To buy it I had to sell all that I had; and I hesitated (Matt 13:46) (8.1.2).... I prayed you for chastity and said: "Grant me chastity and continence, but not yet" (8.7.17).... I was [still] hesitating whether to die to death and to live to life. (8.9.25, italics added)

At this time of the culmination of his hesitation, Augustine had greatly experienced the divine intervention into the internal warfare of his mind. This means that Lady Continence (who might be a messenger of God—"the light of moral goodness and of a beauty"—for guiding Augustine into the life of moral earnestness and purity) had greatly visited his restless heart. Lady Continence had strongly encouraged Augustine to overcome his hesitation and to commit himself to the life of celibacy, as later Augustine recalled and confessed:

> To receive and embrace me she [Lady Continence] stretched out pious hands, filled with numerous good examples for me to follow. There were large numbers of boys and girls, a multitude of all ages, young adults and grave widows and elderly virgins. In every one of them was Continence herself, in no sense barren but "the fruitful mother of children" (Ps 112:9), the joys born of you, Lord, her husband. And she smiled on me with a smile of encouragement as if to say: "Are you incapable of doing what these men and women have done? Do you think them capable of achieving this *by their own resources and not by the Lord their God*? Their Lord God gave me to them. *Why are you relying on yourself*, only to find yourself unreliable? *Cast yourself upon him*, do not be afraid. He will not withdraw himself so that you fall. Make the leap without anxiety; he will catch you and heal you.". . . "Stop your ears to your impure members on earth and mortify them" (Col 3:5). (8.11.27, italics added)

While facing a divine intervention through Lady Continence's request for a life of celibacy, the young Augustine's inner tension mounted and became unbearable. He threw himself down "under a certain tree" which could be a fig (or olive) tree. He let his tears flow freely, and bitterly cried, "How long, O Lord? How long, Lord, will you be angry to the uttermost? Do not be mindful of our old iniquities (Ps 6:4). . . . How long is it to be? Tomorrow, tomorrow. Why not now? Why not an end to my impure life in this very hour" (8.12.28). When he was saying this and weeping in the agony of his heart, Augustine heard a childlike voice chanting from a neighboring house, "Pick up and read, pick up and read"—*Tolle lege, Tolle lege!* (8.12.29). He took this as a divine command because he remembered the conversion story of Antony, who was wholly turned toward the life of asceticism by the reading of a specific verse of the Bible.[96] As later Augustine stated, "For I had heard how Antony happened to be present the gospel reading, and took it as an admonition addressed to himself when the words were read: 'Go, sell all you have, give to the poor, and you shall have treasure in heaven; and come, follow me' (Matt 19:21)" (8.12.29). After hearing the voice of God for demanding the reading of the Bible, Augustine hurried back to the place where his friend, Alypius, was sitting in the garden. He opened one of the Apostle Paul's letters and his eyes fell on the words: "Let us live honorably as in the day, not in reveling and drunkenness, not in debauchery and licentiousness, not in quarreling and jealousy. Instead, *put on the Lord Jesus Christ*, and make no provision for the flesh, to gratify its desires" (Rom 13:13–14, italics added). Here the young Augustine had felt the divine indwelling and intervention through the word of God (8.12.29). As Froehlich points out, "He had experienced God as the master rhetorician in the garden scene where the divine Word had moved him through the chant of a child and the words of the Apostle Paul."[97] Like the case of Antony, through a specific verse of the Bible, God had intervened to transfigure Augustine. Specifically,

---

96. While articulating the correlation between Antony's reading of the Bible and his transformation, Knowles states, "The place was lower Egypt, and the time a year in the last decades of the third century; more precisely, an Egyptian church in AD 271. Antony, son of well-to-do Egyptian peasants, heard the words of Jesus read by a priest: 'If you will be perfect go, sell all thou hast and give to the poor, and come, follow me.' He fulfilled the three-fold command and began to live alone, dedicating himself to a life of prayer and manual work. No doubt individuals had acted in a similar way before. Antony differed from them both in the determination and sanctity of a long life, and in his gift for inspiring and guiding others, the stream of imitators that soon became a flood, begging Antony to tell them the secret of his life" (*Christian Monasticism*, 10).

97. Froehlich, "Take Up," 9.

the word of God hit the heart of Augustine. The Bible had interpreted the rhetorician Augustine through the activity of God's Spirit rather than the teacher of rhetoric interpreting the Bible.[98] This means that the word of God had urged Augustine to look at his wounded soul, his distorted will, which was primarily rooted in his falling away from the ground of Being. This word of God had also triggered the young philosopher Augustine to see his intellectual pride (i.e., his dependency on his own wisdom and virtue) as well as his vacillation to stand humbly before God (8.12.29).[99]

Apparently, God's interaction with Augustine through the Christian Scriptures had played an eminent role in Augustine's transformation in the Milanese garden in light of the correlation between hearing the voice of God and reading a biblical text. More specifically, at the time of divine intervention through the word of God, Augustine had opened his mind to hear the inward divine locution. He had accepted the presence of God in the depths of his soul, at which point he had felt the healing power of God's loving grace in his heart—"As I became unhappier, you came closer. Your right hand was by me, already prepared to snatch me out of the filth (Jer 28:13), and to clean me up" (6.16.26). In the midst of his experiences of divine presence and divine

---

[98]. There is a debate on the issue of the dominant role of Antony or Paul in Augustine's conversion. In emphasizing the influence of Antony the Egyptian monk on Augustine's spiritual change, E. Ann Matter writes, "Paul and Luke are minor elements of the narrative structure compared to the influence of Matthew and Antony" ("Conversion(s)," 25; see, 24). Meanwhile, in line with Fredriksen and Ferrari, Judith C. Stark focuses on the impact of the Apostle Paul on Augustine's transformation— "Augustine's language is strongly reminiscent of Paul's description of the inner conflict of the will" ("Dynamics," 50). While acknowledging the contributions of the previous studies, this study suggests that the role of Antony and the role of Paul in Augustine's conversion process were not separate but interwoven, that is, both Antony and Paul had deeply affected Augustine's spiritual change and his thought. We need to remind that the life of Antony had triggered Augustine to become a servant of God and to establish a new way of the monastic life, and that the Epistles of Paul had affected Augustine to recognize the key difference between the pagan Neoplatonism and Christianity (i.e., the Christian belief of the humble Incarnate Christ) and to experience God's intervention and God's transforming power (by means of Rom 13–14) in the depths of his divided soul.

[99]. Augustine frequently applied and adapted the story of the prodigal son (Luke 15:11–24) and the story of the lost sheep (Luke 15:1–7) to himself (*conf.* 4.16.30; 12.15.21). By using the parables of the prodigal son and the lost sheep, here Augustine recalled and confessed that in spite of his hesitation to become a Christian, God, as a loving Parent, had continuously waited for him.

transfiguring power, the young rhetorician Augustine confessed his restlessness and powerlessness (i.e., his painful condition of the divided self/will) in light of the interaction of the soul and the ground of Being. Augustine had gradually recognized that God was nearer to him than he was to himself. Through his encounter with the divine, he became reconciled to himself and to God and placed himself in the hands of God. While reconstructing new relationships with himself and with God, Augustine's soul began to flow, to merge into God and was purified and transformed by the fire of God's love. This means that God's merciful hands had touched his wounded soul and healed his distorted will.[100] As such, Augustine had overcome his deep sense of existential isolation and shame (i.e., the sickness of the soul); namely, he had experienced his interior transformation from the division of the self (i.e., the split of the will) to the integration of the self (i.e., the transformation of the will)—"God breaks the bonds of sexual [pleasure and worldly fame] and sets him free the deeper bondage of the will."[101] Now Augustine had felt peace in mind—"At once, with the last words of this sentence, it was as if a light of relief from all anxiety flooded into my heart. All the shadows of doubt were dispelled" (8.12.29). He had finally found the safe resting place for his soul in relation to God, as later he recalled and confessed: "Love is the soul's weight" (*pondus meum amor meus*) (13.9.10); "I have loved your beauty and the place of the habitation of the glory of my Lord (Ps 25:7–9)" (12.15.21).

While exploring the complexity and richness of Augustine's narrative conversion, we are able to recognize that the coherent and multiple factors had worked together in the unfolding process of his transformation. More specifically, in the interactive and cumulative conditions of his psychological distress and existential abyss, his quest to know himself and the divine, his affective bonds with others, his participation in the Milanese cathedral and the philosophical group, his cultural

---

100. Paul Tillich claims that "[Augustine's] sin is primarily and basically the power of turning away from God. For this reason, no moral remedy is possible. Only one remedy is adequate—a return to God. This, of course, is possible only in the power of God, a power which man under the conditions of existence has lost" (*Christian Thought*, 160).

101. Vaught, *Encounters*, 68. Influenced by James, Stark views Augustine's conversion as a resolution of the divided will ("the sickness of the soul") ("Dynamics," 56). He pays attention to the correlation between God's grace and Augustine's spiritual change (ibid., 58).

changes impacted by Neoplatonism and Christian monasticism, and his encounters with the divine by way of the messenger of God ("Lady Continence") and the word of God, the young Augustine was converted to Christianity in the Milanese garden in the summer of 386.[102] Augustine had humbly cast himself upon the Incarnate Christ (i.e., "the good pearl") who had mediated the chasm between God and Augustine himself and who had encouraged Augustine to participate in the Christian life of incarnation, death, and resurrection, as Vaught points out: "[Augustine's] putting on Christ is not only a way of embracing the incarnation and sharing the crucifixion, but also a way of participating in the resurrection."[103] In the state of his embrace with the humble Incarnate Christ, Augustine became a Christian, namely, became a newly created being of faith in Christ.[104]

While looking at the process of Augustine's lived experience of conversion, we are also able to realize that his representations of God were positively changed. More specifically, along with his experiences of loving ("good-enough") care and support by other persons within the Christian community and his philosophical and cultural changes (resulted in his reconstruction of identity, worldview, divine nature, and belief) as well as his experiences of the transforming power of divine grace and his acceptance of divine intervention into his life, here Augustine had gradually reformulated the representations of God. As discussed earlier, in the context of his experiences of traumatic injuries (*conf.* 1.9.14–15), the early and adolescent Augustine had formulated his negative self-image as well as his negative representations of God as scourging (8.11.25), mocking (6.6.9), indifferent (1.9.14), and wrathful (3.3.5) in terms of a sense of self-reproach, inability to relate to others/Other, and suffering. Consistent with the formation of his negative

---

102. Later Augustine continuously emphasized the relation between the transforming power of God's grace and Christian conversion: "We have separated ourselves from You, and if You do not turn us around, we will never be converted" (*en. Ps.* 79.4).

103. Vaught, *Encounters*, 98.

104. Kreidler states, "Augustine views his own conversion experience as two tiered. Not only is he asking to be healed of the works of the flesh, which inhibit the search for truth, but he is also asking to be healed of intellectual pride, the mark of the Stoic wise man and the Platonist philosopher. The conversion process is a movement away from the intellectual pride of the philosophers who saw themselves as the source of their own wisdom and virtue to an experience of the humility of the Incarnate Christ as model and healer" ("Conversion," 510–11).

Playing Together

representations of God, later the adolescent and young Augustine (who was influenced by the Manichean dualistic materialism) had improperly understood God as corporeal and divisible (3.7.12).

However, in the midst of his existential predicament, Augustine had experienced loving care and support from significant others, including his spiritual father Ambrose (5.13.23–5.14.25) and his spiritual mentor Simplicianus (8.2.3–5, 8.5.10). In the midst of intellectual disruption in the Manichean materialistic dualism and skeptic thinking, he had undergone his philosophical and cultural changes through his learning of Christian Neoplatonism (*conf.* 7.12.18, 7.18.24, 7.20.26, 7.21.27; *civ. Dei* 10.27–29, 14.11) and Christian monasticism (*conf.* 8.6.14–15, 8.7.17, 8.12.29). In the midst of spiritual abyss, he had encountered God in the Milanese garden. Unlike his early experience of God (who might be in silence to his traumatic situation [1.9.14]), here Augustine had felt God's presence in his heart, that is, he had experienced the initiating activity of God's loving grace (8.12.28–30). This implies that the young Augustine had finally overcome his deep sense of disconnection or isolation, namely, he had re-constructed his proper relationships with himself, others, and the divine. Through these loving relationships, he had undergone progressive restoration and healing in which his negative God representations were transformed into positive God representations.

Here Augustine had reformulated his representations of God as follows:

1) God as loving—"My God, in my thanksgiving I want to recall and confess your mercies over me. Let my bones be penetrated by your love" (8.1.1); "You pierced my heart with the arrow of your love" (9.2.3; see 6.5.7, 6.6.9, 7.8.12, 8.12.30, 10.1.1, 10.6.8, 10.27.38, 10.28.39, 10.29.40, 12.15.21).

2) God as present—"You were with me" (10.27.38); "As I became unhappier, you came closer. Your right hand was by me, already prepared to snatch me out of the filth (Jer 28:13). . . . You are present, liberating [me] from miserable errors, and you put [me] on your way, bringing comfort and saying: 'Run, I will carry you, and I will see you through to the end, and there I will carry you' (Isa 46:4)" (6.16.26; see 5.9.16, 10.6.8).

3) God as healing—"Your scalpel cut to the quick of the wound, so

that I should leave all these ambitions and be converted to you, who are 'above all things' (Rom 9:5) and without whom all things are nothing, and that by conversion I should be healed" (6.6.9); "Your right hand had regard to the depth of my dead condition, and from the bottom of my heart had drawn out a trough of corruption" (9.1.1; see 7.8.12, 9.2.3, 9.4.12, 10.28.39, 10.29.40).

4) God as incorporeal and indivisible—"After reading the books of the Platonists and learning from them to seek for immaterial truth, I turned my attention to your invisible nature understood through the things which are made" (7.20.26); "With all my heart I believe you to be incorruptible, immune from injuries, and unchangeable" (7.1.1; see 3.7.12, 7.1.2, 7.5.7, 7.10.16).

Later Augustine's reformation of his God representations had played an important role in developing a better Christian living in solitude and community which was related to his continuous spiritual journey for union with God, his participation in the Christian monastic community, and his pastoral ministry for others in the Christian church in light of the experiences of self, others, and the divine.[105]

At the time of his experience of the transformation of his representations of God, the garden experience in Milan had enabled Augustine to make a new resolution for reconstructing the rest of his lifetime. Augustine decided both to give up his ambitions for a successful life in this world and to stand firmly upon the rule of Christian faith (which his mother Monica had dreamed about [3.11.19–2 1]). That means that Augustine resigned his professorship of rhetoric and renounced his upcoming legal marriage with a young rich heiress meant to acquire a higher status in Roman society. As such, he was involved in the life of "serving God" (*servire Deo*), at which point he had engaged in the life of celibacy and asceticism in his Christian community (*conf.* 8.12.30; Possidius, *v. Aug.* 2).[106]

---

105. Kreidler discusses "Augustine's use of the image of *Christus Medicus* or Christ the Healer, a term well known in North African Christianity as early as the days of Tertullian and Cyprian. [Later] Augustine often used the image in his sermons, probably because it would have been both appealing and familiar to his congregation" ("Conversion," 510).

106. See Bonner, *Saint Augustine*; Bourke, *Augustine's Quest*; Brown, *Augustine*; Harrison, *Augustine's Early Theology*; Lancel, *Saint Augustine*; Wills, *Saint Augustine*.

Playing Together

While acknowledging the process of Augustine's spiritual change in the garden of Milan, we are able to recognize how Augustine's conversion had affected Alypius' conversion and how the word of God had influenced Alypius' transformation in the same garden. As noted above, Alypius (who was a Manichee) was together with Augustine in the garden. Here Alypius was a witness for Augustine's existential struggle to search for union with God as well as his spiritual change through divine inspiration from the Christian Scriptures. Just as a specific scriptural text (i.e., Rom 13:13–14) had profoundly affected Augustine's transformation and his life of celibacy and asceticism, a specific verse of the Bible had impacted Alypius' spiritual change. Following the example of Augustine, Alypius had read the same book of the Apostle Paul's letters, especially Romans 14:1—"Welcome those who are weak in faith, but not for the purpose of quarreling over opinions." Similar to the case of the adolescent and young Augustine, influenced by both the African temperament of sensual pleasure and the Manichean dualistic materialism, Alypius seriously indulged in the desire to enjoy worldly pleasures—"The whirlpool of Carthaginian morals, with their passion for empty public shows, sucked [Alypius] into the folly of the circus games. . . . He was miserably involved in that [desire of pleasure]" (6.7.11). However, while Alypius was reading the authoritative word of the Christian Scriptures, God was deeply communicating with him in the garden of Milan. Through his experiences of divine interjection into his life, here Alypius had completely overcome his early rash enthusiasm for empty games and was converted to Christianity in the summer of 386 (8.12.30). Furthermore, following Augustine, he had also committed himself to the life of celibacy and asceticism in the Christian community—"Without any agony of hesitation [Alypius] joined me in making a good resolution and affirmation of intention, entirely congruent with his moral principles" (8.12.30).[107]

While looking at the conversion experiences of Augustine and Alypius, we are also able to discover the correlation between Augustine's spiritual change and Monica's transformation. More specifically, after their experiences of conversion through God's grace by the word of God, Augustine and Alypius went to Monica, and told her what had happened in the garden. While sharing their transformative stories, she

---

107. See Quinn, *Companion*, 458–59; TeSelle, *Augustine the Theologian*, 42; Vaught, *Encounters*, 101.

was filled with joy. Monica had earnestly praised God for helping her accomplish more than she could ever expect, as later Augustine stated: "She exulted, feeling it to be a triumph, and blessed you who 'are powerful to do more than we ask or think' (Eph 3:20). She saw that you had granted her far more than she had long been praying for in her unhappy and tearful groans" (8.12.30). Moreover, Monica had humbly accepted God's calling for the newly converted Augustine who had decided to dedicate himself to the life of continence and asceticism as well as the life of the service of the Christian community (8.12.30). At this point, Vaught portrays the transformation of Monica: "Monica is 'converted' when she hears about the conversion of her son, turning her back on the worldly ambitions she entertains for her son, and accepting the fact that Augustine has now become God's son in a richer way than she could have ever imagined. Earlier Monica has wanted marriage, legitimate grandchildren, and professional success for Augustine, together with his conversion to Christianity. Now she is 'converted' when she becomes willing to accept Augustine's Christian conversion to the exclusion of everything else."[108]

Indeed, Augustine's conversion, Alypius' conversion, and Monica's transformation were essential for establishing the new Christian community in faith in Christ. Surprisingly, Augustine's own conversion to Christianity had affected Alypius' conversion and Monica's transformation, much like the transforming stories of Victorinus, Antony, and Ponticianus' two friends had influenced Augustine's own spiritual change. Now his conversion experience had triggered him to participate in the life of asceticism and celibacy. Moreover, it had urged them (i.e., Augustine, Alypius, and Monica) to engage in Christian living in solitude and community, much like Ponticianus' two friends and their fiancées were involved in Christian monastic life.

Consequently, as emphasized in question 5, Augustine's conversion to Christianity was not simply an isolated experience of a person. Rather, it had occurred while developing relationships with himself, others, and the divine. More specifically, it could happen in the complex contexts of his struggle to know himself and the divine, his interactions with others, his participation in the Christian community, his philosophical and cultural changes, and his deep encounter with God. Through his conversion to Christianity in the Milanese garden,

---

108. Vaught, *Encounters*, 102.

Augustine had found a new way of Christian life in solitude and community which was profoundly rooted in the interaction between faith in Christ and Christian friendship.[109]

The Acceptance of Christian Baptism and the Experience of the Vision of Ostia

Along with Augustine's experience of God's intervention and grace in the Milanese garden, this section describes *his acceptance of the sacrament of Christian baptism and his engagement in the vision of Ostia* with Monica. While continuously corresponding to other stages of Rambo's model of conversion, it is deeply relevant to stage 7—*consequences*. In consideration of the continuous effects of Augustine's converting process, this section pays attention to his ongoing transformation for the rest of his life. More specifically, it elaborates the impact of Milanese baptismal liturgy on Augustine's spiritual change and the influence of Ostia experience on his formation of the Christian community.

As such, question 6 asks how Augustine's relationships with himself, others, and the divine were related to human development and spiritual maturity.[110] After his garden experience, Augustine had engaged in the movement of the continuing transformation for the rest of his lifetime. In this way, this question is suitable for discussing the unfolding process of Augustine's change—"converting" or "continued conversion"—which was related to his earnest search for connection and negotiating disconnection and reconnection with himself, others, and the divine. In doing so, it provides us insights into how the ritual performance of Christian baptism (i.e., the Milanese baptismal liturgy) had impacted Augustine's transformation (which was deeply related to the metaphor of spiritual death and rebirth) as well as how Augustine's

---

109. While articulating the correlation between Augustine's conversion, Christian friendship, and the establishment of the new community, Vaught writes, "Friendship is a crucial thread that runs throughout the *Confessions*. It begins in adolescence, appears in a negative form in the pear-stealing episode, and contracts into the frozen isolation of an adolescent waste-land. Now friendship resurfaces, generating an imagistic relation that grounds a new kind of community. Friendship of this kind presupposes that those who have stood alone before God stand together" (*Encounters*, 103; see 79, 101).

110. Question 6 is primarily related to the collaborative dialogue of factors such as the quest for knowing himself and the divine, interactions with others, and participation in Christian communities.

Ostia vision with Monica had affected the construction of Christian life in solitude and community.

The young Augustine became a Christian in the summer of 386, but his life of conversion did not "end in the garden in Milan."[111] After his garden experience, Augustine came to Cassiciacum for retreat with his family (e.g., his mother, Monica; his son, Adeodatus; his brother, Navigius) and his friends (e.g., Alypius) in the fall of 386 (*conf.* 9.2.2–3). Here Augustine and his followers had established a Christian philosophical community—"a community of learned celibates"—which was financially supported by his friend, Verecundus.[112] This Verecundus had provided his country villa at Cassiciacum in order to help Augustine and his followers achieve their intellectual and spiritual journey toward God and community, although Verecundus could not join this group of celibacy due to the status of his married life (9.3.5–6). While citing Verecundus an example of Christian friendship, later Augustine remembered Verecundus' kindness and his support for the Cassiciacum community and was sorry to hear Verecundus' sudden death; as such, he prayed to God for the soul of Verecundus:

> Most generously he offered us hospitality at his expense for as long as were there. . . . For when we were absent during our stay in Rome, he was taken ill in body, and in his sickness departed this life a baptized Christian. . . . We would have felt tortured by unbearable pain. . . . Faithful to your promises, in return for *Verecundus' country estate at Cassiciacum where we rested in you from the heart of the world,* you rewarded him with the loveliness of your evergreen paradise (9.3.5, italics added).

During the time at Cassiciacum, Augustine had suffered from a serious disease in his lungs—"I lost the power to speak, it came into my heart to beg all my friends present to pray for me to you, God of health of both soul and body. I wrote this on a wax tablet and gave it to them to read. As soon as we fell on our knees in the spirit of supplication, the pain vanished. . . . I had experienced nothing like it in all my life" (9.4.12). After recovering his health, Augustine (who was

---

111. See Wills, *Augustine's Conversion*, 6.

112. Wills insists that for Augustine, Christian life "was not a matter of his single salvation but of a philosophical discipline jointly pursued with others" (ibid., 118). Augustine did "finally bring together the partners he needed to pursue the Christian life in community" at Cassisciacum, Thagaste, and Hippo (ibid., 118; see 117, 119).

a Christianized Neoplatonist) resigned his professorship of rhetoric of Milan—"Redeemed by you, I was not now going to return to putting my skills up for sale" (9.2.2); "I no longer had the interest in money which ordinarily enabled me to endure a heavy work-load" (9.2.4; see 9.4.7)—and participated in Christian philosophical discussions with his fellows (9.4.7). In particular, he had made the important decision to be baptized. Augustine wrote a letter to Bishop Ambrose to receive permission for Christian baptism in the Milanese cathedral (9.5.13).

Having been encouraged by Ambrose for his baptism, Augustine came back to Milan. After accepting the order of the catechumen in the Milanese cathedral, he had engaged in the baptismal liturgy on March 10, 387. This means that Augustine began his Lenten catechumenate, which consisted of 1) enrollment and fast, 2) instruction, 3) scrutinies, 4) the creed, 5) holy week, and 6) the vigil. After completing the Lenten catechumenate, Augustine was engaged in the Milanese baptismal liturgy, which was composed of 1) the opening ceremony, 2) the anointing, 3) renunciation and profession, 4) consecration of the waters, 5) immersion, 6) anointing and foot washing, and 7) the white garment and the sealing. At the Easter vigil service April 24–25, 387, Augustine was finally baptized by Bishop Ambrose with his son Adeodatus and his friend Alypius (9.6.14).[113]

While writing the *Confessions*, Augustine did not explicitly depict the ritual process of Christian baptism in the Milanese cathedral (because he might have respected the tradition of the secrecy of the early Christian church which had cloaked both baptism and Eucharist).[114] As such, we are able to reconstruct Augustine's engagement in the Milanese baptismal liturgy by using Ambrose's two mystagogical catecheses, *The Sacraments* and *The Mysteries*:

> [Augustine and the other newly baptized] entered the baptistery itself. . . . The[se] candidates probably stripped at this point and were anointed, perhaps over the whole body. They formally renounced the devil and then turned to the east and proclaimed allegiance to Christ (*De mysteriis* 2.7). . . . Bishop [Ambrose] consecrated the water in the font with prayer and

---

113. See Fenn, "Magic"; Finn, *Death to Rebirth*, "It Happened"; Harmless, *Augustine*; Wright, "Augustine."

114. Harmless, "Baptism," 84–85.

the sign of the cross.[115] After this, candidates descended one by one into the water: "You were asked: 'Do you believe in God the Father almighty?' You said: 'I do believe,' and you dipped.... Again you were asked: 'Do you believe in our Lord Jesus Christ and in his cross?' You said: 'I do believe,' and you dipped.... A third time you were asked: 'Do you believe also in the Holy Spirit?' You said: 'I do believe,' you dipped a third time" (*sacr.* 2.20).... When candidates came up from the font, they were anointed again, this time with chrism poured on the head. After this, in a rite unique to Milan, candidates' feet were washed by the bishop. They were then clothed in new white robes. There followed a consignation, in which the bishop invoked the Holy Spirit, praying for the seven gifts mentioned in Isaiah 11:2, and the candidates were signed with the cross, most likely using chrism.... After baptism the newly baptized were led back to the assembled faithful and would participate for the first time in the liturgy of the Eucharist. Each day during Easter week, Augustine and the other newly baptized would have come to the basilica in their white robes and received a form of instruction known as mystagogy, that is, the "teaching of the mysteries."[116]

Through the sacrament of Christian baptism, Augustine was transfigured. The baptized Augustine had entered into the process of dying and beginning anew which was rooted in a sharing of the death and resurrection of Christ. This means that the holy waters of baptism had enabled Augustine to be recreated and to be anew. The old Augustine died and was buried; now the new one was reborn and was risen. As such, Augustine was delivered from evil, reconciled with God,

---

115. Harmless contends that Ambrose used an epigram with a chiastic rhyme scheme in order to help the neophytes to remember the ritual meaning of the water of the holy font (which related to cleaning the sin of the baptismal candidate through a burial with Christ):

Uidisti	You see
aquam,	the water,
sed non aqua omnis sanat,	but not all water heals;
sed aqua sanat	but water heals
quae habit gratiam	that has the grace
Christi.	of Christ.
Aliud est elementum,	One is an element,
aliud consecratio,	the other, a consecration.
aliud opus,	the one [is] a work,
aliud operatio.	the other, the worker

(*Augustine*, 101; see Ambrose, *sacr.* 1.15).

116. Harmless, "Baptism," 85.

enlightened by the Spirit, and incorporated into the body of Christ, the Church. The newly baptized Augustine was welcomed as a member of the Christian church. He celebrated his first Eucharist with others who was baptized. Finally, Augustine became fully Christian, as later he recalled and confessed:

> *We were baptized*, and disquiet about our past life vanished from us. During those days I found an insatiable and amazing delight in considering the profundity of your purpose for the salvation of the human race. *How I wept during your hymns and songs! I was deeply moved by the music of the sweet chants of your Church. The sounds flowed into my ears and the truth was distilled into my heart.* This caused the feelings of devotion to overflow. Tears ran, and it was good for me to have that experience (*conf.* 9.6.14). . . . The Church at Milan had begun only a short time before to employ this method of mutual comfort and exhortation. The brothers used to sing together with both heart and voice in a state of high enthusiasm. (9.7.15; see 9.7.16, italics added)

Indeed, the Milanese baptismal liturgy had affected Augustine's transformation and his reorganization of the rest of his life. During the rite of his baptism, Augustine had heard the singing of the church members. He was deeply astonished because he already knew the origin of the custom of singing in the Milan cathedral. Here Augustine could remember that Bishop Ambrose (who had kept the Creed of the Council of Nicaea) had encouraged his congregation to sing the sacred songs (in which some were composed by himself) within the basilica, while he and his flock (including Monica) had struggled to defend their church against the Arians (who had been aided by the Empress Justina and the Roman Army [9.7.15]).[117] As such, *these* hymns and songs of the church members had challenged the baptized Augustine to rethink the goal and meaning of his life and to follow the examples of the life of humility for Christ and dedication to the church, as later he stated:

---

117. See Bourke, *Augustine's Quest*, 83. Later Augustine described the impact of the hymns and songs on the congregation in the Milanese cathedral (who were against the Arians) as follows: "That was the time when the decision was taken to introduce hymns and psalms sung after the custom of the Eastern churches, *to prevent the people from succumbing to depression and exhaustion.* From that time to this day the practice has been retained and many, indeed almost all your flocks, in other parts of the world have imitated it" (9.7.15, italics added).

> You pierced my heart with the arrow of your love. . . . The examples given by your servants whom you had transformed from black to shining white and from death to life, crowded in upon my thoughts. They burnt away and destroyed my heavy sluggishness, preventing me from being dragged down to low things. They set me on fire with such force that every breath of opposition from any "deceitful tongue" (Ps 119:2f) had the power not to dampen my zeal but to inflame it the more. (9.2.3)

In the *Confessions*, Augustine had portrayed his long existential and spiritual odyssey to become a baptized Christian as well as a member of the church community. There were four main events of Augustine's life in the *Confessions* related to the theme of Christian baptism: 1) Monica's decision to postpone the boy Augustine's baptism after the recovery of his physical health at Thagaste (1.11.17–18); 2) the Manichee Augustine's mocking of the Christian baptism of his unnamed friend at Thagaste (4.4.7–9); 3) the Manichee and skeptic Augustine's lack of desire for Christian baptism in spite of his serious physical illness at Rome (5.9.16); 4) Augustine's own baptism with Adeodatus and Alypius by Bishop Ambrose of Milan (9.6.14). Based on his transforming experience through the Milanese baptismal liturgy, later Augustine had considered baptism both the sacrament of the remission of sins and the rebirth for the newness of life.[118]

There is an analogous relation between the stories of conversion and the stories of Christian baptism in terms of conversion-baptism. Consistent with the portrayal of his own odyssey for Christian baptism, Augustine had also illustrated others' baptisms which were deeply related to their conversions to Christianity. In that sense, as O'Brien describes Augustine's conversion within others' conversion stories, Wright portrays Augustine's baptism within others' baptisms. While paying attention to the correlation of others' experiences of Christian baptism with Augustine's own experience of the baptismal rite, Wright states, "All the other mentions of baptism in the *Confessions* relate to what I will call, if only by convenient shorthand, believer's baptism or perhaps better conversion-baptism: Monnica's hope for Augustine

---

118. Augustine noted, "I know . . . one baptism consecrated and sealed with the name of the Father, and the Son, and the Holy Ghost" (*ep.* 23.4); "Inasmuch as water, sanctified by the prayer of the priest in the Church, washes away sins, just so much does it multiply sins when infected . . . with the words of heretics" (*bapt.* 6.25.46; see *s.* 213.9; *f. et op.* 20.36).

(6.13.23), the famously public baptism of Victorinus, 'an infant born at your font' (8.2.3–5), Verecundus' death-bed conversion and baptism (9.3.5), that of Nebridius (9.3.6), of Alypius with Augustine himself and his son Adeodatus (9.6.14), of Evodius (9.8.17), of Patricius his father (9.10.22), and even it seems of Monnica herself (9.13.34)."[119] These stories of baptism (including the case of Augustine) help us recognize how Christian baptismal liturgy had affected the transformation of the baptized and how it had stimulated the newly baptized to become a member of the community, namely, to enter into the movement to formulate or reformulate the Christian community.[120]

During and after his conversion to Christianity and his Christian baptism, Augustine had learned "how to love properly" or relate to himself, others, and the divine.[121] More specifically, Augustine became reconciled to himself by entering into the unifying process of his divided self or distorted will. He became reconciled to God by putting himself on the humble Incarnate Christ. As he had greatly recovered his relationships with himself and with the divine, now Augustine had reformulated, implicitly or explicitly, his relationships with others. For example, he became reconciled to his unnamed woman—Adeodatus' mother (who returned Africa, vowing never to live with another man [6.15.25]) by following her example of the life of continence; he became reconciled to his unnamed friend (who was baptized on his deathbed and was angry at Augustine's mocking at his baptism [4.4.7–9]) by receiving his own Christian baptism in the Milanese cathedral;[122] further, he became reconciled to his mother Monica (who was disappointed in her son's involvement in the Manichean sect and had long prayed for his conversion to Christianity [3.11.19–3.12.21]) by abandoning his Manichean belief and by becoming a faithful Christian within the church community.

---

119. Wright, "Augustine," 290–91.

120. Augustine had depicted the impact of his own experience of Christian baptism on the spiritual changes of other persons by using the case of Nebridius. When Nebridius joined the Cassiciacum community, he was a highly intellect, but was not yet Christian. However, Augustine's transformation through the Milanese baptismal liturgy had triggered him to imitate the life of humility and asceticism. Nebridius was finally baptized and became a servant of the Christian community (9.3.6, 9.4.7).

121. See Paffenroth, "Book Nine," 146–52.

122. See Asiedu, "Example of a Woman," 303–4.

Understanding Religious Conversion

Not long after his baptism, Augustine decided to go back to North Africa with his followers in order to establish a new Christian community (i.e., a lay monastic community, as later he noted: "'You make people to live in a house in unanimity' (Ps 67:7).... We were together and by a holy decision resolved to live together. We looked for a place where we could be of most use in your service; all of us agreed on a move back to Africa" (9.8.17). After departing from Cassiciacum, they came to Ostia on the Tiber in order to rest for their long voyage to North Africa.

During their stay at Ostia, Augustine and Monica talked about their spiritual journey toward union with God, as it related to issue of the eternal life of the saints. At the time of their conversation about Christian life for the glory of God, they were profoundly immersed into themselves (as Augustine himself entered into his own mind to know himself and the divine in the Milanese garden). Through their inner spiritual journey toward the existence of Being, they had experienced the divine presence in their hearts and the divine intervention into their lives. Here Augustine and Monica had not undergone simply an isolated experience, but a shared mystical experience of union with God, as later Augustine described:

> Our minds were lifted up by step we climbed beyond all corporeal objects.... We ascended even further by internal reflection and dialogue and wonder at your works, and we entered into our own minds. We moved up beyond them so as to attain to the region of inexhaustible abundance where you feed Israel eternally with truth for food. There life is the wisdom by which all creatures come into being, both things which were and which will be.... Furthermore, in this wisdom there is no past and future, but only being, since it is eternal. (9.10.24)

On that day when they had their spiritual conversation, Augustine and Monica agreed with each other that this world with all its delights became worthless to them. Monica said to Augustine: "My son, as for myself, I now find no pleasure in this life.... My hope in this world is already fulfilled. The one reason why I wanted to stay longer in this life was my desire to see you a Catholic Christian before I die. My God has granted this in a way more than I had hoped. For I see you despising this world's success to become his servant" (9.10.26).

Playing Together

Indeed, Augustine's description of a shared experience at Ostia was crucial for understanding his living in solitude and community.[123] As discussed earlier, the young philosopher Augustine had learned the Neoplatonic method of meditation such as the ascent of the soul toward the One or the return of the soul to the Origin. As such, here Augustine had portrayed his Ostia experience by using this Neoplatonic method of meditation. However, through his experiences of Christian conversion and baptism, he had gradually overcome the Plotinian concept of individualism—"the flight of the alone to the Alone" which tended to overemphasize the isolated individual's philosophical and spiritual inquiry for the truth. Now Augustine had recognized the importance of the life of community or solidarity in faith in Christ, acknowledging the importance of the life of solitude or prayer of the person. Later his recognition of the importance of Christian living in Christian friendship and Christian living in contemplation had led him to integrate his pastoral ministry with his monastic life at Hippo Regius.

After the shared Ostia experience, Monica fell ill and died (9.8.17, 9.11.27–28). During her long spiritual journey, she was involved in the life of continence after the death of her husband (9.13.37). In doing so, she had sacrificed herself for her son and had prayed for his turning away from Manichaeism to Christianity (3.11.19–3.12.21). Especially, Monica committed herself to God and God's church; she had struggled to defend the Milanese cathedral against the Arians (9.7.15). After her son's conversion and baptism, she had dedicated herself to care for the newly established Christian community (i.e., the Cassiciacum community); namely, she had played an preeminent role of spiritual mother in the community in light of faith in Christ and Christian friendship, as later Augustine recalled: "My mother stayed close by us in the clothing of a woman but with a virile faith, an older woman's serenity, a mother's love, and a Christian devotion. . . . Lord—by your gift you allow me to speak for your servants, for before her falling asleep *we were bound together in community in you* after receiving the grace of baptism—she exercised care for everybody as if they were all her children. She served us as if she was a daughter to all of us" (9.4.8, 9.9.22, italics added). As

---

123. While viewing the Ostia experience as "a shared experience," McGinn and McGinn writes, "In comparison with the Milan account, the Ostia experience is presented in language that is more social in context, more affective in rhetoric, and more complex in its appeal to transformed interior sensation" (*Christian Mystics*, 155–56; see Vaught, *Encounters*, 128).

such, Augustine and his fellows had bitterly lamented the death of their spiritual mother, Monica, and had prayed for her soul to rest in peace (9.11.27–9.12.32). Later Augustine had remembered Monica's whole life of humility for Christ and dedication for others (see 9.8.17–9.13.37). Influenced by Monica, Augustine had sincerely attempted to follow her example of humility and dedication within his integrated Christian life of solitude and community.

Apparently, during Augustine's unfolding process of transformation, there is close relation between his experience of divine intervention and grace in the Milanese garden, his acceptance of the Milanese baptismal liturgy, and his Ostia vision with Monica. In the interactive and consummated conditions of his experiences of psychological crisis and existential predicament, his inquiry to know himself and the divine, his intensified interactions with others, his affiliations with the Christian community and the philosophical group, his intellectual and cultural changes, and his encounter with God in the Milanese garden, the convert Augustine was continuously involved in the ongoing transformational process of spiritual life and dedication for the rest of his lifetime. As such, he had participated in the Milanese baptismal liturgy in which he had undergone the spiritual death and rebirth; namely, he publicly became a member of the Christian community. After his baptism, he was engaged in the vision of Ostia with Monica in which they had shared the mystic experiences of divine grace and intervention into their life of pilgrimage.

Engagement in the Service of God and God's People

Along with the description of Augustine's acceptance of Christian baptism and his experience of the Ostia vision, this section investigates *his engagement of the service of God and service of others*. While interrelating to other stages of Rambo's model of conversion, it is consonant with the stage of *consequences*. In this way, this section focuses on Augustine's ongoing spiritual journey of transformation ("converting") and dedication; that is, it articulates how the mature Augustine was involved in his monastic life and his pastoral ministry in light of the symbiotic interplay between love of God and love of neighbor. As such, question 6 is continuously beneficial for discussing the interrelated link between

Playing Together

Augustine's relationships with himself, others, and the divine, and his mental development and spiritual maturity.

In the conditions of the unexpected death of Monica at the seaport of Ostia (as well as the political and social disturbance in the Empire),[124] Augustine and his fellows changed their plans to journey to North Africa. They went to Rome in 387 and remained there for a year. During his stay in Rome, he had participated in philosophical and religious discussions with his fellows. In particular, here Augustine had learned the Pachomian tradition of early Christian monasticism, as he had already learned the Antonian tradition of the ascetic/solitary life through Ponticianus' account of the life of Antony (Possidius, *v. Aug.* 3, 5).[125] As discussed earlier, the Pachomian tradition of the monastic life had been founded and developed by Pachomius the Egypt monk who had pursued to live together with other monks in organized communities in Upper Egypt ("the Pachomian *Koinonia*") and composed the first known monastic rule.[126] In that sense, the Pachomian tradition of monasticism had greatly emphasized the life of the community of the cenobites (e.g., 9.2.2–3; Possidius, *v. Aug.* 3, 5) rather than the life of the solitary hermitage of the desert anchorites (e.g., 8.6.14–15)— in order to overcome the risk of indulging in the isolated life of the individual or individuals. While visiting a number of monasteries in Rome, Augustine was deeply moved into the hallmarks of the Christian monastic life which consisted of shared possessions, chastity, and holiness. As such, he had learned the organized skills of the community and practices of Eastern monasticism (based on the Pachomian tradition) which included the pattern of communal prayer, reading the Scriptures, manual labor, the authority structure, the common life and sharing possessions, fasting, or clothing. Later Augustine's learning of both Antonian anchoritism and Pachomian cenobitism had enabled him to establish a more developed Christian monastic movement in

---

124. Brown states, "The fleet of the usurper, Maximus, a general who had been in command at Caernarvon, was blockading the harbours of Rome; the Emperor Theodosius, a pious Galician general who ruled in Constantinople, was preparing to crush his rival. Because of this blockade, the little group of Africans was brought to a halt in Ostia" (*Augustine*, 121).

125. See E. A. Clark, "Asceticism"; Harrison, *Augustine*; Lawless, *Augustine*; Zumkeller, *Augustine's Ideal*.

126. See Harmless, *Desert Christians*; Schaff, "Monasticism"; Zumkeller, *Augustine's Ideal*.

the Latin West, which had effectively integrated the Christian living in solitude and the Christian living in community in light of the interaction of contemplation and action. (In this way, we are able to recognize that the early desert spirituality of Egypt was crucial for the formation and development of Christian monasticism in the Latin West.)

After learning the Pachomian tradition of Christian monasticism in Rome, Augustine returned to North Africa with his fellows in 388. By way of Carthage, he arrived at his home town, Thagaste. Here Augustine had founded a lay Christian community with his fellows—the "servants of God" (*serui dei*)—in which he had kept a form of shared life with other members and had continued his studies and meditation. As later his biographer Possidius stated:

> When [Augustine] had received the grace of God, he determined, with others of his neighbors and friends who served God with him, to return to Africa to his own home and lands to which he came and in which he was settled for almost three years. He now gave up these possessions and began to live with those who had also consecrated themselves to God, in fastings and prayers and good works, meditating day and night in the Law of the Lord. (Possidius, *v. Aug.* 3; see *ep.* 126.7; *s.* 355.2)[127]

Consistent with his ongoing process of becoming a servant of God through the monastic way of life, Augustine came to Hippo Regius in 391 in order to recruit the members of his community of Thagaste as well as to look for a new place to establish a monastic community. While participating in the worship service of the Hippo cathedral, Augustine was unexpectedly ordained as a priest under the pressure of the old and Greek-speaking Bishop Valerius (who had long sought for an young and Latin-speaking assistant for him) and his congregation (although he had strongly resisted against this appointment) (*s.* 355.2; Possidius, *v. Aug.* 4). However, after accepting Valerius and his congregation's demand as a divine calling, Augustine moved from Thagaste to Hippo Regius with his friends. At that time, much like Bishop Ambrose

---

127. Zumkeller portrays the Thagaste community as follows: "Here in Tagaste something of the spirit of the cenobitism of the Eastern monasteries was revived. And yet Augustine immediately introduced new aspects to this form of living. Manual labor was no longer the companions' sole occupation. Possidius describes Augustine's curriculum: study, teaching, and writing. From the beginning, Augustine devoted much time to study, viewing as his special vocation the reconciling of the Church's asceticism with scientific knowledge and literature" (*Augustine's Ideal*, 25; see 24–32).

Playing Together

of Milan had encouraged the rhetorician Augustine to become a Christian, here Bishop Valerius of Hippo had encouraged the priest Augustine to perform, successfully and effectively, his ecclesiastical obligation for church members. In doing so, he had also helped Augustine to rebuild the lay Christian monastery with his fellows in a garden of the cathedral. While receiving Valerius' support, Augustine became a famous preacher and an influential leader in the African Church (*v. Aug.* 5). In 395, he became the auxiliary bishop of Hippo Regius; after the death of Valerius in 396, Augustine succeeded him (*v. Aug.* 8).[128] Surprisingly, we are able to realize that like Simplicianus and Ambrose of Milan, Bishop Valerius had deeply influenced Augustine in fostering his ongoing spiritual transformation which was deeply related to his involvement into his monastic life [i.e., prayer] and pastoral ministry [i.e., social engagement] in the context of the North African church.

As a monk and a priest/bishop, Augustine had reformulated his Christian monasteries which were based on the spirit and actions of the apostolic community at Jerusalem as described in Acts 4:31–35, while remembering the importance of the heritage of the early Christian monastic movements (i.e., the Antonian tradition of the ascetic/solitary life and the Pachomian tradition of the communal life). In that sense, later Possidius described as follows: "[Augustine] established a monastery within the church and began to live with the servants of God according to the manner and rule instituted by the holy apostles. The principal rule of this society was that no one should possess anything of his own, but that all things should be held in common and be distributed to each one as he had need, as Augustine had formerly done after he returned to his native home from across the sea" (*v. Aug.* 5).

Along with the establishment of the lay monastery, Augustine had also founded the clerics' monastery (*monasterium clericorum*) at the "house of the Bishop" as well as monasteries for women at Hippo Regius. In order to reorganize and manage these lay, clerical, and women's monasteries, Augustine had made the monastic *Rule* around 397 in which all members of the community had attempted to live together in unity and to have "one heart and soul" directed towards God (*reg.* 1.2).[129]

128. See Bonner, *St. Augustine*; Bourke, *Augustine's Quest*; Brown, *Augustine*.

129. See Harrison, *Augustine*; Lawless, *Augustine*, "Rules"; Zumkeller, *Augustine's Ideal*.

Importantly, Augustine's ongoing transformative process of spiritual life was involved in not only turning toward God, but also turning toward neighbors.[130] This means that while participating in the life of Christian monastery, Augustine had also engaged in the life of pastoral ministry for others, including his church members. Augustine's concept of the monastic ideal and life was rooted in "Christian love" (*caritas*) in which community members had intended to engage in "the service of love" of God and neighbor.[131] In that sense, as a monk and a bishop, Augustine had sought to integrate the seemingly disparate but mutually enriching dimensions of Christian living—contemplation and action, as he noted:

> As for the three kinds of life, the life of [sanctified] leisure, the life of action, and the combination of the two, anyone, to be sure, might spend his life in any of these ways without detriment to his faith, and might thus attain to the everlasting rewards.... What does a man possess as a result of his love of truth? And what does he pay out in response to the obligations of Christian love? For no one ought to be so leisured as to take no thought in that [sanctified] leisure for the interest of his neighbour, nor so active as to feel no need for the contemplation of God. (*civ. Dei* 19.19)

Based on the primacy of love of God and neighbor in the Bible (e.g., Matt 22:37–40), Augustine constantly confronted the following issue during his lifetime: To what extent can "the inner life of the spirit" (i.e., a life of prayer/solitude) be harmonized with "an active apostolate and the performance of charitable works" (i.e., a life of community/social engagement)?[132] Indeed, Augustine had struggled to reconcile

---

130. See Canning, *Unity of Love for God and Neighbour*; Clark, *Augustine*, "Eye of the Heart," "Spirituality"; Martin, *Restless Heart*; McGinn and McGinn, *Christian Mystics*.

131. In consideration of the "the practice of love" of God and neighbor within Augustine's monastic communities at Hippo, Van Bavel writes, "The first community of Jerusalem plays the role of an ancient dream which becomes an ideal for the present and for the future. We could characterize the Rule of Augustine as a call to the evangelical equality of all people. It voices the Christian demand to bring all men and women into full community" ("Introduction to the Rule," 8; see 7).

132. For Augustine, there are two opposite kinds of love: 1) *caritas* (*amor Dei*) refers to a God-centered love in which one is subject to God and is turned toward the neighbor; 2) *cupiditas* (*amor sui/mundi*) indicates a self-centered love in which one seeks one's private interest and one looks arrogantly to domination against others (*Gn.*

his early and continuing preference for the contemplative life with the many ecclesiastical duties surrounding his priesthood, and later, his episcopacy (*ep.* 10.1–3, 21.1–6, 48.1–4).[133] In doing so, he was involved in the vigorous and difficult debates with the Manichees, the Donastists, the Arians, and the Pelagians in order to defend the North African church from paganism/heresy. In that sense, Kreider points out, "North Africa was a hard world. As a bishop, Augustine was involved in struggles with religious rivals—especially 'schismatic' Donatists and pagans. These struggles at times also involved him in contests with local power brokers for influence and dominance. So before long Augustine became an active participant in the Christianization, by favor, fiat, and force, of North Africans and their society."[134]

During the long time of his debates, Augustine had dedicated himself to establish more proper Christian guidelines and beliefs (which were deeply related to the themes of 1) God and soul, 2) sin and God's grace, 3) creation, time, and eternity, 4) the unity of the love of God and neighbor, and 5) the Christian church and baptism) in order to lead God's people into a better Christian living within the specific historical and socio-cultural context.[135] Until his last ecclesiastical struggle for protecting his flock and church in the midst of the siege of Hippo Regius by the Vandals in 430, Augustine had successfully committed himself to the service of God and the service of others (*v. Aug.* 29, 30, 31).

Apparently, as emphasized in question 6, Augustine's converting experience did not refer to the alienated withdrawal from the world. Rather, it was continuously involved in the loving relationships with himself, others, and the divine. This means that it had compelled him to move into the healing and transforming process through his life; as

litt. 11.15.19–20; *civ. Dei* 14.28; Van Bavel, "Love," 510).

133. See Torchia, "Contemplation and Action."

134. Kreider, *Change*, 55.

135. Clark insists that "while his [Augustine's] spirituality includes a longing for mystical union with God, it is firmly rooted in the biblical command to love one's neighbor" ("Spirituality," 815). In that sense, for Augustine, transformation into greater likeness to the Trinity by loving God and neighbor (*conf.* 13.22.32) became his goal of spiritual life. Rather than an escape from the material world, the centrality of the "Word made flesh" made his spirituality to be a concrete application of the Gospel to life in the worlds. During his lifetime, Augustine had continuously engaged in "union with God, communion with his neighbors, and [pastoral] ministry to those in need of spiritual and material assistance" (ibid., 814–15).

such, it had led him to engage in the integrated Christian life of solitude and community in the specific social, cultural, and religious context of his time. Indeed, within his newly reconstructed relationships, Augustine could actually dedicate himself to the loving service of God and neighbor in light of the mutual interaction of God, self, and community.

Summary

Augustine was converted to Christianity in the Milanese garden in the summer of 386. His conversion experience was a complicated and multi-layered *process* of existential and spiritual change which brought the total reorientation and transformation of his life, affected by the interaction of personal, social, cultural, and religious components. This study has attempted to portray a more coherent and integrated picture of his conversion process by using the main interdisciplinary question and the six substantive and mutually-informing questions. In doing so, it has articulated what happened in his lifelong process of change ("converting") and dedication in which multi factors had worked simultaneously and cumulatively (much like a range of various voices in the choir had interacted with one another within the spirit of harmony and balance).

Augustine was born in North Africa of the Roman world in which Christianity became an official religion after Constantine's conversion to Christianity in 312. This means that the process of Christianization was widespread and far-reaching in the Roman world, including his hometown, Thagaste. Along with Christianization, there were serious religious conflicts between Christianity and paganism in North Africa. In this context, there were two disparate yet powerful movements: 1) sensual pleasure and materialism and 2) moral earnestness and purity in North African society. Augustine's father Patricius (who was a pagan) might have been more influenced by the former movement, but his mother Monica (who was an ardent Christian) might have been more affected by the latter movement. Although there was no serious hostility between Patricius and Monica within the familial context, their different personalities and religiosity had deeply influenced the formation of the early and adolescent Augustine's personality, worldview, and belief. During his early school life, the boy Augustine had experienced traumatic injuries through his experiences of beatings from school teachers, his parents' laughing at his stripes, and God's silence about it. In the context of his experiences of traumatic injuries, Augustine had negatively formulated his self-images and his representations of God (as scourging, marking, and indifferent).

Before his conversion, the Manichee and skeptic Augustine had accomplished a successful, worldly career (i.e., a municipal chair of rhetoric in Milan). However, he had experienced psychological distress and crisis which were rooted to his sense of inner division, isolation, and restlessness in his mind (the sickness of the soul). Augustine's sense of inner conflict was deeply related to his experiences of early traumatic injuries and his two opposed desires—1) the desire for sensual pleasure and materialism (i.e., the life of seeking for licentiousness and worldly fame) and 2) the desire for moral earnestness and purity (i.e., the life of searching for the Truth)—which were rooted in his parents' different personalities, worldviews, and religiosity. As such, the young rhetorician Augustine had also undergone serious relational problems with others/Other, including his mother Monica, his unnamed friend (the baptized Christian), and his unnamed woman (Adeodatus' mother). In the context of his psychological crisis and distress and his relational problems, he was not able to find the resting place on earth.

Importantly, Augustine's experiences of psychological crisis and existential abyss had triggered him to move into his inner world to know himself and to know the divine. Here the restless Augustine had begun to recollect and reflect on his life history. In doing so, he had attempted to recognize the root of his inner conflict and the cause of his life problem, at which point he was able to open his mind in order to hear the inward divine voice. This means that he had gradually moved into the process of unifying his divided self which was related to his deep experience with the divine/God ("a More").

During his quest for knowing himself and the divine and his struggle for re-establishing purpose and meaning in life, the young Augustine was related to and influenced by significant others. Here Augustine (who was a rhetorician and an active seeker) had experienced loving care and support from other persons (especially Ambrose, Simplicianus, Ponticianus, Alypius, and Monica) within the Christian community. While receiving the hospitality of Bishop Ambrose, Augustine had regularly participated in the worship service in the Milanese cathedral and had heard the sermons of Ambrose. Through Ambrose's gifted interpretations of the Bible, Augustine had learned a new way of reading the Christian Scriptures and had begun to recognize the great depth of Christian faith and living. In particular, Ambrose's sermons (which had reflected Christianized Neoplatonism) had encouraged the young Augustine to embark on an interior journey toward union with God. As such, Augustine had eventually made a decision to depart from the Manichean sect and to become a catechumen within an alternative community (i.e., the Milanese cathedral).

Along with his interactions with Ambrose and his participation in the Christian community, Augustine had met Simplicianus. Simplicianus had advised Augustine to deal with his existential predicament and his spiritual abyss as well as to read the Epistles of the Apostle Paul. In particular, he told Augustine about the conversion story of his old friend Victorinus who was a famous professor of rhetoric in Rome. Before his conversion to Christianity, Victorinus ardently believed in the traditional Roman cults. However, after reading the Christian Scriptures, he put himself on the humble Incarnate Christ and then publicly received Christian baptism, despite knowing that his public confession of Christian faith would cause him to lose his professorship of rhetor by the edict of the emperor Julian. The conversion story of Victorinus had compelled Augustine to look at his state of bondage of the will and his hesitation of becoming a baptized Christian.

During his intimate interactions with Ambrose and Simplicianus, Augustine (and Alypius) received a visit from Ponticianus. Ponticianus had told them about the life story of Antony the Egyptian desert monk and the conversion story of his two friends. Influenced by the life of Antony, these two friends of Ponticianus were converted to Christianity at Trier. After resigning their higher positions in the imperial court, they had dedicated themselves to the life of asceticism and celibacy. Following the example of Ponticianus' two friends, their two fiancées had also devoted to the life of continence. As such, Ponticianus had also decided to become a baptized Christian, although he was not involved in the Christian monastic community. After hearing the life of Antony as well as the conversion stories of Ponticianus' two friends and their fiancées, the rhetorician Augustine was ashamed of himself because he had still remained in the desire for worldly fame and because he had still vacillated to become a Christian.

Indeed, these significant persons had played a preeminent role in the process of Augustine's spiritual change in light of the interaction with companions and a network of Christian friendships. More specifically, Augustine's intensive interactions with others and his participation in the Christian community (i.e., the Milanese cathedral) had helped him to overcome his dualistic materialism and his skeptic thinking in the Academy as well as to fulfill his (psychological) needs (e.g., a sense of belonging and solidarity) and to discover a new way of Christian living in community. In doing so, the interlocking conversion stories of Victorinus, Antony, and Ponticianus' two friends (and their fiancées) had challenged the young Augustine to look at his state of existential predicament and spiritual abyss (which was related to his wounded soul and his desire of worldly ambition) and to imitate their example of humility in faith in Christ.

While fostering his affective bonds and intimate interactions with other people and his intensified affiliations with Christian communities, the intellect Augustine had gradually experienced philosophical and cultural changes which had been profoundly influenced by the Neoplatonic heritage and the Christian monastic movements of his time. In the context of his participation in the Milanese group of intellects and his encounters with Christian Neoplatonists (e.g., Ambrose and Simplicianus), Augustine had read the books of the Neoplatonists (especially those of Plotinus and Porphyry) and had learned about the important Neoplatonic themes, including the ascent of the soul toward the One/the return to the Origin. Through his readings of Neoplatonic books and his meetings with Christian Neoplatonists, the Manichee and skeptic Augustine had reconstructed his conceiving of the divine nature (from the corporeal and divisible being to the incorporeal and invisible being) as well as his understanding of evil (from a real existence to no substance or an absence of good). Augustine's reformulation of his view on the nature of the divine and the nature of good and evil had deeply challenged him to move into his interior journey toward union with the divine in terms of the dynamic interaction of God and soul.

In the conditions of his struggles with an inner journey toward the divine and his intimate interactions with others as well as his readings of the books of the Neoplatonists and his reconstruction of his view on divine nature and the origin of evil, the intellect Augustine had (re)-read the Bible. Through reading the Bible, Augustine had found the crucial difference between the Holy Scriptures and the Neoplatonic books. More specifically, he had realized that Pagan Neoplatonists (e.g., Porphyry) had viewed Christ as a wise man, while emphasizing the virtue of the human nature of Christ rather than the virtue of his divine nature. In particular, he had recognized that unlike the letters of the Apostle Paul, the books of the Neoplatonists did not include the Christian concept of the Incarnate Christ who is a mediator between God and the human and who is a perfect example of humility. (We are able to realize that before his conversion to Christianity, Augustine—the young philosopher—had understood Christ as an excellent man, at which point he had indulged in intellectual pride, regarding himself as a source of wisdom and virtue.)

At the time of his readings of the Bible and his recognition of the key difference between Neoplatonic books and Christian Scriptures, the young Augustine was greatly aware of the early Christian monasticism. As noted above, he had heard from Ponticianus about the early Christian monastic movement, especially the acetic life of the Egyptian Antony who was a founder of desert monasticism. As Ponticianus' two friends were influenced by the life of Antony, here Augustine had been affected by the Antonian tradition of the life of asceticism. More specifically, Augustine's encounter with the anchoritic monasticism of Antony had stimulated Augustine to move from the life of sensual pleasure and worldly ambition to the life of moral earnestness and purity. It had also challenged Augustine to stand humbly before God in the garden of Milan, to become a servant of God ("a monk"), and to follow the example of humility and celibacy.

Consistent with his inner journey toward union with the divine, his newly reconstructed relationships with others, his commitment to the Christian community, and his philosophical and cultural changes by learning Christian Neoplatonism and Christian monasticism, the young Augustine had faced himself and God in the Milanese garden of 386. He had still struggled to find the resting place for his soul, although he had already undergone intellectual transformation about the nature of the divine and the nature of good and evil. In this context, Augustine's inner tension had mounted and became unbearable, and he rushed into the garden. Here Augustine had experienced the divine intervention into his restless mind by means of God's messenger, Lady Continence. While showing many examples of humility and celibacy,

Lady Continence had urged Augustine to overcome his hesitation and to commit himself to the life of asceticism and celibacy. In a state of his weeping bitterly under a tree and his struggling to make a decision, Augustine had heard the divine voice—*Tolle lege, Tolle lege!*—which sounded like the chanting of the neighboring child. While remembering the case of Antony (who had read Matt 19:21 and was transfigured), Augustine had read the book of the Apostle Paul (especially Rom 13:13–14). While reading a specific verse of the Christian Scriptures, Augustine had felt the presence of God in his heart and had accepted the transforming power of God's grace in his wounded soul. Through his encounter with the divine by means of the word of God, he cast himself in the merciful hands of God and became reconciled to himself and to God. This reconciliation had enabled him to overcome his deep sense of existential isolation (i.e., the sickness of the soul), that is, to move in the interior transformation from the division of the self (i.e., the split of the will) to the integration of the self (i.e., the transformation of the will). During his progressive restoration and healing, his early negative God representations were changed into positive God representations as loving, present, and caring. As such, he had discovered the safe resting place for his soul in relation to God. Finally, the young Augustine put himself on the humble Incarnate Christ and had engaged in the renunciation of the worldly ambition and the life of asceticism and celibacy.

Indeed, Augustine's conversion to Christianity was crucial for accomplishing the new Christian community in light of the interaction of faith in Christ and Christian friendship. Augustine's own conversion in the Milanese garden had influenced Alypius' conversion and Monica's transformation, just as the conversion stories of Victorinus, Antony, and Ponticianus' two friends had affected his own spiritual change.[136] After his conversion, the newly converted Augustine had retreated with his family and his friends at Cassiciacum where they had lived together. Augustine and his followers were involved in the life of asceticism and celibacy, as Ponticianus' two friends and their fiancées were engaged in Christian monastic life in faith in Christ. At the Easter Vigil in 387, Augustine was baptized with Adeodatus and Alypius by Bishop Ambrose in the Milanese cathedral. The baptized Augustine had moved into the process of dying and beginning anew—the Christian life of

---

136. See Asiedu, "Example of a Woman.,"

death and resurrection in Christ. He publicly became a member of Christian community. Through his baptismal liturgy of the Milanese cathedral, Augustine had formed his new relationship with God, and then he had felt a sense of belonging and a new responsibility for others (e.g., the Milanese church members who had struggled to protect his church against the Arians; the Cassiciacum community members who had accompanied him on his spiritual journey).

In the context of his experiences of Christian conversion and baptism, Augustine was motivated to keep an ongoing spiritual journey of transformation ("converting") which was deeply related to his establishment of Christian monasteries and his pastoral ministry.[137] After his baptism, by way of Ostia (in which he had shared the mystical experience with Monica), Augustine went to Rome in 387. Here he had learned the Pachomian tradition of Christian monasticism which had emphasized the life of the community of the cenobites. After learning in Rome, Augustine returned to North Africa in 388. As a layperson, Augustine had founded the Christian lay community in his hometown, Thagaste. Later Augustine (who became a monk-priest/bishop) had also established the lay monastery in the garden of the cathedral (391), the clerical monastery at "the house of the Bishop" (395/6), and monasteries for women at Hippo Regius. At the time of his engagement in monastic life, Augustine was associated with the fulfillment of his ecclesiastical duties in the cathedral of Hippo. This means that he had attempted to integrate his monastic life with his pastoral ministry in the context of the North African Church in light of the correlation of Christian living in solitude and Christian living in community. During his ongoing spiritual journey of transformation, Augustine had truly dedicated himself to the life of becoming a servant of the humble Incarnate Christ as well as becoming a humble Christian for God's people.

PROPOSING A HOLISTIC PATTERN OF THE CONVERSION PROCESS FROM THE CONFESSIONS

Following the above reinterpretation of Augustine's conversion process, this section of the chapter additionally provides a holistic pattern of

---

137. Kreider writes, "[Augustine's] conversion involved change not just of [personal] belief but also of belonging and behavior [in the community]" (*Change*, xv; see 109).

the conversion process from the *Confessions*. The *Confessions* is a book of the pilgrim who requires strong solidarity and friendship from his fellows and his readers going through the common struggle to answer the same crucial question that Augustine put to himself.[138] In a related vein, Martin states,

> Augustine saw himself as a pilgrim and seeker, called, stimulated and guided by the Word. His intent was to invite others to make the journey and thus we are meant to share with him the adventures, the joys, the sorrows, the learnings, the demands that came to him during the actual course of his spiritual journey as our own invitation admonition, to enter upon the path of Christ. Thus, to be faithful to Augustine, the story of the Augustinian tradition cannot simply be about him, but likewise about the Christ-journey he proposes for all of us.[139]

While paying attention to both the personal dimension and the universal dimension of religious change, this study generalizes Augustine's narrative of transformation within the modern Christian community in light of a movement from one's personal story of conversion to a universal story of conversion in the religious community. As Van Fleteren points out the theme of the generalization of Augustine's conversion, "Augustine—not to mention ourselves—has a well-known tendency to universalize on his own experience. In the *Confessiones* and elsewhere, he exhibits a conversion mentality, a mentality which undoubtedly arises out of his own experience. He is inclined to wish for others what he himself had experienced. His own conversion served in his mind as a kind of paradigm for all mankind. . . . By coming to a greater understanding of his conversion to Christianity, we may come to a better understanding of ourselves."[140]

As noted earlier, scholars have provided various paradigms of Augustine's conversion process from the *Confessions*.[141] However, previous studies have tended to articulate the pattern of the conversion experi-

---

138. See Dixon, *Augustine*; Gay, "Augustine"; Kotze, *Augustine's Confessions*; McMahon, *Medieval Meditative Ascent*; Niño, "Restoration"; O'Meara, *Young Augustine*; TeSelle, "Augustine as Client"; Vaught, *Encounters*.

139. Martin, *Restless Heart*, 14; see 156–57.

140. Van Fleteren, "Augustine's Theory," 66–67, 73. See Paffenroth, "Book Nine," 144, 146.

141. See McGinn and McGinn, *Christian Mystics*; Niño, "Restoration"; Sisemore, "Augustine's *Confessions*."

ence as founded in the *Confessions* from the perspective of one theoretical discipline. In a more specific and extended vein, using Rambo's interdisciplinary framework, this study suggests an interdisciplinary and multi-layered pattern to elaborate the complex and interrelated factors of Augustine's conversion process. This pattern can be valid for experiencing and reflecting on religious conversion in both the academic field and the Christian community.[142]

The Expression of One's Restless Feelings in Psychological Crisis and Spiritual Darkness

The pattern of the conversion process from the *Confessions* begins with the description of the specific context of the young Augustine in which he had experienced psychological crisis and spiritual darkness. In the summer of 386 in Milan, Augustine had seriously undergone a sense of the divided self within his psychological distress as well as a feeling of restlessness within his deep spiritual abyss (the soul's "falling to pieces"). Moreover, at the time of his experience of the inner division of the mind, Augustine had also experienced relationship problems due to his inability to love other persons (e.g., his dismissal of his unmarried wife—"his long-term partner"—for his worldly ambitions [*conf.* 6.15.25]). In this context of his experiences of both the inner conflict of the mind and the relational problems with others, Augustine confessed, "My two wills, one old, the other new, one carnal, the other spiritual, were in conflict with one another, and their discord robbed my soul of all concentration" (8.5.10); that is, "in my own case . . . the self which willed to serve was identical with the self which was unwilling. It was I. I was neither wholly willing nor wholly unwilling. So I was in conflict with myself and was dissociated from myself. The dissociation came about against my will" (8.10.22; see 8.10.23–24; Rom 7:15, 19). As such, he argued, "My pilgrimage is so wearisome! I have not yet arrived in that homeland where I shall live untroubled by any evil. . . . Why am I not yet there?" (*en. Ps.* 119.6). Importantly, Augustine's experiences of

---

142. In this book, I have struggled with how I can relocate more effectively and practically the conversion narrative of St. Augustine within the context of pastoral care and ministry (and the field of the academy)—in order to facilitate a better understanding of the conversion stories of the church members as well as to enhance the experiences of religious conversion within the Christian community.

psychological crisis and spiritual darkness had compelled him to think about what was the real problem in his life as well as what was the real cause of his inner distortion of the will and feeling of restlessness in his heart. Indeed, Augustine's confrontation with his deep existential predicament and his spiritual abyss had stirred him to enter into an earnest quest for knowing himself and knowing the divine.

Clearly, the theme of Augustine's expression of his restless feelings guides us to realize that one's sense of dividedness and restlessness in a psychological crisis and spiritual darkness is not a simply negative symptom of fragmentation or estrangement, but a positive opportunity to deeply recollect and reflect upon one's life; that is, it compels oneself to acknowledge the roots of one's inner conflict at which point one is able to open one's mind to hear the inward divine locution.

Entrance into One's Inwardness with the Divine

The restless Augustine (who had suffered from "sickness unto death") had entered into his inner world to know himself and the divine (*conf.* 7.10.16) after realizing that he was not able to find a resting place on earth (7.7.11, 8.5.10). In *Soliloquies*, Augustine described his yearning for the knowledge of the self and the knowledge of the divine as follows:

> *Augustine*: There, I have prayed to God.
> *Reason*: What then do you wish to know?
> *Augustine*: All the things for which I prayed.
> *Reason*: Summarize them briefly.
> *Augustine*: I want to know God and the soul.
> *Reason*: Nothing more?
> *Augustine*: Nothing whatsoever. (*sol.* 1.2.7; see 2.1.1, *ord.* 2.18.47)

Here Augustine wanted to know who he was in relation to the divine and to know who God was for him in light of the interaction between God and the soul (see *conf.* 9.1.1). In other words, he had quested for meaning in life as well as his cognitive satisfaction of the Truth. In consideration of the concept of the ascent of the soul to God (the return of the soul to the Origin), Augustine accounted for his intellectual and spiritual apprehension of God and the soul as follows:

> By the Platonic books I was admonished to return into myself. . . . I entered and with my soul's eye . . . saw above that

> same eye of my soul the immutable light higher than my mind (7.10.16). What then do I love when I love my God? Who is he who is higher than the highest element in my soul? Through my soul I will ascend to him. I will rise above the force by which I am bonded to the body and fill its frame with vitality. (10.7.11)

During his inner struggles, both in experiencing himself and experiencing the divine, Augustine had gradually discovered that he was far away from God ("the ground of being"), at which point he had recognized that the primary cause of both his inner division (and his relational problem with others) was deeply derived from his disconnection with the ground of Being (4.10.15).[143] This means that Augustine needed to accept God's presence in the depth of his soul and his life (rather than his worldly ambitions).

Significantly, this theme of Augustine's interior journey toward union with God gives us an insight that one needs to move into one's inner world to know oneself and the divine, if one is to quiet the restlessness of one's heart ("the soul's sickness"). One's interior journey toward encounter with God enables oneself to realize the central problem of one's life which is deeply related to one's turning away from God. This implies that one needs to turn toward God as well as to create a new way of living in light of the interplay between the soul and the ground of its existence.

The Confession of One's Powerlessness to the Divine

During his interior journey toward union with God, Augustine made a decision to open himself to the divine and confessed his powerlessness (i.e., his painful condition of fragmentation—"tragic estrangement") to God in terms of the relation between the soul and the ground of being. Here Augustine had no reason "to hide himself from God" as well as "to hide God from himself"[144]; as such, he wrote, "Lord my God, judge of my conscience, is my memory correct? Before you I lay my heart and my memory. At that time you were dealing with me in your hidden secret providence, and you were putting my shameful errors before your face (Ps 49: 21) so that I would see and hate them" (*conf.* 5.6.11; see 10.1.1).

---

143. See Vaught, *Encounters*, 82.
144. See Capps, "Parabolic Events," 267–68.

Augustine began to put himself within the presence of God—"O God of hosts, turn [me] and show [me] your face, and [I] shall be safe" (4.10.15; see Ps 79:8)—at which point he accepted the divine intervention and grace into his mind and his life—"Augustine *allows himself to be thought by God.*"[145] Now Augustine discovered a resting place in relation to the ground of Being. Augustine confessed, "You stir [me] to take pleasure in praising you, because you have made [me] for yourself, and [my] heart is restless until it rests in you" (1.1.1). After disclosing his hopeless condition and achieving the resting place within the divine presence, Augustine remarkably moved himself to be related to the divine (and others). He accounted for his conviction of the divine indwelling and his dialogue with God: "Your right hand had regard to the depth of my dead condition, and from the bottom of my heart had drawn out a trough of corruption. . . . Already my mind was free of 'the biting cares' of place-seeking, of desire for gain, of wallowing in self-indulgence, of scratching the itch of lust. And I was now talking with you, Lord my God, my radiance, my wealth, and my salvation" (9.1.1). This implies that Augustine entered into the process of interior transformation from the divided self to the integration of the self in relation to his profound experience with the divine (8.12.28–29).

Importantly, the theme of Augustine's confession of his powerlessness before God leads us to recognize the importance of one's fundamental openness to God's presence in order to achieve a permanent resting place (in one's heart and life), as the Apostle Paul says: "I will boast all the more gladly of my weaknesses, so that the power of Christ may dwell in me" (2 Cor 12:9; see Phil 4:13). Within this safe resting place of the divine, one can overcome a sense of inner isolation and then one begins to recover a sense of relationships with the divine and others.

The Experience of Loving Care and Support from Other People in the Christian Community

During the period of the depths of his ontological struggle to know himself and the divine, Augustine was related to and influenced by other persons (e.g., Ambrose [*conf.* 5.13.23–5.14.25, 9.6.14]; Simplicianus

---

145. McMahon, "Book Thirteen," 218.

[8.2.3–5]; Ponticianus [8.6.14–15]; Alypius [8.11.27]; Monica [6.2.2, 9.7.15, 9.10.23–26]; Augustine's unmarried wife [6.15.25]). In other words, Augustine had experienced loving care and support from these persons within Christian communities. These significant persons had affected Augustine to overcome his dualistic materialism (i.e., the Manichean belief [3.7.2, 3.7.12]) and his skeptic thinking in the Academy (5.14.25) as well as to fulfill his (psychological) needs (e.g., a sense of belongingness) and to find a new way of life in the Christian community. In doing so, Simplicianus (who was a spiritual father of Bishop Ambrose of Milan and a Christian Neoplatonist) told the conversion story of his friend Victorinus at Rome (8.2.3–5); Ponticianus (who was a fellow African Christian and a high court official of the Empire) visited Augustine (and Alypius) and he accounted for the conversion stories of his two friends at Trier (who were influenced by the ascetic life of Antony the Egyptian monk) (8.6.13–15). Clearly, Augustine's intimate interactions with significant others in the Christian communities helped him to make up for his frustration with his deprivations in the social and cultural conditions of his time as well as to foster a new ability to live together with others in the community in light of interpersonal bonds and a web of Christian friendships.[146] The conversion stories of other persons ("a story within a story") challenged Augustine to overcome his isolated life-style, to be converted to Christianity, and to follow their example of humility in faith in Christ.[147]

Significantly, the theme of Augustine's experiences of loving care and support from other people in Christian communities provides us with an insight insofar as the experience of the self is deeply related to the experience of others. In other words, one's psychological development and spiritual maturity are deeply affected by one's continuous intimate relationships with other members of the Christian community. Through intensive interactions with significant others and through affiliations with religious groups (a process of "resocialization" or "institutionalization"), one becomes a new member of an alternate community. Here one can overcome a sense of disconnection with (the divine and) others and then one can engage in Christian living in community.

---

146. See Kreider, *Change*; Kreidler, "Conversion"; Meeks, *Christian Morality*; Vaught, *Encounters*; Wills, *Saint Augustine*.

147. See Matter, "Conversion(s)"; O'Brien, "Approach"; Van Fleteren, "Augustine's Theory."

Confrontation with Philosophical and Cultural Changes Resulting in the Reconstruction of Personal (and Religious) Identity, Worldview, and Belief

Along with his intensive interactions with others and his participation in Christian communities, the young Augustine had confronted philosophical and cultural changes that were profoundly rooted in the Neoplatonic heritage and the Christian monastic movement of the late fourth century. That is, Augustine had gradually reconstructed his personal and religious identity, worldview, and belief through his readings of the Platonist books (*conf.* 7.9.14–17.23) and his encounters with Christian Neoplatonists (e.g., Ambrose [5.13.23–5.14.25] and Simplicianus [8.2.3–5]) as well as through his learning of the early Christian monastic movements at Milan and then in Rome (including the Antonian tradition of the ascetic/solitary life [8.6.14–15] and the Pachomian tradition of the community life [Possidius, *v. Aug.* 3, 5]) and his practices of the monastic life at Thagaste and then Hippo Regius. Clearly, Christian Neoplatonism helped Augustine to reformulate his view on the divine nature from the material and divisible being to the immaterial and indivisible being (as well as his concept of evil from a "substance" to "a privation of good"); namely, to make his inner spiritual journey for union with God (in light of knowing God and the soul) (*conf.* 3.7.12, 7.1.1–2, 7.5.7, 7.10.16, 7.20.26; *c. ep. Man.* 15.20).[148] Furthermore, it compelled Augustine to acknowledge the Christian concept of the Incarnate Christ (who is a mediator between the human and the divine and who is a perfect example of humility). In doing so, the early Christian monastic movements had challenged the new convert Augustine to enter into the life of celibacy within the Christian philosophical community at Cassiciacum and then in Rome. Moreover, these movements (especially Antonian anchoritism and Pachomian cenobitism) had affected Augustine to become a servant of God ("a monk"), at which point the lay-monk Augustine established a monastery/lay Christian community at Thagaste in North Africa, and then the priest/bishop-monk Augustine found the lay and clerical monasteries

---

148. See Ayres and Barnes, "God"; Cary, *Augustine's Invention*; Chadwick, *Augustine*; Kenney, "Augustine's Inner Self"; Kevane, "Christian Philosophy"; Lancel, *Saint Augustine*; Markus, "Life"; McMahon, *Medieval Meditative Ascent*; O'Meara, *Young Augustine*.

at Hippo Regius in light of the mutual interaction of Christian life in solitude and Christian life in community.[149]

The theme of Augustine's reconstruction of personal/religious identity, worldview, and belief (which was influenced by the Neoplatonic heritage and the Christian monastic movement in the late fourth century) shows the impact of institutional and cultural-philosophical forces on the process of human transformation. This implies that one's intellectual development and spiritual maturity do not exist "in a vacuum." Rather, they are inherently related to the specific context of one's philosophical and cultural changes which results in the reformation of one's personal and religious identity, worldview, and belief (a process of "acculturation" or "cultural revitalization").

The Experience of the Transformation of the God Representation

Augustine's God representations had evolved throughout his lifetime. There is an inherent link of the transformation of the young (and adult) Augustine's God representations with his interpersonal relationships within the Christian communities, and his experiences of the philosophical and cultural changes of his time, and his encounters with the divine intervention and grace in the midst of his existential predicament and spiritual abyss. The aged Augustine revealed the process of the formation and reformation of his own God representations in his works (especially the *Confessions*), while reflecting on his lifetime before God and his readers, including his community members (*conf.* 10.1.1, 10.4.4; *retr.* 2.6.1). Augustine's early traumatic injuries ("emphatic failure" or "internalized bad objects" [*conf.* 1.9.14–15; *civ. Dei* 21.14]) had negatively affected the construction of his self-image which was relevant to his sense of low self-esteem (*conf.* 1.12.19, 1.19.30, 2.2.4, 4.6.11, 4.16.30). While disclosing his negative self-image, the child and young Augustine had characterized his representations of God as harsh (1.12.19, 2.2.4), discarding (1.9.14, 5.9.16), vindictive (6.6.9, 9.4.12), laughing (4.1.1, 6.6.9), and material/corruptible ("being a bodily thing")—"God [is] confined within a corporeal form" (3.7.12).

However, during his intimate interactions with other persons, his participation in Christian communities, his learning about Christian

---

149. See E. A. Clark, "Asceticism"; Harrison, *Augustine*; Lawless, *Augustine*; Zumkeller, *Augustine's Ideal*.

Neoplatonism and Christian monasticism of the fourth century, and his experiences of the loving grace of the divine, Augustine had gradually experienced philosophical and cultural changes (which were related to his transformation/change of his personal and religious identity, worldview, and belief), at which point his negative God representations were changed into the positive God representations. This means that Augustine began to re-create his relationships with himself, others, and the divine by entering into the process of restoration and healing. Now Augustine had positively re-characterized his representations of God as follows:

1) God as merciful—"But you, Lord 'abide for eternity and you will not be angry with us for ever' (Eccl 18:1; Ps 84:6). You have mercy on dust and ashes, and it has pleased you to restore my deformities in your sight (Ps 18:15)" (7.8.12).

2) God as encouraging—"With your word you pierced my heart, and I loved you . . . there is a light I love, and a food, and a kind of embrace when I love my God—a light, voice, odour, food, embrace of my inner man, where my soul is floodlit by light which space cannot contain . . . and where there is a bound of union that no satiety can part" (10.6.8).

3) God as restoring—"I do not hide my wounds. You are the physician, I am the patient. You are pitiful, I am the object of the pity" (10.28.39).

4) God as incorporeal and incorruptible—"God is a Spirit (John 4:24), not a figure whose limbs have length and breadth and who has a mass" (3.7.12; see *c. ep. Man.* 15.20).

Significantly, the theme of Augustine's transformation of his God representations leads us to realize that one's God representations have evolved throughout one's life span, influenced by the complex and rich interplay of the person with personal, social, cultural, and religious forces.[150] In doing so, it guides us to be aware that the formation and reformation of one's representations of God have affected and have been affected by one's relationships with oneself, others, and the divine (within the specific social and cultural contexts). In that sense, one's recovery of the positive representations of God is essential for mak-

---

150. See Rizzuto, *Birth*; Spero, *Religious Objects*; Spiro, "Collective Representations."

ing a better Christian living in which one involves mental health, good friendship, and spiritual awakening.

The Re-Creation of One's Loving Relationships with Oneself, Others, and the Divine

Consistent with his long struggles with his sense of inner division, his interior quest for knowing himself and the divine, his honest confession of powerlessness to God, his intensive interactions with others within the Christian communities, his philosophical and cultural changes in the context of the influence of the Neoplatonic heritage and the Christian monastic movement of the fourth century, his experience of the reformation of his God representations, now the young Augustine converted to Christianity in the Milanese garden in 386; that is, he made a decision to be a servant of God and to enter into the life of asceticism and celibacy. In other words, Augustine made a resolution to engage in the renunciation of his worldly ambition for a successful career, then committed himself to the service of God and to the service of God's people in light of Christian life in solitude and community. Indeed, before his conversion to Christianity (especially the time of his existential predicament and spiritual abyss), the Manichee and skeptic Augustine was in the midst of relational problems, as he noted: "I was on the way [in which] I had committed against you, against myself, and against others" (*conf.* 5.9.16). However, (during and) after his conversion to Christianity, he had earnestly attempted to re-create his (empathic) relationships with himself, others, and the divine in light of the reciprocity of the love of God and neighbor.

Clearly, through his conversion experience, Augustine was involved in the process of dying and beginning anew (11.7.9). This means that Augustine entered into the process of progressive restoration, that is, he had experienced healing of his whole being—"When I shall have adhered (Ps 72:28) to you with the whole of myself, I shall never have 'pain and toil' (Ps 89:10), and my entire life will be full of you" (10.28.39; see 5.1.1, 6.6.9, 10.6.10, 13.22.32; Phil 4:13).[151] Within his loving relationships with himself, others, and the divine, the new convert Augustine had "restored strength and true courage" in order

---

151. See Canning, *Unity of Love for God and Neighbour*; Clark, *Augustine*; Martin, *Restless Heart*.

to serve God and God's children for the rest of his life. In particular, as a monk-priest/bishop, Augustine had founded the lay and clerical monasteries at Hippo as well as he had served the cathedral of Hippo and had taken care of the members of the church community (especially the poor). He had kept a balance between the life of contemplation and the life of church ministry in light of the interaction between his monastery and his church (*civ. Dei* 19.19; *conf.* 12.25.35, 13.22.32; *Trin.* 6.5.7; see Matt 22:37–40). Augustine made the monastic *Rule* in which all members of the community had attempted to become "one heart and soul" directed towards God (*reg.* 1.2). He had earnestly participated in continuous and difficult debates with the Manicheans, the Donatists, the Arians, and the Pelagians in order to protect both God's people and the North African Church from paganism/heresy as well as to establish more appropriate Christian guidelines and doctrines for a better Christian living in the specific historical and social context. Until his last ecclesiastical struggle for defending his flock and church in the midst of the blockade of Hippo by the Vandal army, Augustine had successfully lived in the service of love of God and God's people (Possidius, *v. Aug.* 29, 30, 31).

Importantly, the theme of Augustine's re-creation of loving relationships with himself, others, and the divine guides us to recognize that one's conversion experience is not simply a "once and for all event," but an ongoing process of change in one's whole lifetime. One's conversion experience does not refer to the isolated withdrawal from the world. Rather, it stirs one to enter into the healing process of relationships with oneself, others, and the divine; that is, it encourages one to engage in the cooperative and integrated life of solitude and community in the specific cultural and social context of one's time. Indeed, within one's renewed relationships, one can actually and continuously commit oneself to the loving service of God and neighbor in light of the experiences of the self, others, and the divine, as Augustine points out:

> What do I want? What do I desire? What do I burn for? Why am I sitting here? Why do I live? There's only one reason: so that we may live together with Christ. This is my intense desire, this my honor, this my richness, this my joy, this my glory. . . . I DO NOT WANT TO BE SAVED WITHOUT YOU—*quid autem volo? Quid desidero? Quid cupio? Quare hic sedeo? Quare vivo? Nisi hac intentione, ut cum Christo simul vivamus. Cupiditas mea ista est, honor meus iste est, possessio mea ista est, gaudium*

> *meum hoc est, gloria mea ista est . . . NOLO SALVUS ESSE SINE VOBIS.* (s. 17.2)[152]

Summary

I present a more holistic and multi-dimensional pattern of Augustine's conversion process for experiencing and reflecting on religious conversion in both the academy and the Christian community. In other words, by using Rambo's interdisciplinary framework of religious change, I characterize more effectively and practically the pattern of conversion experience as described in the *Confessions* (and other works of Augustine). As such, I intend to universalize Augustine's conversion within the Christian community in order to understand better not only Augustine's conversion narrative, but also our own conversion stories within the pastoral care situations and various historical and social/cultural contexts. This integrative and multi-dimensional pattern helps us to pay attention to the importance 1) to express one's restless feelings in psychological crisis and spiritual darkness, 2) to enter into one's inwardness with the divine, 3) to confess one's powerlessness to the divine, 4) to experience loving care and support from other people in the Christian community, 5) to confront with philosophical and cultural changes resulting in the reconstruction of personal and religious identity, worldview, and belief, 6) to experience the transformation of the God representation, and 7) to re-create one's loving relationships with oneself, others, and the divine.

---

152. Quoted in Martin, *Restless Heart*, 159–60.

6

Sharing the Conversion Narrative in Our Midst

Reflections and Implications

> Autobiography [which is inherently related to "the metaphor of the self in the process of becoming"] enables an author to struggle with the question: "What is becoming of me?" But, in the final analysis, we read autobiography because we want to know: "What is becoming of us?"
>
> —Donald Capps[1]

THIS BOOK ESTABLISHED AN integrated perception of the complexity and richness of religious conversion from an interdisciplinary perspective. It employed the systemic stage model of conversion proposed by Lewis Rambo in order to articulate how personal, social, cultural, and religious components had impacted the unfolding process of Augustine's change. While examining the complicated and multi-layered process of Augustine's conversion, this study integrated religious and social science perspectives to understand his lifelong transformation as well

---

1. Capps, "Parabolic Events," 272.

as to demonstrate the benefits of coordinating a range of approaches in the study of his conversion.

This interdisciplinary study demonstrated that Augustine's conversion experience was engaged in the interactive and cumulative contexts of his experience of psychological distress and existential predicament, his inquiry to know himself and the divine, his interpersonal bonds with others, his affiliations with the Christian community, his philosophical and cultural changes, and his encounter with the divine, his acceptance of Christian baptism, his experience of the vision of Ostia, and his engagement in the service of God and others. Following the integrated understanding of Augustine's conversion, this study additionally proposed a holistic and multi-dimensional pattern of the conversion process as found in the *Confessions* (and other works of Augustine).

The coherent portrayal of Augustine's narrative of transformation enables us to appreciate that Augustine's conversion was involved in an evolving process of his lived experience of change in which multiple factors interacted with and reinforced one another, calling for the continuous transformation and commitment of his whole life in light of the experiences of the self, others, and the divine. The findings of this study provide some significant implications for scholars of conversion, for pastoral caregivers in the Christian community, and for future researchers of religious change.

IMPLICATIONS FOR SCHOLARS OF RELIGIOUS CONVERSION

In line with Rambo's approach to conversion, this book contributes to the literature by enhancing the interdisciplinary study of religious change. As such, this book provides insights for scholars of conversion (especially those of Augustine's conversion experience) by fostering effectively the integrated understanding of the complex phenomenon of religious conversion through the reinterpretation of the process of Augustine's narrative of change.

The findings of this study, first of all, help scholars to recognize that the interdisciplinary approach to religious change is a good tool for achieving a richer and more accurate perception of human transformation by way of a collaborative dialogue among religious and social science studies of conversion, as Rambo (1993) points out: "For conversion to be understood in all its richness and complexity, the disciplines of anthropology, sociology, psychology, and religious studies must all be taken into account."[2] More specifically, this interdisciplinary study is able to become a bridge or mediator among various disciplines—especially psychology, sociology, anthropology, and religious studies—in order to enhance the respect of another unique account ("voice") of the conversion narrative, to overcome indifferent and juxtaposed stances from one discipline to another, and thus to facilitate a more critical and mutually-informing conversation of religious change. In this way, this study encourages scholars of conversion (who have neglected the social scientific interpretation of human transformation) to pay attention to the personal, familial, socio-cultural, and philosophical issues/forces in the process of human change; it also encourages academics in the social sciences (who have ignored the religious factor [e.g., the divine intervention and grace] in the process of religious change) to respect the role of the divine in one's lived experience of change.

As such, this study challenges scholars to enter together into the meaningful and valid work of coordinating a range of approaches to the study of conversion as well as to share together the benefits of constructing an interdisciplinary approach to religious change. That is, it enables them to achieve an insight into depicting a more integrated picture of how the complicated and multiple factors involved in the conversion narrative are knit together (as if the members of an orchestra perform together in a spirit of harmony and balance in order to show successfully the richness and meaning of a song itself).[3]

2. Rambo, *Religious Conversion*, 7.

3. During his lifetime, Augustine had continuously opened his mind to establish his theological reflections and answers to his existential predicaments and philosophical questions in the historical and social/cultural context. Although Augustine had paid attention to the priority of faith—"faith precedes reason (*crede ut intelligas*) because unless you believe, you will not understand" (see *ench.* 5)—from the time of his garden experience until his death, he had continuously struggled with keeping a balance between faith (*fides*) and reason (*ratio*), and between the transformation of the will and the transformation of the knowledge (see Cushman, "Faith and Reason," 271; Quinn, *Companion*, 390; Ramirez, "Reason over Faith," 123, 131; Van Fleteren, "Authority and Reason," 70–71). H. Richard Niebuhr views Augustine as the "theologian of cultural transformation by Christ" who had involved a continuous dialogue between the Christian gospel and culture of his time (*Christ and Culture*, 207–8). Following Niebuhr, I would like to contend that Augustine's earnest attempt to integrate the life of knowing and the life of believing (in light of mutual interaction of his

IMPLICATIONS FOR PASTORAL CAREGIVERS IN THE CHRISTIAN COMMUNITY

This book contributes by applying Rambo's model of religious conversion within the context of pastoral care and ministry in order to understand better not only the conversion narrative of Augustine, but also the conversion stories of members of the Christian community. In doing so, this study has characterized and advanced the pattern of Augustine's conversion as described in the *Confessions* (and his other works). As such, it provides implications for pastoral caregivers in the Christian community who have helped persons to cope with their psychological crisis, existential predicament, and spiritual abyss as well as to re-establish their relationships with themselves, others, and the divine. Indeed, in the context of pastoral ministry, many Christian pastoral caregivers (who might be only theologically-oriented to understand religious conversion) have tended to be unaware of (or to ignore) the influence of personal, social, and cultural factors on the process of human transformation, as Rambo points out: "Religious people . . . consider this [sacred] dimension [e.g., the divine grace] absolutely essential to the whole process of human transformation; other factors are subordinate to it."[4]

Broadly, Rambo's interdisciplinary approach to religious conversion is deeply rooted in the critical correlational method in that it facilitates an essentially equal conversation among various disciplines. Along with this line, this interdisciplinary study of (the pattern of) Augustine's conversion is placed in the critical correlational method. As such, it is also relevant to (or is inspired by) a practical theological approach to pastoral care and ministry, which leads caregivers to engage in the experience of and reflection on Augustine's transformational process within the faith community. Don S. Browning defines fundamental practical theology as "critical reflection on the church's dialogue with Christian sources and other communities of experience and interpretation with the aim of guiding its action toward social and individual

---

intellectual knowledge of Neoplatonism and his Christian faith of God) challenges the modern scholars of conversion (as well as the pastoral caregivers of the Christian community) to recognize the importance of the interdisciplinary approach to religious experiences within specific human conditions.

4. Rambo, *Religious Conversion*, 10.

transformation."[5] By using Tillich's term "method of correlation,"[6] Browning remakes a "revised correlation method" for promoting a critical dialogue between traditional Christian resources and human science resources. Browning's revised correlational method involves a movement of practice to theory to practice. Browning's practice-theory-practice model begins with practices, proceeds to identification of the theory implicit in the practices, and, in interdisciplinary conversation with that theory, moves back or modifies the practices in which they are involved. Browning emphasizes the role of practice as prior to theory, and is clear in overcoming the notion that practical theology is the application of theory to concrete situations (the theory-practice model).[7] Based on practice-theory-practice movement, Browning's revised correlational method involves an interdisciplinary movement for bringing theological texts and Christian traditions into critical conversation with sources from other disciplines (psychology, sociology, ethics, etc). His method calls on the Christian community to relate to and critically reflect on various "interpretations" of human experiences in order to assess the "relative adequacy" of any given interpretation for moral guidance in a pluralistic world. As such, it leads persons (Christian or not) to better understand particular human situations, and to make better actions in pastoral care situations.

While acknowledging the critical correlational method within Browning's practical theological framework, this interdisciplinary study of the pattern of Augustine's conversion process gives the members of the community an insight into a need for appropriate pastoral care and ministry in various historical and social/cultural contexts. In doing so, it helps us to recognize the importance of correlating questions and answers from interpretations of Christian faith with questions and answers from other interpretations of ordinary human experience. More

5. Browning, *Practical Theology*, 36.

6. Paul Tillich defines the "method of correlation" as a way of uniting Christian message and human situation. The method of correlation provides theological answers for the existential questions arising in human situations (*Systematic Theology*, vol. 1, 8, 60).

7. Traditionally, practical theology has been conceived as theological reflection on the tasks of the ordained ministers and leaders of the church for preaching, teaching, liturgy, and counseling. The traditional type of theological reflection involves a movement from theory to practice, originating in theological ideas and concepts which are then applied to practical aspects of ministry.

specifically, this study guides pastoral caregivers to enter into collaborative dialogue between traditional Christian resources and modern human science resources, between practice and theory, between the church and the university, and between the sacred and the secular; as such, it provides an insight into promoting a mutual and critical correlation between the Christian tradition and the contemporary situation.

In a more critical and integrative way, the major findings of this study of Augustine's conversion (as discussed in chapter 5) help pastoral caregivers of the religious community to foster an ability for critically integrating religious and social science perspectives for a better understanding of religious conversion, and to recognize how the multiple factors involved in religious change are knit together. More specifically, this study leads pastoral caregivers to attend to the interrelated link between one's spiritual journey toward God and one's sense of belonging with others within Christian communities in light of knowing/experiencing oneself, others, and the divine. It also leads them to look at how one has gradually reshaped one's identity, worldview, and belief through intimate interactions with other people and through participation in religious groups, influenced by the specific social and cultural conditions of one's time.

In emphasizing the value of the integrated conversation between traditional Christian and human science resources, this study guides pastoral caregivers to be aware of the importance of (re)-establishing one's connections with the divine and others within the process of one's transformation. In this vein, scholars have paid attention to the inherent link between the recovery/development of one's relationships with God/others and the experience of one's change/healing in the various conditions of pastoral care or spiritual direction. Influenced by Browning, John Patton describes pastoral care as "a ministry of the Christian community" in order to broaden the focus of pastoral care beyond the individual pastor to the larger group of cares within the Christian community.[8] In the emphasis on pastoral care within the interrelatedness of the community members, Patton defines pastoral care as "the person-to-person response that grows out of participation in a caring community and which seeks to enable persons to give and receive care and to experience community."[9] While presenting the communal contextual

---

8. Patton, *Pastoral Care*, 6, 15.
9. Ibid., 27.

paradigm of pastoral care, Patton argues that the central act of pastoral care is not so much problem solving, but "hearing and remembering in relationship."[10] At this point, for Patton, the effective way in pastoral care is not critical judgment, but mutual understanding of one another in a web of relationships. In line with Browning and Patton, Chris R. Schlauch insists that pastoral (clinical) care is a kind of collaborative conversation in which both the pastoral caregiver and the troubled person engage in healing relationships. More specifically, in this collaborative conversation, the pastoral caregiver faithfully companions and collaboratively translates with the troubled person ("faithful companioning"); that is, through empathy, the caregiver introspects as if the caregiver is the troubled in order to feel together the inner experience of the other; as such, both are involved in the process of experiencing and reflecting, practicing and theorizing, together. Schlauch asserts that healing is not simply the absence of something (e.g., the symptoms of depression). Rather, healing as a process lies in faithful companioning and loving relationships between the caregiver and the troubled (and between the divine and the believer).[11] In a related vein, Margaret Guenther elucidates spiritual direction within relationships in terms of listening to and sharing the stories of spiritual pilgrimage. Guenther contends that the purpose of spiritual direction is "to help people discover how to define themselves in relation not only to the world, but also to God."[12] From a feminist perspective, Guenther describes the context of spiritual direction as "holy listening." For Guenther, holy listening refers to not domination and submission in the hierarchical structure, but hospitality, friendship, and intimacy in the mutual relationship. Guenther presents the metaphor of hospitality to and welcoming the stranger which is cheerful and valid for making a safe place or space for the directee as well as for listening to and sharing the story of the other. For Guenther, both ordinary persons, the director and the directee, are able to join together in inviting God into their space: "Here we are, you and I, and I hope a third, Christ, is in our midst."[13] Holy listening grows with the light of God's unseen presence.

---

10. Ibid., 40; see 15–37.
11. Schlauch, *Faithful Companioning*, 141; see 131.
12. Guenther, *Holy Listening*, 69.
13. Ibid., 15.

Corresponding with the literature of pastoral care and spiritual direction, this interdisciplinary study contributes by enhancing the formation and reformation of one's relationships with the divine and with other community members in the specific contexts of pastoral care or spiritual direction. In doing so, this study encourages the members of the faith community to reconstruct their religious tradition in a wider world of experience and meaning. It helps persons to understand themselves in relation to God as well as in relation to the self and others. As such, this study guides us to pay attention to the inherent link between the self, suffering, and healing, between psychological development and spiritual maturity, between the transcendent and the immanent, between the interior and the exterior, between the sacred and the secular, and between the human yearning for holiness ("spiritual awakening") and the human yearning for belongingness ("living human web").

Importantly, this interdisciplinary study provides an insight into re-describing (or re-locating) Augustine's conversion experience within the modern Christian community in light of "universalizing Augustine's story" of conversion. In the *Confessions*, Augustine disclosed his spiritual journey toward God and invited his fellows and readers into sharing his lived experience of change. In this way, Augustine described the goal of his *Confessions*: "The thirteen books of my *Confessions*, whether they refer to my evil or good, praise the just and good God, and stimulate the heart and mind of man [the human reader] to approach unto Him [God]" (*retr.* 2.6.1; see *conf.* 10.1.1). While emphasizing spiritual friendships between Augustine and his readers as well as between Augustine and the divine, McMahon writes,

> Augustine aimed to befriend his readers in God. The *Confessions* directly enacts Augustine the narrator's intimacy with God and catches readers up into his prayer. It thereby brings readers into intimacy with the narrator's life and mind. Some readers accept this intimacy and grow into it; others find Augustine unsympathetic and resist. In any event, the *Confessions* labors to establish relationship between Augustine and his readers. The narrator does not say so, and the author cannot. Nevertheless, the long history of responses to the *Confessions* shows how successful Augustine has been at creating a sense of intimacy with his readers.[14]

---

14. McMahon, *Medieval Meditative Ascent*, 129.

Along the same line, this study encourages Christian believers to enter into a creative and critical conversation between Augustine's conversion story in the late fourth century and our own conversion stories in the twenty-first century. It helps the members of the Christian community to look at the inherent link of Augustine's story of spiritual journey with our own stories of spiritual pilgrimage in various pastoral care situations in light of the continuity of conversion in the Christian community. In the case of Augustine, he had struggled with the process of self-becoming: "What[/How] is *becoming* of me?" Through a critical and integrative dialogue between Augustine's transforming narrative and our own transforming stories, we Christian believers can establish our own existential question for a more mature spiritual journey— "What[/How] is *becoming* of us" in our own historical and social/cultural milieu? As such, this creative and integrative conversation enables us to realize both the personal dimension and the universal dimension of religious conversion, which are separate yet mutually-informing, in the process of human transformation in light of a movement from Augustine's personal story of conversion to a universal story of conversion in the community.

More importantly, by commending a creative conversation between Augustine's conversion narrative and our own conversion stories, this interdisciplinary study guides the members of the Christian community to appreciate that Christian conversion experience does not occur in isolation ("in a vacuum"), but in relational contexts of oneself, others, and God; as such, it takes place within historical and social/cultural contexts. This implies that Christian conversion does not mean withdrawing from the world, but rather engaging in both the service of God and the service of others, as Karl Rahner states: "[Christian conversion] is love for the neighbor, because only in conjunction with this can God really be loved, and without that love no one really knows with genuine personal knowledge who God is."[15] In that sense, this study leads Christian believers not only to achieve a better understanding of Augustine's conversion, but also to imitate (or engage in) his life, which was interwoven by the cooperative life of solitude and community in

---

15. Rahner, "Conversion," 206. While acknowledging the value of Christian life in solitude, Claire E. Wolfteich pays attention to the value of Christian life in community: "[Christian] spirituality must be studied in historical and cultural context. Spirituality is 'an experience rooted in a particular community's history'" (*American Catholics*, 8–9; see Leech, *Spirituality*, 14).

light of the interaction of the love of God and the love of neighbor. Especially when re-describing Augustine's lived experience of change within our life of pilgrimage, he has encouraged us to join the Christian spiritual journey; as such, he has given a new direction to Christian ideals of living in terms of the interplay of prayer (contemplation of God in his monastic life) and social engagement (action for others in his pastoral ministry).[16] In this way, while emphasizing the interrelatedness between a servant of "the humble Incarnate Christ" and a "humble Christian" for others in light of the personal transformation and the network of Christian friendships, Kreidler writes,

> Augustine of Hippo's pastoral practice is directly related to his experience of conversion. That is, Augustine's pastoral practice flowed directly from his own experience of the humble Christ of the Gospel manifested in, and in relationship to Christ's body the Church. Specifically, Augustine's appropriation of the Christ of Scripture was the foundation of his understanding of conversion both for himself and for the community. . . . Augustine knew that any theology of ministry was the result of identification with the humble Incarnate Christ and his identification with his brothers and sisters . . . in the process of conversion.[17]

While paying attention to Augustine's transforming life of relationships with himself, others, and the divine during his lifetime, this interdisciplinary study challenges us to recognize afresh that Christian conversion experience is usually involved in an ongoing process of religious change that inherently requires the continuing change—"converting"—and dedication of the person's whole life in terms of the reciprocity of turning toward God and turning toward others. In other words, Augustine's converting life story of relationships encourages us to involve the integrated life of contemplation (the transformation of the self) and action (the transformation of the community/world) within various historical and social/cultural conditions. Indeed, along with our web of transforming relationships, Christian believers are able to commit, continuously and actually, ourselves to the loving service of God and neighbor in light of our experiences of the self, others, and the divine.

---

16. See *civ. Dei* 19.19.

17. Kreidler, "Conversion," 510.

RECOMMENDATIONS FOR FUTURE RESEARCH

This book has actively and critically engaged in the interdisciplinary study of religious conversion. As such, it encourages future researchers to establish more interdisciplinary studies of religious conversion, that is, to integrate critically the religious and human science perspectives as well as to portray a more coherent and integrated picture of how personal, social, cultural, and religious components interact with one another in the process of religious change.

This book has reflected on how to use Rambo's model of religious conversion more creatively and practically in order to relocate Augustine's conversion experience within the contemporary Christian community in terms of universalizing the story of religious conversion. In that sense, the present study of the holistic and multi-dimensional pattern as described in the *Confessions* (and other works of Augustine) is an attempt to better understand both Augustine's conversion story and our own conversion narratives in various pastoral care situations. As such, it contributes by guiding the members of the Christian community to realize the correlation between Augustine's narrative of spiritual journey and our own stories of spiritual pilgrimage in various historical and social/cultural contexts. Moreover, this interdisciplinary study also contributes by enhancing a mutual and critical correlation between the Christian tradition and the contemporary situation, at which point it stirs us to engage in a creative and integrative dialogue between traditional Christian and modern human science resources.

While paying attention to movement *from* the discontinuity of one's solitary story of conversion *to* the continuity of a universal story of conversion in the community, this book primarily uses the case of St. Augustine and, additionally, the cases of other persons' conversion experiences (e.g., the conversion of Alypius) from the *Confessions* in order to explore the process of religious change. As such, this study encourages us to understand the transformation of a person in the context of the Christian community ("one's journey from unbelief to faith"). In that sense, it contributes by attempting to universalize (or generalize) Augustine's story of conversion in the religious group in light of a movement from the personal to the universal narrative of transformation.

This study did not attempt to use other various conversion stories within the context of different cultures and different times in order to achieve a richer and more appropriate perception of the complex phenomenon of religious change as well as to universalize effectively the story of conversion. For this reason, I hope that future researchers will do more to compare the differences and similarities of a variety of conversion experiences in various human conditions (e.g., the conversion stories of the early Egyptian monk [e.g., Antony] and the modern American monk [e.g., Thomas Merton], or the conversion narratives of the Christian Platonist in the West and the Christian Confucianist in the East). Moreover, there is a need for continued examination of the conversion process of entire religious groups as well as the conversion process of individuals in other religious or non-religious environments.

Appendix
The Implications of the Role of Augustine's Unnamed Woman in His Conversion

WHILE PAYING ATTENTION TO the implications of the vow of Augustine's unnamed woman in the process of his transformation, Asiedu repudiates a dualistic view of two women—Augustine's unnamed woman and his mother, Monica—which emphasizes the link between Augustine's dismissal of the concubine and his "surrender to Monica": 1) Augustine's unnamed woman was a pagan, at which point she had continuously interrupted Augustine to become a Christian; in contrast, 2) Augustine's mother was a Christian, at which point she had discharged this unnamed woman in Milan in order to help his son, to be a Christian. This means that Asiedu rejects the description of two women in Augustine's lifetime from a point of view of "juxtaposition" and contradiction. While acknowledging the role of Monica in Augustine's conversion to Christianity, Asiedu emphasizes the role of the mother of Adeodatus in his transformation.[1]

In this book, I basically follow Asiedu's view of two important women in Augustine's conversion and his life. As such, I agree with view on the positive role of Monica in Augustine's transformation.[2] In that sense, this study attempts to articulate how the Christian mother Monica had deeply affected his son's conversion to Christianity in 386. However, like Asiedu, I am unable to agree with the above dualistic view—Monica was a Christian and Augustine's concubine was a pagan

---

1. Asiedu, "Example of a Woman," 295–306.
2. See Burrell, "Reading the *Confessions*," 340–42; Elledge, "Augustine," 76–86; Fenn, "Magic," 81.

Appendix

because this juxtaposed and contradictory view on two women might portray Augustine's unnamed woman as a symbol of evil and might depict Monica as a symbol of good. This implies that this dualistic view might have (too negatively) described Augustine's unnamed woman as a serious obstacle to Augustine of becoming Christian, at which point Augustine (who was a religious victim for a long time) made a proper decision to dismiss his woman in order to return to his mother's true religion, Christianity. As such, I suggest paying attention to Garry Wills' statement that the adolescent and young Augustine (who was a Manichee) had interrupted the Christian life of his unlawful wife. Wills writes, "Una was a Catholic. . . . [Augustine's] treatment of Una would justify the self-condemning language Augustine uses. He was not merely persuading Una to live with him, but to make a break with her church (and, no doubt, her Catholic parents). Augustine would later reproach himself bitterly for trying to persuade a dear friend to give up Catholicism."[3] Although Wills' argument could be controversial, I am easily unable to reject his view that the young Augustine might have persuaded his unlawful wife in order to let her turn away from the traditional Christian faith and later the mature Christian Augustine might regret his behavior. In order to make a richer and more accurate evaluation of Wills' statement, we need to recognize that the young Augustine (who was a Manichee and an able scholar of rhetoric) had continuously attempted to convert his Christian friends, including his unnamed friend, to Manichaeism—"I had turned him away from the true [Christian] faith" (*conf.* 4.4.7; see 4.4.8–9), although Monica was angry at Augustine for his anti-Christian behaviors—"For my mother, your faithful servant, wept for me before you more than mothers weep when lamenting their dead children" (3.11.19).[4]

In consideration of Wills' view on the Manichee Augustine's anti-Christian position against his unnamed woman, I also suggest reminding that after the dismissal of his concubine, Augustine had another concubine (6.15.25); at the same time, Augustine had waited for his lawful marriage with a young aristocratic heiress. As such, I raise some questions as follows: "Who was a Christian? Augustine's another concubine or his young fiancée?"; "What was the real cause of Augustine's dismissal of his first concubine?"; "Was Augustine's

3. Wills, *Saint Augustine*, 16–17.
4. See Bourke, *Augustine's Quest*, 23–24.

first concubine (who was Adeodatus' mother) really an obstacle to the process of becoming a Christian?"; "Who was actually the victim at the time of dismissal? Augustine or Adeodatus' mother?" Now we have no accurate evidence that Augustine's second concubine and his young noble fiancée were Christians, although Starnes tends to depict Augustine's young fiancée as a Christian.[5] We need to look at Augustine's own depiction that many high-class people of the late Empire were pagans rather than Christians (8.2.3). Following above questions, I cast a doubt on the view that Augustine's first woman was a just pagan, as well as view that Augustine was a victim. We need to pay attention that Augustine dismissed, primarily and explicitly, Adeodatus' mother because she was *not* an impediment to Christianity *but* an impediment to his lawful marriage for his worldly fame and money—"she was a *hindrance* to my [socially acceptable] marriage" (6.15.25, italics added). As such, Adeodatus mother could be a "victim of [Augustine's] pursuit of a more advantage marriage"[6] and "an obscure victim of the . . . principles [of the concubinage of the Christian Church] and great snobbery of the Milanese."[7]

Honestly, I (who have lived with my wife for fifteen years and who have two children) have experienced pain and difficulty for understanding the theme of Augustine's discharge of his "unlawful" wife, although unlawful wives were normally dismissed in the late Roman world—"Neither Augustine nor Monica was snobbishly cold or cruel in the dismissal of his concubine. Because of her inferior social station, she simply could not hope to marry him. At that time . . . women did not expect, let alone campaign for, equality of rights with respect to marriage. Once Augustine decided upon a suitable marriage, he was compelled to separate from his beloved concubine."[8] I suggest looking at Eric Plumer's argument as follows: "Attempts have been made to cast Augustine's dismissal of her in a less offensive light, noting that common-low wives were normally dismissed in Roman society in order that socially acceptable marriages could be entered into. But

5. Starnes, *Augustine's Conversion*, 159, 166.
6. Miles, *Desire*, 27.
7. Brown, *Augustine*, 52; see Hippolytus, *apost. const.* 16.23; Leo I, *ep.* 167.
8. Quinn, *Companion*, 326; see E. A. Clark, "Asceticism," 68; O'Meara, *Young Augustine*, 123–24.

Appendix

while such arguments may be valid, they have left most modern readers dissatisfied."[9]

I am sorry to hear the silent cry of "a helpless, unnamed woman" who belonged to the low-class in the Roman world and who lived in the social and cultural milieu of *concubinage* of the late Roman Empire.[10] My view is that the theme of Augustine's dismissal of his unmarried wife involved a sad yet precious (love) story between the young Augustine and his lover. In this sense, the young Augustine's woman was not merely a concubine but a lover, although he began to live with her in order to satisfy his sexual desires. Basically, I agree with some scholars' view on Augustine's unnamed woman that she was a Christian.[11] As noted earlier, there was a far-reaching movement of Romanization in the Empire of Augustine's time; as such, Christianity became the official religion of the Roman world. This means that there was a strong process of Christianization in North African society. In this official movement of Christianization, Augustine's woman might have become a Christian. In particular, we need to pay attention to Augustine's own description about his separation with her as follows: "She had returned to Africa vowing that she would never go with another man. . . . I was unhappy, incapable of following a woman's example of [continence]" (*conf.* 6.15.25). This depiction of Augustine gives us a hint or an insight that his woman was not simply a pagan, but a Christian. Moreover, it leads us to recognize that at the time of the painful separation, Augustine's unlawful wife made a decision to enter into the life of celibacy and asceticism based on the movement of Christian monasticism. If Augustine's woman had been more influenced by the African temperament of sensual pleasure than the (Christian) monastic movement, she might have preferred to enter into the life of licentiousness and materialism than the life of continence.

Here I am also sorry to look at the deep silence of Augustine about her name (which was profoundly rooted in his own deep existential abyss). However, I suggest that the unnamed woman's life of continence might have influenced Augustine's spiritual transformation. That is,

9. Plumer, "Book Six," 105.

10. Asiedu, "Example of a Woman," 295–306; Plumer, "Book Six," 104–5; Vaught, *Journey*, 152–53.

11. Brown, *Augustine*, 80; Finn, *Death to Rebirth*, 216; Wills, *Saint Augustine*, 16–18, 41–42.

The Implications of the Role of Augustine's Unnamed Woman

her life of continence had challenged the young rhetorician Augustine to look at his own deep division of the mind as well as to reconstruct the purpose and meaning of his life (6.16.26). Indeed, after his conversion to Christianity, like his unnamed lover, the newly converted Augustine decided to engage in the Christian life of asceticism and celibacy, and dedicated himself in the service of God and others for the rest of his life. Later Augustine (who was a mature bishop) had urged the newly baptized not to imitate those who had lived in concubinage (*s.* 221.4.4). Here Augustine was strict for the married who had taken a concubine—"That's why I've got this to say to you, my brothers, my sons, those of you that have wives, don't go looking for anything else; those of you who haven't, and wish to marry, keep yourselves chaste for them, just as you want them to come chaste to you" (*s.* 224.3).[12] In the newly transformed context of Augustine's life of the service of God and others as well as his woman's life of continence, the story of the young Augustine and his woman has challenged us to join a new Christian living or spiritual marriage in Christian faith in Christ (see *conf.* 8.11.25–27; Possidius, *v. Aug.* 2). As such, I would like to conclude that now the story of Augustine and his unlawful wife could be our own story for the life of Christian pilgrimage across cultures and times in light of interaction of joy in encounter, pain in separation, and silence in longing/remembering.

---

12. See Quinn, *Companion*, 336.

Bibliography

Abraham, William J. "The Epistemology of Conversion: Is There Something New?" In *Conversion in the Wesleyan Tradition*, edited by Kenneth J. Collins and John H. Tyson, 175–91. Nashville: Abingdon, 2001.

Aguilar, Mario I. "African Conversion from a World Religion: Religious Diversification by the Waso Boorana in Kenya." *Africa* 65 (1995) 525–44.

Allison, Joel. "Recent Empirical Studies in Religious Conversion Experiences." *Pastoral Psychology* 17 (1966) 21–34.

———. "Religious Conversion: Regression and Progression in an Adolescent Experience." *Journal for the Scientific Study of Religion* 8 (1969) 23–38.

Ammerman, Nancy Tatom. *Bible Believers: Fundamentalists in the Modern World*. New Brunswick, NJ: Rutgers University Press, 1987.

———. "Religious Identities and Religious Institutions." In *Handbook of the Sociology of Religion*, edited by Michele Dillon, 207–24. Cambridge: Cambridge University Press, 2003.

———. "Telling Congregational Stories." *Review of Religious Research* 35 (1994) 289–301.

Asiedu, F. B. A. "Following the Example of a Woman: Augustine's Conversion to Christianity in 386." *Vigiliae Christiange* 57 (2003) 276–306.

Augustine. *Against Julian, an Unfinished Book*. In *The Works of Saint Augustine: A Translation for the 21st Century*. pt. I: vol. 25, edited by John E. Rotelle. New York: New City Press, 1999. [Cited hereafter as *WSA*]

———. *Against the Epistle of Manichaeus Called Fundamental*. In *A Select Library of the Nicene and Post-Nicene Fathers of the Christian Church*, vol. 4, edited by Philip Schaff, 126–50. Grand Rapids: Eerdmans, 1956. [Cited hereafter as *NPNF*]

———. *City of God*. Translated by Henry Bettenson. London: Penguin, 1984.

———. *Commentary on the Letter to the Galatians*. In *WSA* pt. I: vol. 17 (1990).

———. *Confessions*. Translated by Henry Chadwick. New York: Oxford University Press, 1991.

———. *Divine Providence and the Problem of Evil (On Order)*. In *The Fathers of the Church*, vol. 1, edited by Ludwig Schopp, 227–332. New York: Cima, 1948. [Cited hereafter as *FC*]

———. *The Enchiridion (On Faith, Hope, and Love)*. In *NPNF* vol. 3 (1980) 229–76.

———. *Expositions of the Psalms* (33–50). In *WSA* pt. III: vol. 16 (2000).

———. *Expositions of the Psalms* (99–120). In *WSA* pt. III: vol. 19 (2003).

———. *Expositions of the Psalms* (121–150). In *WSA* pt. III: vol. 20 (2004).

Bibliography

———. *Homilies on the First Epistle of John*. In *NPNF* vol. 7 (1956) 453–529.
———. *Homilies on the Gospel of John*. In *NPNF* vol. 7 (1956) 1–452.
———. *Letters of St. Augustine*. In *NPNF* vol. 1 (1956) 210–593.
———. *The Literal Meaning of Genesis*. In *Ancient Christian Writers: The Worksof Fathers in Translation*, vols. 41–42, edited by W. J. Burghardt and Thomas Comeford. Lawler. New York: Newman, 1982. [Cited hereafter as *ACW*]
———. *Miscellany of Eighty-Three Questions*. In *WSA* pt. I: vol. 12 (2008) 13–157.
———. *Miscellany of Questions in Response to Simplician*. In *WSA* pt. I: vol. 12 (2008) 159–231.
———. *On Baptism, Against the Donatists*. In *NPNF* vol. 4 (1956) 407–514.
———. *On Christian Doctrine*. In *NPNF* vol. 2 (1956) 519–34.
———. *On Faith and Works*. In *ACW* vol. 48 (1988).
———. *On Grace and Free Will*. In *NPNF* vol. 5 (1971) 433–65.
———. *On Nature and Grace*. In *NPNF* vol. 5 (1971) 115–51.
———. *On Rebuke and Grace*. In *NPNF* vol. 5 (1971) 467–91.
———. *On the Grace of Christ and Original Sin*. In *NPNF* vol. 5 (1971) 213–55.
———. *On the Greatness of the Soul*. In *FC* vol. 2 (1947).
———. *On the Happy Life*. In *FC* vol. 1 (1948) 27–84.
———. *On the Holy Trinity*. In *NPNF* vol. 3 (1980) 1–228.
———. *On the Merits and Remission of Sins, and on the Baptism of Infants*. In *NPNF* vol. 5 (1971) 11–78.
———. *On the Predestination of the Saints*. In *NPNF* vol. 5 (1971) 493–519.
———. *On the Soul and Its Origin*. In *NPNF* vol. 5 (1971) 313–71.
———. *On the Two Soul, Against the Manichaeans*. In *NPNF* vol. 4 (1956) 91–107.
———. *Reply to Faustus the Machichaean*. In *NPNF* vol. 4 (1956) 151–345.
———. *The Retractions*. In *FC* vol. 60 (1968).
———. *The Rule of Saint Augustine*. Translated by Raymond Canning. New York: Image, 1986.
———. *Sermons*. In *WSA* pt. III: vols. 2[20–50], 3[51–94], 4[94A–147A], 5[148–83], 6[184–229Z], 7[230–72B], 10[341–400] (1990).
———. *Soliloquies: Augustine's Inner Dialogue*. Translated by Kim Paffenroth. Hyde Park, NY: New City Press, 2000.
———. *Teaching Christianity*. In *WSA* pt. I: vol. 11 (1990).
———. *To Cresconius, a Donatist Grammarian*. In *WSA* pt. I: vol. 22 (1990).
———. *To the Letters of Petilian, the Donatist*. In *NPNF* vol. 4 (1956) 515–628.
Austin-Broos, Diane. "The Anthropology of Conversion: An Introduction." In *The Anthropology of Religious Conversion*, edited by Andrew Buckser and Stephen D. Glazier, 1–12. New York: Rowman & Littlefield, 2003.
Aviad, Janet. *Return to Judaism: Religious Renewal in Israel*. Chicago: University of Chicago Press, 1983.
Ayres, Lewis, and Michel R. Barnes. "God." In *Augustine through the Ages: An Encyclopedia*, edited by Allan D. Fitzgerald, 384–90. Grand Rapids: Eerdmans, 1999.
Babcock, William S. "Augustine and the Spirituality of Desire." *Augustinian Studies* 25 (1994) 179–99.
———. "Cupiditas and Caritas: The Early Augustine on Love and Human Fulfillment." In *Augustine Today*, edited by Richard John Neuhaus, 1–34. Grand Rapids: Eerdmans, 1993.

Bibliography

Bainbridge, William Sims. "The Sociology of Conversion." In *Handbook of Religious Conversion*, edited by H. Newton Malony and Samuel Southard, 178–91. Birmingham, AL: Religious Education, 1992.

Bakan, David. "Some Thoughts on Reading Augustine's *Confessions*." *Journal for the Scientific Study of Religion* 5 (1965) 149–52.

Barclay, William. *Turning to God: A Study of Conversion in the Book of Acts and Today*. Grand Rapids: Baker, 1975.

Barth, Karl. "The Awakening to Conversion." In *Conversion: Perspectives on Personal and Social Transformation*, edited by Walter E. Conn, 35–49. New York: Alba, 1978.

Berger, Peter, and Thomas Luckmann. *The Social Construction of Reality: A Treatise in the Sociology of Knowledge*. New York: Penguin, 1991.

Bonner, Gerald. *St. Augustine of Hippo: Life and Controversies*. 3rd ed. Norwich: Canterbury, 2002.

———. "Starting with Oneself; Spiritual Confessions—Saint Augustine's *Confessions*." *The Expository Times* 101 (1990) 163–67.

Bourke, Vernon J. *Augustine's Quest of Wisdom: Life and Philosophy of the Bishop of Hippo*. Milwaukee, WI: Bruce, 1945.

———. "Socio-Religious Issues in Augustine's Day." *Augustinian Studies* 4 (1973) 205–12.

Bouyer, Louis. "The Origins of Monasticism." "The Latin Fathers: From St. Ambrose and St. Jerome to St. Augustine." "Latin Monasticism from St. Augustine to St. Gregory." In *The Spirituality of the New Testament and the Fathers*, 303–30; 455–94; 495–522. New York: Seabury, 1963.

Brown, Peter. *Augustine of Hippo: A Biography*. Berkeley: University of California Press, 2000.

———. *Authority and the Sacred: Aspects of the Christianization of the Roman World*. Cambridge: Cambridge University Press, 1995.

Browning, Don S. *A Fundamental Practical Theology: Descriptive and Strategic Proposals*. Minneapolis: Fortress, 1991.

———. "The Psychoanalytic Interpretation of St. Augustine's *Confessions*: An Assessment and New Probe." In *Psychoanalysis and Religion*, edited by Joseph H. Smith and Susan A. Handelman, 136–59. Baltimore: The Johns Hopkins University Press, 1990.

Buckser, Andrew. "Social Conversion and Group Definition in Jewish Copenhagen." In *The Anthropology of Religious Conversion*, edited by Andrew Buckser and Stephen D. Glazier, 69–84. New York: Rowman & Littlefield, 2003.

Burns, J. Patout. "Grace." In *Augustine through the Ages: An Encyclopedia*, edited by Allan D. Fitzgerald, 391–98. Grand Rapids: Eerdmans, 1999.

———. "Providence as Divine Grace in St. Augustine." In *Augustinus afer*, edited by Pierre-Yves Fux et al., 211–18. Fribourg, Suisse: Éditions Universitaires, 2003.

Burrell, David. "Reading the *Confessions* of Augustine: An Exercise in Theological Understanding." *The Journal of Religion* 50 (1970) 327–51.

Byasse, Jason. *Reading Augustine: A Guide to the Confessions*. Eugene, OR: Cascade, 2006.

Callen, Barry L. "A Mutuality Model of Conversion." In *Conversion in the Wesleyan Tradition*, edited by Kenneth J. Collins and John H. Tyson, 145–59. Nashville: Abingdon, 2001.

Bibliography

Campbell, Ted A. "Conversion and Baptism in Wesleyan Spirituality." In *Conversion in the Wesleyan Tradition*, edited by Kenneth J. Collins and John H. Tyson, 160–74. Nashville: Abingdon, 2001.

Canning, Raymond. "Augustine on the Identity of the Neighbour and the Meaning of True Love for Him 'as Ourselves' (Matt. 22.39) and 'as Christ Has Loved Us' (Jn. 13.34)." *Augustiniana* 36 (1986) 161–239.

———. "Love of Neighbour in St. Augustine." *Augustiniana* 33 (1983) 5–57.

———. "'Love Your Neighbour as Yourself' (Matt. 22.39): Saint Augustine on the Lineaments of the Self to Be Loved." *Augustiniana* 34 (1984) 145–97.

———. "The Unity of Love for God and Neighbour." *Augustiniana* 37 (1987) 38–121.

———. *The Unity of Love for God and Neighbour in St. Augustine*. Heverlee, Belgium: Augustinian Historical Institute, 1993.

———. "Uti/frui." In *Augustine through the Ages: An Encyclopedia*, edited by Allan D. Fitzgerald, 859–61. Grand Rapids: Eerdmans, 1999.

Cao, Nanlai. "The Church as a Surrogate Family for Working Class Immigrant Chinese Youth: An Ethnography of Segmented Assimilation." *Sociology of Religion* 66 (2005) 183–200.

Capps, Donald. "Augustine as Narcissist: Comments on Paul Rigby's 'Paul Ricoeur, Freudianism, and Augustine's *Confessions*.'" *Journal of the American Academy of Religion* 53 (1985) 115–27.

———. "Augustine: The Vicious Cycle of Child Abuse." In *The Destructive Power of Religion*, edited by J. Harold Ellens, 127–49. Westport, CT: Praeger, 2004.

———. "Augustine's *Confessions*: Self-Reproach and the Melancholy Self." *Pastoral Psychology* 55 (2007) 571–91.

———. "Augustine's *Confessions*: The Scourge of Shame and the Silencing of Adeodatus." In *The Hunger of the Heart: Reflections on the Confessions of Augustine*, edited by Donald Capps and James E. Dittes, 69–92. West Lafayette, IN: Society for the Scientific Study of Religion, 1990.

———. "Augustine's *Confessions*: The Story of a Divided Self and the Process of Its Unification." *Pastoral Psychology* 55 (2007) 551–69.

———. *The Depleted Self: Sin in a Narcissistic Age*. Minneapolis: Fortress, 1993.

———. "Parabolic Events in Augustine's Autobiography." *Theology and Today* 40 (1983) 260–72.

Cary, Philip. *Augustine's Invention of the Inner Self: The Legacy of a Christian Platonist*. New York: Oxford University Press, 2000.

———. "Book Seven: Inner Vision as the Goal of Augustine's Life." In *A Reader's Companion to Augustine's Confessions*, edited by Kim Paffenroth and Robert P. Kennedy, 107–26. Louisville: Westminster John Knox, 2003.

———. "Interiority." In *Augustine through the Ages: An Encyclopedia*, edited by Allan D. Fitzgerald, 454–56. Grand Rapids: Eerdmans, 1999.

Castro, Emilio. "Conversion and Social Transformation." In *Christian Social Ethics in a Changing World*, edited by John C. Bennett, 348–66. New York: Association, 1966.

Chadwick, Henry. *Augustine*. New York: Oxford University Press, 1986.

———. "Introduction and Notes." In *Confessions*, by Augustine, translated by Henry Chadwick. New York: Oxford University Press, 1991.

Christensen, Carl W. "Religious Conversion in Adolescence." *Pastoral Psychology* 16 (1965) 17–28.

Clair, Michael. *Human Relationships and the Experience of God: Object Relations and Religion*. New York: Paulist, 1994.
Clark, Elizabeth A. "Asceticism." In *Augustine through the Ages: An Encyclopedia*, edited by Allan D. Fitzgerald, 67–71. Grand Rapids: Eerdmans, 1999.
Clark, Gillian. *Christianity and Roman Society*. New York: Cambridge University Press, 2004.
Clark, Mary T. *Augustine*. New York: Continuum, 2000.
———. "Augustine: The Eye of the Heart." In *Spiritualities of the Heart: Approaches to Personal Wholeness in Christian Tradition*, edited by Annice Callahan, 23–32. New York: Paulist, 1990.
———. "Spirituality." In *Augustine through the Ages: An Encyclopedia*, edited by Allan D. Fitzgerald, 813–15. Grand Rapids: Eerdmans, 1999.
Cleaver, Eldridge. *Soul on Fire*. Waco, TX: Word, 1978.
Clement, Fabrice. "The Pleasure of Believing: Toward a Naturalistic Explanation of Religious Conversions." *Journal of Cognition and Culture* 3 (2003) 69–89.
Collinge, William J. "Developments in Augustine's Theology of Christian Community Life After A.C. 395." *Augustinian Studies* 16 (1985) 49–64.
Conn, Walter. *Christian Conversion: A Developmental Interpretation of Autonomy and Surrender*. New York: Paulist, 1986.
———. "Conversion." In *The New Westminster Dictionary of Christian Spirituality*, edited by Philip Sheldrake, 214–15. Louisville: Westminster John Knox, 2005.
Corrigan, Kevin. "Love of God, Love of Self, and Love of Neighbor: Augustine's Critical Dialogue with Platonism." *Augustinian Studies* 34 (2003) 97–106.
Cushman, Robert E. "Faith and Reason in the Thought of St. Augustine." *Church History* 19 (1950) 271–94.
Daly, Lawrence J. "Psychohistory and St. Augustine's Conversion Process." *Augustiniana* 28 (1978) 231–54.
———. "St. Augustine's *Confessions* and Erick Erikson's *Young Man Luther*: Conversion as 'Identity Crisis.'" *Augustiniana* 31 (1981) 183–96.
DeSimone, Russell J. "Augustine: On Being a Christian." *Augustinian Studies* 19 (1988) 1–35.
Dittes, James E. "Continuities between the Life and Thought of Augustine." *Journal for the Scientific Study of Religion* 5 (1965) 130–40.
Dixon, Sandra Lee. *Augustine: The Scattered and Gathered Self*. St. Louis, MO: Chalice, 1999.
Dodds, E. R. "Augustine's *Confessions*: A Study of Spiritual Maladjustment." In *The Hunger of the Heart: Reflections on the Confessions of Augustine*, edited by Donald Capps and James E. Dittes, 43–54. West Lafayette, IN: Society for the Scientific Study of Religion, 1990.
Dubay, Thomas. *Deep Conversion/Deep Prayer*. San Francisco: Ignatius, 2006.
Elledge, W. Paul. "Embracing Augustine: Reach, Restraint, and Romantic Resolution in the *Confessions*." *Journal for the Scientific Study of Religion* 27 (1988) 72–89.
Epstein, Seymour. "The Implications of Cognitive-Experiential Self-Theory for Research in Social Psychology and Personality." *Journal for the Theory of Social Behavior* 15 (1985) 283–310.
———. "Integration of the Cognitive and the Psychodynamic Unconscious." *American Psychologist* 49 (1994) 709–24.
Erikson, Erik H. *Childhood and Society*. New York: Norton, 1963.

Bibliography

Fenn, Richard. "Magic in Language and Ritual: Notes on Augustine's *Confessions*." *Journal for the Scientific Study of Religion* 25 (1986) 77–91.

Ferrari, Leo C. "Book Eight: Science and the Fictional Conversion Scene." In *A Reader's Companion to Augustine's Confessions*, edited by Kim Paffenroth and Robert P. Kennedy, 127–36. Louisville: Westminster John Knox, 2003.

———. "The Boyhood Beatings of Augustine." *Augustinian Studies* 5 (1974) 1–14.

———. *The Conversion of Saint Augustine*. Villanova, PA: Villanova University Press, 1984.

———. "Paul at the Conversion of Augustine (*Conf.* VIII, 12, 29–30)." *Augustinian Studies* 11 (1980) 5–20.

Finn, Thomas M. *From Death to Rebirth: Ritual and Conversion in Antiquity*. New York: Paulist, 1997.

———. "It Happened One Saturday Night: Ritual and Conversion in Augustine's North Africa." *Journal of the American Academy of Religion* 58 (1990) 589–616.

Fisher, Humphrey J. "Conversion Reconsidered: Some Historical Aspects of Religious Conversion in Black Africa." *Africa* 43 (1973) 27–40.

———. "The Juggernaut's Apologia: Conversion to Islam in Black Africa." *Africa* 55 (1985) 153–73.

Fitzgerald, Allan D. "Adeodatus." "Alypius." In *Augustine through the Ages: An Encyclopedia*, edited by Allan D. Fitzgerald, 7, 16–17. Grand Rapids: Eerdmans, 1999.

Fortin, Ernest L. "City of God." In *Augustine through the Ages: An Encyclopedia*, edited by Allan D. Fitzgerald, 196–202. Grand Rapids: Eerdmans, 1999.

Fowler, James W. *Becoming Adult, Becoming Christian: Adult Development & Christian Faith*. San Francisco: Jossey-Bass, 2000.

———. *Stages of Faith: The Psychology of Human Development and the Quest for Meaning*. New York: Harper San Francisco, 1981.

Fredriksen, Paula. "Augustine and His Analyst: The Possibility of a Psychohistory." *Soundings* 61 (1978) 206–27.

———. "Christians in the Roman Empire in the First Three Centuries CE." In *A Companion to the Roman Empire*, edited by David S. Potter, 587–606. Malden, MA: Blackwell, 2006.

———. "Paul and Augustine: Conversion Narratives, Orthodox Traditions, and the Retrospective Self." *Journal of Theological Studies* 37 (1986) 3–34.

Freud, Sigmund. *Civilization and Its Discontents*. Edited and Translated by James Strachey. 1930. Reprint. New York: Norton, 1989.

———. *The Ego and the Id*. 1923. Reprint. New York: Norton, 1989.

———. *The Future of an Illusion*. 1927. Reprint. New York: Norton, 1989.

———. *Leonardo da Vinci and a Memory of His Childhood*. 1910. Reprint. New York: Norton, 1989.

———. "Mourning and Melancholia." In *The Standard Edition of the Complete Psychological Works of Sigmund Freud*, edited and translated by James Strachey, 14:243–58. 1917. Reprint. London: Hogarth, 1957.

———. *New Introductory Lectures on Psycho-Analysis*. 1933. Reprint. New York: Norton, 1989.

———. "Obsessive Acts and Religious Practice." In *The Standard Edition of the Complete Psychological Works of Sigmund Freud*, edited and translated by James Strachey, 9:117–27. 1907. Reprint. London: Hogarth, 1953.

———. *The Psychopathology of Everyday Life*. 1960. Reprint. New York: Norton, 1989.

———. "A Religious Experience." In *Collected Papers*, edited by James Strachey, 5:243–46. 1928. Reprint. London: Hogarth, 1957.

———. *Totem and Taboo: Some Points of Agreement between the Mental Lives of Savages and Neurotics*. 1913. Reprint. New York: Norton, 1989.

Froehlich, Karlfried. "'Take Up and Read': Basics of Augustine's Biblical Interpretation." *Interpretation* 3 (2004) 5–16.

Gaiser, Frederick J. "A Biblical Theology of Conversion." In *Handbook of Religious Conversion*, edited by H. Newton Malony and Samuel Southard, 93–107. Birmingham, AL: Religious Education, 1992.

Gaventa, Beverly Roberts. "Conversion in the Bible." In *Handbook of Religious Conversion*, edited by H. Newton Malony and Samuel Southard, 41–54. Birmingham, AL: Religious Education, 1992.

———. *From Darkness to Light: Aspects of Conversion in the New Testament*. Philadelphia: Fortress, 1986.

Gay, Volney. "Augustine: The Reader as Selfobject." *Journal for the Scientific Study of Religion* 25 (1986) 64–76.

Geertz, Clifford. "Religion as a Cultural System." "'Internal Conversion' in Contemporary Bali." In *The Interpretation of Cultures: Selected Essays*, 87–125, 170–89. New York: Basic, 1973.

Gelpi, Donald L. *Charism and Sacrament: A Theology of Christian Conversion*. New York: Paulist, 1976.

———. *The Conversion Experience: A Reflective Process for RCIA Participants and Others*. New York: Paulist, 1998.

Georgiou, Steve T. *The Last Transfiguration: The Quest for Spirituality Illumination in the Life and Times of Saint Augustine*. Grand Rapids: Phanes, 1994.

Gibbs, Eddie. "Conversion in Evangelistic Practice." In *Handbook of Religious Conversion*, edited by H. Newton Malony and Samuel Southard, 278–94. Birmingham, AL: Religious Education, 1992.

Gillespie, V. Bailey. *The Dynamics of Religious Conversion: Identity and Transformation*. Birmingham, AL: Religious Education, 1991.

Gilson, Etienne. *The Christian Philosophy of St. Augustine*. New York: Random, 1960.

Glock, Charles Y., and Rodney Stark. *Religion and Society in Tension*. Chicago: McNally, 1965.

Gonzáez, Justo L. *A History of Christian Thought: From Augustine to the Eve of the Reformation*. Vol. 2. Nashville: Abingdon, 1987.

Gopnik, Alison. "Explanations as Orgasms." *Minds and Machines* 8 (1998) 101–18.

Gorman, Michael M. "Aurelius Augustinus: The Testimony of the Oldest Manuscripts of Saint Augustine's Works." *Journal of Theological Studies* 35 (1984) 475–80.

Greeley, Andrew M. "Religious Musical Chairs." In *In Gods We Trust: New Patterns of Religious Pluralism in America*, edited by Thomas Robbins and Dick Anthony, 101–26. New Brunswick, NJ: Transaction, 1981.

Greenberg, Jay R., and Stephen A. Mitchell. *Object Relations in Psychoanalytic Theory*. Cambridge, MA: Harvard University Press, 1983.

Greil, Arthur L., and David R. Rudy. "Conversion to the Worldview of Alcoholics Anonymous: A Refinement of Conversion Theory." *Qualitative Sociology* 6 (1983) 5–28.

Bibliography

Griffin, Emilie. *Turning: Reflections on the Experience of Conversion*. New York: Doubleday, 1980.
Guder, Darrell L. *The Continuing Conversion of the Church*. Grand Rapids: Eerdmans, 2000.
Guenther, Margaret. *Holy Listening: The Art of Spiritual Direction*. Boston: Cowley, 1992.
Gutierrez, Gustavo. "A Spirituality of Liberation." In *Conversion: Perspectives on Personal and Social Transformation*, edited by Walter E. Conn, 307–13. New York: Alba, 1978.
Haight, Roger. *The Experience and Language of Grace*. Mahwah, NJ: Paulist, 1979.
Hamilton, N. Gregory. *Self and Others: Object Relations Theory in Practice*. Northvale, NJ: Aronson, 1990.
Häring, Bernard. "The Characteristics of Conversion." In *Conversion: Perspectives on Personal and Social Transformation*, edited by Walter E. Conn, 213–23. New York: Alba, 1978.
Harmless, William. *Augustine and the Catechumenate*. Collegeville, MN: Liturgical, 1995.
———. "Baptism." In *Augustine through the Ages: An Encyclopedia*, edited by Allan D. Fitzgerald, 84–91. Grand Rapids: Eerdmans, 1999.
———. *Desert Christians: An Introduction to the Literature of Early Monasticism*. Oxford: Oxford University Press, 2004.
Harrison, Carol. *Augustine: Christian Truth and Fractured Humanity*. Oxford: Oxford University Press, 2000.
———. *Rethinking Augustine's Early Theology: An Argument for Continuity*. Oxford: Oxford University Press, 2006.
Hefner, Robert W. "World Building and the Rationality of Conversion." In *Conversion to Christianity: Historical and Anthropological Perspectives on a Great Transformation*, edited by Robert W. Hefner, 3–44. Berkeley: University of California Press, 1993.
Heirich, Max. "Change of Heart: A Test of Some Widely Held Theories about Religious Conversion." *American Journal of Sociology* 83 (1977) 653–80.
Heschel, Abraham J. *Who Is Man?* Stanford, CA: Standford University Press, 1965.
Hiebert, Paul G. "Conversion in Hinduism and Buddhism." In *Handbook of Religious Conversion*, edited by H. Newton Malony and Samuel Southard, 9–21. Birmingham, AL: Religious Education, 1992.
Hiltner, Seward. "Toward a Theology of Conversion in the Light of Psychology." *Pastoral Psychology* 17 (1966) 35–42.
Hindsley, Leonard P. "Monastic Conversion: The Case of Margaret Ebner." In *Varieties of Religious Conversion in the Middle Ages*, edited by James Muldoon, 31–46. Gainesville, FL: University Press of Florida, 1997.
Hippolytus. *Apostolic Constitutions*. In *The Treaties on the Apostolic Tradition of St Hippolytus of Rome*. Edited by Gregory Dix and Henry Chadwick, xxii–xxviii, 27–28. London: Alban, 1992.
Holt, Laura. "Original Sin." In *Augustine through the Ages: An Encyclopedia*, edited by Allan D. Fitzgerald, 607–15. Grand Rapids: Eerdmans, 1999.
Holtzen, Thomas L. "The Therapeutic Nature of Grace in St. Augustine's *De Gratia et Libero Arbitrio*." *Augustinian Studies* 31 (2000) 93–115.
Holy Bible. Rev. ed. Nashville: Nelson, 1989.

Bibliography

Horton, Paul C. *Solace: The Missing Dimension in Psychiatry.* Chicago: University of Chicago Press, 1981.
Horton, Robin. "African Conversion." *Africa* 41 (1971) 85–108.
———. "On the Rationality of Conversion (Pt. I & II)." *Africa* 45 (1975) 219–35, 373–99.
Hudson, Deal W. "The Catholic View of Conversion." In *Handbook of Religious Conversion*, edited by H. Newton Malony and Samuel Southard, 108–22. Birmingham, AL: Religious Education, 1992.
Iannaccone, Laurence R. "Why Strict Churches Are Strong?" *American Journal of Sociology* 99 (1994) 1180–211.
Innes, Robert. "Integrating the Self through the Desire of God." *Augustine Studies* 28 (1997) 67–109.
James, William. *The Varieties of Religious Experience.* 1902. Reprint. New York: Penguin, 1982.
Johnson, Cedric B., and H. Newton Malony. *Christian Conversion: Biblical and Psychological Perspectives.* Grand Rapids: Zondervan, 1982.
Jones, James W. *Contemporary Psychoanalysis & Religion: Transference and Transcendence.* New Haven: Yale University Press, 1991.
———. *Religion and Psychology in Transition: Psychoanalysis, Feminism, and Theology.* New Haven: Yale University Press, 1996.
Jonte-Pace, Diane. "Augustine on the Couch: Psychohistorical (Mis)readings of the *Confessions*." *Religion* 23 (1993) 71–83.
Kahn, Peter J., and A. L. Greene. "'Seeing Conversion Whole': Testing a Model of Religious Conversion." *Pastoral Psychology* 52 (2004) 233–58.
Kamaleson, Samuel T. "The Call to Personal Conversion to Jesus Christ Today." *The Ecumenical Review* 44 (1992) 442–52.
Kasdorf, Hans. *Christian Conversion in Context.* Scottsdale, PA: Herald, 1980.
Kelley, Dean M. *Why Conservative Churches Are Growing: A Study in Sociology of Religion with a New Preface for the ROSE Edition.* Macon, GA: Mercer University Press, 1995.
Kenney, John P. "Augustine's Inner Self." *Augustinian Studies* 33 (2002) 79–90.
Kevane, Eugene. "Christian Philosophy: The Intellectual Side of Augustine's Conversion." *Augustinian Studies* 17 (1986) 47–83.
Kilbourne, Brock K., and James T. Richardson. "The Communalization of Religious Experience in Contemporary Religious Groups." *Journal of Community Psychology* 14 (1986) 206–12.
———. "Paradigm Conflict, Types of Conversion, and Conversion Theories." *Sociological Analysis* 50 (1988) 1–21.
Kildahl, John P. "The Personalities of Sudden Religious Converts." *Pastoral Psychology* 16 (1965) 37–44.
Kligerman, Charles. "A Psychoanalytic Study of the *Confessions* of St. Augustine." In *The Hunger of the Heart: Reflections on the Confessions of Augustine*, edited by Donald Capps and James E. Dittes, 98–108. West Lafayette, IN: Society for the Scientific Study of Religion, 1990.
Knowles, David. *Christian Monasticism.* New York: McGraw-Hill, 1977.
Knuuttila, Simo. "Time and Creation in Augustine." In *The Cambridge Companion to Augustine*, edited by Eleonore Stump and Norman Kretzmann, 103–15. Cambridge: Cambridge University Press, 2001.

Bibliography

Kohut, Heinz. *How Does Analysis Cure?* Chicago: University of Chicago Press, 1984.

———. *The Restoration of the Self.* New York: International Universities Press, 1977.

Kohut, Heinz, and Ernest Wolf. "The Disorders of the Self and Their Treatment: An Outline." *International Journal of Psychoanalysis* 59 (1978) 413–25.

Kotze, Annemare. *Augustine's Confessions: Communicative Purpose and Audience.* Boston: Brill, 2004.

Kraft, Charles H. "Cultural Concomitants of Higi Conversion: Early Period." *Missiology* 4 (1976) 431–42.

Kreider, Alan. *The Change of Conversion and the Origin of Christendom.* 1999. Reprint. Eugene, OR: Wipf and Stock, 2007.

Kreidler, Mary Jane. "Conversion: Augustine's Theology of Ministry." *Review for Religious* 49 (1990) 509–22.

Lacan, Dom Marc-Francois. "Conversion and Grace in Old Testament." In *Conversion: Perspectives on Personal and Social Transformation*, edited by Walter E. Conn, 75–96. New York: Alba, 1978.

Lancel, Serge. *Saint Augustine.* Translated by Antonia Nevill. London: SCM, 2002.

Lawless, George. *Augustine of Hippo and His Monastic Rule.* Oxford: Clarendon, 1987.

———. "Rules, Monastic." In *Augustine through the Ages: An Encyclopedia*, edited by Allan D. Fitzgerald, 739–40. Grand Rapids: Eerdmans, 1999.

Lee, Roland R., and J. Colby Martin. *Psychotherapy after Kohut: A Textbook of Self Psychology*, Hillsdale, NJ: Analytic, 1991.

Leech, Kenneth. *Spirituality and Pastoral Care.* 1989. Reprint. Eugene, OR: Wipf and Stock, 2005.

Leo the Great. *Letters.* In *The Fathers of the Church: A New Translation*, vol. 34, edited by Roy Joseph Deferrrari, 1–312. Washington, DC: Catholic University of America Press, 1963.

Lichtenstein, Aharon. "On Conversion." *Tradition* 23 (1988) 1–18.

Lienhard, Joseph T. "Friendship, Friends." In *Augustine through the Ages: An Encyclopedia*, edited by Allan D. Fitzgerald, 372–73. Grand Rapids: Eerdmans, 1999.

Lofland, John, and Norman Skonovd. "Conversion Motifs." *Journal for the Scientific Study of Religion* 20 (1981) 373–85.

Lofland, John, and Rodney Stark. "Becoming a World-Saver: A Theory of Conversion to a Deviant Perspective." *American Sociological Review* 30 (1965) 862–75.

Lohfink, Gerhard. *Jesus and Community: The Social Dimension of Christian Faith.* Philadelphia: Fortress, 1984.

Lohse, Bernhard. *A Short History of Christian Doctrine: From the First Century to the Present.* Philadelphia: Fortress, 1985.

Lonergan, Bernard. "Theology in Its New Context." In *Conversion: Perspectives on Personal and Social Transformation*, edited by Walter E. Conn, 3–21. New York: Alba, 1978.

MacDonald, Scott. "The Divine Nature." In *Augustine's Confessions: Critical Essays*, edited by William E. Mann, 85–105. New York: Rowman & Littlefield, 2006.

MacMullen, Ramsay. *Christianizing the Roman Empire (A.D. 100–400).* New Haven: Yale University Press, 1984.

Mahoney, Annettee, and Kenneth I. Pargament. "Sacred Changes: Spiritual Conversion and Transformation." *Journal of Clinical Psychology* 60 (2004) 481–92.

Mallard, William. "The Incarnation in Augustine's Conversion." *Recherches Augustiniennes* 15 (1980) 80–98.
Mann, William E. "Augustine on Evil and Original Sin." In *Augustine's Confessions: Critical Essays*, edited by William E. Mann, 71–83. New York: Rowman & Littlefield, 2006.
Markham, Paul N. *Rewired: Exploring Religious Conversion*. Eugene, OR: Pickwick, 2007.
Markus, Robert A. *The End of Ancient Christianity*. New York: Cambridge University Press, 1990.
———. "Life, Culture, and Controversies of Augustine." In *Augustine through the Ages: An Encyclopedia*, edited by Allan D. Fitzgerald, 498–504. Grand Rapids: Eerdmans, 1999.
Marquardt, Manfred. "Christian Conversion: Connecting Our Lives with God." In *Rethinking Wesley's Theology for Contemporary Methodism*, edited by Randy L. Maddox, 99–111. Nashville: Kingswood, 1998.
Martin, Thomas F. "Augustinian Spirituality." In *The New Westminster Dictionary of Christian Spirituality*, edited by Philip Sheldrake, 136–38. Louisville: Westminster John Knox, 2005.
———. *Our Restless Heart: The Augustinian Tradition*. Maryknoll, NY: Orbis, 2003.
Matter, E. Ann. "Conversion(s) in the *Confessiones*." In *Collectanea Augustiniana—Augustine: Second Founder of the Faith*, edited by Joseph C. Schnaubelt and Frederick Van Fleteren, 21–28. New York: Lang, 1990.
McClanahan, John Howard. "The Psychology of the Self in the Writings of Augustine." ThD diss., Southern Baptist Theological Seminary, 1957.
McDargh, John. "Creating a New Research Paradigm for the Psychoanalytic Study of Religion: The Pioneering Work of Ana-Maria Rizzuto." In *Religion, Society, and Psychoanalysis: Readings in Contemporary Theory*, edited by Janet Liebman Jacobs and Donald Capps, 181–99. Boulder, CO: Westview, 1997.
———. *Psychoanalytic Object Relations Theory and the Study of Religion*. Lanham, MD: University Press of America, 1983.
McGinn, Bernard, and Patricia Ferris McGinn. *Early Christian Mystics: The Divine Vision of the Spiritual Masters*. New York: Crossroad, 2003.
McKim, Donald K. "The Mainline Protestant Understanding of Conversion." In *Handbook of Religious Conversion*, edited by H. Newton Malony and Samuel Southard, 123–36. Birmingham, AL: Religious Education, 1992.
———, editor. *Westminster Dictionary of Theological Terms*. Louisville: Westminster John Knox, 1996.
McKnight, Scot. *Turning to Jesus: The Sociology of Conversion in the Gospels*. Louisville: Westminster John Knox, 2002.
McLynn, Neil. "Ambrose." In *Augustine through the Ages: An Encyclopedia*, edited by Allan D. Fitzgerald, 17–19. Grand Rapids: Eerdmans, 1999.
McMahon, Robert. "Book Thirteen: The Creation of the Church at the Paradigm for the *Confessions*." In *A Reader's Companion to Augustine's Confessions*, edited by Kim Paffenroth and Robert P. Kennedy, 207–23. Louisville: Westminster John Knox, 2003.
———. *Understanding the Medieval Meditative Ascent: Augustine, Anselm, Boethius, & Dante*. Washington, DC: Catholic University of America Press, 2006.

Bibliography

McVann, Mark. "Conversion and Community: The Challenge of Being Human Humans." In *Conversion: Voices & Views*, edited by Frank P. Cervone et al., 64–80. Romeoville, IL: Christian Brothers Conference, 1988.

Meeks, Wayne A. *The Origins of Christian Morality: The First Two Centuries*. New Haven: Yale University Press, 1993.

Meissner, William W. *Psychoanalysis and Religious Experience*. New Haven: Yale University Press, 1984.

Mendez-Moratalla, Fernando. *The Paradigm of Conversion in Luke*. London: T. & T. Clark, 2004.

Miles, Margaret R. *Desire and Delight: A New Reading of Augustine's Confessions*. New York: Crossroad, 1992.

———. "Infancy, Parenting, and Nourishment in Augustine's *Confessions*." *The Journal of the American Academy of Religion* 50 (1982) 349–64.

Monagle, John F. "Friendship in St. Augustine's Biography: Classical Notion of Friendship." *Augustinian Studies* 2 (1971) 81–92.

Montgomery, Robert L. "The Spread of Religions and Macrosocial Relations." *Sociological Analysis* 52 (1991) 37–53.

Morris, George E. *The Mystery and Meaning of Christian Conversion*. Nashville: Discipleship Resources, 1981.

Newton, John Thomas. "The Importance of Augustine's Use of the Neoplatonic Doctrine of Hypostatic Union for the Development of Christology." *Augustinian Studies* 2 (1971) 1–16.

Ng, Kwai Hang. "Seeking the Christian Tutelage: Agency and Culture in Chinese Immigrants' Conversion to Christianity." *Sociology of Religion* 63 (2002) 195–214.

Niebuhr, H. Richard. *Christ and Culture*. San Francisco: Harper San Francisco, 2001.

Niebuhr, Reinhold. "Graces as Power in, and as Mercy towards, Man." In *Conversion: Perspectives on Personal and Social Transformation*, edited by Walter E. Conn, 27–34. New York: Alba, 1978.

Niño, Andrés G. "Restoration of the Self: A Therapeutic Paradigm from Augustine's *Confessions*." *Psychotherapy* 27 (1990) 8–18.

Nissiotis, Nikos A. "Conversion and the Church." *The Ecumenical Review* 19 (1967) 261–70.

Nock, Arthur Darby. *Conversion: The Old and New in Religion from Alexander the Great to Augustine of Hippo*. Baltimore: The Johns Hopkins University Press, 1933.

Norris, Rebecca Sachs. "Converting to What? Embodied Culture and the Adoption of New Beliefs." In *The Anthropology of Religious Conversion*, edited by Andrew Buckser and Stephen D. Glazier, 171–81. New York: Rowman & Littlefield, 2003.

O'Brien, William J. "An Approach to Teaching Augustine's *Confessions*." *Horizons* 5 (1978) 47–62.

O'Connell, Robert J. "Sexuality in St. Augustine." In *Augustine Today*, edited by Richard John Neuhaus, 60–87. Grand Rapids: Eerdmans, 1993.

———. *St. Augustine's Confessions: The Odyssey of Soul*. Cambridge, MA: Belknap, 1969.

Oden, Thomas C. *The Transforming Power of Grace*. Nashville: Abingdon, 1993.

O'Donnell, James J. *Augustine: A New Biography*. New York: Ecco, 2005.

———. *Augustine: Confessions*. Vol. 1: Introduction and Text; Vol. 2: Commentary on Books 1–7; Vol. 3: Commentary on Books 8–13. Oxford: Clarendon, 1992.

Olson, Daniel V. A., and Paul Perl. "Variations in Strictness and Religious Commitment within and among Five Denominations." *Journal for the Scientific Study of Religion* 40 (2001) 757–64.

Olson, Roger E. *The Westminster Handbook to Evangelical Theology*. Louisville: Westminster John Knox, 2004.

O'Meara, John J. *The Young Augustine: The Growth of St. Augustine's Mind up to His Conversion*. Rev. ed. New York: Alba, 2001.

Paffenroth, Kim. "Book Nine: The Emotional Heart of the *Confessions*." In *A Reader's Companion to Augustine's Confessions*, edited by Kim Paffenroth and Robert P. Kennedy, 137–54. Louisville: Westminster John Knox, 2003.

———. "God in the Friend, or the Friend in God?: The Meaning of Friendship for Augustine." *Augustinian Heritage* 38 (1992) 123–36.

Pargament, Kenneth I. *The Psychology of Religion and Coping: Theory, Research, Practice*. New York: Guilford, 1997.

Parsons, William B. "St. Augustine: 'Common Man' or 'Intuitive Psychologists'?" *Journal of Psychohistory* 18 (1990) 155–79.

Patton, John. *Pastoral Care in Context: An Introduction to Pastoral Care*. Louisville: Westminster John Knox, 1993.

Peace, Richard V. *Conversion in the New Testament: Paul and the Twelve*. Grand Rapids: Eerdmans, 1999.

Peel, J. D. Y. "Conversion and Tradition in Two African Societies: Ijebu and Buganda." *Past and Present* 77 (1977) 108–41.

———. "History, Culture and the Comparative Method: A West African Puzzle." In *Comparative Anthropology*, edited by Ladislav Holý, 88–118. Oxford: Blackwell, 1987.

Plotinus. *The Six Enneads*. Translated by Stephen MacKenna and B. S. Page. Chicago: Encyclopaedia Britannica, 1952.

Plumer, Eric. "Book Six: Major Characters and Memorable Incidents." In *A Reader's Companion to Augustine's Confessions*, edited by Kim Paffenroth and Robert P. Kennedy, 89–105. Louisville: Westminster John Knox, 2003.

Possidius. *The Life of Saint Augustine: A Translation of the Sancti Augustini Vita*. Translated by H. Terbert Weiskotten. Merchantville, NJ: Evolution, 2008.

Power, Kim. "Concubine/Concubinage." In *Augustine through the Ages: An Encyclopedia*, edited by Allan D. Fitzgerald, 222–23. Grand Rapids: Eerdmans, 1999.

———. *Veiled Desire: Augustine on Women*. New York: Continuum, 1996.

Pruyser, Paul W. *The Play of the Imagination: Toward a Psychoanalysis of Culture*. New York: International Universities Press, 1983.

———. "Psychological Examination: Augustine." *Journal for the Scientific Study of Religion* 5 (1966) 284–89.

Quinn, John M. *A Companion to the Confessions of St. Augustine*. New York: Lang, 2007.

———. "Eternity." "Time." In *Augustine through the Ages: An Encyclopedia*, edited by Allan D. Fitzgerald, 318–20, 832–38. Grand Rapids: Eerdmans, 1999.

Rahner, Karl. "Conversion." In *Conversion: Perspectives on Personal and Social Transformation*, edited by Walter E. Conn, 203–11. New York: Alba, 1978.

Rambo, Lewis R. "Bibliography: Current Research on Religious Conversion." *Religious Studies Review* 8 (1982) 146–59.

Bibliography

———. "Conversion: Toward a Holistic Model of Religious Change." *Pastoral Psychology* 38 (1989) 47–63.

———. "The Psychology of Conversion." In *Handbook of Religious Conversion*, edited by H. Newton Malony and Samuel Southard, 159–77. Birmingham, AL: Religious Education, 1992.

———. *Understanding Religious Conversion*. New Haven: Yale University Press, 1993.

Rambo, Lewis R., and Charles E. Farhadian. "Converting: Stages of Religious Change." In *Religious Conversion: Contemporary Practices and Controversies*, edited by Christopher Lamb and M. Darrol Bryant, 23–34. New York: Cassell, 1999.

Ramirez, J. Roland E. "The Priority of Reason over Faith in Augustine." *Augustinian Studies* 13 (1982) 123–31.

Reidhead, Mary Ann, and Van A. Reidhead. "From Jehovah's Witness to Benedictine Nun: The Roles of Experience and Context in a Double Conversion." In *The Anthropology of Religious Conversion*, edited by Andrew Buckser and Stephen D. Glazier, 183–97. New York: Rowman & Littlefield, 2003.

Rennie, Robert A. "Elements of Christian Conversion." DMin diss., Acadia University, 1995.

Reta, Jose Oroz. "Conversion." In *Augustine through the Ages: An Encyclopedia*, edited by Allan D. Fitzgerald, 239–42. Grand Rapids: Eerdmans, 1999.

Rigby, Paul. "Paul Ricoeur, Freudianism, and Augustine's *Confessions*." *Journal of the American Academy of Religion* 53 (1985) 93–114.

Rizzuto, Ana-Maria. *The Birth of the Living God: The Psychological Study*. Chicago: University of Chicago Press, 1979.

Russell, Frederick H. "Augustine: Conversion by the Book." In *Varieties of Religious Conversion in the Middle Ages*, edited by James Muldoon, 13–30. Gainesville, FL: University Press of Florida, 1997.

Salzman, Leon. "The Psychology of Religious and Ideological Conversion." *Psychiatry* 16 (1953) 177–87.

———. "Types of Religious Conversion." *Pastoral Psychology* 17 (1966) 8–20.

Savage, Sara. "A Psychology of Conversion—From All Angles." In *Previous Convictions*, edited by Martyn Percy, 1–18. London: SPCK, 2000.

Schaff, Philip. "Monasticism." In *History of the Christian Church*, 147–233. Grand Rapids: Eerdmans, 1950.

Schlauch, Chris R. *Faithful Companioning: How Pastoral Counseling Heals*. Minneapolis: Fortress, 1995.

Scroggs, James R., and William G. T. Douglas. "Issues in the Psychology of Religious Conversion." *Journal of Religion and Health* 6 (1967) 204–16.

Sisemore, Timothy A. "Saint Augustine's *Confessions* and the Use of Introspection in Counseling." *Journal of Psychology and Christianity* 20 (2001) 324–31.

Smith, Gordon T. *Beginning Well: Christian Conversion & Authentic Transformation*. Downers Grove, IL: InterVatsity, 2001.

———. *Transforming Conversion: Rethinking the Language and Contours of Christian Initiation*. Grand Rapids: Baker, 2010.

Snow, David A., and Richard Machalek. "The Sociology of Conversion." *Annual Review of Sociology* 10 (1984) 167–90.

Snow, David A., et al. "Social Networks and Social Movements: A Microstructural Approach to Differential Recruitment." *American Sociological Review* 45 (1980) 787–801.

Sorabji, Richard. "Time, Mysticism, and Creation." In *Augustine's Confessions: Critical Essays*, edited by William E. Mann, 209–35. New York: Rowman & Littlefield, 2006.

Spero, Moshe Halevi. *Religious Objects as Psychological Structures: A Critical Integration of Object Relations Theory, Psychotherapy, and Judaism*. Chicago: University of Chicago Press, 1992.

Spiro, Melford E. "Collective Representations and Mental Representations in Religious Symbol Systems. In *On Symbols in Anthropology: Essays in Honor of Harry Hoijer*, edited by Jacques Maquet, 45–72. Malibu, CA: Undena, 1982.

Starbuck, Edwin Diller. *The Psychology of Religion. An Empirical Study of the Growth of Religious Consciousness*. 3rd ed. New York: Scott, 1912.

Stark, Judith Chelius. "The Dynamics of the Will in Augustine's Conversion." In *Collectanea Augustiniana—Augustine: Second Founder of the Faith*, edited by Joseph C. Schnaubelt and Frederick Van Fleteren, 45–64. New York: Lang, 1990.

Stark, Rodney, and William Sims Bainbridge. "Networks of Faith: Interpersonal Bonds and Recruitment to Cults and Sects." *American Journal of Sociology* 85 (1980) 1376–95.

Starnes, Colin. *Augustine's Conversion: A Guide to the Argument of Confessions I–IX*. Waterloo, ON, Canada: Wilfrid Laurier University Press, 1990.

Stewart, Charles W. "The Religious Experience of Two Adolescent Girls." *Pastoral Psychology* 17 (1966) 49–55.

Straus, Roger A. "Changing Oneself: Seekers and the Creative Transformation of Life Experience." In *Doing Social Life*, edited by John Lofland, 252–73. New York: Wiley & Sons, 1976.

———. "Religious Conversion as a Personal and Collective Accomplishment." *Sociological Analysis* 40 (1979) 158–65.

Sun, Han-Yong. *Time and Eternity in St. Augustine*. Seoul: The Christian Literature Society of Korea, 1998.

Tack, Theodore E. *As One Struggling Christian to Another: Augustine's Christian Ideal for Today*. Collegeville, MN: Liturgical, 2001.

TeSelle, Eugene. "Augustine as Client and as Theorist." *Journal for the Scientific Study of Religion* 25 (1986) 92–101.

———. *Augustine the Theologian*. Eugene, OR: Wipf and Stock, 2002.

Teske, Roland J. "Augustine's Theory of Soul." In *The Cambridge Companion to Augustine*, edited by Eleonore Stump and Norman Kretzmann, 116–23. Cambridge: Cambridge University Press, 2001.

———. "Soul." In *Augustine through the Ages: An Encyclopedia*, edited by Allan D. Fitzgerald, 807–12. Grand Rapids: Eerdmans, 1999.

Tillich, Paul. *The Essential Tillich: An Anthology of the Writings of Paul Tillich*. Edited by F. Forrester Church. Chicago: University of Chicago Press, 1987.

———. *A History of Christian Thought*. New York: Harper & Row, 1968.

———. *Systematic Theology*. 3 vols. Chicago: University of Chicago Press, 1951–63.

Tippett, Alan R. "Conversion as a Dynamic Process in Christian Mission." *Missiology* 5 (1977) 203–21.

———. "The Cultural Anthropology of Conversion." In *Handbook of Religious Conversion*, edited by H. Newton Malony and Samuel Southard, 192–208. Birmingham, AL: Religious Education, 1992.

Bibliography

Toon, Peter. *Born Again: A Biblical and Theological Study of Regeneration.* Grand Rapids: Baker, 1987.

Torchia, N. Joseph. "Contemplation and Action." In *Augustine through the Ages: An Encyclopedia*, edited by Allan D. Fitzgerald, 233–35. Grand Rapids: Eerdmans, 1999.

Ulanov, Ann B. *Finding Space: Winnicott, God, and Psychic Reality.* Louisville: Westminster John Knox, 2001.

Ullman, Chana. *The Transformed Self: The Psychology of Religious Conversion.* New York: Plenum, 1989.

Van Bavel, Tarsicius J. "Church." "Love." In *Augustine through the Ages: An Encyclopedia*, edited by Allan D. Fitzgerald, 169–76, 509–16. Grand Rapids: Eerdmans, 1999.

———. "The Double Face of Love Augustine." *Augustinian Studies* 17 (1986) 169–81.

———. "Introduction to the Rule." "Commentary on the Rule." In *The Rule of Saint Augustine*, 3–8, 39–120. New York: Image, 1986.

Van Fleteren, Frederick. "Ascent of the Soul." In *Augustine through the Ages: An Encyclopedia*, edited by Allan D. Fitzgerald, 63–67. Grand Rapids: Eerdmans, 1999.

———. "Authority and Reason, Faith and Understanding in the Thought of St. Augustine." *Augustinian Studies* 4 (1973) 33–71.

———. "St. Augustine's Theory of Conversion." In *Collectanea Augustiniana—Augustine: Second Founder of the Faith*, edited by Joseph C. Schnaubelt and Frederick Van Fleteren, 65–80. New York: Lang, 1990.

Vaught, Carl G. *Access to God in Augustine's Confessions: Books X–XIII.* Albany, NY: State University of New York Press, 2005.

———. *Encounters with God in Augustine's Confessions: Books VII–IX.* Albany, NY: State University of New York Press, 2004.

———. *The Journey toward God in Augustine's Confessions: Books I–VI.* Albany. NY: State University of New York Press, 2003.

Vessey, Mark. "Possidius." In *Augustine through the Ages: An Encyclopedia*, edited by Allan D. Fitzgerald, 668–69. Grand Rapids: Eerdmans, 1999.

Walker, Williston. *A History of the Christian Church.* 3rd ed. New York: Scribners's Sons, 1970.

Wallace, Anthony F. C. "Handsome Lake and the Great Revival in the West." *American Quarterly* 4 (1952) 149–65.

———. "Revitalization Movements." *American Anthropologist* 58 (1956) 264–81.

Weininger, Benjamin. "The Interpersonal Factor in the Religious Experience." *Psychoanalysis* 3 (1955) 27–44.

Weintraub, Karl J. *The Value of the Individual: Self and Circumstance in Autobiography.* Chicago: University of Chicago Press, 1978.

Wells, David F. *Turning to God: Biblical Conversion in the Modern World.* Grand Rapids: Baker, 1989.

Williams, Daniel D. "The Significance of St. Augustine Today." In *A Companion to the Study of St. Augustine*, edited by Roy W. Battenhouse, 3–14. Grand Rapids: Baker, 1979.

Wills, Garry. *Saint Augustine.* New York: Viking, 1999.

———. *Saint Augustine's Conversion.* New York: Viking, 2004.

Winnicott, Donald W. *Playing and Reality.* New York: Routledge, 1971.

Bibliography

Witherup, Ronald D. *Conversion in the New Testament.* Collegeville, MN: Liturgical, 1994.

Wolfteich, Claire E. *American Catholics through the Twentieth Century: Spirituality, Lay Experience, and Public Life.* New York: Crossroad, 2001.

Wolterstorff, Nicholas. "God's Speaking and Augustine's Conversion." In *Augustine's Confessions: Critical Essays*, edited by William E. Mann, 161–74. New York: Rowman & Littlefield, 2006.

Woodberry, J. Dudley. "Conversion in Islam." In *Handbook of Religious Conversion*, edited by H. Newton Malony and Samuel Southard, 22–40. Birmingham, AL: Religious Education, 1992.

Woollcott, Philip. "Some Considerations of Creativity and Religious Experience in St. Augustine of Hippo." *Journal for the Scientific Study of Religion* 5 (1966) 273–83.

Wright, David F. "Augustine and the Transformation of Baptism." In *The Origins of Christendom in the West*, edited by Alan Kreider, 287–310. New York: T. & T. Clark, 2001.

Wulff, David M. *Psychology of Religion: Classic & Contemporary.* 2nd ed. New York: Wiley & Sons, 1997.

Zehnder, David J. *A Theology of Religious Change: What the Social Science of Conversion Means for the Gospel.* Eugene, OR: Pickwick, 2011.

Zinnbauer, Brian J., and Kenneth I. Pargament. "Spiritual Conversion: A Study of Religious Change among College Students." *Journal for the Scientific Study of Religion* 37 (1998) 161–80.

Zumkeller, Adolar. *Augustine's Ideal of the Religious Life.* Translated by Edmund Colledge. New York: Fordham University Press, 1986.

Name Index

Abraham, William J., 64–65
Aguilar, Mario I., 48–50
Allison, Joel, 24
Alypius, 4, 102, 107–8, 112, 114–15, 142, 192, 197n155, 198–99n158, 293, 302–4, 321, 329
Ambrose, 4, 104–6, 105n22, 111, 142, 183, 196, 214, 293–96, 299, 327, 339–40
Ammerman, Nancy Tatom, 42–43
Antony, 107, 189, 191, 214n207, 218–19, 224, 225n245, 239, 241, 299–300, 309, 316n98
Arius, 132
Asiedu, F. B. A., 151, 285–86, 369
Augustine, 3, 95–150, 263–344
Austin-Broos, Diane, 12, 52–53
Aviad, Janet, 62–63n137
Ayres, Lewis, and Barnes, Michel R., 134n90

Babcock, William S., 122n67, 143n112, 234n274
Bainbridge, William Sims, 12, 35
Bakan, David, 158–59, 162, 164n39
Barclay, William, 71–72, 79–80
Barth, Karl, 79n183
Berger, Peter, and Luckmann, Thomas, 36, 43
Bonner, Gerald, 97n4, 113n44, 117n55, 142n109, 146n118, 147n119–22, 148n123–25, 303n75
Bourke, Vernon J., 99n10, 110n38, 221n231, 226n250, 303n75

Bouyer, Louis, 208n189, 210n195, 214n207
Brown, Peter, 99n9, 106n27, 112n42, 163n34, 171n59, 178, 182n107, 245, 267, 270n15, 273–74, 296n66, 303n75
Browning, Don S., 179n98, 333n124, 360–61
Buckser, Andrew, 40–41
Burns, J. Patout, 139n103
Burrell, David, 168, 229–30
Byassee, Jason, 241n299

Caelestius, 135–36, 140
Callen, Barry L., 65n146, 80
Campbell, Ted A., 77n175
Canning, Raymond, 145n115, 251–52
Cao, Nanlai, 35–36
Capps, Donald, 169–70, 172–76, 259n356, 276–79, 280n36, 281n38, 289, 357
Cary, Philip, 205–8, 294–95, 308n83
Castro, Emilio, 79n183
Chadwick, Henry, 95–96, 97n5, 100n11, 107n29–30, 296n66
Christensen, Carl W., 23n27
Cicero, 100n11, 264, 275
Clair, Michael, 181n104, 257–58n349
Clark, Elizabeth A., 106n27, 219n223, 224n243, 284
Clark, Gillian, 270n14, 270–71n16
Clark, Mary T., 98n6, 252–53, 337n135
Cleaver, Eldridge, 55–56
Clement, Fabrice, 28, 32,

393

Name Index

Collinge, William J., 221n231, 226n250
Conn, Walter, 2, 29n45, 31–33, 66n147
Corrigan, Kevin, 252n341
Cushman, Robert E., 359n3

Daly, Lawrence J., 164n38, 171n59
DeSimone, Russell J., 252n341
Dittes, James E., 158–62, 164n39, 186, 230
Dixon, Sandra Lee, 176, 179–81, 186–87
Dodds, E. R., 153–55, 162, 170, 186, 281n38
Donatus, 127
Dubay, Thomas, 79n183

Elledge, W. Paul, 166–69, 186–87, 244n308, 290, 302
Epstein, Seymour, 27, 32
Erikson, Erik H., 29

Faustus, 102–3, 149, 275
Fenn, Richard, 168n48, 243–44
Ferrari, Leo C., 242–43n303, 259n356, 274n27, 279–80
Finn, Thomas M., 74, 104–5n22, 246–48
Fisher, Humphrey J., 49N103
Fitzgerald, Allan D., 115n51, 142n110, 303n75
Fortin, Ernest L., 146n118
Fowler, James W., 29n45, 30–31, 33
Fredriksen, Paula, 164n38, 171–72, 242–43n303, 270–71n16
Freud, Sigmund, 16–18, 152–53
Froehlich, Karlfried, 237–38, 252n341, 315

Gaiser, Frederick J., 66n147, 68–69
Gaventa, Beverly Roberts, 64n140, 68
Gay, Volney, 176–78, 186–87
Geertz, Clifford, 47
Gelpi, Donald L., 74–75
Georgiou, Steve T., 241n298, 246n317
Gibbs, Eddie, 59
Gillespie, V. Bailey, 29–30, 33

Gilson, Etienne, 120n61, 123n70, 134n90, 140n105
Glock, Charles Y., and Stark, Rodney, 34
Gonzáez, Justo L., 120n61, 122n68, 124n72
Gopnik, Alison, 28
Gorman, Michael M., 272n21
Greeley, Andrew M., 38n73
Greenberg, Jay R., and Mitchell, Stephen A., 181n104
Greil, Arthur L., and Rudy, David R., 38–39
Griffin, Emilie, 63–64
Guenther, Margaret, 363
Gutierrez, Gustavo, 79

Haight, Roger, 233n270
Hamilton, N. Gregory, 181n104
Häring, Bernard, 79n183
Harmless, William, 193n137, 214n207, 216n211, 220n229, 225n245, 245–46, 269, 326n115
Harrison, Carol, 213–18, 267–72, 308n83
Hefner, Robert W., 47–48
Heirich, Max, 38
Heschel, Abraham J., 62
Hiebert, Paul G., 62–63n137
Hiltner, Seward, 29n45
Hindsley, Leonard P., 64n140
Hippolytus, 99n10, 106n27
Holt, Laura, 137n99
Horton, Paul C., 181n104
Horton, Robin, 46–47
Hudson, Deal W., 74n168

Iannaccone, Laurence R., 44

James, William, 5, 12, 20–22, 29n45, 32–33, 155, 165–66, 169, 186–87, 277, 288–89
Johnson, Cedric B., and Malony, H. Newton, 66n147, 73–74
Jones, James W., 257–58n349
Jonte-Pace, Diane, 171n59

Name Index

Kahn, Peter J., and Greene, A. L., 87n207, 91n218
Kamaleson, Samuel T., 79n183
Kasdorf, Hans, 66n147, 79n183
Kelley, Dean M., 43–44
Kenney, John P., 351n148
Kevane, Eugene, 213n204
Kilbourne, Brock K., and Richardson, James T., 38n75
Kildahl, John P., 19
Kligerman, Charles, 155–58, 162, 186
Knowles, David, 269n13, 270–71n16, 315n96
Knuuttila, Simo, 123n69, 123n71–72, 125n76
Kohut, Heinz, 171n58, 173n66, 175n78
Kohut, Heinz, and Wolf, Ernest, 173n66
Kotze, Annemare, 345n138
Kraft, Charles H., 51–52
Kreider, Alan, 201–4, 344n137
Kreidler, Mary Jane, 199–201, 293, 318n104, 320n105, 366

Lacan, Dom Marc-Francois, 64n140
Lancel, Serge, 112n42, 211–13, 272n21
Lawless, George, 141n108, 218–23
Lee, Roland R., and Martin, J. Colby, 175n78
Leech, Kenneth, 365n15
Leo I, Pope, 106n27
Lichtenstein, Aharon, 72n162
Lienhard, Joseph T., 195n145
Lofland, John, and Skonovd, Norman, 27–28
Lofland, John, and Stark, Rodney, 34, 38n75
Lohfink, Gerhard, 250n332
Lohse, Bernhard, 130n83, 136n97, 138n100
Lonergan, Bernard, 79n183

MacDonald, Scott, 119n59, 125n76
MacMullen, Ramsay, 96n2, 270–71n16
Mahoney, Annettee, and Pargament, Kenneth I., 26, 33
Mani, 100

Mann, William E., 137n98, 138n100
Markham, Paul N., 74n166, 77n175
Markus, Robert A., 101n13, 126n79, 269n13, 270–71n16, 271
Marquardt, Manfred, 60, 80n186
Martin, Thomas F., 195n145, 249–51, 263, 345
Matter, E. Ann, 190–92, 241n299, 242–43n303, 298, 316n98
McClanahan, John Howard, 268–69, 281n37
McDargh, John, 257–58n349, 258–59n352
McGinn, Bernard, and McGinn, Patricia Ferris, 9, 248–49
McKim, Donald K., 12,
McKnight, Scot, 77n175, 79n181
McLynn, Neil, 104–5n22
McMahon, Robert, 195n145, 364
McVann, Mark, 77n175, 79n183
Meeks, Wayne A., 202n170
Meissner, William W., 257–58n349
Mendez-Moratalla, Fernando, 71
Miles, Margaret R., 171n59, 184n115, 285–86n46
Monagle, John F., 195n145
Montgomery, Robert L., 39–40
Morris, George E., 65–66, 72–73, 79n183

Newton, John Thomas, 208n189
Ng, Kwai Hang, 52
Niebuhr, H. Richard, 359n3
Niebuhr, Reinhold, 79n183
Niño, Andrés G., 8, 176–87
Nissiotis, Nikos A., 74n166, 78
Nock, Arthur Darby, 190
Norris, Rebecca Sachs, 53–54

O'Brien, William J., 188–90, 239n289, 298
O'Connell, Robert J., 99n10; 124n73, 277n30–31, 308n83
Oden, Thomas C., 64
O'Donnell, James J., 104n22, 107n32, 109n36, 196n150, 294n63
Olson, Daniel V. A., and Perl, Paul, 44n93

Name Index

Olson, Roger E., 76–78
O'Meara, John J., 106n27, 164n38, 209–11, 283

Pachomius, 220n229, 224, 225n245, 333
Paffenroth, Kim, 184–86, 195n145
Pargament, Kenneth I., 24–26, 32–33
Parsons, William B., 181–84, 186–87
Patton, John, 362–63
Peace, Richard V., 64n140, 66n147, 70–71
Peel, J. D. Y., 49n103
Pelagius, 134–35, 140
Plotinus, 104n20, 123, 206–9, 257, 306–8
Plumer, Eric, 286, 290, 371–72
Ponticianus, 4, 107, 189–92, 194, 197, 214, 218, 299–301
Porphyry, 104n20, 209, 306, 308
Possidius, 111, 114, 116, 117n55, 148n125, 303n75
Power, Kim, 99n10, 106n27
Pruyser, Paul W., 160n25, 181n104, 186, 257–58n349

Quinn, John M., 106n27, 126n78, 240–43, 245n314, 283, 311

Rahner, Karl, 78, 365
Rambo, Lewis R., 3–4, 10–12, 15, 19–20, 81–94, 255, 360
Rambo, Lewis R, and Farhadian, Charles E., 82n188, 90n216
Ramirez, J. Roland E., 359–60n3
Reidhead, Mary Ann, and Reidhead, Van A., 56–58
Rennie, Robert A., 1
Reta, Jose Oroz, 12n22
Rigby, Paul, 161–63, 186
Rizzuto, Ana-Maria, 10n16, 183n110, 258, 257–58n349

Salzman, Leon, 18–19
Savage, Sara, 16
Schaff, Philip, 220n229, 224n244
Schlauch, Chris R., 171n58, 257–58n349, 363

Scroggs, James R., and Douglas, William G. T., 18n11
Simplicianus, 4, 104–5n22, 107n29, 189, 194–99, 292–99, 306–8
Sisemore, Timothy A., 8
Smith, Gordon T., 64–65, 69–70, 76–77, 245n314
Snow, David. A., and Machalek, Richard, 37
Snow, David A., et al., 41
Sorabji, Richard, 124n72–73
Spero, Moshe Halevi, 10n16, 259
Spiro, Melford E., 10n16, 259
Starbuck, Edwin Diller, 21–23, 33
Stark, Judith Chelius, 190n128, 191n132, 264–65, 316n98, 317n101
Stark, Rodney, and Bainbridge, William Sims, 41–42
Starnes, Colin, 232–34, 281n37, 310n87, 311n89, 371
Stewart, Charles W., 24–25, 33
Straus, Roger A., 37
Sun, Han-Yong, 112n42, 115n50, 124n73, 145n115

TeSelle, Eugene, 178n93, 230–32, 238–40, 241n299
Teske, Roland J., 121n63–64
The apostle Paul, 108, 191, 301–2n72, 316n98
Tillich, Paul, 60–61, 126n78, 131n87, 140n106, 317n100, 361n6
Tippett, Alan R., 50–51
Toon, Peter, 75–76
Torchia, N. Joseph, 145n116

Ulanov, Ann B., 257–58n349
Ullman, Chana, 23–24, 33
Una, 274, 370 (see, 4, 99, 106, 116, 284–87, 369–73)

Valerius, 116–18, 217, 334–35
Van Bavel, Tarsicius J., 132n88, 143n112, 218n220, 253n347, 336n131
Van Fleteren, Frederick, 192–93, 241n298, 298, 306n79, 345

Vaught, Carl G., 190n130, 196–99, 234–37, 285–86n46, 289–90, 296n68, 318, 322, 323n109
Vessey, Mark, 148n125
Verecundus, 110, 324
Victorinus, 107, 189, 192–93, 297–99, 340

Walker, Williston, 104n20, 132n89, 136n96, 270–71n16, 295n65
Wallace, Anthony F. C., 54–55
Weininger, Benjamin, 38n75
Weintraub, Karl J., 178n91, 178n93
Wells, David F., 66n147, 74n166
Wills, Garry, 189n122, 193–96, 274, 285–87, 303, 324n112, 370

Winnicott, Donald W., 171n58, 181n104, 257–58n349
Witherup, Ronald D., 64n140, 66–67, 74n166, 79
Wolfteich, Claire E., 365n15
Woodberry, J. Dudley, 63n137
Woollcott, Philip, 182n109
Wright, David F., 244–45
Wulff, David M., 21n19

Zehnder, David J., 77n175
Zinnbauer, Brian J., and Pargament, Kenneth I., 25–26, 32–33
Zumkeller, Adolar, 201n167, 223–27, 334n127

Topical Index

A story within a story, 189, 291, 301–2, 350
Athanasius, 214n207
Augustine
  a baptized Christian, 111–12, 325–28
  a catechumen, 97, 111, 296
  a convert to Christianity, 108–9, 314–20
  a Manichee, 100–1, 275, 293
  a monk and priest/bishop, 116–48, 334–37
  a Neoplatonist, 104–5, 305–6
  a skeptic, 103–4, 293
  at Cassiciacum, 110–11, 310, 324–25
  at Hippo Regius, 116–48, 334–37
  at Ostia, 112–13, 330–32
  at Thagaste, 97–102, 114–16, 272–73, 334
  at the cathedral of Milan, 104–5, 111–12, 293–94, 325–27
  at the cathedral of Hippo, 116–48
  at the Milanese garden, 108–9, 312–18
  his birth, 97, 272
  his brother Navigius, 97, 273, 324
  his death, 147–48, 337
  his early years, 97–99, 272–75, 277–83
  his father Patricius, 5, 97–98, 101, 156, 162, 273, 281–82
  his (re)formation of the God representations, 182–84, 259–60, 280, 318–20, 352–53
  his former student Eulogius, 114
  his monastic rules, 141–42, 216–17, 221–22, 333
  his mother Monica, 4, 97–98, 101, 103, 105–6, 108, 112, 156, 192, 197–98, 273–74, 281–85, 296, 330–32, 369
  his reading of Cicero's *Hortensius*, 100, 191, 284, 294, 300
  his reading of the books of Neoplatonists, 104, 305–6
  his reading of the Epistles of Paul, 108, 191, 307–9, 315, 343
  his sister Perpetua, 97
  his son Adeodatus, 99, 106, 111–12, 114–16, 274, 324, 329
  his unmarried wife, 4, 99, 106, 116, 274, 284–87, 369–73
  impact of the sacred songs, 327
  in Carthage, 99–103, 114, 274–75, 333
  in Rome and Milan, 103–13, 275–76, 293–96, 313–20, 325–27, 333–34
Augustine's Conversion
  psychological studies, 5–6, 152–88
    regressive psychopathology, 5–6, 152–65; unification of his divided self, 5–6, 165–71; mental development, 6, 171–86
  sociological studies, 6–7, 188–204
    influence of others conversion stories, 6–7, 188–93; interpersonal bonds and the Christian community, 6–7, 193–204

399

Topical Index

anthropological studies, 6–7, 205–28
  influence of the Neoplatonic heritage, 6–7, 205–13; Christian monastic movement, 6–7, 213–27
theological studies, 7, 228–54
  transforming power of God's grace, 7, 229–37; Christian Scriptures, 237–43; Christian baptism, 243–48; reciprocity of the love of God and neighbor, 248–53
Augustine's conversion process
  context of Augustine's time, 266–76
  psychological distress and crisis, 4, 108, 169, 255–56, 276–77
  quest to know himself and the divine, 4, 256, 287–91
  encounters with significant others, 4, 256, 291–303
  participation in Christian communities, 4, 257, 291–303
  philosophical and cultural change, 4, 257, 304–11
  divine intervention and grace, 4, 312–23
  Christian baptism, 325–30
  vision of Ostia, 330–32
  service of God and God's people, 332–38
Augustine's life-changing experiences
  beatings at school, 98, 277–81
  pear-stealing episode, 98–99, 274
  death of his unnamed friend, 102, 284
  disappointment in Faustus and Manichean cosmology, 102–3, 275
  escape from his mother, 103, 284
  dismissal of his unmarried wife, 106, 284–87
  relationships with his spiritual mentors, 106–8, 293–304
  famous garden experience, 108–9, 313–16
  baptism by Bishop Ambrose, 111–12, 325–27
  mystical vision at Ostia, 112–13, 330–31

  monastic life and church ministry, 116–48
  last ecclesiastical struggle for his flock and church, 147–48
Augustine's thought, 96
  God and the soul, 119–22
  sin and God's grace, 134–41
  creation, time, and eternity, 122–26
  Christian church and baptism, 126–32, 140–41
  Trinity, 132–34
  contemplation and action, 142–46
  uti(use) and *frui*(enjoyment) 144–45
Augustine's works
  Against Julian, an Unfinished Book, 137
  Against the Epistle of Manichaeus Called Fundamental, 119
  City of God, 146
  Confessions, 3, 8, 118, 148, 151, 153, 158–61, 163, 171, 174–75, 182, 184–85, 190, 192, 198, 229, 231n260–61, 232, 259, 264, 345, 364, 367
  Debate with Fortunatus the Manichee, 117
  Debate with Maximinus, an Arian Bishop, 133
  The Enchiridion (On Faith, Hope, and Love) 136
  Miscellany of Eighty-Three Questions, 118
  On Baptism, against the Donatists, 127
  On Continence, 119
  On Free Will, 114
  On Genesis against the Manichees, 114–15
  The Literal Meaning of Genesis, 118
  On Nature and Grace, 136
  On Order, 110
  On Rebuke and Grace, 137
  On the Faith and the Creed, 117, 132
  On the Grace of Christ and Original Sin, 136
  On the Greatness of the Soul, 113

Topical Index

On the Happy Life, 110
On the Holy Trinity, 133
On the Merits and Remission of Sins, and on the Baptism of Infants, 136
On the Nature of the Good, 119
On the Teacher, 115
On the True Religion, 115
On the Two Souls, against the Manichaeans, 118
On the Usefulness of Belief, 118
Psalm against the Donatists, 127
Reply to Faustus the Manichean, 119
The Retractions, 147
The Soliloquies, 110
To Cresconius, a Donatist Grammarian, 128
To the Letters of Petilian, the Donatist, 128
The Unity of the Church, 128

Born again/regeneration, 75–76, 325–27

Cases of conversion/transformation: Alypius, 197–98, 321; Antony, 191, 239, 343; Monica, 97–98, 321–22; Ponticianus, 300; Ponticianus' two friends (and their fiancées) 191, 194–95, 214–15, 299–302; Simplicianus, 196–97, 297; the Emperor Constantine, 213–14, 270, 338; Victorinus, 189–90, 297–99
Change, 2, 12, 81–82,
Christian living in solitude and community, 81, 194, 216–18, 248–53, 354–55, 365–66
Christian Monastery, 213–27, 225n245, 269, 335–36
 anchoritic life, 214–15, 225n245
 asceticism/celibacy, 213, 216–19, 223
 cenobitic life, 215–16, 220, 224, 225n245, 333, 351
 desert monasticism, 214, 218–19
 Life of Antony, 214n207

monk, 225n245
one heart and soul, 217, 222, 335
Communal/contextual paradigm of pastoral care, 362–63
Complexity of religious change, 2, 80–91, 93, 261–62, 265
Concubinage, 99n10, 106n27
Conversion event, 1
Conversion process, 1–2, 12, 264, 338, 357–58
Convert, 91–93
 spiritual life, 79–80
Converting, 82n189, 92, 109, 323, 332, 338
Conservative churches, 43
Continence, 194, 285–86, 314, 329, 340
Council of Nicaea, 104–5n22, 118n57, 132
Culture, 11
Cultural factors, 45–59, 205–28, 304–12
Cultural transformation, 52–53

Death to rebirth/life, 74, 243–48, 325–27, 354
Discordant personality/discordancy, 169–70
Donatism, 126–32
 Diocletian persecution, 126–27
 Donatus, 127

Embodiment of cultures, 54
Embrace, 167–69, 290
Emotional crisis, 20, 24
Encapsulation, 89–90
Encultured being(s), 12, 53
Epicurean philosophy of pleasure, 268–69, 310–11
Estrangement, 60–61, 284–86, 348
Ethnographic settings, 52

Faithful companioning, 363
Fundamental practical theology, 360–61
Fundamentalism, 42
Fundamentalist church, 42

401

Topical Index

God's calling, 78, 237-43, 253, 315, 334
God's grace, 60-65, 229-37, 312-23
God's revelation to humanity, 238
Ground of Being, 289, 348
Group conversion, 51

Healthy-minded person, 21
Holy listening, 363
Human development and spiritual maturity, 260-61, 350
Human ontological anxiety(nonbeing) 61-62

Identity crisis/formation, 29-30
Illusion, 16, 181n104
Integrated, 1n2
Interior journey, 255-56, 287-91
Integrated understanding of the conversion process, 93-94, 261-66
Interdisciplinary approach, 1-2, 10-11, 94, 255, 263-64, 367
Interdisciplinary questions, 255-61
Interlocking stories of conversion, 190-93, 297-304

Julian's edict, 107n30, 298

Knowing/experiencing one self, others, and the divine, 7, 265, 292, 320, 355, 366

Lack of parental empathy, 173
Living human web, 364

Manichaeism, 100-101
Metaphor of the choral performance, 266
Method of correlation, 361
Milanese baptismal liturgy, 325-26
Morbid-minded person, 21
Multiple factors of Augustine's conversion, 4, 265, 358

Narcissism/narcissistic/traumatic injury, 171-72, 175-76, 179-80, 185, 277-80
Neoplatonism, 9, 104n20, 205-13

ascent of the soul the One, 9, 207-8, 213, 306, 347
Milanese circle of the intellects, 211, 293, 305-6
Network of Christian friendship, 193-204, 321-22
New being, 61, 313-20, 325-27

Object relations theory, 181n104
Odedipus complex, 18, 152-53, 155, 158-61, 183-84
One-ness and many-ness, 180
One's journey from unbelief to faith, 367
ongoing-containing Korean/Chinese box of stories of conversion, 190n130, 291
Ongoing(/evolving) process of conversion, 1, 11, 79, 92, 338, 355, 358

Pachomian *Koinonia*, 333
Pattern of the conversion process, 8-10, 344-56
  expression of restless feelings, 9, 346-47
  inwardness with the divine, 9, 347-48
  experience of care and support, 9, 349-50
  philosophical and cultural changes, 9, 351-52
  transformation of the God representation, 10, 352-54
  re-creation of relationships, 10, 354-56
Person, 11
Personal factors, 16-33, 152-87, 276-87
Practice-theory-practice movement, 361
Pre-oedipal experiences, 171-72, 177-78
Process of acculturation/cultural renewal, 50 58
Process of Christianization(/converting) 88, 203, 213-14, 270-73, 338, 372

Topical Index

Process of resocialization/institutionalization, 36–44, 201–4, 292, 350
Process of self-becoming/self-exposure, 171–72, 176–78, 181, 290, 365

Rambo's model of religious conversion, 3–4, 10–11, 81–94
conversion motifs:
  intellectual, 82; mystical, 82; experimental, 82; affectional, 82–83; revivalism, 83; coercive, 83
metaphor of tracks of the metropolitan train yard, 15
systemic stages:
  context, 83–84, 266; crisis, 84–85, 276; quest, 86–87, 287–88; encounter, 87–89, 291; interaction, 89–90, 291, 304; commitment, 91–92, 305; consequences, 92–93, 312, 323, 332
Rationality theory, 46
Relationships (with oneself, others, and the divine) 10, 61, 64, 78–80, 177–78, 260–61, 266, 319, 354–56, 364
Religion, 11
Religious conversion:
  definition, 1, 11–12
  psychological studies, 2, 16–33
    regressive psychopathology, 16–20; unification of the divided self, 20–26; intellectual arousal and cognitive satisfaction, 26–28; human development process, 29–32
  sociological studies, 2, 33–45
    deprivation and religious affiliation, 33–36; social influences, 36–41; member recruitment and religious institutions, 41–44
  anthropological studies, 2, 45–59
    rationality, 46–50; acculturation, 50–54; cultural revitalization, 54–58
  theological studies, 2, 59–81
    encounter with God, 60–65; the Scriptures, 65–71; ritual act of baptism, 71–78; reciprocity of the love of God and neighbor, 78–80
Religious coping process, 25–26
Religious factors, 59–81, 228–54 312–28
Remission of sin, 243–48, 328
Resting place, 287–88, 291, 296, 313, 317
Restlessness of the heart, 108, 287, 313–15, 348
Revised correlational method, 361
Romanization of the Empire, 267–68, 273

Self-reproach/depletion/fragmentation, 172–78, 180, 279
Self-transcendence, 31–32, 61, 178–79
Sense of belonging and solidarity, 200–4, 292–93, 304
Sense of coherence/integration, 179
Sense of deprivation, 33–36, 284
Sense of inner isolation, 173–74, 180, 277, 279–84, 313
Servant of God and for others, 81, 222, 248–53, 332–38, 355, 366
Shame experience, 171–76, 179–80,
Sickness of the soul, 22, 287, 293, 313, 317, 343
Silent cry, 372
Skepticism, 96, 102–3, 149
Social and institutional factors, 33–45, 181–204, 291–304
Social attachments/networks, 36–38
Social influence theory, 36
Social transformation, 56
Society, 11
Submission/transformation of intellect, 209–13
Submission/transformation of will, 209, 234–35
Spiritual awakening, 364
Spiritual maladjustment, 155, 169
Spiritual pilgrimage, 96, 365, 367
Spirituality of liberation, 79
Strain theory, 33–34
Strict churches, 44
Strictness, 43

403

Topical Index

The Arians, 132–34
The converted community, 198, 202
The Easter Vigil(April, 24–25, 387) 111, 325
The God representation, 10n16, 257–59, 353–54
The Incarnation/the Incarnate Christ, 139–40, 210n192
The Pelagians, 134–41
The Vandals, 147–48
Theory of revitalization movements, 54–55
Therapy of self-examination, 182–83
Togetherness, 79–80, 197

Tolle lege (take up and read) 108, 236–43, 315, 343
Traditional African cosmologies, 46–47, 283
Traditional Roman-African temperament, 268–69, 372
Turning, 12, 65–67, 70–71, 79, 249–50, 366

Universal obsessive neurosis, 17
Universalizing Augustine's story of conversion, 9–10, 364, 367

Waso Boorana, 49

www.ingramcontent.com/pod-product-compliance
Lightning Source LLC
Chambersburg PA
CBHW071228290426
44108CB00013B/1332